THE NAKED TRUTH

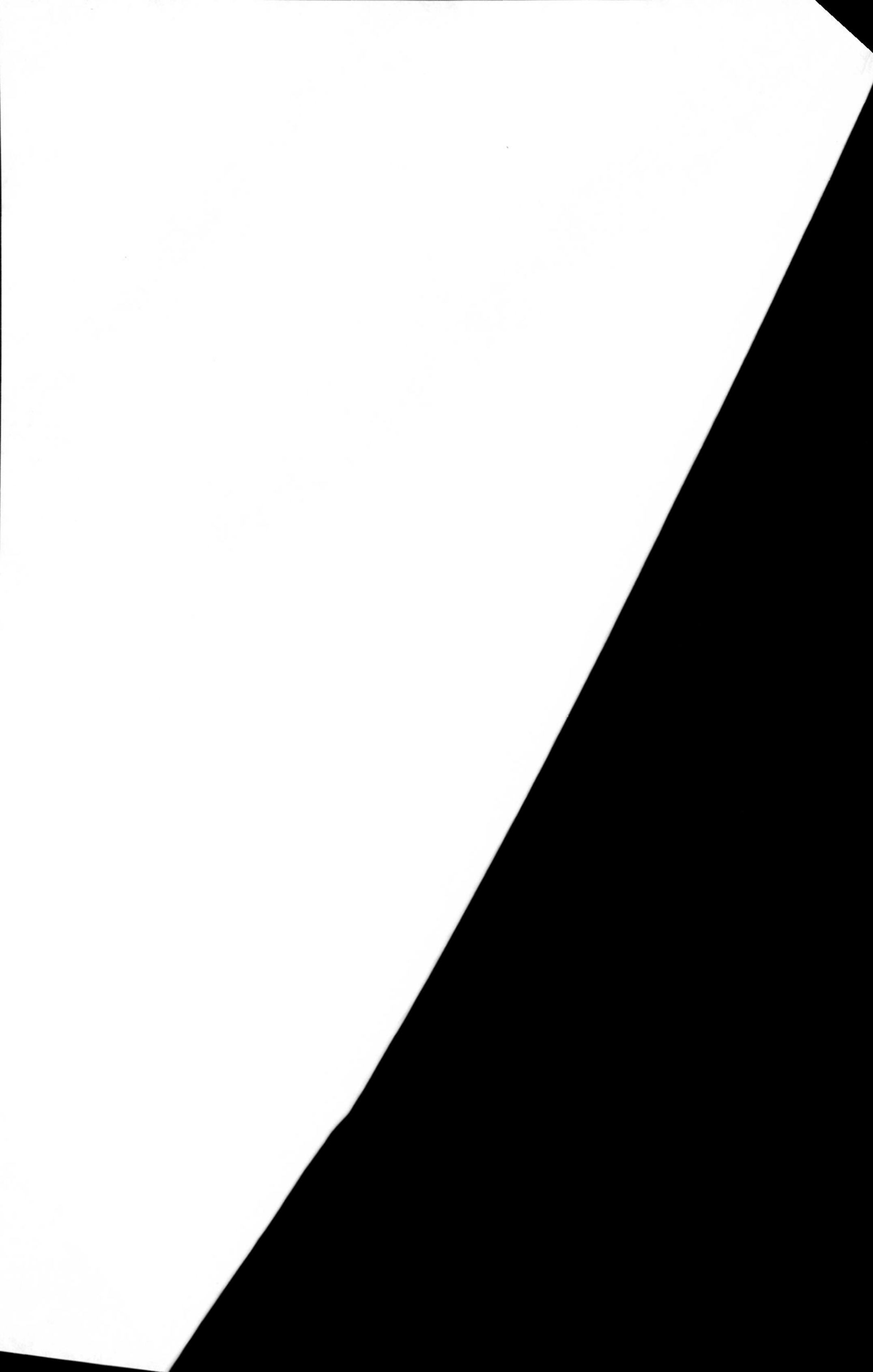

THE NAKED TRUTH

Viennese Modernism and the Body

ALYS X. GEORGE

THE UNIVERSITY OF CHICAGO PRESS
CHICAGO AND LONDON

The University of Chicago Press, Chicago 60637
The University of Chicago Press, Ltd., London

Published 2020
Printed in the United States of America

29 28 27 26 25 24 23 22 21 20   1 2 3 4 5

ISBN-13: 978-0-226-66998-4 (cloth)
ISBN-13: 978-0-226-69500-6 (e-book)
DOI: https://doi.org/10.7208/chicago/9780226695006.001.0001

Library of Congress Cataloging-in-Publication Data

Names: George, Alys X., author.
Title: The naked truth : Viennese modernism and the body / Alys X. George.
Description: Chicago : University of Chicago Press, 2020. | Includes bibliographical references and index.
Identifiers: LCCN 2019049797 | ISBN 9780226669984 (cloth) | ISBN 9780226695006 (ebook)
Subjects: LCSH: Human body—Austria—Vienna—History—19th century. | Human body—Austria—Vienna—History—20th century. | Human figure in art. | Human body in literature. | Human body in popular culture. | Modernism (Art)—Austria—Vienna—History—19th century. | Modernism (Art)—Austria—Vienna—History—20th century.
Classification: LCC HM636 .G47 2020 | DDC 128/.6—dc23
LC record available at https://lccn.loc.gov/2019049797

♾ This paper meets the requirements of ANSI/NISO Z39.48-1992 (Permanence of Paper).

. . . There are moments when the body is as numinous
as words, days that are the good flesh continuing.
—Robert Hass, "Meditation at Lagunitas"

CONTENTS

List of Illustrations ix

Note on Translations xi

Introduction 1

1. The Body on Display: Staging the Other, Shaping the Self 23

   Science and Spectacle: "Exotic" Bodies on Display 25

   Fictional Encounters? Peter Altenberg's *Ashantee* (1897) 38

   Somatic Utopias: Viennese Hygiene Exhibitions 44

   Literary Life Reform: Peter Altenberg's *Pròdrŏmŏs* (1906) 56

   Nature and Culture on Stage 63

2. The Body in Pieces: Viennese Literature's Anatomies 68

   Becoming the Blade: Vivisection as the Primal Scene 71

   In the Dissecting Room: Arthur Schnitzler and Marie Pappenheim 75

   Viennese Symptoms, Human Fragments: Joseph Roth's Journalism 88

   The Politics and Poetics of Viennese Corpses: Carry Hauser and Joseph Roth 101

   Corpse as Capital: Ödön von Horváth's *Faith, Hope, and Charity* (1932) 108

3. The Patient's Body: Working-Class Women in the Clinic 115

Finding a Voice: The Poetics of Pregnancy (Marie Pappenheim and Ilka Maria Ungar) 120
Egon Schiele in the Clinic 127
In the Women's Clinic: Architecture, Gaze, Film 140
Speaking for Suffering Mothers: Else Feldmann and Carry Hauser 149
The Politics and Public Visibility of Workers' Bodies 156

4. The Body in Motion: Staging Silent Expression 168

Body Language and Crisis of Language 171
Hugo von Hofmannsthal and the Power of Pantomime 177
Self and Other: Exploring Identity through Free Dance 185
Making Modern Dance Viennese 194
Celluloid Gestures and the Cinematic Body 203
The Worker's Body: Modern Dance, Machine Culture, and Social Democracy 214

Epilogue 229

Acknowledgments 237
Notes 241
Index 311

ILLUSTRATIONS

1 Hermann Bahr with Gustav Klimt's *Nuda Veritas*, circa 1905 2
2 "Daily Bodily Hygiene," 1929 8
3 "Contrasts of Two Human Bodies," 1930 11
4 "The Ashanti Chief with His Royal Court," 1897 27
5 Egon Schiele, physiognomic drawings, 1917 33
6 Anthropometric photographs, 1886 35
7 First edition cover of Peter Altenberg's *Ashantee*, 1897 39
8 Commemorative postcard, General Hygienic Exhibition, 1906 45
9 Peter Altenberg on the Lido, 1913 46
10 "Air and Sunbathing on the Schafberg," 1925 48
11 Postcard from the Vienna Hygiene Exhibition, 1925 50
12 Photograph of Erna Morena, inscribed by Peter Altenberg, 1918 55
13 Franz Zelezny, statuette of Peter Altenberg, 1909 57
14 Max Thun-Hohenstein, gymnastic demonstration, 1926 65
15 Franz Matsch, *Anatomy*, circa 1900 70
16 Carry Hauser, *War Victim*, 1922 96
17 Josef Eberle, poster for the Imperial Employment Agency for War Invalids, 1917 98
18 Dancing war invalid, 1915 98
19 Leg prostheses mounted on classical sculptures, 1915 99
20 Carry Hauser, plate from *The Book of the City*, 1921 105
21 Viennese corpse tram, after 1945 107
22 Gustav Klimt, *Medicine*, 1901 116
23 Gustav Klimt, *Hope I*, 1903 118
24 Egon Schiele, *Pregnant Woman*, 1910 129

25 Egon Schiele, *Pregnant Woman*, 1910 130
26 Egon Schiele, *Pregnant Woman*, 1910 131
27 Egon Schiele, *Portrait of Dr. Erwin von Graff*, 1910 134
28 Lecture hall of the Vienna Women's Clinic, circa 1911 144
29 Film still from *Marital Hygiene*, 1922 147
30 Carry Hauser, illustration for Else Feldmann's *The Body of the Mother*, 1923 154
31 Leaflet for *Woman and Child* exhibition, 1928 158
32 Advertisement for layette package, 1932 159
33 Bruno Frei, cover for *Vienna's Misery*, 1921 164
34 Mother and children, Bruno Frei, *Vienna's Misery*, 1921 165
35 Ruth St. Denis in *Radha*, 1906 187
36 Grete Wiesenthal in *Donauwalzer*, circa 1907 197
37 Erwin Lang, woodcut of Grete Wiesenthal in *The Wind*, 1910 199
38 Rhythmic gymnastic exercises, New Hellerau School, 1920s 216
39 Advertisement for Hilde Holger's New School for Movement Art, 1920s 219
40 Gymnastic exercises, Schwarzwald School, 1915 221
41 Gertrud Bodenwieser, *Demon Machine*, 1939 224
42 Hilde Holger, *Mechanical Ballet*, 1926 226

NOTE ON TRANSLATIONS

Wherever possible, I have used published translations of the works cited. These are noted in the text, as are any alterations I have made to them. However, since many of the sources drawn from are lesser known and not yet translated into English, I have, in large part, provided my own translations. Where not otherwise indicated, the translations are mine.

INTRODUCTION

They are an odd pair, the man and the woman depicted in the photograph. His stout figure, draped neck to toe in a heavy cassock, is curiously abstract. A luxuriant beard seamlessly extends the long, dark column of his body nearly to his piercing eyes, which widen, askance, to a bright punctuation mark in the grayscale interior landscape. She trains her vivid gaze no less directly on the viewer, yet her frontal nudity—unabashed, concrete, shimmering off the canvas—is the antipode to his physical concealment. Look at us, the twosome seems to challenge. She throws down the gauntlet, though, by matter-of-factly holding up a mirror all the while. Look at yourselves, she dares us. What do you see?

One half of this esoteric couple, the writer-director Hermann Bahr (1863–1934), was the godfather of the Young Vienna literary circle. As a torch-bearing critic, he sought, with uncommon persistence and verbiage, to define what exactly constituted modernism, and Viennese modernism specifically. His counterpart, the formidable redhead in the painting to which this book's title alludes, is Gustav Klimt's (1862–1918) allegorical *Nuda Veritas* (1899). Bahr acquired the alluring Truth from Klimt in autumn 1900 for four thousand crowns, roughly twenty-five thousand euros. What seems in contemporary terms like a steal, a deal brokered between an artist and one of his staunchest supporters, is rendered moot by the knowledge that the sum was one-third of what Bahr paid for the construction of the entire villa that housed the painting—and himself—in Ober St. Veit, a neighborhood of Vienna's Hietzing district.[1] Designed by Joseph Maria Olbrich (1867–1908), right down to the specially fashioned wood paneling surrounding the canvas, the villa was a Gesamtkunstwerk of Viennese modernism, and *The Naked Truth* its iconographic centerpiece.

Fig. 1. Hermann Bahr in the study of his villa in Ober St. Veit with Gustav Klimt's *Nuda Veritas*. Photograph by Aura Hertwig, ca. 1905. Image courtesy of KHM-Museumsverband, Austrian Theater Museum, Vienna.

The photograph, shot by Aura Hertwig around 1905, stages the canvas's supertitle in Bahr's defiant posture: "If you cannot please everyone through your deed and your artwork, please just a few. Pleasing many is terrible."[2] The sharp polemic was as much a rebuke to the critics of the Vienna Secession as it was a programmatic statement of purpose for the city's artistic avant-garde at large. My eye is drawn, however, to Truth's mirror, rendered as a milky moonstone in the painting. I am reminded of Michel Foucault: "It is the mirror that teach[es] us . . . that we have a body."[3] *Körper haben* and *Leib sein*—*to have* a body (from the Latin *corpus*) and *to be* a body (from the Middle High German *lip*, both "body" and "life")—these central distinctions of philosophical anthropology are implicated in Hertwig's image of Bahr and Truth, dauntless, her mirror aloft.[4] In the defining image of Viennese modernism, *Nuda Veritas*, the body is front and center, at once an invitation and a provocation. Why, then, has the body been neglected in the cultural history of Vienna?

A full decade before positioning his writing desk in the sight line of—and facing—the two-meter-tall, naked Truth, Bahr had already identified the body as a key locus of modernist cultural production. His early programmatic texts document a restless quest to define a specifically Austrian form of modernism that could rival those of Paris and Berlin. "The Modern" (Die Moderne), a groundbreaking essay from 1890, details the characteristics of a new direction in Viennese art and literature. Truth, life, and, consequently, the purpose of modern art were to be found, according to Bahr, in the threefold exploration of emotions, thoughts, and the body.[5] Two of the three paradigms Bahr pinpointed, the interior worlds of human emotions and thoughts, proved prognostic.

Like *Nuda Veritas*, Sigmund Freud's (1856–1939) *The Interpretation of Dreams* (Die Traumdeutung) was completed in late 1899, although it was postdated to 1900 to coincide symbolically with the dawn of a new century. Freud's theories provided unparalleled insights into the life of the human mind, as well as impulses that influenced the cultural production of his age and far beyond. Moreover, they have offered an irresistible frame of reference for subsequent historiography on Viennese modernism. Carl Schorske's groundbreaking scholarship of the 1960s and 1970s, a series of essays united in the Pulitzer Prize–winning *Fin-de-Siècle Vienna: Politics and Culture* (1979), identified *homo psychologicus* (psychological man) as the emblematic manifestation of Viennese culture.[6] Two elegant, powerful theses defined Schorske's understanding of modernist cultural production in Vienna. It was premised, first, in Freud's wake, on a fascination with the psyche, the unconscious, and subjectivity; it was distinguished, second, by a withdrawal into the life of the mind resulting from the failure of Austrian liberal politics, which Schorske characterized as an ahistorical retreat into the garden of aestheticism.[7] Since then, the psyche has been the enduring paradigm and an inward turn the central gesture of Viennese modernism.[8]

But what of Bahr's third wellspring of truth, life, and art: the body? As he formulates a blueprint for modern cultural production in 1890, Bahr appeals directly to his Viennese contemporaries: "We want to observe the bodies, individual and in aggregate, in which humankind lives; want to study the laws they obey, the destinies they experience; the births from whence and the deaths toward which they march; want to document it as it is."[9] Bahr's peers took up the directive in spades at the fin de siècle. Using their pens and stages, drafting tables and brushes, and, soon after, their new Kodaks and movie cameras, they observed, studied, and documented bodies—their own and those of others. From its very origins, Viennese modernism was as attuned to *homo physiologicus*, the physiological human being, with all its attendant naked truths, as it was to psychological man. This search in the arts was nourished by a refashioning of knowledge about the human body in medicine, the sciences, and philosophy in the second half of the nineteenth century. A full generation before Vienna became the hothouse for Freudian psychoanalysis, it was the world leader in anatomy and pathology under the second Vienna medical school. The prominence of these disciplines, the social networks that existed between doctors and artists in Vienna, and the popularization of medical knowledge around 1900 help to explain why the cultural production of Viennese modernism—literature, the visual arts, and the performing arts—engaged so unflaggingly with the body—as material, trope, and metaphor.

This book, an interdisciplinary cultural history of the long Viennese fin de siècle (1870–1938), recovers the forgotten history of the human body in Viennese modernism. It restores *homo physiologicus* to his—and her—rightful place alongside *homo psychologicus* in the story of Vienna's cultural production from the late imperial period through the interwar years. By centering on the body culture that occupied the addressees of Bahr's artistic mandate, it seeks to understand how Viennese society's attitudes toward the body shaped its cultural production. It puts, in other words, *culture* back into the historical study of body culture, while also positioning body culture as a crucial yet long overlooked facet of Viennese modernism. It therefore significantly deepens our knowledge about Viennese modernism, adding vital nuance and complexity to a historical era which itself has evolved into a culture industry of powerful proportions.[10] Moreover, it allows us to view familiar players from the Viennese cultural scene in new light, while also reinscribing forgotten cultural figures—many of them long disregarded on the basis of gender, class, or ethnicity—to their rightful places in the narrative of Viennese modernism.

Body culture, in its broadest sense, is the intersection of scientific knowledge about the body with aesthetic, popular, and social representations of it. The history of the body is a field, that is, where thought and life intersect. The notion of body culture is distinct from, but encompasses, the related concept of physical culture. As Karl Toepfer has noted in his significant study *Empire of Ecstasy*, the body's determinacy, its ostensible finitude as physical matter, belies the scope of what might immediately come to mind under the rubric of body culture. In point of fact, a wide array of endeavors is subsumed under the term. It includes, but is by no means limited to, "the performing arts, literature, the fine arts, sports, athletics, medicine, sex, sexology, fashion, advertising, labor, ergonomics, architecture, leisure activities, music, physiognomic study, and military discipline."[11] Toepfer argues that modernist culture "physicalize[s] modernity within the body" and perceives "the body itself as a manifestation of modernist desire."[12] Body culture thus bespeaks a way of interrogating traditional boundaries between "mind and body, subject and object, self and the world,"[13] categorical distinctions that were increasingly being called into question in the decades around 1900.

While Hermann Bahr laid the body as a programmatic cornerstone in the search for the modern and for truth, this central aspect of Viennese modernism has never been considered systematically from a scholarly vantage point. Yet Viennese modernists both partook in and contributed to the wider European "rediscovery of the human body" that historian George Mosse identified as a distinctive feature of European society at the turn of the nineteenth to the twentieth century.[14] In a recent attempt to synthesize the key intellectual program points of Viennese modernism, Hubert Christian Ehalt identified a new consciousness about the body as one of the era's central features.[15] Years ago, though, the art historian Werner Hofmann and the writer Hilde Spiel had already remarked on the centrality of the body in Viennese modernist cultural production.[16] Both criticize the antitheses through which Viennese modernism has so often been read: dream and reality—as the Historical Museum of the City of Vienna's pathbreaking 1985 exhibition *Dream and Reality: Vienna 1870–1930* (Traum und Wirklichkeit: Wien 1870–1930) positioned it—or ornament and austerity—the two poles of the Jugendstil decorative impulse and its rejection by Adolf Loos, Karl Kraus, and others. If we step outside of these conceptual antinomies, as Hofmann suggests, it is possible to note a golden thread throughout the cultural production of Viennese modernism, one absolutely central to the exploration of the visual arts, philosophy, psychology, literature, and social theory: the impulse, as Hofmann phrases it, "to recognize the flesh, to apprehend the human being in its creatureliness."[17]

This unique attentiveness to the materiality of the human body in Viennese culture stems, I argue, from the centrality of the materialist conception of disease under the second Vienna medical school. Called to life in the 1830s and 1840s, it reigned paramount in the second half of the nineteenth century.[18] While Freud would later make his life's work the exploration of people's psychic creatureliness, his training was fully under the spell of Viennese materialism. Writing in the 1920s, Freud himself cautioned against a mythic creation narrative of psychoanalysis. While it "may be said to have been born with the twentieth century," he wrote, "it did not drop from the skies ready-made." How it developed must take into account the contextual circumstances that informed it and with which it was in dialogue, as well as its specific prehistory.[19] It was his medical training in anatomy and physiology at the University of Vienna, more than any philosophical or artistic antecedent, that shaped Freud's worldview.[20] His strongest early influence was the scientific materialism that was Viennese medicine's unique hallmark, one that grew out of a reactionary stance to the early nineteenth-century speculative idealism of *Naturphilosophie*.[21] That scientific materialism was, as David Luft has argued, the defining factor that characterized the Viennese tradition[22]—and the body its central object. Long before Freud became a groundbreaking psychoanalyst, he was a "radical materialist."[23] Before the psyche became the watchword of a generation, in other words, the guiding principle was the body.

When Freud began his medical studies in 1873, Vienna was the "Mecca of medicine," as Rudolf Virchow famously termed it. Working as the second Vienna medical school, together with Josef Škoda (1805–81) and Josef Hyrtl (1810–94), the legendary Carl von Rokitansky (1804–78) had fundamentally retooled diagnostic medicine around the discipline of pathological anatomy.[24] They replaced a largely observational and descriptive medicine with the localization of clinical symptoms traced to pathological changes in organs and specific parts of the body. Such knowledge was best won not at the bedside but on the autopsy table. From autopsies, doctors could conduct detailed analyses and, ultimately, diagnoses of the pathological changes that had resulted in illnesses. Late in his life, Rokitansky once claimed to have performed over eighty thousand dissections, and he elevated the corpse—the material facticity of the human body—to the central source of medical knowledge in Vienna in the second half of the nineteenth century. The Viennese privileging of postmortem examination led to the city's status as the worldwide center of pathological anatomy, and doctors from across the globe flocked to its lecture halls and dissecting rooms. It also, however, was the central feature of what William Johnston calls Vienna's characteristic "therapeutic nihilism," which he used as a conceptual lens through which to interpret Austrian intellectual history.[25] For decades, Viennese medicine stood under the sign of understanding illness rather than treating it. It is this propensity for examination and diagnosis, often absent a therapeutic impulse, that we find reflected time and again in the cultural production of the long fin de siècle.

If we follow Freud's directive and chart the genealogy of psychoanalysis to his own training in the anatomical sciences, with the body as their material basis, we must analogously interrogate the origins of Viennese modernism, since its own creation myth has been linked inextricably to a psychological turn. The prehistory of that psychological turn is, as this study claims, a corporeal turn. The fascination with the body in Viennese culture not only predated the allure of psychoanalysis as an interpretive lens but ran parallel to it into the interwar years. The alternative genealogy I propose for Viennese culture in the long fin de siècle allows us to draw an arc that springs from the centrality of the body in Viennese medicine of the middle- to late-imperial period and extends to the communal socialist politics of the First Republic, whose health and hygiene initiatives foregrounded the body with a centrality perhaps unmatched worldwide. The materialist theory of disease that prevailed under the second Vienna medical school in the second half of the nineteenth century had raised the body to a central position in Viennese thought and culture long before the psyche achieved predominance. Anatomy's and pathology's concern with the corporeal colored Viennese culture for decades to come, not least in Freud and Josef Breuer's early work on hysteria, which emphasized the legibility of the body as a text. As scientific and medical knowledge filtered outward from universities and clinics, the idea of controlling the body through dietetics, hygiene, fitness, and—taken to the extreme—through social-Darwinist eugenics, racial hygiene, and criminology permeated public discourse. Popular illustrated newspapers such as *Der Kuckuck* regularly devoted entire pages, for example, to everyday hygiene matters and health concerns. Philipp Sarasin speaks of a "culture of bodily knowledge" that transformed the ancients' philosophical dictum "Know thyself!" into a bourgeois educational directive from 1850 onward.[26] That mandate became the catchphrase of Viennese hygiene and public education initiatives, as well as of pedagogical reforms for the working classes, particularly in the interwar First Austrian Republic.

The fascination with the human body in Viennese culture stems not only from the centrality of the materialist conception of disease under the second Vienna medical school, as I argue, but also, as Werner Hofmann notes, from the Austrian Catholic tradition, with its dogma of the word become flesh.[27] David Luft, moreover, identifies one of the distinctive

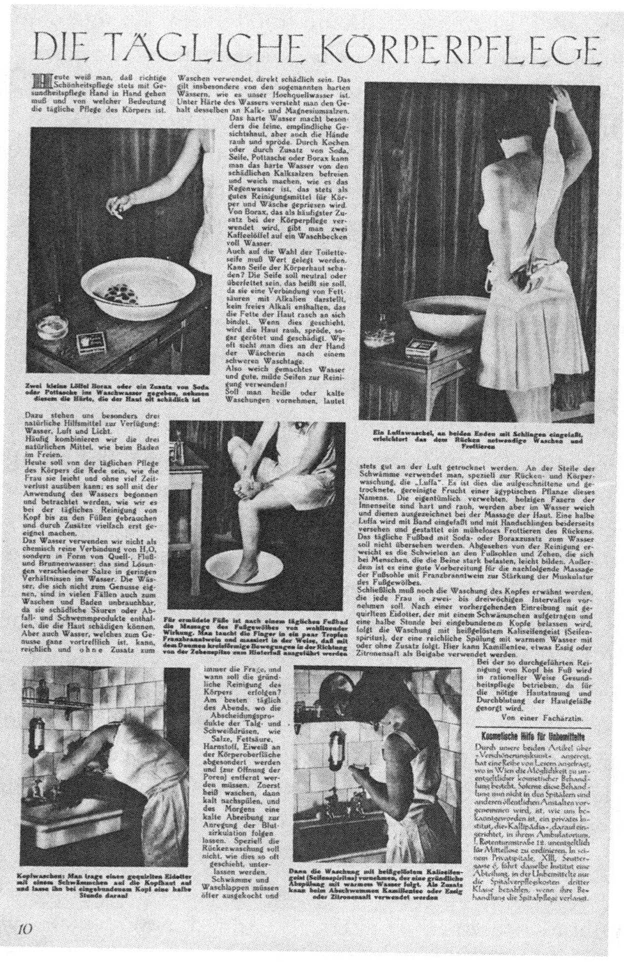

DIE TÄGLICHE KÖRPERPFLEGE

Heute weiß man, daß richtige Schönheitspflege stets mit Gesundheitspflege Hand in Hand gehen muß und von welcher Bedeutung die tägliche Pflege des Körpers ist.

Dazu stehen uns besonders drei natürliche Hilfsmittel zur Verfügung: Wasser, Luft und Licht.
Häufig kombinieren wir die drei natürlichen Mittel, wie beim Baden im Freien.
Heute soll von der täglichen Pflege des Körpers die Rede sein, wie die Frau sie leicht und ohne viel Zeitverlust ausüben kann; es soll mit der Anwendung des Wassers begonnen und betrachtet werden, wie wir es bei der täglichen Reinigung von Kopf bis zu den Füßen gebrauchen und durch Zusätze vielfach erst geeignet machen.
Das Wasser verwenden wir nicht als chemisch reine Verbindung von H_2O, sondern in Form von Quell-, Fluß- und Brunnenwasser; das sind Lösungen verschiedener Salze in geringen Verhältnissen im Wasser. Die Wässer, die sich nicht zum Genusse eignen, sind in vielen Fällen auch zum Waschen und Baden unbrauchbar, da sie schädliche Säuren oder Abfall- und Schwemmprodukte enthalten, die die Haut schädigen können. Aber auch Wasser, welches zum Genusse ganz vortrefflich ist, kann, reichlich und ohne Zusatz zum Waschen verwendet, direkt schädlich sein. Das gilt insbesondere von den sogenannten harten Wässern, wie es unser Hochquellwasser ist. Unter Härte des Wassers versteht man den Gehalt desselben an Kalk- und Magnesiumsalzen.
Das harte Wasser macht besonders die feine, empfindliche Gesichtshaut, aber auch die Hände rauh und spröde. Durch Kochen oder durch Zusatz von Soda, Seife, Pottasche oder Borax kann man das harte Wasser von den schädlichen Kalksalzen befreien und weich machen, wie es das Regenwasser ist, das stets als gutes Reinigungsmittel für Körper und Wäsche gepriesen wird. Von Borax, das als häufigster Zusatz bei der Körperpflege verwendet wird, gibt man zwei Kaffeelöffel auf ein Waschbecken voll Wasser.
Auch auf die Wahl der Toiletteseife muß Wert gelegt werden. Kann Seife der Körperhaut schaden? Die Seife soll neutral oder überfettet sein, das heißt sie soll, da sie eine Verbindung von Fettsäuren mit Alkalien darstellt, kein freies Alkali enthalten, das die Fette der Haut rasch an sich bindet. Wenn dies geschieht, wird die Haut rauh, spröde, sogar gerötet und geschädigt. Wie oft sieht man dies an der Hand der Wäscherin nach einem schweren Waschtage.
Also weich gemachtes Wasser und gute, milde Seifen zur Reinigung verwenden!
Soll man heiße oder kalte Waschungen vornehmen, lautet immer die Frage, und wann soll die gründliche Reinigung des Körpers erfolgen? Am besten täglich des Abends, wo die Abscheidungsprodukte der Talg- und Schweißdrüsen, wie Salze, Fettsäure, Harnstoff, Eiweiß an der Körperoberfläche abgesondert werden und (zur Öffnung der Poren) entfernt werden müssen. Zuerst heiß waschen, dann kalt nachspülen, und des Morgens eine kalte Abreibung zur Anregung der Blutzirkulation folgen lassen. Speziell die Rückenwaschung soll nicht, wie dies so oft geschieht, unterlassen werden.
Schwämme und Waschlappen müssen öfter ausgekocht und stets gut an der Luft getrocknet werden. An der Stelle der Schwämme verwendet man, speziell zur Rücken- und Körperwaschung, die „Luffa". Es ist dies die aufgeschnittene und getrocknete, gereinigte Frucht einer ägyptischen Pflanze dieses Namens. Die eigentümlich verwebten, holzigen Fasern der Innenseite sind hart und rauh, werden aber im Wasser weich und dienen ausgezeichnet bei der Massage der Haut. Eine halbe Luffa wird mit Band eingefaßt und mit Handschlingen beiderseits versehen und gestattet ein müheloses Frottieren des Rückens.
Das tägliche Fußbad mit Soda- oder Boraxzusatz zum Wasser soll nicht übersehen werden. Abgesehen von der Reinigung erweicht es die Schwielen an den Fußsohlen und Zehen, die sich bei Menschen, die die Beine stark belasten, leicht bilden. Außerdem ist es eine gute Vorbereitung für die nachfolgende Massage der Fußsohle mit Franzbranntwein zur Stärkung der Muskulatur des Fußgewölbes.
Schließlich muß noch die Waschung des Kopfes erwähnt werden, die jede Frau in zwei- bis dreiwöchigen Intervallen vornehmen soll. Nach einer vorhergehenden Einreibung mit gequirltem Eidotter, der mit einem Schwämmchen aufgetragen und eine halbe Stunde bei eingebundenem Kopfe belassen wird, folgt die Waschung mit heißgelöstem Kaliseifengeist (Seifenspiritus), der eine reichliche Spülung mit warmem Wasser mit oder ohne Zusatz folgt. Hier kann Kamillentee, etwas Essig oder Zitronensaft als Beigabe verwendet werden.
Bei der so durchgeführten Reinigung von Kopf bis Fuß wird in rationeller Weise Gesundheitspflege betrieben, da für die nötige Hautatmung und Durchblutung der Hautgefäße gesorgt wird.

Von einer Fachärztin.

Zwei kleine Löffel Borax oder ein Zusatz von Soda oder Pottasche ins Waschwasser gegeben, nehmen diesem die Härte, die der Haut oft schädlich ist

Ein Luffawaschel, an beiden Enden mit Schlingen eingefaßt, erleichtert das dem Rücken notwendige Waschen und Frottieren

Für ermüdete Füße ist nach einem täglichen Fußbad die Massage des Fußgewölbes von wohltuender Wirkung. Man taucht die Finger in ein paar Tropfen Franzbranntwein und massiert in der Weise, daß mit dem Daumen kreisförmige Bewegungen in der Richtung von der Zehenspitze zum Hinterfuß ausgeführt werden

Kopfwaschen: Man trage einen gequirlten Eidotter mit einem Schwämmchen auf die Kopfhaut auf und lasse ihn bei eingebundenem Kopf eine halbe Stunde darauf

Dann die Waschung mit heißgelöstem Kaliseifengeist (Seifenspiritus) vornehmen, der eine gründliche Abspülung mit warmem Wasser folgt. Als Zusatz kann beim Abschwemmen Kamillentee oder Essig oder Zitronensaft verwendet werden

Kosmetische Hilfe für Unbemittelte

Durch unsere beiden Artikel über »Verschönerungskunst« angeregt, hat eine Reihe von Lesern angefragt, wo in Wien die Möglichkeit zu unentgeltlicher kosmetischer Behandlung besteht. Soferne diese Behandlung nun nicht in den Spitälern und anderen öffentlichen Anstalten vorgenommen wird, ist, wie uns bekanntgeworden ist, ein privates Institut, die »Kallipädia«, darauf eingerichtet, in ihrem Ambulatorium, I. Rotenturmstraße 12, unentgeltlich für Mittellose zu ordinieren. In seinem Privatspitale, XIII, Seuttergasse 6, führt dasselbe Institut eine Abteilung, in der Unbemittelte nur die Spitalverpflegskosten dritter Klasse bezahlen, wenn ihre Behandlung die Spitalpflege verlangt.

10

Fig. 2. "Daily Bodily Hygiene" (Die tägliche Körperpflege). *Der Kuckuck*, November 17, 1929, 10. ANNO/Österreichische Nationalbibliothek, Vienna.

features of the Viennese intellectual and cultural world as an accent on the "powerful role of feelings and the body in human experience." Accompanied by a pessimistic existential bent, one Luft reads through Otto Weininger, Robert Musil, and Heimito von Doderer, the centrality of the body in Viennese culture resulted from the confluence of scientific materialism—especially as manifest in medicine—and philosophical irrationalism in the second half of the nineteenth century.[28] Luft has a wider perspective in mind on the latter point, but in our context, Nietzsche's wise man in *Zarathustra* springs to mind: "Body am I through and through," he says, "and nothing besides; and soul is just a word for something on the body. The body is a great reason, a multiplicity with one sense, a war and a peace, one herd and one shepherd."[29] It is, in other words, everything.

Underlying this book's focus on the specifically Viennese interest in the body in the decades surrounding the turn of the century is the body's centrality within the wider contextual landscape of modernity. The task Bahr laid out for his contemporaries in fin-de-siècle Vienna—to investigate the body and its determinants, to analyze its destinies, births, and deaths—amounts to nothing less than an early appeal for the "corporeal turn" that has lately received sustained scholarly attention.[30] The rubrics *body studies* and *body history* have become common cross-disciplinary parlance since the 1980s, following on the heels of Foucault's foundational studies about the sexuality, illness, and disciplining of bodies and the rediscovery of Norbert Elias's monumental *The Civilizing Process* (1939).[31] The reams of critical literature produced in recent decades attest to a persistent interest in the body, as well as in its cultural, social, philosophical, and historical construction.[32] The din around the body has been so resonant in academic circles over the past four decades that the medievalist Caroline Bynum was prompted early on to ask (one senses not without a trace of exasperation), "Why all the fuss about the body?"[33] Interest in the body as an object of inquiry has proliferated in fields as far ranging as ethnography and anthropology; art history and literary studies; feminist, gender, and sexuality studies; sociology and urban studies; and philosophy and historical studies of all stripes—from political, social, and cultural history to the histories of science and medicine.

The corporeal turn has been framed by the notion—building on Foucault and articulated most trenchantly by feminist scholars such as Judith Butler, Susan Bordo, Elizabeth Grosz, and others—of the body as a historical, sociocultural, and political construct.[34] The body is, in other words, not merely a biological given but is discursively created and subject to the inscription of power and knowledge. Bordo, for example, views the body as a cultural text, open, like other forms of cultural creation, to reading and interpretation. Similar to cultural studies' and new historicism's view that artists and their aesthetic production are inseparable from their surroundings, Bordo views the body as equally mutable and subject to change according to its sociocultural context. Her important study *Unbearable Weight: Feminism, Western Culture, and the Body* probes the sociohistorical underpinnings that have influenced perceptions of the (female) body. Arguing with both feminist theory and Foucault, Bordo maintains that attitudes toward the body have evolved over time, in accordance with the powerful influence of institutions, media, and other hegemonic forces. As a result, the body—and perceptions of it—are far from enduring; instead, they are impermanent, subject to reappraisal and modification, and compelled to adapt in accordance with their varying contexts.[35]

This fact is significant not just for the framing of women's bodies but also for the bodies of other marginalized populations, including those distinguished by class and ethnicity. While feminist scholars have highlighted how women's bodies are sites where discursive power is exercised, the same holds true for Jewish bodies and the bodies of the working classes. Particularly in the context of medicine, which forms one of the focal points of this study, Sander L. Gilman has demonstrated how Jewish "difference"—and the purported difference of many others—has been historically constructed through medical discourses.[36] Gilman and Klaus Hödl have documented the dangerous seamlessness between the scholarly study of biology, anatomy, and other human sciences, on the one hand, and the biology of "race" as a constructed category, on the other, that characterized late nineteenth- and early twentieth-century scientific and medical discourses.[37]

Especially salient in our context is Caroline Bynum's pinpointing of two distinct sets of theoretical constructs frequently deployed in contemporary studies on the body. Either the body is referred to in terms of its limits, locatedness, boundaries, and constraints—whether in biological, physical, or social terms—she argues; or the body is referred to in the context of its limitlessness, desire, or potentiality, as a flexible construct or a malleable representation.[38] Both of these conceptions of the body were, however, already present at the turn of the century. Around 1900, the body was either conceived of as constraining/constrained and limiting/limited, something to be overcome, improved upon, or mastered; or it was viewed in terms of its potential, its seeming limitlessness, its versatility and flexibility. And, as we will see, sometimes the boundaries between the groupings collapsed.

While Bordo's contextual perspective and Bynum's conceptual outline inform my approach to the body in Viennese modernism, it is also important to keep in mind, as the art historian Lynda Nead reminds us,

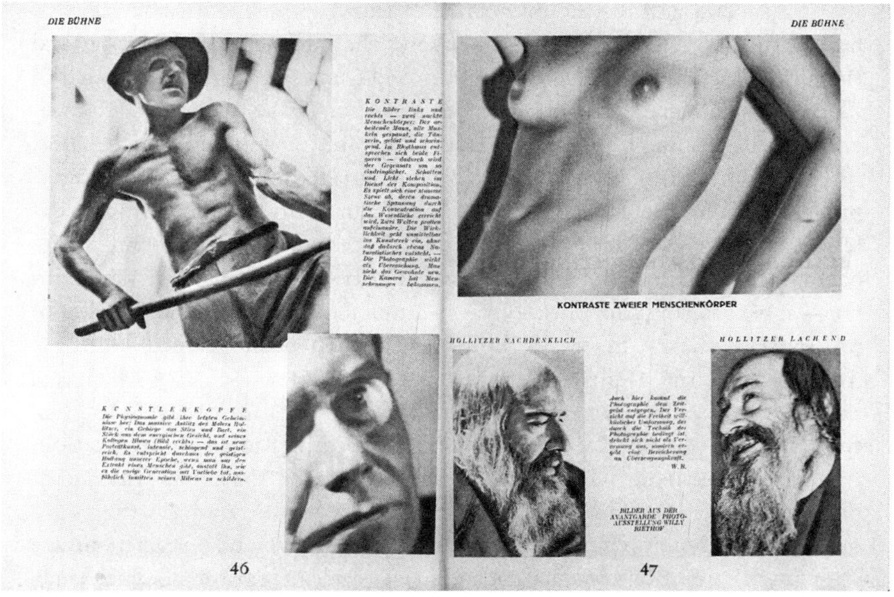

Fig. 3. "Contrasts of Two Human Bodies" (Kontraste zweier Menschenkörper), two-page spread. *Die Bühne*, February 1, 1930, 46–47. Photographs by Willy Riethof. ANNO/Österreichische Nationalbibliothek, Vienna.

that cultural representations—literary, visual, and mental—always produce bodies. "There is no recourse to a semiotically innocent and unmediated body," she contends.[39] For this reason, my approach to the body is not strictly historical but focuses primarily on a wide variety of representations and theories of the body from the time frame covered. It moreover investigates the social practices and material cultures—themselves historically contingent—that mark and frame historical bodies.[40] These materialities and practices, it is worth remembering, necessarily inform the ways in which we "read" and make sense of the bodies at hand. Published in *Die Bühne* in 1930, a striking photo spread by Willy Riethof (1905–94) invites viewers, for example, to consider the "contrasts of two human bodies." An image of a bare-chested worker is juxtaposed with that of a dancer's nude torso; both are surrounded by physiognomic photo studies of artists' countenances. The caption does not merely alert us to the social and cultural practices that shaped the bodies we see depicted here but also notes that "two worlds collide" in the image assemblage. That the "camera has gained human eyes," according to the commentary, also bears witness to debates about the mutual influence of bodies and media.

The second half of the nineteenth century witnessed a sea change in how bodies were perceived, and—beyond the advances in medicine and the natural sciences I have already sketched—any number of factors led to its centrality in the culture of the fin de siècle. These included the physical culture craze; prevailing philosophical and epistemological debates, in particular those about the status of language; processes of industrial modernization; and a changed and rapidly changing media-technological landscape. It is no great leap to imagine that the sweeping epochal shifts occurring in these and other arenas at the turn of the century led many to feel—appropriating Marx and Engels's famous formulation and the title of Marshall Berman's important work—as if all that had seemed solid was melting into air.[41] Hence, the persistence of the term *crisis* with regard to modernity and its effects. In Schorske's reading of fin-de-siècle Vienna, that crisis was one of the liberal ego; in Jacques Le Rider's interpretation, it was a generational identity crisis; for John Boyer, the crisis was one of party politics.[42] Beyond specific local manifestations, though, the pages of past and contemporary reflections on modernity and modernism are strewn with mentions of crises of the senses and perception, of experience, language, and representation, of the self. Sara Danius has suggested that the artistic practices we classify under the rubric of modernism are, when viewed in this frame of reference, many different kinds of "crisis management."[43] If modernity was characterized by a pervasive sense of crisis, and if modernism is a collection of various forms of crisis management, what, then, could serve as stable grounding, as a counterweight to all the upheaval of an era W. H. Auden famously called "the age of anxiety"?

In response to an epochal sense of unmooring, Auden's sonnet sequence "In Time of War" (1939), written on the brink of World War II and in the year after the Austrian "Anschluss"—that is, at the close of the era this book considers—offers an answer: "We have no destiny assigned us: / Nothing is certain but the body."[44] Ulrich, the protagonist of Robert Musil's monumental, unfinished novel *The Man without Qualities* (Der Mann ohne Eigenschaften), similarly proclaims, in 1913, the dawn of "an era of physical culture, for the only thing that gives ideas some sort of foothold is the body to which they belong."[45] As the categorical distinctions between self and the world, subject and object, *Geist* and *Gesellschaft*, were increasingly destabilized in the decades around 1900, the materiality of the body appeared to offer substance, stability, and certitude—particularly vis-à-vis the shadowy, immaterial depths of the psyche, which Freud had begun to plumb. In her landmark study *The Body in Pain*, Elaine Scarry argues that historical watersheds of philosophical and social crisis result in recourse to the body. When belief is undermined—that is, when central philosophical or religious tenets, key ideologies, and accepted cultural constructs are called into question—Scarry maintains that people appeal to "the sheer material factualness of the human body" in order to imbue their lifeworlds with "the aura of 'realness' and 'certainty.'"[46] The fascination with the corporeal in Viennese modernism corroborates Scarry's assertion. The body was looked to as a kind of somatic and semiotic utopia, which seemed to offer answers to pressing questions in an era of unsettling change. It shows that modernity was not merely a "condition," a series of crises and efforts at crisis management, but that it was also "performed and experienced." Modernity thus not only acts *on* bodies but is also acted out *with* bodies—and representations of them.[47] An array of desires was projected onto the body, as people sought to create "presence," enhance "immediacy," recover "naturalness," and adequately express the "authenticity" of lived experience. Such questions were asked across a range of aesthetic genres—including literature, painting, pantomime, modern dance, and silent film.

Let us recall for a moment Hermann Bahr's appeal to his Viennese contemporaries in 1890 to observe, investigate, and depict bodies. For Bahr, that utopian call to aesthetic action had taken a more reflective philosophical turn after the fin de siècle. Writing in his journal in 1906, Bahr pointed to the disconnect between the bodies his generation felt they *should* have—embodiments of a highly developed civilizational spirit—and the bodies they *actually* had. "We are all suffering from the fact that our bod[ies] are not keeping pace with [our] will[s]," he remarked. "It is as if we had already achieved the spirit of a higher human form, but the body we are schlepping behind us from the earlier [form] cannot satisfy the [new spirit]. And perhaps we must suffer so much from this affliction that from it strength will one day spring forth, [the strength], commensurate with the strong new spirit, that will at last form the body anew." If those of the younger generation believe they can simply declare themselves to be Nietzschean Übermenschen, they are sorely mistaken, he opines. Bahr describes the process necessary to achieve correspondence between mind and body: "First, a crisis. This becomes a powerful yearning. From it, the spirit forms an image. The growth of the body follows from that. We are currently engaged in devising the image of a new human being. And are feeling the labor pains." The quest for a "new human being," the goal of a "new body"—both of which should be ideal manifestations of the era's "new spirit"—are, Bahr argues in the same entry, the "longing of the entire generation."[48]

What follows in *The Naked Truth*, then, are generational snapshots of a wide-ranging search to better understand the self and others, to create a sense of belonging, to access "truth" and meaning in the modern world—through the body. The subsequent chapters crisscross six decades, frame dozens of figures, and traverse aesthetic and scientific domains. Each chapter focuses on a recurrent corporeal topos that occurred across genres of cultural production: bodies on display; bodies in pieces; patients' bodies; and bodies in motion. Taking a thematic approach allows us to regard from a variety of vantage points how and why the works of various writers and artists engage, often very differently, with the body.

The Naked Truth makes the case for the centrality of the body in Viennese modernist cultural production in four narrative chapters, each revolving around a constellation of protagonists. Canonical figures in Viennese culture—Peter Altenberg, Adolf Loos, Arthur Schnitzler, Ödön von Horváth, Egon Schiele, Vicki Baum, and Hugo von Hofmannsthal—are brought into dialogue with other fascinating yet often overlooked figures, such as the author and doctor Marie Pappenheim, the poet Ilka Maria Ungar, the journalist Else Feldmann, the visual artist Carry Hauser, the film theorist Béla Balázs, and the dancers Grete Wiesenthal, Gertrud Bodenwieser, and Hilde Holger, for example. The individual chapters, each centering on a specific trope of the body, likewise allow different modes of cultural production—literature, popular exhibitions, painting, the performing arts (pantomime, dance), and silent film—to intersect. This thematic approach enables the diachronic consideration of genres and authors, while simultaneously highlighting the synchrony of the era's interart relations, sociocultural networks, and crossover between aesthetic production and medico-scientific discourses.

Chapter 1 examines how human bodies were staged and represented in popular public exhibitions at the fin de siècle. Initially, the Viennese sought to define themselves vis-à-vis cultural others. The late imperial period's large-scale human displays, so-called ethnographic exhibitions, were implicated in both science and spectacle. Austro-Hungarian anthropology and ethnography—disciplines that emerged directly from (pathological) anatomy as Vienna's leading medical specialization—developed corporeal taxonomies on the basis of measurements taken from the peoples on display. As new display modes increasingly invited physical transgression, spectators were invited to become armchair scientists at the expense of exhibition participants. Later, after the turn of the century, it was the body of the self that was put on display in blockbuster hygiene exhibitions, which showcased the achievements of both Austria's medical sciences and its imperial aspirations. Much like the life reform movements of the same period, the hygiene exhibitions pursued utopian goals of improving the body to create a healthy, classless *Volksgemeinschaft* (people's community) of equals as a civilizational corrective to the perceived ills of modern society. In the interwar years, the discourses, displays, and visual codes shifted again, as "new humans" took center stage in Social Democratic biopolitics. This chapter connects medical science and social history as reflected in exhibition culture to Viennese cultural production in the work of a leading Viennese modernist author, Peter Altenberg. Altenberg's literature was uniquely attuned to the human body, and his books *Ashantee* (1897) and *Pròdrŏmŏs* (1906) coincided with—and spotlighted in prose—the bodies on display in the exhibitions.

Chapter 2 uncovers a hidden geography of medical institutions in Viennese modernist literature by attending to the body in pieces. From the 1880s to the 1930s, Viennese literature repeatedly presented the dissecting room as the birthplace of knowledge, and, as under the second Vienna medical school, the corpse was the object on which the search for truth was carried out. Two doctor-writers, Marie Pappenheim and Arthur Schnitzler, employ the trope in this fashion. Schnitzler, long acclaimed as an "anatomist of the soul"—his writing regarded as the literary counterpart to Freud's theories of the unconscious—shows that key works, including *Dream Story* (Traumnovelle, 1925–26), were indebted to his training as a bona fide anatomist. Following World War I, the corpse comes to serve a different, social function, as in Joseph Roth's early journalistic work and Carry Hauser's graphic art. The University of Vienna's Anatomical Institute subsequently took on dubious social relevance in Ödön von Horváth's drama *Faith, Hope, and Charity* (Glaube Liebe Hoffnung, 1932), which fictionalizes a Viennese trade in cadavers. The text reveals much about the desperation of the working poor, whose bodies were conceived of as commodities to be capitalized on in the hopes of alleviating their misery. The corpse as a central topos in Viennese modernist literature functions as a truth-teller, whether in epistemological or social terms.

Chapter 3 brings to light an interface between cultural production and institutional medicine in Vienna—one that intersects on the patient's body, and more specifically on the pregnant bodies of working-class women. The chapter tracks how changing conceptions of motherhood were reflected in Viennese literature, visual art, and medicine in the first three decades of the twentieth century. It embeds these representations in a historical framework that renders visible operations of gender, class, and power (per Foucault) to show that in Vienna between 1900 and 1930, the working-class mother's body became an increasingly contested site. Early in the twentieth century, forgotten poets such as Marie Pappenheim and Ilka Maria Ungar sought to give a literary voice to working-class mothers on their own terms. Meanwhile, contemporary painters such as Egon Schiele were granted direct access to patients as models in institutional medical settings by doctors, who were at once advocates, benefactors, and patrons. The pregnant female body was made tractable by new clinical architecture, which structured the gaze. It also included film sets that turned out popular "enlightenment" films, underwritten by central architects of the famous interwar Viennese welfare state, which embedded medical knowledge about the female body in fictional frame narratives to educate mass audiences. Else Feldmann's fiction and reporting take on interwar biopolitical initiatives to regulate the expectant mother's body from a critical perspective, while socially conscious photojournalism and visual art brought representations of working-class bodies into wide circulation in the visual and textual vernacular of early twentieth-century Vienna. "Red Vienna" elevated the working-class mother to a key role in the city's sociopolitical fabric, but the clinical facticity of patients' bodies meanwhile influenced aesthetic developments within Viennese visual art.

Chapter 4 traces the interdependence of three modes of cultural production—pantomime, dance, and silent film—that eschew spoken and written language in favor of body language from the 1890s to the 1930s. What began as a response to a perceived crisis of language was increasingly seen as a way to address pressing social problems. Initially, authors and directors such as Bahr, Schnitzler, Hugo von Hofmannsthal, and Max Reinhardt revived the folk tradition of pantomime in the 1890s, turning to gesture as an idealized mode of communication. The development of free dance in Vienna, largely through Grete Wiesenthal after 1900, merged with this trend. Viennese cultural producers, including Hofmannsthal and the writer Vicki Baum, moreover used pantomime and dance to negotiate questions of Jewish identity. By the 1920s, Viennese dancers such as Gertrud Bodenwieser and Hilde Holger had begun critiquing the social implications of urban industrial modernization in their expressive dance (*Ausdruckstanz*). The gestural principles and performative presence underlying pantomime and dance were important templates for silent film. Béla

Balázs penned the first book-length work of film theory in German while living in exile in interwar Vienna, but he was preceded by Hofmannsthal's similarly inflected theoretical texts. Chapter 4 demonstrates that in Viennese modernist dance, pantomime, and film, gesture was viewed as a kind of urlanguage, a seemingly more truthful, immediate, and universal form of communication than written language. That notion operated on the premise, informed by Vienna's nineteenth-century anatomical and physiological traditions, that bodies are not only fundamentally legible but also sources of initially hidden knowledge. The chapter moreover brings into focus the significant, often ignored contributions of Viennese modern dancers, most of them women, within this developmental trajectory.

Vienna was, of course, no vacuum. Both before and after the First World War, which transformed it from the first city of a multinational empire to the socially progressive capital of a widely unloved rump republic, Vienna was woven into the wider fabric of a vibrant central and eastern European cultural network. For all its range, the development of Viennese body culture paralleled that of Berlin and Munich, Prague, Budapest, Zagreb, and Lviv—let alone that of New York, London, and Paris.[49] A truly transnational history of the body in central Europe remains to be written, but in order to treat the Viennese aspect of that larger history with the necessary analytical depth, this study's geographic area of inquiry is delimited.

While the geography of this study is restricted to Vienna, my viewfinder is trained on a wider temporal vista, which—along with the aforementioned geographic question prompted by such an undertaking—is best conceived of metaphorically, to speak with Scott Spector, as the thin ridge of a mountain range.[50] Each step toward it reveals an ever more sweeping panorama beyond, in other words, and it becomes increasingly difficult to separate the fin de siècle proper from that which came after it. More conventional historiography tends, whether for utilitarian or ideological reasons, to hew close to definitive political or existential fracture lines. Salient examples in the Austrian context would be the Austro-Hungarian Compromise of 1867; the end of World War I, and with it the Habsburg monarchy, in 1918; and the so-called Anschluss of 1938. Yet such a rupture-foregrounding approach is apt to minimize, or even obscure, significant political, intellectual, and aesthetic continuities—to say nothing of the persistence of discursive patterns—over the course of decades.[51] The necessity of taking a long chronological view, not merely of the nineteenth century but also of the fin de siècle and modernism, is particularly vital when biopolitical discourses are in play, as they are in this study.[52] In this case, adhering to conventional chronological boundaries runs the risk of downplaying discursive continuities about the body or turning a blind eye to the "unitary context," as Geoff Eley has phrased it, that gave rise to the specific confluence of modern rationalistic, eugenic, hygienic, racist, and nationalist thought in Germany, Austria, and central Europe at large—all centered on questions of difference and belonging defined through the human body.[53] The National Socialist mobilization of these corporeal discourses is not the focus of the present study. Rather, I look at discourses of the body and body-based practices from the perspective of their formation and evolution rather than their disastrous co-option. However, the epilogue spells out their catastrophic convergence in the Viennese context, thus also looking beyond convenient historical fracture lines.

The stakes of such a transdisciplinary, synthetic approach are manifold. First, it significantly revises and expands our knowledge about and understanding of modern Austrian history and Viennese cultural history as a whole. Challenging Carl Schorske's notion of *homo psychologicus* as the paradigmatic instantiation of Viennese modernist culture, the present study offers a new examination of Viennese cultural production in the decades surrounding the fin de siècle. Under the broad rubric of "rethinking Vienna 1900," Steven Beller, Allan Janik, Scott Spector, and Pieter Judson have, along with the Austrian scholars Wendelin Schmidt-Dengler, Hubert Christian Ehalt, Evelyne Polt-Heinzl, and others, stressed the need for a revision of the "Schorskean paradigm."[54] I argue that such a counterparadigm is found in the body and its history.[55]

Second, *The Naked Truth* applies the historical concept of the long fin de siècle to the Viennese cultural field. Strictly defined, Viennese modernism is understood as an aesthetic movement in literature, the arts, and music in the two decades between 1890 and 1910.[56] But more recent scholarly work has begun to argue for the necessity of broadening the approach to include its antecedents and, particularly, its descendants.[57] The editors of the seminal *Metropolis Vienna: Textures of Modernism* (Metropole Wien: Texturen der Moderne, 2000), for example, recognized the necessity of integrating interwar Red Vienna into a *longue durée* of Viennese modernism.[58] This perspective had earlier been modeled by the Historical Museum of the City of Vienna's monumental exhibition *Dream and Reality: Vienna 1870–1930* in 1985, as well as by William Johnston's comprehensive historical framework for understanding Viennese culture and thought, both of which highlighted the richness and diversity of modernist cultural and intellectual production over a wide temporal span.[59] I adopt a similar sweep. While detailed studies and exhibitions focusing exclusively on the interwar years have done much to upend the hegemonic "Vienna 1900" myth,[60] the caesuras of 1918 and 1919—World War I, the dissolution of the Habsburg empire, and the founding of the First Austrian Republic—still persist as historically convenient divides. The ruptures in human experience wrought in these pivotal years are incontrovertible, and they make good sense when the point of departure is political. This book, however, is concerned foremost with cultural production, which certainly registers critical historical and political events but does not break off neatly according to years and dates. Rather, each chapter contains an arc that couches the cultural production of the late-imperial fin de siècle proper between that of the nineteenth-century liberal era and interwar Red Vienna. This approach pinpoints aesthetic continuities, and maps the evolution of discursive trajectories about the body across the boundaries imposed by political historiography.

Third, in its emphasis on interdisciplinary connections, *The Naked Truth* builds on the tradition of prior, influential historiography on Viennese thought and culture, including that of Schorske and many others.[61] However, my approach diverges sharply from earlier studies of Viennese modernism by incorporating discussions of popular culture. Genres the study takes seriously, such as the mass press, photography, silent film, dance, pantomime, and exhibition cultures, are not traditionally treated alongside literature, painting, architecture, and music in work on Viennese modernism. Considering popular culture enables us to recover neglected works by canonical artists and authors, many of whom exhibited a concentrated, lifelong engagement with such forms. Hofmannsthal's understudied works for pantomime, dance, and film—genres he worked in from the early 1890s until the end of his life—are perhaps the best case in point. In this regard, my research looks beyond previous secondary literature on Viennese modernism to current developments within modernist studies at large.[62]

When I speak of "culture," certainly one of the more hackneyed concepts in scholarly debates, I have in mind three separate yet intimately intertwined forms of expression of the modern human experience: canonical "high" art, "popular" culture, and common societal practices and customs. In this respect, I am indebted, of course, to Andreas Huyssen's foundational work to bridge the "great divide" between elite and popular culture.[63] But equally decisive is Mary Gluck's call to "rethink Vienna 1900" by conceiving of culture in terms of the widest possible range of responses people have when they attempt to create values and meanings in the face of epochal change such as that of the fin de siècle.[64] While I do not claim to offer a new theoretical model for cultural history, the spectrum of cultural creations I consider corroborates in practical terms how accounting for the richest and most varied forms of cultural production can pry open the rigid historiographic mythology of Vienna 1900. It took several decades for a revisionist perspective to emerge, but since roughly our own fin de siècle, historians have registered no small amount of "discontent" about the reification of "Vienna 1900" as a discursive subject.[65] Austrian historians such as Siegfried Mattl, Wolfgang Maderthaner, Lutz Musner, Alfred Pfoser, Roman Horak, and Gerhard Meissl have been instrumental in reappraising the Schorskean paradigm. A good deal of their criticism has hinged precisely on the fact that an artificial split between "high" and "low" forms of cultural production was erected and then sustained for decades by bracketing popular culture out of analyses of Viennese modernism.

Historiography's lacunae, though, have not been limited to the cultural products themselves. By adopting an interdisciplinary methodology that considers popular cultural forms alongside "high culture," *The Naked Truth*, fourth, gives overdue consideration to a host of forgotten figures from the Viennese cultural sphere, many of them relegated to the periphery of or erased from cultural histories altogether on account of gender, ethnicity, or class. Much recent work has been done to show that it was not just the collective Oedipal revolt of a young generation of Viennese sons, as Schorske framed it, that made Viennese modernism what we know today. Crucial revisions have drawn increased attention to *who* created Vienna modernism and *under what conditions*. That women, Jews, and the working classes were for too long largely omitted from the founding narratives of turn-of-the-century Vienna is now being redressed. Just how vitally women cocreated Viennese modernism has been demonstrated in literature by Lisa Silverman, in the visual arts by Julie Johnson, and in politics, building on Harriet Anderson's formative study.[66] Viennese culture would have been unthinkable without its high number of Jewish cultural creators and the pivotal role of Jewish patrons in sponsoring the avant-garde. As Stefan Zweig famously wrote, "nine-tenths of what the world of the nineteenth century celebrated as Viennese culture was in fact culture promoted and nurtured or even created by the Jews of Vienna."[67] The work of scholars such as Steven Beller, Lisa Silverman, Marsha Rozenblit, Abigail Gillman, Elana Shapira, Alison Rose, Elisabeth Malleier, Klaus Hödl, and Hillary Hope Herzog has offered necessary correctives, bringing the contributions of Viennese Jewish writers and artists back into the very center of Viennese cultural life, where they rightfully belong.[68] Scott Spector has worked from Vienna's social margins to provide us with a more nuanced picture of how Viennese from across the social spectrum experienced their lifeworlds, while Wolfgang Maderthaner and Lutz Musner's revisionist social history of Vienna crucially recovered the working classes on "the other side of fin-de-siècle Vienna."[69] A spate of exhibitions on the role of women in the work of Klimt, Schiele, and Oskar Kokoschka has also begun to redress the gender imbalance in public-facing knowledge about Viennese modernism.[70] This study extends such efforts, but goes further by incorporating them in the wider framework of a leading cultural trope.

Lastly, *The Naked Truth* makes a significant contribution to a growing field of historical scholarship that has recently begun to investigate how Viennese modernism was inextricably intertwined with the era's scientific and medical cultures.[71] Such connections were frequently created, whether consciously or unconsciously, through individual cultural multipliers, who forged intellectual matrices of influence. Through the activities of key figures, the arts, the sciences, politics, and social concerns were brought into dialogue with one another. Implicitly, my work supports the "Vienna circles" model of network-based thinking put forth by Edward Timms.[72] By mapping the cultural field of Viennese modernism, Timms revealed how various groups of artists, writers, philosophers, journalists, and politicians coalesced and interacted.[73] *The Naked Truth* profits from such network-based thinking, while bringing to light other as yet unrecognized connections and advancing the case for links between medical science and cultural production. This approach is reminiscent of a remark by Robert Musil in his essay "The Obscene and Pathological in Art" (1911): "To experience the need for (artistic) representation . . . means to depict something: to represent its connections to a hundred other things; because objectively nothing else is possible, because only in this way can one make something comprehensible and tangible, . . . as even scientific understanding can only arise through comparisons and connections, and as this is the only way human understanding can arise at all."[74] Musil's network theory serves as my guide in what follows.

The resulting historically and disciplinarily synthetic model enables a novel perspective on Viennese culture and society between 1870 and 1938. This study sheds light on the extent to which figures from across the artistic, political, and intellectual spectrum engaged with the body both as a material source of knowledge and as a site of utopian possibility. Such an analysis likewise opens up new avenues of investigation for post–World War II Austrian culture, since the fascination with the corporeal has persisted unabated until today. Questions about how we view and define ourselves—both as individuals and as a society—are unremitting; they are the fundamental questions of life. We will never cease to look to our own bodies and those of others for answers. But as Paul Valéry reminds us, "We speak of [the body] to others as of a thing that belongs to us; but for us it is not entirely a thing; and it belongs to us a little less than we belong to it."[75] Valéry's insight returns us once more to the Viennese study of Hermann Bahr and Klimt's naked Truth, her painted mirror aloft. To whom does the body belong? This question reverberates throughout the case studies that follow.

CHAPTER ONE

The Body on Display: Staging the Other, Shaping the Self

The postal ship arriving from Budapest on the afternoon of July 10, 1896, docked at the Weißgerberlände on the Danube canal in Vienna's third district. Local newspapers had been trumpeting the ship's arrival days in advance, and a crowd over two thousand strong turned out to welcome the vessel. Journalists from the *Illustrirtes Wiener Extrablatt*, the *Neues Wiener Tagblatt*, and other dailies were on the scene that day and reported how, with "thunderous jubilation, like at an electoral victory," the throngs cheered the visitors and surged toward the quay, each person straining to catch a glimpse of the disembarking party. The police, anticipating such a commotion, had fenced off and restricted public access to the landing earlier in the day. Despite their best efforts, though, the authorities could maintain crowd control only with great effort.[1] What could have incited the normally decorous Viennese to such feverish anticipation? The arriving contingent consisted of close to seventy natives from Africa's Gold Coast, and the *Extrablatt*'s writer remarked that the Viennese people "would have lifted the black people onto their shoulders if they could have."[2] "Ashanti fever" had gripped Vienna.[3]

The thirty men, eighteen women, and twenty children[4]—purportedly members of the Ashanti people of what is today south-central Ghana—had arrived to take part in the latest in a series of so-called ethnographic or anthropological exhibitions, also known as *Völkerschauen* (shows of peoples), and which I will refer to here as human displays.[5] The human display was a form of popular entertainment that became ever more fashionable in Europe around the turn of the century. Vienna alone was host to more than fifty such exhibitions between 1870 and 1910, averaging more than one per year for forty years straight.[6] Audiences likewise swarmed to another kind of exhibition staged after the turn of the century, with increasing frequency into the interwar years: hygiene exhibitions. Both trends hinged on the public staging and display of the human body for consumption and comparison. While human displays profited from exploitation and voyeuristic spectatorship in their stagings of the "exotic" body of the cultural Other, hygiene exhibitions trafficked in knowledge about the bodily Self. Despite their marked differences, both phenomena posited surprisingly homologous utopian concepts of "natural" and "authentic" living and "natural" and "ideal" bodies, which acted as foils for the anxieties of modern society.

Advances in medicine and hygiene in the second half of the nineteenth century had afforded people lives that were healthier and longer than ever before. The popularization of discoveries from the life sciences and medicine gave more and more Austrians knowledge about their bodies, allowing them to reflect on and tailor their lifestyles to achieve improved health and longevity. While modernization and scientific progress certainly bettered the lives of many, the heightened attention to individual and social disciplining of the body also revealed a gap between physical ideals to be striven for and people's corporeal realities. The longing of an entire generation for "new men" and "new women"—in short, for a modern human being, who became a paradigm of twentieth-century revolutionaries, reformers, and dictators alike—necessitated a new relationship with the body and new discourses of the body.[7] At work here is a process of identity construction, both individual and collective, a process that occurs through the staging, visualization, and representation of two bodies: the body of the Self and the body of the Other. As this chapter proposes, the shaping of individual and collective corporeal identities commensurate with turn-of-the-century Viennese modernism and modernity at large was played out in the display of human bodies in popular culture.

At work in all of these contexts is a sense of longing—a desire to recover something lost, to make present something absent, or to access something (or someone) forbidden or unapproachable. From their inception, human displays were designed to give the impression of authentic encounter. Just as such exhibitions sold audiences the premise that they were seeing authentic native peoples who live in closer alignment with nature, the life reform and hygiene movement promised physiological optimization—an approach to the body's "authentic" state—through improved lifestyles. At the heart of this longing, in both cases, is the human body. And the sciences and medicine were, as we will see, deeply implicated in the objectification and instrumentalization of the body—its display, exoticizing, documentation, eroticizing, comparison, and classification—that permeated Viennese life in the decades around the turn of the century. These domains also filtered into Viennese modernism.

Read together, the issues outlined here find a prominent place in the cultural production of one of the leading players in fin-de-siècle Vienna, but one typically read as a quixotic, bohemian contrarian: Peter Altenberg. Altenberg's oeuvre is a remarkable nexus for the phenomena highlighted above—the vogue for human displays and the life reform movement—as well as for the diverse elements of the cultural discourse of the body around 1900. Perhaps more than anyone else at work in turn-of-the-century Vienna, Altenberg took up Hermann Bahr's call to engage with the body and create a "new man" to go along with the modernist spirit. In turn, Altenberg's experiments shed light on processes of personal and collective identity construction through the body in fin-de-siècle Vienna.

SCIENCE AND SPECTACLE: "EXOTIC" BODIES ON DISPLAY

The jubilant reception that greeted the Ashantis at the Weißgerberlände in July 1896 was crowned by a celebrity parade in typical Viennese style. *Fiaker*, the horse-drawn carriages so characteristic of the city's image even today, ferried the participants from the quay to the city center and around the Ringstraße, before arriving at the zoological garden in the Prater park.[8] The Ashanti village was very literally a human zoo inside a zoo. There, the "villa colony," as it was called, consisted of roughly a dozen huts, arranged in circular fashion around an open tract, where it would remain for more than three months.[9] While earlier human displays had aroused ample journalistic attention, the Ashanti village's size, scale, and detail kindled unprecedented public and media excitement. The exuberant crowds that had met the arriving ship turned out en masse for the duration of the exhibition, breaking all prior box office records. Fifteen thousand visitors attended on the opening afternoon alone; for the month of July one hundred and six thousand attendees were counted. On Sundays, the exhibition regularly drew up to thirty thousand paying visitors, and some days were so full that entry had to be restricted.[10] Both highbrow Viennese newspapers, such as the liberal *Neue Freie Presse*, and the popular press kept curious readers current about the daily goings-on at the Ashanti village in great detail. The *Neues Wiener Tagblatt* and *Illustrirtes Wiener Extrablatt*, for example, dedicated significant column space to the events. Stories and dispatches—often with prominent front-page or feuilleton placement—

appeared nearly every day for the show's tenure. "'Ashanti' has become the ultimate word *du jour* in Vienna," remarked Robert Franceschini, science feuilletonist for the *Neues Wiener Tagblatt*. He continued:

> It is as if there were only few other interests to be had in Vienna that are more important than a visit to the Negro village. . . . Since the black caravan came here from Budapest, almost only one stereotypical question is heard in public places and when people meet on the street: "Have you been to [see] the Ashantis?" And there is hardly any get-together without the Ashanti village sooner or later being the topic of conversation. The public displays a virtually feverish attention for it, and like people at archery and singing festivals [*Schützen- und Sängerfesten*], who are happy when they get to shake the hand of an archer or singer, now they are happy when they can sit at a table with Negroes or carry a black child in their arms. Brotherhoods are toasted to, friendships forged, and some European enthusiasts even attempt gallant overtures toward the beauties from the Gold Coast.[11]

Franceschini's summary captures something of the enthusiasm the exhibition aroused. Even decades later, the memories of visiting the exhibition remained vivid, as an article from the *Arbeiter-Zeitung* from 1928 by the journalist Else Feldmann documents.[12] While such accounts highlight the Viennese public's sustained desire for contact with the peoples on display, they do not, for the most part, reflect critically either on how these people came to be on display in Vienna or on their experiences.

The 1896 Ashanti village was an unmatched box office hit, but it was hardly the first such exhibition in Vienna. Human displays date back to the first third of the nineteenth century, and the Ashanti were among the first to arrive in Vienna. In 1833, for example, the *Wiener Zeitung* ran advertisements announcing an exhibition of "Africans from the warmongering nation of the Ashantis."[13] Beginning in the early 1870s and continuing well into the 1920s and 1930s, a steady stream of indigenous peoples—Sudanese, Swahili, Sinhalese, Zulu, Australian Aborigines, Native Americans, Bedouins, Siamese, Samoans, Burmese, Inuits, American cowboys, and countless others—populated Vienna's public exhibitions grounds. Exhibitions of this kind were fixtures in the popular entertainment landscape of the 1860s and early 1870s throughout Europe. The German impresario Carl Hagenbeck (1844–1913), however, knew to capitalize on this trend and coined the term *Völkerschau* to describe the live visual displays of humans that would make him famous. Hagenbeck had already made

Fig. 4. "The Ashanti Chief with His Royal Court" on display in Vienna, 1897. *Wiener Bilder*, May 16, 1897, 3. Photographer unknown. ANNO/Österreichische Nationalbibliothek, Vienna.

a name for himself with his family-run animal menagerie and zoological garden in Hamburg by 1875, when he began importing and exhibiting non-Western peoples for "ethnographic" purposes. Traveling performances such as Hagenbeck's ranged from a single person to ensembles of hundreds, and each exhibition was designed to present a specific geographical region or a particular national, cultural, or ethnic group. The troupes traveled from city to city, appearing at world's fairs, museums, and other popular entertainment venues across Europe. Most frequently, though, they ended up in zoological gardens like the one in Vienna's Prater park—which were undergoing a transformation in purpose in the late nineteenth century. Here, entire villages were constructed, complete with dozens of "authentic" huts, places of worship, and ritual grounds for dances and other cultural performances. Often, such native villages were set up alongside sculpted botanical and zoological landscapes that displayed flora and fauna native to the region in question.[14]

The human display craze in fin-de-siècle Vienna and elsewhere can be read in the context of a wider culture of what Vanessa R. Schwartz has called "spectacular realities," which emerged from and played a pivotal role in the entertainment industry of the late nineteenth century. These included such popular cultural forms as the mass illustrated press, wax museums, dioramas and panoramas, early film, and anatomical, pathological, and ethnographic museum collections, all of which purported to represent contemporary life "realistically," but in fact relied on sensationalism to reach the broadest possible audiences.[15] In Vienna, the majority of human displays were concentrated in the Prater, the park that became a focus of Viennese public life after Emperor Joseph II opened it for general recreation in the mid-eighteenth century. By the late nineteenth century, the Prater—with its central attraction, the Wurstelprater amusement zone, immortalized by Felix Salten in his 1911 book[16]—had become a "doubly exotic" site of twin spectatorial pursuits: masses crowding the exhibition spaces to catch glimpses of "exotic" peoples; and an educated, bourgeois audience purporting to observe the "primitive" gawking behavior of a broad mass public.[17] "Exotic" behaviors and "exotic" bodies alike were the subjects of study.

Among the visitors were not only the usual Prater habitués, the working classes, but also the heir presumptive Archduke Franz Ferdinand and the Viennese artistic set, including Richard Beer-Hofmann, Arthur Schnitzler, Felix Salten, and Peter Altenberg, many of whom rendered their encounters in literature.[18] Theodor Herzl, for example, expressed amazement about the exhibitions on view in "The Human Zoo" (Der Menschengarten), which ran in the *Neue Freie Presse* in April 1897. "Well now I have seen everything!" he marveled in the article, whose title is a play on the word *Tiergarten* ("animal garden," or zoo). "In the Prater there are any number of 'wild' people and animals currently assembled, brought here by entrepreneurs for curious onlookers who could never travel to such faraway places. One sees Samoans, Singhalese, and Ashantis, and in the cages, pens, pits, and enclosures all manner of beasts, worms, and birds. . . . In what forms the species that want to survive take refuge! And what terrors the struggle for survival generates."[19] The liberal *Neue Freie Presse*—for which Herzl was the Paris correspondent during the Dreyfus affair in the mid-1890s, and of which he became feuilleton editor at the same time his Zionist activities were intensifying—was not alone in its uncritical remarks that the native peoples exhibited in the Prater satisfied the spectatorial voyeurism of audiences incapable of traveling to experience foreign cultures in situ. Carl Hagenbeck's first biographer asserted that human displays "gave to the millions of people who are unable to search out other kinds of fellow humans living in remote parts of the earth, in their homeland, the sight of them among us."[20] Like souvenirs acquired on travels abroad, these human displays are generated and driven by narratives told only through the active intervention of the possessor or stager. Such narratives say everything about the longings of the stager and reveal nothing about the thoughts or identity of the staged, for they are not given a voice.[21] The encounter with the Other—and with the body of the Other—brought spatially and temporally closer through human displays, and under the guise of "knowledge," serves as a foil to understand and construct one's own identity.

The stagings had become so much in vogue that by 1893 they warranted an entry in a contemporary German encyclopedia. *Meyers Konversations-Lexikon* described "anthropological exhibitions" as "performances of representative foreign peoples for the satisfaction of visual pleasure and the dissemination of anthropological knowledge."[22] This definition clearly points to two separate but related premises of these spectacular takes on reality, which included human displays: performance and consumption and the spread of knowledge (in the case of the *Völkerschau*, "anthropological" knowledge). These self-professed goals were manifest in a process of exchange between forms of popular visual culture and more traditional educational and scientific institutions, such as national history museums. As the historians Siegfried Mattl and Werner Michael Schwarz have noted, around 1900, museums and scientific institutions began to draw on popular culture techniques of the spectacle in their display practices in order to entice wider audiences into classical educational settings. Alongside traditional display formats, museums, like Vienna's Natural History Museum, opened in 1889, began integrating lifelike forms of presentation—including dioramas, wax figures, and mannequins—into their visual repertoires, aiming to transmit to viewers a sense of completeness and realism. The goal was to make information palatable, to make education easily digestible in the formal museum setting.[23] Simultaneously, mass entertainment culture, including Hagenbeck's human displays and Hermann Präuscher's Anatomical Museum in the Prater, began relying on scientific attestations and a light educational agenda to gain legitimacy and to veil, albeit thinly, the mere profit-orientedness of such ventures.[24] In short, venerable museums, in open competition with edutainment, were beginning to use popular spectacular culture to increase their commercial viability, aiming to position themselves as more respectable but still entertaining educational and scientific venues. At the same time, popular cultural forms like human displays were mobilizing real scientists and (pseudo)scientific knowledge to gain a semblance of respectability while returning a financial gain. Human bodies provided the capital for this process of exchange. Normtransgressing bodies—the "spectacular," "pathological," and "exotic"—were staged in both contexts for commercial profit and intellectual edification.[25] In the last two decades of the nineteenth century, two trends converged: the commercialization of science and the scientifization of commercial entertainment.[26]

Reporting on two events, in particular, illustrates the focus on the indigenous people's corporeality in the context of fin-de-siècle Vienna's craze for human displays. On October 12, 1896, for example, the *Neues Wiener Tagblatt* reported that an Ashanti man ran into trouble with local authorities after striking an exhibition attendee with apparently characteristic "southern passion." The newspaper stated that the Ashanti was provoked when the Viennese man and his wife "showered" him with "pinches and other caresses."[27] The couple claimed that they had only wanted to touch the man, to feel his skin. A similar incident even led to a court case, when Hermine Schandl, a cashier at the "Venice in Vienna" theme park, adjacent to the Prater zoo, brought charges against the Ashanti chief's wife, Jabolëh Domëi. Schandl claimed to have been rendered unable to work for three days after reportedly having been slapped in the face by the chief's wife. Now Schandl was suing to recover lost wages. Questioned by the judge about the circumstances that led to the incident, Schandl recounted having attended the exhibition after work one day with a colleague, Wessely. Schandl testified that she had wanted only to show Wessely "the lustrous, velvety-soft skin of the chief's wife . . . and to this end she claims to have used her hand to caress the [woman's] black neck." Wessely's deposition, however, told a different story. He stated that Schandl was "exceedingly curious" and alleged she lifted up the woman's shawl "in order to touch the body."[28] The court ruled in favor of the Ashanti chief's wife, finding that she had acted in self-defense. Although the case Schandl brought was merely dismissed and Domëi was not compensated for her own grievance, the physical violation against Domëi was duly noted by the court.

Such incidents of transgressive physical contact between the exhibited people and exhibition attendees not only were made possible but were also fueled by several converging factors. First, new kinds of "semipermeable" exhibition spaces arose in the second half of the nineteenth century.[29] The trend toward more open exhibition spaces was manifest perhaps most saliently in the transformations of museum and zoological displays of the age. Museums, for instance, began integrating dioramas visitors could walk through instead of being separated from exhibited objects in closed glass vitrines.[30] Likewise, menageries, assortments of tropical birds and exotic fauna in elaborate cages, underwent a significant shift in the late nineteenth century. The terms *zoologischer Garten* and *Tiergarten*—literally, "zoological garden" and "animal garden," respectively—originated around this time and reflect the relative freedom of movement afforded both animals and spectators.[31] Semipermeable exhibition spaces, among which the Ashanti village and other human displays can be counted, invited a different relationship between the audience and the exhibited persons or objects. Inherent to newer display practices was the potentially transgressive enticement to cross the line, tempting audience members to breach the boundaries between themselves and the humans on display.[32]

Hagenbeck recognized the attraction of allowing direct contact between exhibition participants and visitors relatively early on in his ventures. During the "Singhalese Caravan" he brought to Vienna in 1885, spectators were encouraged to interact with the natives. The interactive quality of the shows, albeit staged, fostered a sense of "immediacy," "presence," and "authentic" encounter among viewers.[33] This effect was further underscored by the fact that everyday activities, such as family affairs (births, nursing, baptisms, funerals, etc.), schooling, and work, were exhibited at the Ashanti village. Eric Ames maintains that—by commingling foreign cultural traditions with everyday events that would have appeared familiar to European viewers—live, interactive displays such as the Ashanti exhibitions of 1896 and 1897 in Vienna "de-exoticized the other, rendering it familiar and comprehensible, without destroying the lure of the exotic."[34] Thus, the semipermeability of boundaries and the transgressive potential were twofold: not only were the borders between the exhibited humans and audience members made penetrable; the dividing line between the exotic or spectacular and the commonplace or quotidian was also, to a certain extent, lifted. But lawsuits brought by exhibition visitors such as Hermine Schandl show the exhibitions' true dividing line: it is less the semipermeability of spaces—valid of course from only one side, that of the spectator—and far more the body, physical contact, which is revealed to be the real boundary.

The second facet fueling direct, often transgressive, interaction between natives and spectators at the human displays was a dominant and uniform thread in journalistic coverage over their duration: ceaseless reporting, often in elaborate detail, about the Ashantis' bodies.[35] All of these descriptions, Herzl's included, read like objectifying, anthropological analyses, clearly guided by the scientific racism of the age. Favoring a sensational, subjective reporting style, the newspapers focused on the natives' nudity from the day of their arrival. The *Extrablatt* reported that "the dark bodies, only their loins covered, almost gleamed in the blazing sun," while the *Tagblatt* wrote of "half-naked" Africans, whom the police had directed to cover up their "Adam-like exposed bodies."[36] That the Ashantis' often revealing, "authentic" tribal dress would, for European viewers, be at once scandalous and riveting was a selling point certainly not lost on the exhibition organizers. By commercializing ethnographic depictions, news outlets and impresarios routinely profited from the effect that nude or partially clothed black bodies had on white, European audiences still firmly under the sway of nineteenth-century mores governing morality, respectability, and sexuality.[37]

Herzl's and others' journalistic portrayals of the Ashanti point to a final aspect that encouraged the transgression of semipermeable boundaries between exhibition audiences and exhibited peoples: the role of science and pseudoscience in the context of human displays. In *Die Fackel*, Karl Kraus, one of the few critics of such shows among his contemporaries, stridently censured Herzl and others for their ostensibly "scientific" and "empirical" approach. Were Herzl merely an "idle gawker" or a "thoughtless spectator," his observations could perhaps be passed over as base ignorance, Kraus argued. Instead, ominously, "such shows prompt him [Herzl] to serious reflections, to scientific conclusions." Kraus countered, "Frankly, I find it shameless and scandalous to put human beings on display and to charge money to contribute to the exposure and distortion of their national characteristics; and all that just to accommodate the thirst for knowledge of 'comfortable researchers' and to satisfy their 'ethnographic participation.'"[38] Kraus was virtually alone in recognizing the application of scientific knowledge to justify cultural and racial prejudice for profit.

As the nineteenth century waned, ethnography and anthropology were gaining increasing legitimacy as disciplines in their own right. As Andrew Zimmerman has noted, the very roots of anthropology as a scientific discipline in the European context are to be found in popular culture in general, and in human exhibitions in particular—and even more specifically in the rapid growth of popular scientific discourse within the public sphere.[39] At the same time, fields that would today be considered pseudosciences—craniology, phrenology, physiognomy, anthropometry, graphology, and the like—contributed to the reification of these scientific fields. But both the sciences and the pseudosciences concurrently attained a significant degree of popular authority by purporting to establish links between subjects' physical appearance and alleged psychological traits.[40] Even an artist as significant as Egon Schiele was engaged to fashion physiognomic illustrations for an anthropogeographic treatise as late as 1917.[41]

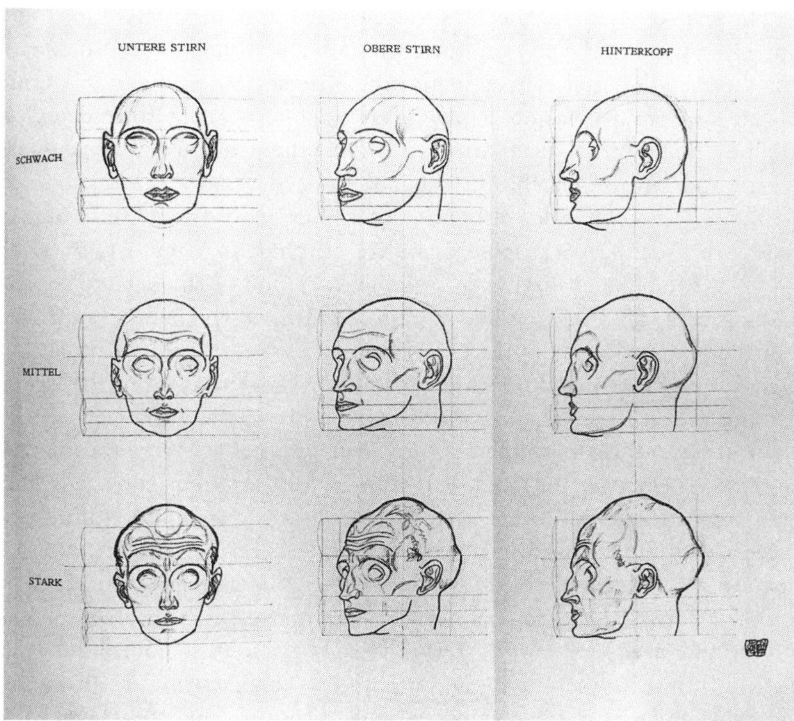

Fig. 5. Egon Schiele, physiognomic drawings of human heads. Erwin Hanslik, *Wesen der Menschheit*, Schriften des Instituts für Kulturforschung 5 (Vienna: Verlag Institut für Kulturforschung, 1917), n.p.

From the inception of the human display as a cultural phenomenon, the organizers integrated science and the pseudosciences into their presentations. In order to substantiate the participants' "authenticity," the exhibition promoters commonly elicited attestations and endorsements from scientists and researchers. In the early days of the exhibitions, the impresarios turned to linguists, who would conduct interviews with the exhibited people and determine whether they were native speakers of the languages of the ethnic groups they claimed to represent. The scientists then issued attestations, which were often widely published in newspapers and magazines or excerpted in advertisements. Significant for the present study is that the focus on determining veracity and authenticity through language shifted. As the years went on, the natives' bodies, their physical constitution, were increasingly seen as more accurate grounds on which to establish authenticity.[42]

The case of Carl Hagenbeck's Viennese debut is instructive in this regard. He arrived in the city in June 1878 with a fifteen-person "Nubian caravan," part of a larger "animal caravan." The setting was suitably grand: Hagenbeck's troupe was on display in the Prater's soaring Rotunde exhibition hall, built for the 1873 World's Fair. But the influence of Hagenbeck's human and animal exhibition was not limited to fairground audiences; he made it onto the order of the day of a meeting of the Anthropological Society in Vienna (Anthropologische Gesellschaft in Wien, AGW), which had been established just three years before. One of the society's founding members, the geologist and explorer Ferdinand Hochstetter (1829–84), took the podium at a committee meeting in early June 1878 to talk about Hagenbeck's traveling exhibition. Hochstetter held sway among the scientific community; he had, after all, been appointed inaugural director of the imperial natural history collection in 1876.[43] Standing before the committee in 1878, Hochstetter urged it to support not only Hagenbeck's troupe but also similar exhibitions. Emphasizing the "considerable interest" of Hagenbeck's "living and dead ethnographic material," Hochstetter reasoned to his colleagues that it would be desirable, perhaps even advisable, to offer a formal endorsement to such enterprises, in this first instance by issuing Hagenbeck an attestation from the scientific community. The meeting minutes document the outcome of Hochstetter's petition: "On the speaker's motion, the committee rules to certify that Mr. Hagenbeck's enterprises are not conventional shows, but a commendable undertaking that promotes science appreciably."[44] With a single vote, the Viennese academic community had granted Hagenbeck's human displays and others like them an unprecedented degree of scientific legitimacy, elevating them from mere fairground entertainment.

But one hand washed the other. Even as institutionalized organizations such as the Anthropological Society played a significant role in legitimizing enterprises like Hagenbeck's, the scientists were often invited in kind to take anthropometric measurements of the exhibition participants' bodies—the "ethnographic material" Hochstetter referenced—for their scientific research. Scientists in essence bartered scientific legitimacy for research subjects. The AGW's official academic journal, for example, frequently published research based on data collected from research subjects who were brought to Vienna as part of human displays in the Prater. For the first German Colonial Exhibition in 1896, Austrian anthropologist Felix von Luschan developed a detailed form, on which he recorded the physical details and measurements of more than one hundred African exhibition participants for a governmental report.[45] This form included the

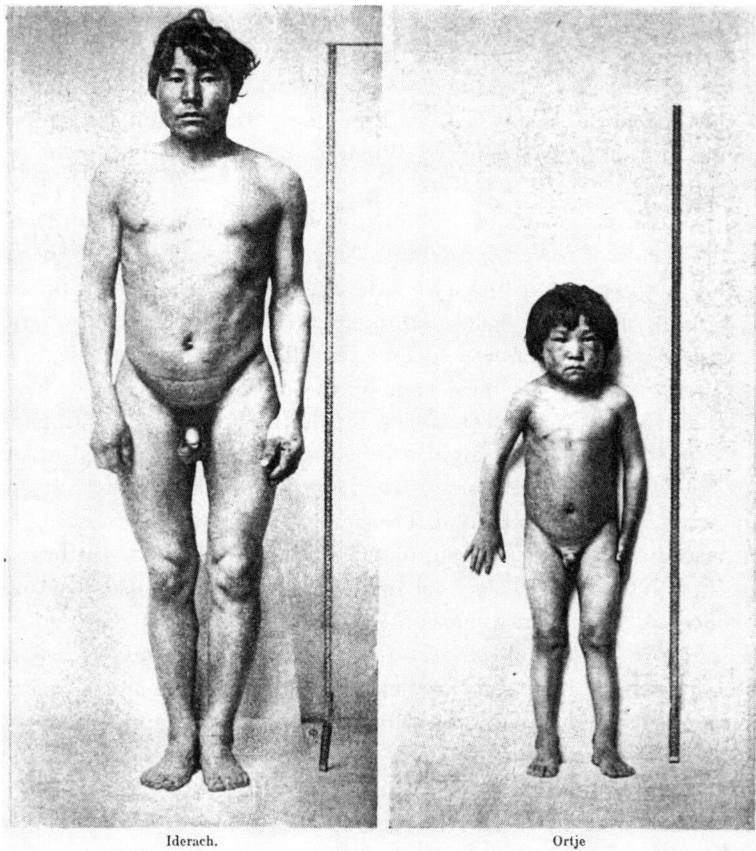

Fig. 6. Anthropometric photographs of Samoyed man (Iderach) and boy (Ortje). *Mittheilungen der Anthropologischen Gesellschaft in Wien* 16 (1886), plate 4, n.p. Photographer unknown.

standard measurements—height, weight, age, and the like—but was utterly exhaustive, including twelve possible main iris colors and a separate category with seven different colors for the very innermost part of the iris; entries for five different parts of the nose; type of eyelashes ("long, short; straight, curved; cut, pulled out"); space for a comprehensive dental record; detailed craniological measurements; and many other categories.[46] Luschan, a doctor by training, became the first university instructor in an anthropological discipline, but was approved only because he was interested foremost in physical ethnography, that is, in the physical study of the human body—an aspect of the field that made sense to the board of the medical school, steeped in the anatomical focus of the second Vienna medical school. Luschan's career demonstrates paradigmatically how the discipline of physical anthropology emerged in part from the medical school at the University of Vienna, and particularly from anatomy and physiology.[47]

Within the framework of the Anthropological Society in the 1870s, anthropology was conceived of foremost as a natural science and as the study of humankind's natural history.[48] Like many of its cousins in other European countries—more or less all founded in the three decades between 1860 and 1890—the Viennese society centered on empirical research, inductive reasoning, monogenesis, and (in the case of Austria, in contrast to Germany) Darwinism. Nevertheless, medicine—and anatomy in particular—assumed foundational significance in the emerging discipline of anthropology by the 1870s.[49] Doctors made up the single largest professional group among the Anthropological Society's members and founding functionaries. The pathological anatomist Carl von Rokitansky—the beacon of the second Vienna medical school and he of the eighty thousand autopsies, if we recall from the introduction—was the AGW's first president. And while physical anthropology may not have been a central research concern of the society initially, Rokitansky's focus on the material matter of the human body certainly cast a corporeal light on the entire endeavor. His inaugural lecture for the AGW, for example, repeatedly emphasized anatomy and physiology as the "cardinal foundations" of anthropology.[50]

The strong link between ethnography and human displays such as the Viennese Ashanti exhibitions of 1896 and 1897 is of significance here. If anthropologists could not travel to colonies to document various ethnic groups and cultures, they could take up the position of armchair scientists and let the natives come to them, as they did in the human displays of the last decades of the nineteenth and first decades of the twentieth centuries. Writing in the respected scientific journal *Zeitschrift für Ethnologie* in 1906, Luschan, by then working in Berlin, noted the high level of "scientific interest" in the people on display at the Abyssinian village exhibition held in Berlin at Castans Panoptikum the year prior. Luschan, however, is palpably disappointed, commenting that the Abyssinians would neither allow themselves to be measured or photographed "in a scientific manner," nor give hand- or footprints for anthropometric study. "Regrettable," he calls the situation, that serious scientists are limited to "a wholly superficial inspection." He wonders whether the anthropological society can exert professional influence on the exhibition organizers to convince the native people to allow more comprehensive exams, because it is "a *nobile officium* [noble mission] to examine, measure, and photograph people with precision" in the service of science.[51]

Within the context of the disciplinary reification of ethnography and anthropology, the exhibition participants served as objects of study, their bodies as scientific objects for observation and assessment. They were cataloged and objectified on the basis of their physical constitution, and the exhaustive, intricate, detailed physical descriptions of the exhibited peoples emphasized their status as scientific objects.[52] Whereas the ethnic veracity of the natives had formerly been determined by their language, dress, behavior, and disposition (in short, by their habitus, in the sense of Marcel Mauss, Norbert Elias, and Pierre Bourdieu)—all things that could ostensibly be learned—their "authenticity" was later determined on the basis of their physical bodies. As Werner Michael Schwarz writes, "The human being was reduced to that which apparently could not be falsified: to his body and above all his face, from which a person's aptitude, character, and value could be determined. . . . The person was identifiable based on that, conceived of more or less naked, just as it was carried out in reality with complete disrespect on 'exotic' people who were made to stand naked before the scientist's eye and camera lens."[53] Because the corporeal cannot be falsified or adulterated, the body, in the end, was thought to be the only true measure of identity, of cultural belonging, of "authenticity."

Just as the exhibition participants were staged in purportedly realistic village settings, the exhibition organizers staged the audience too. The promoters encouraged viewers to assume the mantle of the seemingly impartial ethnologists or anthropologists, inviting them to adopt an "anthropological gaze,"[54] similar to Kraus's notion of "ethnographic participation." The establishment of such clear anthropological boundaries was not merely scientific posturing. Far more, it allowed the culture drawing the lines—determining the us/them, civilized/primitive hierarchies—to assert the supremacy of its own cultural identity and its own race.[55] Know thyself, these human displays invited their audiences, by purporting to know the Other.

That statement of purpose is significant because it underscores the anthropological boundary as a subjective construct, the establishment and subsequent transgression of which crosses and therefore belies that other demarcation, the one between science and popular cultural entertainment. Here, again, knowledge about the human body is the epistemological staging ground for such debates. Both science and entertainment were participants in a deeper cultural shift regarding the relationship with and significance of the body. These changes were processed through public demonstrations of how the body—"exotic" bodies, in particular, but also "scientifically noteworthy" bodies—should be seen, examined, or otherwise encountered. In both the human displays and the institutional environment (whether popular or academic)—the focus was often on the human body as guarantor of "authentic" identity—be it the spectacular body, the "exotic" body, or physical pathology; in short: the body of the Other. A large portion of the fascination of the human exhibitions hinged on the fact that they put people on display, made objects intended for viewing out of their bodies. In Schwarz's words, human displays "did not simply show 'exotic' people; to put it plainly, [they showed] simply people, *bodies*, the material via which all questions of difference—social, racial, sexual, or moral difference—were negotiated in the late nineteenth century."[56] Physical difference, in other words, was the primary means by which the cultural Other was defined, enabling in turn a more concrete, if fabricated, definition of the Self. These matters of self-definition flowed into the cultural production of Viennese modernism, as a controversial, late nineteenth-century work of fiction demonstrates.

FICTIONAL ENCOUNTERS? PETER ALTENBERG'S *ASHANTEE* (1897)

"I am living in paradise," the author and *Lebenskünstler* Peter Altenberg declared in a letter to his sister Gretl Engländer from August 1896.[57] The Eden to which Altenberg referred was the Ashanti village at the zoological garden in the Prater, where the starry-eyed writer was nearly as much a fixture as the native people on display in 1896 and 1897. Altenberg was so enthralled by the Ashanti that he wrote a book about his experiences. *Ashantee*, published in 1897, was "dedicated to my black [girl] friends, the unforgettable 'paradise people' Akolé, Akóshia, Tíoko, Djôjô, Nāh-Badûh."[58] The inscription is at once a testament to the high regard in which he held the five young African women, an introduction to the book's main characters, and a reflection of Altenberg's own spurious cultural assumptions, which spring from a European colonialist and racist worldview.[59] Purporting to give the Ashanti a voice, Altenberg problematically identifies himself as one of the Ashanti and turns the liberal, bourgeois spyglass around by observing and critiquing the gawking Viennese audiences. *Ashantee* attempts—and fails—to transcend the speciously "enlightened relativism" of the liberal ideology toward the human display craze in the late nineteenth century. The text thus documents Altenberg's

Fig. 7. First edition cover of Peter Altenberg's *Ashantee*, 1897. Wien Museum, Vienna.

ill-fated efforts to encounter the Africans authentically, while simultaneously revealing the fundamentally misguided weaknesses of his own cultural and authorial perspective. For Altenberg, like Rilke and other writers of his time, fails to realize that his encounters with and subsequent writings about the Africans serve, as Ulrich Baer has written, only "the purpose of defining themselves [as Europeans], of perceiving the Africans not on their own terms but as other."[60]

Just as I cited *Meyers Konversations-Lexikon* above, Altenberg, too, opens *Ashantee* with an abridged entry from the same encyclopedic source, this one defining the Ashanti people (7). By citing a lexical entry in condensed fashion,[61] Altenberg achieves two related aims. As Sander Gilman points out, Altenberg drew on a quasi-academic source—a "textual ethnological museum" of sorts—relying on the capacity of "science" and purporting to dispel popular myths about the cultural Other, while undercutting the spectacular and objectifying pretenses of the human display as an attraction with mere entertainment value.[62] At the same time, Altenberg critiques the liberal, bourgeois notions of *Bildung* and culture, while satirizing this class's hypocritical regard for science.[63]

Altenberg introduces this critical perspective in the book's first vignette, "The Tutor" (Der Hofmeister), which is related by an omniscient narrator. The title character, a thinly veiled Altenberg, is a self-styled private tutor, master of ceremonies, and tour guide, who holds court in the Ashanti village and attempts to educate the Viennese about the exhibited people and enlighten them about themselves. The scene begins with the *Hofmeister* leading two children, Fortunatina and Oscar, through the exhibition. Appalled by the young boy's condescension toward the Ashanti children, the *Hofmeister* provides a corrective admonishment to Oscar's conduct: "Do not draw such lines between us and them. . . . Do you believe that because the dumb *Volk* places itself above them, treats them like exotic animals?! Why?! Because their epidermis contains dark pigment cells?!" (9). In a letter to Ännie Holitscher, Altenberg likewise scathingly criticized the bourgeois Viennese audiences—which he describes as "wretched animals of culture"—for not regarding the Ashanti as equals and for treating them with disrespect. Unleashing an adjectival invective, Altenberg writes, "a chasm separates them [the Ashanti] from you [the public], you impertinent, dumb, vain, hypocritical, cowardly beasts!!!"[64]

The author was no less condemnatory in a commentary published in the *Wiener Allgemeine Zeitung* in October 1897, following the departure of the second Ashanti group. Here, Altenberg again contrasts the Viennese ("Unseeligen der Cultur") with the Ashanti ("Seeligen des Primitiven"). He views the human displays in romanticizing terms, as a vaccine of sorts (*Medikament*) or restorative treatment (*Regenerations-Cur*) for "the overburdened, overfed and yet poorly nourished souls" of the Viennese and for "the old, tired, European culture-soul [*Cultur-Seele*]."[65] Speaking directly to an "enlightened" audience, Altenberg adopts a rhetoric established around the poles of belonging and not belonging, enlightenment and ignorance, a kind of us versus them mentality, whereby it is clear to which category the author presumptuously counts himself. "Yes indeed, those who conquered the pathetic and sick prejudices in themselves and encountered the blacks . . . with friendship and regard spent beautiful hours" in the exhibition, he remarked.[66] Though this statement sounds progressive for its time, Altenberg consistently succumbed to a different kind of myth-building, centered on the reasons he found the Ashanti preferable: the body and notions of "authenticity" and "naturalness."

Like the journalistic accounts sketched in the previous section, Altenberg, too, excessively thematized the Ashantis' physicality, turning their bodies into a focal point of his writing. While assuming the mantle of an enlightened equal, rather than a voyeuristic visitor, Altenberg, in actuality, falls prey to the same objectifying practices he critiques. The trap for Altenberg is the body of the cultural Other, which, like the pubescent female body, he considered transcendent, close to nature, and unblemished by civilization's harmful influences. This fundamental paradox becomes evident in the *Wiener Allgemeine Zeitung* commentary from 1897, in which Altenberg contrasted unhealthy Viennese bodies with an idealized image of the Ashantis' bodies: "Like a breath of a Greek sense of beauty, [the Ashanti exhibition] came over these all-too-fat or all-too-thin people [the Viennese], somewhat depressed and troubled, and they spoke of the delicate wrists, the beautiful lines of the arms, the regal body shapes of the black girls."[67] In a letter to Gretl Engländer, he described the Ashanti in a poeticized version of the anthropological physical inventories we encountered previously, as "the most noble figures, flawless from head to toe, skin like silk, complexion, teeth, hands marvelous."[68] Altenberg engaged in this physically objectifying discourse, writing repeatedly about the "ideal" physical qualities of the Ashanti. The vignettes "The Physiological" (Physiologisches) and "Dinner" (Souper) even show him participating in the ethnological classification practices of the time. In "Dinner," he describes the phenotype of Akóshia, one of the Ashanti women: "Slavic facial type. Madonna by Hynais, Bohemian-French. . . . Flawless physical build. Skin like silk" (22). The cultural and ethnographic frame of reference Altenberg applies is not merely European but specifically Austro-Hungarian, with the reference to the physiognomy of the monarchy's ethnic groups and to the Czech painter Vojtěch Hynais (1854–1925), schooled in Paris and Vienna. Seen in this light, Altenberg does not regard Akóshia as Akóshia, but as a physical manifestation of European culture. Her body is a screen onto which the author's sensibility, interpretation, and cultural frame of reference are projected.

Altenberg's problematic objectification of the Ashanti women and their bodies contrasts with a genuinely compassionate depiction of the physical and psychological humiliation and discomfort suffered by the Ashanti at the hands of the impresarios and exhibition visitors. "Conversation" (Gespräch), the second vignette in *Ashantee*, recounts an exchange between the narrator and Tíoko about the arrival of an early fall cold snap in Vienna and its effects on the residents of the Ashanti village.[69] The narrator comments on the frosty damp and wonders why the Ashanti are naked in such weather. Tíoko responds that Clark, one of the exhibition's impresarios, will not allow them to wear weather-appropriate clothing to protect themselves from the frigid wind. Tíoko reports, "We are not allowed to wear any clothes, Mister, no shoes, nothing, we even have to take off the headscarf. 'Take it off,' says Clark, 'take it off. Do you intend to present yourself as a lady?!'" When the narrator probes further, Tíoko explains that they must embody stereotypical exotic, primitive Africans. "We must act as wild people, Mister, Africans. It is complete foolish. We could never be like that in Africa. Everyone would laugh. Like 'men of the bush,' yes, those. No one lives in such huts. Those are for dogs where we come from, gbé. Quite foolish. They want us to act like animals. . . . Clark says: 'Hey, there are enough of those in Europe. Why does one need you?! Of course you have to be naked'" (14).[70] Here, a contradiction becomes apparent that replays throughout the text. By calling attention to the fact that the Ashanti would never go out unclothed in such weather at home, Altenberg undermines, perhaps unwittingly, the notion of the natives as "authentic primitives."[71] Whereas behavior is adaptable based on context, he holds to the body as the true marker of authenticity. Nevertheless, Altenberg seems to insist, throughout *Ashantee* and elsewhere, on upholding precisely that notion of the Other's authenticity in his treatment of them. Moreover, it is precisely the women's exposed bodies that make possible the kind of prurient voyeurism that characterizes the whole of the text.[72] This becomes clear in *Ashantee* when the narrator imagines what Tíoko is doing in the village that evening: "Tíoko quivers in the garden, lays the thin, heliotrope-colored calico cloth over her marvelous, light-brown breasts, which otherwise lived in freedom and beauty, as God created them, giving the noble male eye an image of world perfections [*Weltvollkommenheiten*], an ideal of strength and blooming" (12).

The flawed idea of a "noble male gaze" with purely aesthetic, asexual interest in the Ashanti women is consistently bolstered by a rhetorical subtext that recurs throughout *Ashantee*, indeed throughout Altenberg's work and his fascination with pubescent girls. That subtext is the discourse of "naturalness,"[73] which is perhaps most evident in the vignette "Culture" (Cultur). Peter A., the author's fictional alter ego, and the two Akolés—"big" Akolé (seventeen years old) and "bibi" Akolé (seven years old)—have been invited to a dinner party in Vienna at the home of Frau H., during which both of the girls, to the surprise of the guests, proved to be well mannered and educated. Their table manners, the narrator comments, were comparable to those of "English ladies from the queen's court" (28), and both received dolls as gifts from the hostess. The older of the two proceeded to unknot the top of her toga, revealing her "ideal" torso and breasts, and began to nurse the doll. The Viennese dinner guests responded in wonderment at the self-evident naturalness of the elder Akolé's action, with the host, Frau H., remarking that "it was the holiest moment of her life" (29). Altenberg's impassioned exclamations—such as "This is how it was in paradise. Naked, wonderfully formed, free people with peace"[74]—and his consistent emphasis on the Ashantis' physicality and naturalness make it easy to interpret his focus on bodies and an idealizing rhetoric of naturalness as the product of an aestheticizing, eroticizing male gaze.

Regarding "nature" and "naturalness" merely as smoke screens for sexualized male voyeurism belies the true complexity of these concepts in Altenberg's work, however. The tropes of naturalness and the physical ideal—present not just in *Ashantee,* but throughout Altenberg's oeuvre—do far more to explain his fascination with the cultural Other, with pubescent girls, and with nature and the natural world as such. These three categories form leitmotifs in his work, but all three come together neatly in the "Culture" vignette in *Ashantee.* Conversing with Fräulein D. about the "paradise-people," Peter A. explains that Africans, children, and nature arouse in him similar feelings: "Negroes are children. Who understands them?! These Negroes are like the sweet, mute nature. They make you sound out, while they themselves are music-less. Ask what the forest is, the child, the Negro?! They are something that brings us to sound out [Etwas sind sie, was uns zum Tönen bringt], the conductors of our symphony orchestra. They play no instrument, they conduct our souls" (28–29). Altenberg had already formulated these thoughts in an earlier letter to Ännie Holitscher. Explaining the motivation behind his almost daily visits to the Ashanti exhibition in the summer of 1896, he wrote: "The nature that I enjoy in these beloved black men is more beautiful than that of the Salzkammer region, or far more it is the same. It is mute nature, which gives her wonderful being, sings symphonies in us, while they themselves are toneless."[75] The fact that in both texts, all three categories referred to—the cultural Other, the child, and nature—are "toneless" and "play no instrument" points precisely to Altenberg's construction of them as screens onto which unfulfilled or thwarted desires for freedom, naturalness, innocence, physical vigor, and vitalism can be projected. For Altenberg, life in the city—with its endless sea of apartment blocks, its insalubrious smog—was tantamount to sheer antinature, which led only to physical and psychological incapacity. In an essay on Altenberg, W. G. Sebald described Altenberg's plight as a perpetual inability to be at home in the city, which resulted in a longing to recover something of a lost, romanticized natural *Heimat*.[76] Altenberg searched for, and found, screens onto which to project this desire: the female, pubescent body; the body of the Other; and nature, even if that version of nature was an artificially constructed African village within the Prater's confines. He once described the Ashanti village as an "'oasis of romanticism,' in Vienna, the unforgiving metropolis."[77] All three are aggregated under the labels "nature" and "natural," which denote a kind of utopian, distinctly nonurban state of existence unaffected by human interference. And it is that desire for a pure, natural existence that will allow us to contextualize the significance of the life reform movement in his later work, *Pròdrŏmŏs* (1906).

SOMATIC UTOPIAS: VIENNESE HYGIENE EXHIBITIONS

Ten years after the Ashanti people arrived to such fanfare in Vienna and took up residence in the Prater, another type of exhibition was staged there. It was as much of a blockbuster as the human displays, and this time, too, the subject was the human body. The exhibition's focus was, however, the body of the self, not the body of the Other. The setting for the Viennese General Hygienic Exhibition (Allgemeine Hygienische Ausstellung), mounted from May 12 to July 15, 1906, was spectacular: like Hagenbeck's human display from 1878, the General Hygienic Exhibition was held in the Prater's Rotunde, a soaring circular steel construction erected for the 1873 World's Fair.[78] The space was chock-full of close to 1,200 exhibitors from all corners of the Habsburg Empire plying their newest innovations. Everything from mineral waters, naturopathic supplements, and medicines to bathtubs, reform clothing, washing machines, mattresses, cleaning products, literature about hygienic ways of living, and much more was on proud display.[79] According to the exhibition's organizers, the goal was to present hygiene "as applied knowledge and applied art."[80] Viennese eager to learn about ways to improve their physical health and well-being flocked to the Prater. Open from 9 a.m. to midnight every day for its run, the exhibition drew nearly half a million visitors over the course of three months.[81] That meant, in concrete terms, that roughly one in every four residents of Vienna visited the show, and the opening hours were clearly tailored to enable the working classes, in particular, to attend after their shift work. A postcard from the exhibition emphasizes this

Fig. 8. "The People's Diet" (Volksernährung), commemorative postcard from the General Hygienic Exhibition (Allgemeine Hygienische Ausstellung), Vienna, 1906. Author's collection.

democratic impulse. It depicts four mothers in traditional folk attire tending to infants, one of them breastfeeding, under the rubric of "People's Nourishment."

The Viennese were far from alone in their enthusiasm for public hygiene exhibitions. Such shows were mounted across Europe in London, Paris, Berlin, and Dresden in the first decades of the twentieth century. The huge 1906 exhibition in Vienna was a forerunner, though, predating the well-known International Hygiene Exhibition in Dresden by a full five years. In addition to the 1906 exhibition, two further shows were staged in Vienna in 1925 and 1937. Such large-scale exhibits aimed to reach the broadest possible audience by combining medical science about the body and hygiene, targeted at laypeople, with concrete directives about how to best improve one's physical constitution. The goal of hygiene exhibitions was to show people how their bodies could be—that is, to create a kind of static exhibition of body techniques that modeled how to achieve aspirational physical ideals. "Know thyself," the ancient Delphic maxim, was the motto that applied to such displays about the human body. The inscription on a photograph of Peter Altenberg in a bathing costume on the Lido in 1913 gives pointed expression to the stakes at the heart of these exhibitions and the life reform movement, more broadly: "Show me how

Fig. 9. Peter Altenberg on the Lido, with an inscription by Altenberg, 1913. Photographer unknown. Wien Museum, Vienna.

you are 'built,' and I will tell you who you are."[82] Viennese attended such exhibitions to gain knowledge about their bodies, but also, in Altenberg's terms, to learn what it meant, constitutionally, to be modern, urbane, and healthy members of Austrian society.

The spatial overlap and temporal parallel between the performative displays of real human bodies in the Prater, which I analyzed previously, and the 1906 hygiene exhibition is striking. In one case, visitors were invited to view cultural Others as a foil against which to define themselves; in the other, they were trained to cultivate an appreciation for the Self as a fully realizable, perfectible ideal. They were supplied strategies for shaping their lives and refining their bodies. As Michael Hau has detailed, the body is the site of a cult of continuous progress; it is subject to improvement, perfection, and fortification.[83] The knowledge about the human body staged at public health and hygiene exhibitions encapsulated an illusion of the human body as healthy, efficient, controlled, and perfectible. Over the course of the first three decades of the twentieth century, this conception of the body would expand from a personal, individual pursuit to a national ideal.

The public display of information about physical health and hygiene around the turn of the century must of course be viewed in the wider context of the life reform movement (*Lebensreformbewegung*).[84] As in much of central Europe, the life reform movement had gained significant momentum in Vienna by the late nineteenth century, drawing interest from a diverse, primarily urban populace. Vienna had even been home to an early magazine that espoused many of the tenets that would later characterize life reform. The *Popular Austrian Health Newspaper* (Populäre Österreichische Gesundheits-Zeitung), subtitled "A Warning for the Healthy and a Comfort for the Suffering," was published twice weekly in Vienna from 1830 to 1840 and promoted life reform teachings among the Viennese long before the notion of life reform was formally articulated. The term *life reform movement* was first used in the programmatic contexts of health and nutrition circles in the 1890s, but comparable terminology had existed at least since the first third of the nineteenth century.[85] By 1900, *life reform* had become an umbrella term for a complex network of corresponding and often competing projects, orientations, and discourses, ranging from animal rights and environmentalism, peace movements, women's suffrage, penal reform, and homeopathy to abstinence and vegetarianism, child protection, educational reform, land reform and garden city movements, and naturism, among others.

The concept of life reform was manifest on three levels: personal self-improvement (*Selbstreform*); collective enterprises, including clubs, associations, and coalitions; and institutional ventures, such as schools, restaurants, sporting grounds, and health-food stores.[86] The life reform movement was a relatively decentralized movement, consisting of countless figureheads and international, national, regional, and local groups of widely varying membership that cut a broad swath across gender, class, and ethnicity—with individual organizations targeting every possible self-identification. Despite its many branches, the common idea was that

Fig. 10. "Air and Sunbathing on the Schafberg" (Luft und Sonnenbad am Schafberg), 1925. Advertisement for *Pflegestätte für Körperkultur, Sport und Spiel*. Printed by Ed. Danziger. Wienbibliothek im Rathaus, Vienna, Plakatsammlung, P-65110.

a healthy body was the foundation for success in modern society.[87] One aspect of the broader life reform movement, "body-oriented" reform, is relevant to the present study. The notion of reforming the body included several branches: personal hygiene; naturopathy, nutrition reform, abstinence, and drug prevention; physical education and sports movements, including gymnastics, alpinism, and dance; clothing reform; spa and bathhouse culture; and nudism (the latter often subsumed under the rubric of *Freikörperkultur*, literally, "free body culture").[88] A flyer for air and sunbaths on the Schafberg in Vienna featured, for example, a vivacious-looking young woman in a modern swimming costume, while extolling the facility's body culture offerings, among them sport, swimming, and proximity to nature. Body-oriented life reform proffered the notion of the body as "a phantasm of health, performance, mastery, and perfection" in the modern age, as Philipp Sarasin phrased it.[89] The hygiene exhibitions considered here were clearly designed to advance many of the tenets of the body-oriented life reformers.

If we recall the vast array of products on display in the Rotunde in 1906—from bathtubs and bicycles to supplements and clothing made from natural materials, and everything in between—it becomes clear that the Vienna General Hygienic Exhibition was designed with body-oriented life reform in mind. The show reaped a certain amount of criticism from the press for its commercial orientation though.[90] This probably has much to do with the fact that the templates for such exhibitions were World's Fairs, those encyclopedic agglomerations of modern technology, knowledge, and commerce. This situation began to change as new didactic strategies were developed and implemented in museum and exhibition settings for transmitting information about people's bodies. Increasingly, rather than pitching a vast palette of consumer products to benefit people's physical health and hygiene, focus was instead given to educating people about their bodies. Such approaches became ever more popular in the interwar years, when imperial aspirations yielded to Social Democratic communal politics that advocated the centrality of a robust body as a cornerstone of the health of the First Republic. By the early 1930s, notions of improving one's body had become firmly rooted in Viennese political culture, with physical fitness raised to a national imperative. One way this was manifested was in the proliferation of exhibitions about the body, hygiene, and physical culture in the interwar years. This transition becomes visible if we contrast two later examples with the 1906 hygiene exhibition.

A second Viennese Hygiene Exhibition was held in 1925 at the Messepalast, the centrally located, repurposed imperial stables, known today as the Museumsquartier. Like the 1906 exhibition, this one, too, was a blockbuster hit, counting 100,000 visitors in its first week alone.[91] The essayist Alfred Polgar remarked, "he who goes into this exhibition goes into himself."[92] The exhibition comprised three parts: the hygiene exhibition itself, which included sections about sports, nutrition, clothing, sanitation, municipal housing, education, and childcare; the famous exhibition *The Human Being* (Der Mensch), which was widely successful in Dresden from its debut at the 1911 German Hygiene Exhibition and was later the foundational collection for the German Hygiene Museum in Dresden, built between 1927 and 1930; and *The New Household* (Der neue Haushalt), an exhibition of the Council of Austrian Women's Organizations (Bund Österreichischer Frauenvereine). *The Human Being* was perhaps the biggest draw. Polgar's description of what he saw in that pavilion is both vivid and clever. The exhibition, he writes, "shows how one lives [*lebt*] and how one lives in his body [*leibt*], how he sees, hears, smells, tastes, feels, breathes, digests, wears down and regenerates, how his heart robots [*robotet*], his nerves play, his kidneys filter, his muscles flex, his hair sprouts, his intestines and his brain gracefully wind, in short, it [the exhibition] shows everything that takes place under, in, and on the living human skin. Oh, there are things between the top of the skull and the sole of the feet that your academic ignorance cannot even dream of!"[93]

On display in the exhibition pavilion for *The Human Being* was the Dresden exhibit's widely admired "Transparent Man" or "Glass Man" model, constructed entirely of anatomical preparations covered by a see-through "skin," crafted from the new plastic Cellon. The model allowed

Fig. 11. Postcard with two views of the Hygiene Exhibition, Vienna, 1925. Interior view: "The Working Heart" display; exterior view: visitors queuing to enter "The Transparent Man" exhibition. Photographs by Atelier Ch. Scolik, Vienna. Author's collection.

viewers to peer not only into the human body but through it completely, as in the display of "The Working Heart," which Polgar had singled out for mention. It was in some sense a three-dimensional amplification of the effects of radiographic technology, but combined with new techniques for anatomical preparation.[94] The exhibition guidebook sang its praises, calling it "a triumph of modern museum technology." The model imparted, in plastic form, "an entire school of anatomy," one which reiterated and summed up the more traditional didactic displays in the adjacent rooms. The Transparent Man, however, conveyed knowledge about the human body "in so beautiful and artistic a presentation technique that one can claim that hardly ever before has a single field of science presented something so consummate, and most certainly never the field of anatomy."[95] The combination of the display of anatomical knowledge, framed in a scientific fashion, alongside the achievements of the Viennese municipal welfare system and the Council of Austrian Women's Organizations' exhibit on the modern household demonstrates just how decisively knowledge about the human body infused thinking about municipal politics, right down to the very architectonic structure of communal architecture.

Anatomy was, in a meaningful sense, not only the basis for knowledge of the self but also for Austrian state welfare systems of the interwar years. Julius Tandler, the famed anatomist and then the head of interwar Vienna's Welfare Office, summed it up in his introductory remarks for the exhibition catalog. He wrote that the typical kind of exhibition is designed to display the achievements of humankind's creations. Here, we might imagine the vast commercial displays at the World's Fairs, or the earlier General Hygienic Exhibition from 1906. The 1925 exhibition is, Tandler argues, entirely different: "It shows . . . how man lives, or better said, how he should live." While other exhibitions might present the "content of life" (*Lebensinhalt*), Tandler remarked that the 1925 exhibition instead staged the "way of life" (*Lebensweise*). More specifically, he afforded centrality to such exhibitions in municipal politics as sites for the communal dissemination of information about a "rational way of life." Information, examples, demonstrations, and instruction can lead people to such a rational lifestyle, but ultimately the only path to actually achieving it is by exposure to scientific knowledge from birth forward. "The human being can be brought up [*erzogen*] to a way of life, but not taught about it. The Hygiene Exhibition therefore serves as human education [*menschliche Erziehung*]." The task is a generational one: parents must be educated, so that their offspring will be born into a healthy environment. Tandler continues on to explain how the City of Vienna conceives of the term *hygiene*, namely not in the narrower sense of personal cleanliness but in the broadest possible terms, as encompassing "general social welfare," "all disciplines and categories of human social welfare."[96]

The exhibition presented the healthy human body functionally, that is, as a system of networked organ systems working together to sustain life, as demonstrated in the model of the Working Heart. This analogy of the body both as machine and organizational model had been translated visually by artists of the time, such as in Fritz Kahn's breathtaking rendering of "Man as Industrial Palace" (Der Mensch als Industriepalast), contained in his richly illustrated, five-volume *The Life of Man* (Das Leben des Menschen, 1922–31). Kahn, German and a gynecologist by training, gave strikingly modern form to of-the-moment anatomical knowledge about various organ systems. Applying principles of manufacturing and industry to human anatomy and physiology, Kahn attempted to make biological processes more comprehensible to a wide populace. He did so not just by showing people what their bodies looked like but by explaining how they worked.[97] His books had precedents in the tradition of folding anatomical models for popular knowledge included in books about naturopathy and health, such as Friedrich Eduard Bilz's so-called Bilz book, *The New Healing Practice: Textbook for Natural Healing and Healthcare* (Das neue Heilverfahren: Lehrbuch der naturgemäßen Heilweise und Gesundheitspflege, 1888)—which went through countless editions and sold millions of copies, even into the middle of the twentieth century.[98] In Austria, an atlas of foldout anatomical models was planned as early as 1844, though never published, by Anton Franz Perger (1809–76), the visual artist who held the anatomy professorship at the Vienna Academy of Fine Arts.[99]

Another example of the dissemination of medical knowledge to a broad public was the exhibition *Gymnastics—Sports—Play* (Turnen—Sport—Spiel) held at the Austrian Museum (Österreichisches Museum) from April to July 1931. These were the few months leading up to the Second International Workers' Olympics, which began in July 1931, and for which the Vienna stadium in the Prater had been built. Spread out over eighteen rooms, the exhibition combined anatomical and physiological knowledge with diagnostic and therapeutic advice. Eight of the rooms made the body didactically accessible to audiences through posters and models of the skeleton, joints and musculature, circulation and breath. Anatomical preparations were on display in another room, as were apparatuses for the analysis of movement. The latest in X-ray technology and light therapy treatments were advocated in diagnosis and treatment, and visitors could learn about historical and current trends in various branches of physical education, including swimming, skiing, and running.

The exhibition guide contained an essay by Emmerich Czermak, minister of education, titled, simply, "Why Physical Training?" (Warum Leibesübungen?). Czermak argued—as had Hugo von Hofmannsthal in "The Substitute for Dreams" (see chap. 4)—that urban industrialization was forcing more and more people into "one-sided labor," the execution of repetitive motions at the assembly line or on the factory floor. The dominance of an economically driven way of life was inflicting suffering on great numbers of people, according to Czermak. It was not just their minds that wasted away in the face of such capitalist industrial processes but also their bodies. Physical training of the body through gymnastics, sports, and play were the solutions Czermak and many others advocated to prevent the body from atrophying in the face of the demands of modern working life. The comprehensive, holistic approach espoused by the Austrian government through exhibitions such as this one sought to restore the balance between body and mind that a modern urban lifestyle had disrupted. Czermak argued for physical education and the restoration of this balance as a moral imperative, one which is the "duty of the people"

(*Volkspflicht*). Stronger individuals, he hoped, would in turn result in a stronger community.[100]

This is a moment where we can mark a concrete historical shift in how physical culture was perceived: it has evolved from individual physical betterment—as in the early life reform movement or in a definitional sense vis-à-vis the body of the Other—to the idea of a *Volkskörper*, or "body of the people"—a notion central to Viennese communal politics of the interwar years. The reciprocal influence between Viennese politics and culture on this point is illustrated by the architect Adolf Loos's "Guidelines for a Ministry of Culture" (Richtlinien für ein Kunstamt), originally published in the short-lived pacifist journal *Der Friede* on March 29, 1919.[101] Written after the end of World War I and the dissolution of the monarchy, Loos explicitly positions his reflections as a political intervention in this pivotal time of Austrian national self-determination. The place of culture within the new republic was essential, Loos argues. While the emperor had been the protector of the arts in the monarchy, in the republic that protective role must be taken over by the people (*das Volk*).[102] People, however, must be educated to assume their new role, which is why Loos considers such programmatic guidelines necessary.

Under the schooling section for the people, Loos includes nine program points that should be adhered to, among others guidelines on penmanship and less formal forms of spoken address. Two key points interest us in the context of the mainstreaming of the life reform movement and hygiene efforts. All schoolchildren should, Loos argues, be given instruction in hygiene and what he calls "external culture" (*äußere Kultur*). Though he provides few details, the focus is on self-care and maintenance of one's physical health. Noteworthy here is that Loos calls the care of one's body "culture." He summarily dispenses with the distinction between physical existence, on the one hand, and culture as the life of the mind, on the other. Next, Loos argues for a free school meal program for all children up to fourteen years of age. Breakfast, for example, should consist of oatmeal and a piece of fruit. Loos's nutritional recommendations mirror those of the life reformers, naturopaths, and popular guides to healthy living and diet. Finally, Loos calls for physical education (*Turnunterricht*) for all. German gymnastics, as a relic of the eighteenth century, are to be abandoned in favor of Swedish gymnastics and the Dalcroze system of eurythmics. Furthermore, all girls were to receive dance instruction beginning in the sixth year of life (see chap. 4).[103] Loos's thinking on the role of physical education in curricular guidelines for the First Republic was likely influenced by his earlier affiliation with Eugenie "Genia" Schwarzwald's

(1872–1940) progressive Viennese girls' school, where he taught architecture.[104] One primary goal of the guidelines Loos advanced for the new First Austrian Republic in 1919 was to cultivate a health body and body awareness in children from the youngest possible age. Loos later stated that he considered his "Guidelines for a Ministry of Culture" the most important essay he had ever written.[105]

While the vehemence with which the centrality of the body was positioned at this foundational moment of Austrian identity formation was new, the concrete reflections contained in Loos's "Guidelines" were not. They were an outgrowth of thoughts he had earlier formulated in popular lectures, such as "On Standing, Walking, Sitting, Sleeping, Eating, and Drinking" (Vom Stehen, Gehen, Sitzen, Schlafen, Essen und Trinken, 1911). Loos held this lecture repeatedly around Europe—in Berlin, Prague, Munich, and elsewhere—before delivering it in Vienna to a packed house in the Musikverein's great hall. Some two decades before the French sociologist Marcel Mauss's significant lecture "Techniques of the Body" (1934), Loos argued in a similar vein for the human habitus as a culturally and historically specific set of socially learned and coded expressions and gestures.[106]

Loos's thoughts differed from Mauss's later talk in the notion that the human habitus encapsulates the relative modernity of a particular culture—a thought in keeping with his views on architecture and material culture, manifest most potently in his famous lecture "Ornament and Crime" (Ornament und Verbrechen, 1908).[107] It was an idea likewise present in a commentary by Loos's close friend Peter Altenberg. One of the many thousands of collectible photographs Altenberg amassed, an image of Erna Morena, the German silent-film star, her head tilted alluringly, is inscribed with several layers of text in the author's hand onto and over the image. Altenberg's inscription reads: "Anyone who does not walk, run, sit, move like this is no human being! Utmost ideal of human movement-grace [*Bewegungs-Anmuth*]! PA. My utmost life-ideal! All others are cripples. 1918!"[108] Altenberg's personal, effusive commentary reads like a shorthand version of Loos's—or Mauss's—attentiveness to the correspondence between people's habitus and their level of civilizational development. Even more radically, Altenberg correlates physical grace with humanity as such, arguing implicitly that graceful gestures—which can be learned and acquired—are corporeal cultural ideals to be striven for.

Loos's remarks and his guidelines for cultural politics and educational policy show just how central thinking about the body had become by the late imperial period. His engagement with this topic indicates, first,

Fig. 12. Collectible photograph of actress Erna Morena, with an inscription by Peter Altenberg, 1918. Photographer and date unknown. Wien Museum, Vienna.

that (cultured, healthy) bodies were shifted into the very center of interwar Viennese cultural and social politics from the beginnings of the First Republic. Second, it demonstrates, perhaps surprisingly, that it was not just municipal politicians, such as the anatomist Tandler, from whom such assertions would be expected, but also key cultural figures, such as Loos, who made the body the very heart of their cultural programs in Red Vienna.

Given the transition of life reform efforts from fringe movements in the late nineteenth-century imperial years to mainstream political hygiene advocacy in the First Republic, Peter Altenberg's curious book *Pròdrŏmŏs* (1906), a self-described attempt at a *"physiological romanticism,"* was a timely authorial enterprise.[109] Even though it was not on display at the 1906 Hygiene Exhibition, it would have fit right in, since it in many ways epitomizes the cultural project of turning personal body culture into a national—and human—ideal.

LITERARY LIFE REFORM: PETER ALTENBERG'S *PRÒDRŎMŎS* (1906)

The wooden statuette depicts a peculiar figure: the tall crook in his right hand suggests a shepherd, while the string of beads held in his outstretched left hand implies a hawker. The natty plaid suit, its jacket ill fitting, evinces, perhaps, a down-market dandy. In point of fact, the person depicted was something of all three. The heavy, walrus-like mustache lends the gentleman a hirsute frown, and if the figure were not identifiable on the basis of his distinctive facial hair alone, the sculpture's pedestal features his name—Peter Altenberg—just below the title of his latest book, *Pròdrŏmŏs*. The carving, by Franz Zelezny (1866–1932), among the leading Viennese figural sculptors of his generation, is dated 1909. Even more eccentric than the figure himself are the phrases carved into the pedestal on which he stands: "Eat cheese cakes. Buy P. Altenberg beads. Brush your teeth with Dr. Guin [*sic*] de Boutemard paste. And take Tamar Indien Grillon as a laxative." This is strange fare for a sculpture, let alone for a literary text, yet the directives, formulated in the imperative, sum up both the content and tone of Altenberg's book *Pròdrŏmŏs*. Its publication by S. Fischer in 1906 secured its author's status as the "uncle of all of us, the righteous Life Reform Peter A.," as the German writer and anthologist Kurt Pinthus would later call him.[110] By the year of Altenberg's death in 1919, the book was already in its fifth edition. It had clearly fallen on fertile ground.

Altenberg's *Pròdrŏmŏs*, conceived of as a gospel of dietetics and hygiene, was nourished by the surge toward body-oriented life reform efforts around the fin de siècle and anticipated the first major public hygiene exhibition in Vienna. Its title—Greek for *precursor* or *forerunner*—was literally a harbinger, in 1906, of the strength that the life reform movement would soon achieve in Vienna and elsewhere in the interwar years.[111] Though Altenberg was by no means the only author interested in life reform, his book is the only one that treated the topic so thoroughly in literary form.[112] By the time *Pròdrŏmŏs* was published, Altenberg had already

Fig. 13. Franz Zelezny, Pròdrŏmŏs statuette of Peter Altenberg, Vienna, 1909. Egon Friedell, ed., *Das Altenbergbuch* (Leipzig: Verlag der Wiener Graphischen Werkstätte, 1921), n.p.

made a name for himself in the literary establishment with his subjective, impressionistic literary short forms, texts he called *Momentaufnahmen*, or snapshots. *As I See It* (Wie ich es sehe, 1896), *Ashantee* (1897), and *What the Day Brings Me* (Was der Tag mir zuträgt, 1901) were all characterized, as we saw with *Ashantee*, by a laconic yet effusive style. *Pròdrŏmŏs*, however, marked something of a break from Altenberg's prior writings. Rather than the prose sketches and vignettes that characterized his earlier books, the first half of *Pròdrŏmŏs* consists chiefly of aphorisms, bon mots, advice, laconicisms, and aperçus, but also contains short dialogues, recipes, and advertising language. The second half of the book consists largely of the kind of short prose texts that would have been familiar to Altenberg's readers.[113] It touches on topics as wide-ranging as dietetics, abstinence, hygiene, animal rights, clothing, workers' rights, and physical fitness, all of which Altenberg (rightly) predicted would be the "emblem of future generations" (13). The reform he calls for in all of these domains carries not only practical but also ethical and philosophical implications. Moreover, with *Pròdrŏmŏs* Altenberg transformed himself from author to self-anointed hygienist, cultural pedagogue, and advertising guru.[114]

Recurring throughout the book as leitmotifs, the terms *hygiene* and *dietetics* represent a linguistic repertoire that carries with it the potential to function as civilizing and civilizational correctives.[115] But they serve, above all, as techniques for reclaiming the self.[116] In Altenberg's universe, dietetics almost harkens back to a holistic, Galenic conception of the term. In contrast to what we would consider dietetics in the far narrower contemporary conception, ancient medicine envisioned it in a broader fashion. Dietetics encompassed, of course, everything we eat and drink, but also provided directives governing sleep and wakefulness, the proper relation of work and leisure time, and sexual relations. The goal for the ancients was to achieve eucrasia, or physical well-being, through an ideal balance of humors.[117] This classical language of dietetics became the basis of a modern discourse of hygiene a century before *Pròdrŏmŏs* was published.[118]

While Altenberg's notions of dietetics and hygiene aligned in their broad usage with the all-encompassing classical vision, his text strongly advocated regulating these domains to achieve not balance and harmony but a surplus of energy, something Simon Ganahl relates to Nietzsche's posthumously published *Ecce homo* (1888/1908)—and which might be productively related to Anson Rabinbach's notion of "the human motor."[119] Altenberg believed that this surplus of energy was attainable only through knowledge about one's own body, and his book, though deeply flawed, pursued goals similar to those of the hygiene exhibitions of the age. The common end, as Altenberg viewed it, was "every organism's inescapable longing for its possible ideal state," and the means for achieving it was "*conscious wisdom*" (85). Framed against the backdrop of body-oriented life reform, *Pròdrŏmŏs* is a programmatic and vital, if subjective, contribution to a kind of physical evangelism that sought to create intentional knowledge—and here we are reminded of Julius Tandler's later appeals for a "rational way of life"—about how to better one's body and, consequently, one's existence.

For Altenberg, the stakes were formidable. He wrote in no uncertain terms that "the evolution of humanity in relation to spirit and soul [*in geistig-seelischer Beziehung*] depends exclusively on the *application* of the laws of dietetics and hygiene. We are monsters [*Untiere*]. But we already *know* how we could become gods! It is a long, long path" (18). If his readers are willing to follow his advice, they will not only strengthen their "organic powers" (27), but will find a wellspring for humanity's regeneration and evolution (26). Altenberg understood his forward-thinking reformism as a positive contribution to the creation of a kind of modern, "new man," understood, as the expressionists would later formulate it, as one with the ability to live freer and better than preceding generations.[120] This redemptive vision of future humankind—Altenberg called it a "philosophy of optimism" (48)—is a leitmotif throughout *Pròdrŏmŏs*. The site of that idealism, in the context of *Pròdrŏmŏs*—and in Altenberg's own life—was the body, which becomes a kind of "somatic utopia," as Viktor Žmegač has termed it.[121]

One passage in particular summarizes many of the methods Altenberg advises regarding physical self-care. Altenberg positions himself as a physician, dispensing recommendations on drink, sleep, nutrition, and food, as well as their proper dosages. The simple sentences and direct orders go so far as to instruct readers as to *how* to implement his prescriptions: "Vino Condurango, one liqueur glass after a meal, drunk in small sips. Tamar Indien Grillon, in the morning before breakfast, one lozenge, chewed well. Vibration massage, applied extensively until the first sign of fatigue. Sleeping with open windows, the bed positioned close to the windowsill. Eating the fare of convalescents and new mothers, easily digestible and nutritious. Being able to wait for hunger, for a mountain climber's hunger!" (59–60).[122] The goal of Altenberg's strategies to control and master the body, to discipline one's physiological sensations, is to optimize well-being, amplify the body's physical potential, and thus heighten lived experience, which can then be accumulated like capital.[123] It is an economy of temperance, in which self-restraint in the here and now results ideally in greater future returns on one's investment. Altenberg writes, "In this way you will become a John Rockefeller of your life-capital [*Lebens-Kapital*]!" (60). By focusing on austerity and abstemiousness, Altenberg maintains, people have the potential to multiply their stakes, becoming, in the end, small-time Rockefellers of life-energy, with which they can bankroll subsequent creative endeavors.

The peremptory tenor and elliptical economy of language Altenberg employs in the aphorisms that made up the first part of *Pròdrŏmŏs* took their cue from the contemporary advertising language with which newspapers were littered.[124] Particular products recur again and again in Altenberg's compendium of concrete recommendations: he advises readers to turn to pills (Veronal and Hedonal, two brand-name barbiturates he deemed "harmless") and alcohol to induce sleep (9–10); he endorses a particular kind of wine (Vino Condurango), French laxative lozenges (Tamar Indien Grillon), or toothpaste (Boutemard). The catchy and sometimes rhythmic language he uses for his declarations is drawn from popular advertising, designed to stick in consumers' minds. In some cases, the author even tells his readers explicitly where such products could be purchased in Vienna. He advocates a particular kind of earplug, the "Antiphon," for example, to facilitate sleep. He describes the physical properties of the earplug and calls it the "faithful guardian of a deep . . . sleep. The aide of nature itself, which lovingly does the night-work to repair the day's damage. . . . For purchase at purveyors of surgical instruments. In Vienna at Breuer's, first district, Führichgasse" (78).

In addition to explicitly recommending where to purchase products he considered particularly beneficial, Altenberg incorporated another technique familiar from advertising and marketing campaigns: that of the testimonial. Describing an encounter, he writes: "I said to a young woman: 'You are very beautiful. But you could become a thousand times more beautiful! With *Vino Condurango* and *Tamar Indien Grillon*!' She took me for a grown fool. But she purchased herself these two products. When I saw her again, she said: 'You are not half as mad as I thought——.' I bowed silently" (60). Altenberg thought that by directing his readership toward specific products, he was making a concrete contribution toward helping them better their lives and care for their bodies, which were increasingly succumbing to such maladies as neurasthenia. Here, private encounters with public commodities facilitate the production of distinctly modern kinds of art. In this fashion, Altenberg's repurposing of advertising language and technique runs parallel to his textual-photographic "fabrications"[125]—the likes of which we saw with Erna Morena above—which transform the mere consumption of images to artistic production. What is more, Altenberg's textual production—whether between the covers of a book or inscribed spontaneously onto a cabinet card—both emanates from and refers back to the body.

This strategy of making targeted recommendations for specific products in a literary work was influenced both by the advertisements that crowded pages of newspapers and magazines and by the consolidated public displays of individual manufacturers and suppliers at shows such as the 1906 General Hygienic Exhibition. But Altenberg had another cue for the technique in his friend and supporter Adolf Loos, who published an influential series of articles in the late 1890s that adopted the same strategy. Loos named designers and manufacturers he admired, thus steering his readers toward specific essential products, including carriages, men's hats, and undergarments.[126] His goal was to be a tastemaker and multiplier in moving Austrian culture toward a more modern way of living—and this decades before he articulated his cultural-political vision for Austria in the wake of World War I in the "Guidelines." Like Altenberg, Loos believed modernity correlated directly with style, so modern clothing and accessories must correspond to the modern disposition.[127]

In *Pròdrŏmŏs*, Altenberg coupled the modern language of advertising with Zarathustrian ardor for the body.[128] It was Thomas Mann who first picked up on this connection between Altenberg and Nietzsche in both aphoristic compositional style and timeliness of concerns.[129] Both authors moreover appeal to the body as an alternative to the detachment of rationalism. Altenberg summed up the thrust of his book: "In a word: mens sana in corpore sano" (a healthy mind in a healthy body) (34). Altenberg viewed the physical body as the "building of your worldly soul" (*Gebäude deiner Welten-Seele*) (67), but he also found a more modern analogy for the interactions between body and soul, writing that "the soul alone is the motor of this delicate life-machine, 'modern man'!" (64).

Altenberg's frequent parallels between body and machine hinge not on a dualistic, mechanistic conception of mind and body, but point far more to a sometimes ambivalent interdependence between the two. In this sense, Altenberg's thoughts share a family resemblance with a kind of "aesthetic functionalism" à la Adolf Loos.[130] In *Pròdrŏmŏs*, Altenberg did not set out to prove that the human body functioned like a dryly scientific, physiological closed circuit (as in the Transparent Man model), but instead demonstrated his belief in the body as a site of continuous progress and improvement through dietary, social, physical, and medical hygiene.[131] While the soul might be the motor, that motor is useless, Altenberg asserts, if the apparatus that houses it—the body—is out of order.[132] In a later supplement to the book, Altenberg plays the confounded devil's advocate: "You want to be repaired from the spirit, from the soul?!? No, the machinery must be repaired!"[133] He formulates the relationship in plain terms elsewhere in the text: "The spirit is the necessary, inescapable consequence of the body." Deploying the metaphor of a gas lamp, Altenberg explains that, so long as the lamp's inner workings are free from soot, its light will shine bright. So, too, the relationship between body and soul: "Only the body gets sooted: the ailing [*schlimm*] spirit, the dim light, is a consequence of the neglected body! If wick, lamp, and air are right, the spirit always burns bright!"[134] For this reason, his call to arms is focused on the body, which requires perpetual mindfulness to be not merely an ideal conduit for the creative spirit but also, far more importantly, a producer of energy as a resource to nourish that very spirit. This perspective is reminiscent of Nietzsche's assertion in *The Gay Science* that "great health" is something "that one does not merely have but also acquires continually, and must acquire."[135] For both Nietzsche and Altenberg, dietetics and hygiene were first and foremost techniques of self-recovery.[136]

Altenberg's designation of *Pròdrŏmŏs* as a first attempt at a kind of "*physiological romanticism*" (110) makes clear the unity between art and life, mind and body, that the author strove for as the "natural," "authentic" state of the Austrian body. He writes, "*Aesthetics* is *dietetics*! What is *beautiful* is *healthy*. Everything else is diabolical heresy!" (128). Nevertheless, there is a significant gap between the book's doctrinaire program and Altenberg's actual life. The prescriptions of the reform-oriented *Pròdrŏmŏs* stood in often flagrant contradiction to the author's own behavior and lifestyle—his sanatorium visits, mental lability, alcoholism, and chronic physical ailments are all well documented—such that the word *romanticism* in the description could well point to the disparity between the physical reality of Altenberg's own life and the somatic utopia he envisioned.[137] But he was cognizant of this gap and in fact even thematized it in the book. In anticipation of the criticism Altenberg knew he was bound to reap for this discrepancy—and for the very fact of having published such a partially poetic advice manual at all—he introduced a third-person, reflexive narrative layer into *Pròdrŏmŏs* that anticipates, and even satirizes, the reactions of both his readers and the press. The author prophylactically imagines a reviewer lambasting him: "Peter Altenberg's newest book presents a tremendous disappointment to his many admirers. One does not expect much from his limited talents. But more or less accurate aphorisms about how to lead one's life! Why else do we have our doctors and hygienists! A writer is supposed to surprise us. Well, surprise us he did!" (14). "Surprising" was perhaps a euphemistic assessment on Altenberg's part. Thomas Mann's pronouncement that *Pròdrŏmŏs*'s content was little more than "terrible nonsense" pointedly summed up the sentiments of many, who believed that Altenberg's first book, *As I See It*, had been a revolution in literary style. Mann, for example, had described his reaction to that book as "love at first listen" (*Liebe auf den ersten Laut*).[138]

Altenberg also had his share of prominent admirers, though, including Theodor W. Adorno, Hermann Bahr, Karl Kraus, and Adolf Loos.[139] Kraus, caustic as ever in *Die Fackel* in late 1906, critiqued *Pròdrŏmŏs*, anticipating that readers "might be satirically inclined against both Altenberg's doctrinal, salvationist messaging and his newest brew of a spiritual-economic world view, which preaches the purchase of a toothpaste while denying sexual sensations."[140] But Kraus praises Altenberg's "humanity" and "temperament" elsewhere, writing that even a single, laconic sentence by Altenberg outweighed the average Viennese novel.[141] It was Hugo von Hofmannsthal, however, in an otherwise critical review, who recognized the core of Altenberg's reform-minded thinking long before *Pròdrŏmŏs* was a glimmer in Altenberg's eye. In a review of *As I See It* from 1896, Hofmannsthal remarked that Altenberg's prescriptions in that book for baths, food, sports, clothing, and the like are "not dry treatises, but small poems, like those classical fragments of the first physicians and teachers of natural history, who were drunk on the naiveté and joy of their subject."[142] But *Pròdrŏmŏs* bears far more authentic witness to an era under the sign of concrete, body-oriented notions of hygiene and life reform, as well as to that age's striving for the utopian ideals of a perfectible, healthy, and capable body and for a better way of life, lived in greater accordance with nature. In doing so, Altenberg's text was, as Hermann Bahr believed it to be, a sincere, if dilettantish, expression of the hunger of an entire generation, suffering under the unbearable weight of their own bodies.[143]

NATURE AND CULTURE ON STAGE

The bodies of the self and the other on display in the long fin de siècle and interwar years converged on two stages in a single evening in Vienna. It was March 1, 1928. Josephine Baker (1906–75), the renowned African American, later French, dancer and icon of the famed banana skirt, having conquered Paris and other European capitals, made her much-anticipated Viennese debut. Performing in the revue *Black on White* (Schwarz auf Weiß), Baker was poised to take the stage at the Johann Strauß Theater. Also black on white was the striking, horizontally striped villa that the architect

Adolf Loos, a close ally of Peter Altenberg, had designed for Baker in 1927–28 after only a fleeting Parisian acquaintance with the dancer the year before.[144] Now Baker's Viennese run, preceded by both feverish expectation and heated debates, had split the city largely along party and religious lines. At stake was the "erotic," "exotic," "indecent" content of her famed nude performances. Some welcomed an authentic American representative of Jazz Age culture in Vienna, and major dailies published columns documenting the minutest details of her arrival, such as the "Josephine Baker-Bulletin."[145] Yet others, many to the right of the political spectrum, were outraged. The conservative press lamented the "Americanization" of Viennese culture in the most derisive, racist terms. Riots by National Socialists were anticipated in protest of the presence of Baker's nude black body onstage in the city on the Danube. The furor was so intense that when Baker arrived in Vienna one month earlier, she had required a police detail to protect her from right-wing, German nationalist university students, who were pressuring the ruling government to ban her impending performances. The show went on, but not without a fierce parliamentary dispute about the limits of morality and propriety in a special session the week before. Nearby churches even attempted to counter the scandal, tolling their bells and offering additional masses for repentant Baker fans.[146]

Meanwhile, there was the physiologist and nobleman Dr. Maximilian Graf von Thun und Hohenstein (1887–1935), pioneer of a reform system of "biological gymnastics" (biologische Gymnastik), based on what he called "organic movement study" (organische Bewegungslehre). His live demonstrations, too, had been touted in the press weeks in advance, though with considerably less fanfare than Baker's. In the Viennese Konzerthaus, Thun-Hohenstein had, however, designed his own attraction: a custom-installed aquarium, in which four small monkeys—constant companions that had earned him the moniker "Monkey-Thun" (der Affen-Thun)—could demonstrate their aquatic talents alongside the doctor's gymnastic performances. On the evening of March 1, in the concert hall's grand auditorium, Thun-Hohenstein took the stage just a stone's throw from where Baker was performing in the fourth district—and also took off his clothes. Feats of physical strength, dexterity, and flexibility ensued, interspersed with instructive interludes on comparative human and animal anatomy, physiology, and locomotion. Humans can move more efficiently if we look to our animal predecessors, he claimed, and even primates, like humans, enjoy a good swim. One of Thun-Hohenstein's monkeys escaped the stage and tore through the audience; the spectators shrieked and applauded, dissolving into laughter.[147] The *Neue Freie Presse* called the nude doctor "a male Josephine Baker."[148]

Fig. 14. Physiologist and gymnast Max Thun-Hohenstein demonstrating a leap "in the manner of a horse." *Das interessante Blatt*, December 23, 1926, 5. ANNO/Österreichische Nationalbibliothek, Vienna.

The underlying philosophy of Thun-Hohenstein's system of movement and gymnastics was a return to nature. It was hardly a unique selling proposition, given the long history of various life reform movements by this point. What set Thun-Hohenstein's method apart was his appeal to study the animal world, primates foremost but also other four-legged creatures with elegant gaits, such as horses, as models for human movement and posture. Human locomotion, he argued, was little more than the vertical version of vertebrate animals' horizontal quadrupedal motion. But modern life and an upright gait had resulted in us bipeds, according to Thun-Hohenstein, expending far too much energy in inefficient movement sequences.[149] The bottom line in the new gymnastic system was that "humans should learn the rhythm and economy of their movements from animals."[150] To this end, Thun-Hohenstein founded the Scientific Society for the Cultivation of Natural Movement (Wissenschaftliche Gesellschaft für natürliche Bewegungspflege) in Vienna, an institution that took a more academic approach to the study of bodies in motion, though it included the School for Gymnastic Education (Schule für gymnastische Erziehung), which sought to transmit his principles to eager pupils of all ages.[151] He also took his ideas on the road in lecture tours and demonstrations that had him galloping like a horse onstage before well-heeled, paying audiences.

Writing in the *Arbeiter-Zeitung* a few days later, Eugen Hajnal was the only journalist who meaningfully connected the dots between the two performances' coincidence. He noted the moral outrage at Baker's revue by the kind of bourgeois, Christian Social Konzerthaus audiences that went to see Thun-Hohenstein's performance to point out the hypocrisy of Viennese culture: "From a moral standpoint, I must conclude that—even though the majority of the auditorium [at Thun-Hohenstein's event] was comprised of precisely those circles who most wanted to stone poor Josephine—no one was disturbed in the slightest by the doctor's nakedness." Hajnal for his part asserted that, were he attending a nude performance, he would have much preferred to see Baker, someone with clear talent, onstage at the Konzerthaus, instead of the—in his eyes—relatively pointless spectacle of Thun-Hohenstein's antics. Why should Baker be pilloried so mercilessly in Vienna, if a white man can walk naked onto the stage of one of the city's prime venues and perform gymnastics with apes? Where exactly is the line between "nature" and "culture"? Why the hypocrisy, Hajnal asks?[152]

The answer to these questions rests of course with the types of bodies on display in Vienna on March 1, 1928, and on following nights. One was black, the other white; one female, the other male; one was a working-class American advanced to international cultural sensation, the other homegrown Austrian nobility. Race, gender, and class took center stage, in other words, and the contrasting Viennese responses mirrored the starkness of the two naked bodies' juxtaposition in their respective spotlights that evening, barely miles apart. Baker's and Thun-Hohenstein's performances threw into sharp relief the cultural antinomies of interwar Vienna. Moreover, as we saw with the earlier human displays in the Prater, such debates were encoded in discourses about science and entertainment. Whereas Thun-Hohenstein, a physiologist, could stage his nude gymnastics for profit with a legitimizing veil of medical knowledge, Baker had no such recourse. Though she was a skilled cultural entrepreneur, deftly navigating difficult prejudicial terrain by playing with cultural codes for her own gain, it was impossible to escape the ever-present racist, gendered, sexualized, imperial, and, ultimately, spectacular gaze.[153]

These issues crystallized in Adolf Loos's unique—and apparently unbidden—villa design for Baker, as Beatriz Colomina and Anne Anlin Cheng have shown. The structure's interior, a sleek, modern construction that would have put the house's intended inhabitant on display, was encased in a black-and-white exterior "skin," or cladding. It thus architecturally embodied the boundaries between inside/outside and self/other we have seen thematized, frequently in racist terms, throughout this chapter. It moreover demonstrates that questions about the modern body—its substance and essence, its purported naturalness or culturedness—were debated in and through cultural production, in this case through architecture and in our other cases through exhibitions and literature.[154]

What bears mentioning, additionally, in the case of Baker in Vienna is her role beyond the muse of a famous, powerful architect and the "exotic" object of a predominantly white, male gaze.[155] She claimed agency, as she strategically reshaped her Paris revue for its Viennese staging.[156] Not content to be a mere fetish in Vienna, she crafted the program of *Black on White* to include more than just her famous dances. It was a series of over forty scenes in sum, with Baker starring in just five. Instead of resorting solely to her wheelhouse, she interwove her signature performances with Viennese content, much of it focused on the city's natural setting and cultural pride: "a spring scene in the woods, during which Easter Bunny girls dance the Charleston"; a "Return to Schubert" mini-revue, featuring song and dance to classic Viennese melodies; a monologue by the famous German-born Viennese actor and later *Burgtheater* director Hugo Thimig.[157] Baker attempted to turn the tables on matters of belonging and identity through her Viennese program; she deliberately blurred the lines between "native" and "foreign," self and other. Whether motivated by profit or personal conviction, that she spliced content in this fashion shows her questioning what it might mean to be "Viennese," what it might mean to be "other." What this story does not account for is how the Viennese—beyond the uproar that surrounded Baker's visit—viewed themselves through their response to Baker. A journalist for the *Wiener Allgemeine Zeitung* put a fine point on it: "Vienna wants to stay a cosmopolitan city, begs everywhere to be seen as such. In a cosmopolitan city, however, high, pure art has the same right to exist as entertainment. This—and nothing else—is what Josephine Baker is all about."[158] Culture and nature, self and other: regardless of who wields the power in determining the boundaries between these categories, it is clear that questions of identity were pressing in Vienna and that they were negotiated around, on, and through bodies on display. The coincidental performances of March 1, 1928, are perhaps the most fitting illustration of how such matters were debated. They moreover raise issues about performance in general, and these will surface again when we turn our lens to bodies in motion in chapter 4.

CHAPTER TWO

The Body in Pieces: Viennese Literature's Anatomies

> [Clarisse] had come to loathe from the depths of her soul everything voluptuary in art, and was drawn to everything lean and austere, whether it was the metageometry of the new atonal music or the clarified will of classic form, stripped of its skin, like a muscle about to be dissected.
> —Robert Musil, *The Man without Qualities*

> . . . And one without a name
> lay clean and naked there, and gave commands.
> —Rainer Maria Rilke, "Washing the Corpse"

Er ist mit dem 71er gefahren—"he took a ride on the 71." When I first heard this Viennese idiom, its meaning escaped me. Puzzled, I asked a friend, a native of the city's Simmering district, home to Vienna's Central Cemetery, the Zentralfriedhof. Opened in 1874, it was once the largest cemetery in Europe. (Today it is the second largest, though still with the greatest number of interred.) You can almost see its high, ivy-covered walls from the window of my friend's home, and I like to imagine that his characteristically dark Viennese humor was somehow nourished by his lifelong proximity to the burial grounds. "Kick the bucket. Go the way of all flesh," he explained. "That's the English equivalent."

Since 1918, the way all dead flesh goes in Vienna is via the 71 tramline, from the city center out to Simmering, to the Central Cemetery. In the aftermath of World War I, when the number of deaths rose due to catastrophic social conditions, a dedicated "corpse tram"—the so-called *Leichenbim* in the Viennese vernacular—was among the regular stable of streetcars on the rails of the 71 line. Before that, the ceaseless, daily procession of horse-drawn carts transporting Vienna's departed to the necropolis had sparked outcry about hygiene among residents. Already in 1874, the city's municipal council had considered a most modern and efficient solution to the problem: an underground, pneumatic tube system to transport corpses from Vienna's inner districts to the Central Cemetery—at speeds of up to twenty-seven kilometers per hour.[1] Although the project was never realized, the very fact of the proposal's existence says something important about the increasing rationalization of dealings with corpses in Vienna. We will encounter the *Leichenbim* again in the following pages, but we must first investigate what it so prominently conveyed: the dead, with the corpse as their emblem and exemplar.

This chapter centers on literary depictions of these most abject bodies in the works of Arthur Schnitzler, Marie Pappenheim, Joseph Roth, Carry Hauser, and Ödön von Horváth. The figure of the corpse appears in two forms in the examples we will encounter: first, in representations of actual human remains, which are present throughout the decades around the turn of the century; and second, in depictions of "living corpses"—social outcasts and wounded soldiers inhabiting war-torn bodies—which became a powerful symbolic incarnation of Viennese civic turmoil following the First World War.

The cadaver became a somber leitmotif throughout Viennese modernist art and literature, even participating in the aesthetic innovations of the era. In Klimt's sensuous *Water Serpents II* (1904–7) or in Jugendstil graphic art by Koloman Moser, smooth, luminously rendered skin and the pleasingly depicted human form were coupled with the undulating line of organic forms drawn from nature, and this aesthetic was likewise applied to the dead body. Franz Matsch's *Anatomy* spandrel for the University of Vienna's Great Hall, for example, features a human cadaver on a dissecting table framed by dense thickets of stylized foliage.[2] The cadaver's face is turned away from us and fixed in rigor mortis, its angular chin jutting skyward. Matsch's panel is remarkable because, unlike earlier anatomy paintings, it does not glorify—or even depict at all—the doctor and his science.[3] It showcases only the object of study: the human body, rendered naturalistically in its deathly pallor, yet with the distinctive Jugendstil grace of line and form.[4] However, Viennese literature from the fin de siècle and the interwar years often willfully interrogated this ideal. The corpse, that anti-ideal of the human form, is a persistent revenant. In refusing to be vanished, it reveals a decisive cultural shift.

The historian Thomas Laqueur has persuasively shown that the dead perform cultural work that is central to human community, "mak[ing] civilization on a grand and an intimate scale, everywhere and always."

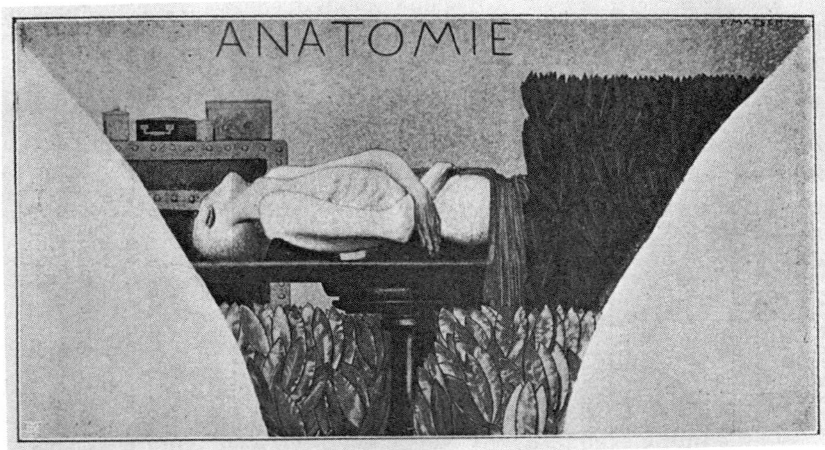

Fig. 15. Franz Matsch, *Anatomy*, drawing for a spandrel in the Great Hall of the University of Vienna. From Adolf Kronfeld, *Die Entwicklung des Anatomiebildes seit 1632* (Vienna: Moritz Perles, 1912), 26.

They persist as active historical agents, even when modernity may have written them off as "nothing and nowhere."[5] In our case, the cadaver represents a search for the underpinnings of truths about life and death, as in the medical tradition described by Foucault in *Birth of the Clinic*. With advances in anatomy, and particularly pathological anatomy, around 1800, death became charged with epistemological promise rather than ontological defeat. In dissecting rooms and anatomical theaters, Foucault writes, "the living night is dissipated in the brightness of death."[6] Viennese doctor-writers such as Marie Pappenheim and Arthur Schnitzler thematized anatomy in this way. Even while it harbors potential as a material source of knowledge of the self, the body-in-pieces often marks a sense of lost totality and broken epistemic order. Depictions of the "living dead" by Joseph Roth, Carry Hauser, and Ödön von Horváth—part of a new visibility of the corpse in the wake of World War I's mass casualties—served this purpose.[7] In the literature and visual art of Viennese modernism, we moreover encounter not only corpses but also renderings of the institutional sites that are their native domain: the dissecting room and the morgue, for example. In Vienna, these settings, commonly the purview of medical specialists, were in some cases opened up to artists and the larger populace. In addition, then, to identifying cadavers, the Anatomical

Institute, and dissection (material, site, and procedure) as central topoi in Viennese modernism, this chapter investigates the transfer of anatomical knowledge from institutions to a lay public.

As the exemplary figure of alterity, the corpse and representations of it offer cultures ways of framing the fact of human mortality and debating cultural norms.[8] In *Over Her Dead Body*, Elisabeth Bronfen argues that aestheticized representations of (female) corpses are palatable articulations of a culture's unconscious knowledge of death—a subject often too threatening to thematize directly, but one which nevertheless exerts a powerful pull. When framed beautifully, death can be visualized in a less sinister fashion; it allows us to play hide-and-seek with the certainty of our own demise.[9] But what of the corpses that populate Viennese modernism, many of which are rendered in a most gruesome, matter-of-fact fashion? Such representations of cadavers are no less symptomatic of the culture from which they emanate. In fact, they are likewise fulcrums of individual transformation and social critique. As Julia Kristeva reminds us, the corpse *is* death, death embodied, unlike, for example, the flat line of a cardiogram—a signifier of death: "as in true theater, without makeup or masks, . . . corpses *show me* what I permanently thrust aside in order to live." The cadaver, she asserts, is "the utmost of abjection. It is death infecting life." As the waste of the self—the "'I' . . . expelled"—it manifests the breakdown of the ordering boundaries between self and world, between being and otherness.[10] Attention to the dead on Laqueur's and Kristeva's terms—that is, to Viennese modernism's bodies-in-pieces—unlocks access to historical and epistemological debates that Viennese modernists were working out over and through their dead.

BECOMING THE BLADE: VIVISECTION AS THE PRIMAL SCENE

Before turning our attention to Viennese modernism's corpses and mortuaries, let us reflect on the significance of the *procedure* of dissection. Both Robert Musil and Sigmund Freud position a potent metaphor at the very center of their self-understanding as thinkers: that of vivisection—surgery conducted on a living organism, usually for experimentation or research in pathology and physiology. The notable aspect of Musil's and Freud's textual vivisections is that the authors are, in both cases, vivisector and vivisected at once. The operative procedure allows them to be simultaneously subject and object, observer and observed—and their own bodies are the material sites of experimentation that result in cognition. Furthermore, their self-vivisections serve as moments of identity construction: through the procedure, Musil and Freud become authors.

The first entry in Musil's diary opens with a declaration of self-identification: "Recently I invented a very fine name for myself: 'monsieur le vivisecteur.' . . . My life: the wanderings and adventures of a vivisectionist of souls at the beginning of the twentieth century!" Reflecting on the figure he has just named, Musil, not yet twenty years old, weighs whether the vivisectionist is possibly a designation "typical of the human being to come, 'Brain Man'—perhaps?"[11] Musil was in the midst of his engineering studies when he noted these thoughts and still years away from composing his dissertation on the influential physicist-philosopher Ernst Mach (1838–1916). Mach's *The Analysis of Sensations and the Relation of the Physical to the Psychical* (Die Analyse der Empfindungen und das Verhältnis des Physischen zum Psychischen, 1886) was a central point of reference for the Viennese modernists, concerned as they were with the boundaries between self and world, appearance and reality.[12] Mach's philosophical positivism, premised on empirical phenomenalism and a physiology of pure sensations, provided a persuasive scientific lens with which to validate the characteristically Viennese late nineteenth-century cultural and philosophical pessimism Jean-François Lyotard made note of.[13] Musil's notion of the vivisection—with himself as object and subject—supplies an appropriately empirical metaphor that allows him to be both inside and outside himself at once.

In the same diary entry, Musil recalls once having looked at a specimen of a fly encased in rock crystal and having the distinct sensation of looking from the outside in. This sensation is now replicated as he gazes out his window onto the street below. If viewed in close-up, he reflects, those objects would certainly have "offended" him. But now, wearing his positivistic goggles, he takes pleasure: viewed from a distance, with this thick filter between observer and object of observation, he experiences "a certain aesthetic satisfaction, a reverberation of sympathy. So now I look from outside to inside and, summa summarum, this moving from outside to inside and from inside to outside gives me the contemplative peace of the philosopher" (2). He takes the same approach when focusing on himself. In a step once removed from the authoring of the "Book of the Night," the name he gave to his diaries, he regards his own writings as the subject of a scientific analysis. Not unlike his view of the fly fixed in the crystal, Musil relishes reading his own reflections. The vivisection stands thus for an analytical step beyond authorship, though originating first in authorship itself. For in the self-vivisection the writer is transformed into his "own historian or the scholar who places his own organism under the microscope and is pleased whenever he discovers something new" (4). In observing himself as he would observe the frozen fly or the goings-on of the world from his window perch, Musil mobilizes vivisection as the objective, scientific procedure capable of establishing both authorial and philosophical authority. This is possible only by adopting a perspective that frees the object of observation from its conventional context and affords analytic precision. The goal is to win knowledge about the soul by observing the functional connections between internal physical systems. It is, in the end, the seemingly objective analysis of subjective production.

In addition to being influenced by Mach, Musil was also reading Nietzsche at the time and perhaps borrowed the notion of intellectual vivisection from the philosopher.[14] Nietzsche deploys vivisection as a metaphor repeatedly throughout his work, even positioning this procedure as the starting point for his critique of metaphysics, as well as for the search for both self-knowledge and knowledge as such. His posthumous fragments include the directive: "Vivisection—that is the point of departure!"[15] Writing in 1888 in the epilogue to *The Case of Wagner*, Nietzsche, with the aim of pursuing "a *diagnosis of the modern soul*," ponders where such a diagnosis would begin: "With a resolute incision into this contradictoriness of instincts, by separating out its opposing values," he concludes, "by performing a vivisection on its most *instructive* case."[16] In this context, the case study is, of course, Wagner. In *On the Genealogy of Morality*, Nietzsche comments on the necessity of analyzing artists and their creative products separately. Insight into the genesis of a work is more important than the person who created it; this, Nietzsche argues, is central for "physiologists and vivisectionists of the mind," concerned as they are with interpreting the signs of the times.[17] In fact, the vivisection metaphor is central to Nietzsche's understanding of the characteristics of the philosophy of his age, distinguished by hubris vis-à-vis oneself: "for we experiment with ourselves in a way we would never permit ourselves to experiment with animals, and carried away by curiosity, we cheerfully slice open our living souls."[18]

Musil's self-conception as *monsieur le vivisecteur*, though perhaps adapting Nietzsche's terminology, is far more centrally concerned with how we relate to and interpret our own experiences—hence the gesture of reading back over the diary and analyzing what he has written. In this regard, Musil sets out, perhaps, to adhere to Nietzsche's directive in *The Gay Science* to rigorously investigate our beliefs and experiences so as to not succumb to deception. Nietzsche comments, "But we, we others who thirst after reason, are determined to scrutinize our experiences as severely as a scientific experiment, hour after hour, day after day. We ourselves wish to be our own experiments and guinea pigs."[19] Nietzsche's injunctions to shift the focus of epistemological inquiry onto our bodies, to vivisect our experiences and the assertions of others as case studies from which to proceed with an experimental philosophy directed at winning knowledge, proved formative for Musil.

Freud, too, deployed the vivisection metaphor in *The Interpretation of Dreams*. Here, as for Musil, it marks the birth of his self-understanding as an author. Freud recounts at length a formative dream, to which he returns three times in the course of the section on "The Dream-Work."[20] He recalls having experienced "a clear expression of astonishment" at its content: a self-vivisection. Freud finds himself in the physiology laboratory of Ernst von Brücke, his revered teacher and mentor and an influential figure in the second Vienna medical school. Freud writes, "*Old Brücke must have set me some task;* STRANGELY ENOUGH, *it related to a dissection of the lower part of my own body, my pelvis and legs, which I saw before me as though in the dissecting-room, but without noticing their absence in myself and also without a trace of any gruesome feeling. . . . The pelvis had been eviscerated, and it was visible now in its superior, now in its inferior, aspect, the two being mixed together*" (5:452). Freud goes on to describe an arduous hike he subsequently undertakes "*with a constant feeling of surprise*" in the dream, because of the fact that his legs should not be functioning properly under these odd circumstances. After a complete retelling of the dream, he breaks off with the pronouncement: "*I awoke in a mental fright*" (5:453). Freud teases out several facets of the dream that appear significant to him in retrospect. The dream of dissecting his own body, Freud determines, represents his personal self-analysis, a process that necessitated reporting his dreams in detail (5:454). Freud's dreams form a cornerstone of *The Interpretation of Dreams*, but the thought of laying bare his psychic life so completely had, in actuality, paralyzed him. He describes the self-analysis the publication necessitated as a process "so distressing to me in reality" that he had delayed the book's printing for over a year (5:477).

The self-vivisection dream as wish-fulfillment came into play in two senses, both hinging on the absence of a "gruesome feeling" (*Grauen*) in the face of such an obviously grisly task. On the one hand, Freud wanted to surmount the distress and "feeling of distaste" regarding the necessity of laying himself bare in order to publish the book (5:477). On the other, and in the second sense of the word *grauen*—to go gray—Freud was cognizant of his advancing age and could not bear the thought of delaying the appearance of his magnum opus any longer, lest his children be left to issue it posthumously (5:478). Freud explains Brücke's laboratory as the location for the dreamed self-vivisection by way of the significance of Brücke, who surfaced in the dream, Freud reckoned, not simply by chance. For it was his mentor who had in the past pushed him to publish his work (5:454). Both the dreamwork as an aspect of self-analysis and the publication of his theories were thus linked inextricably to the procedure of dissection. Freud's key work only became public when he acknowledged that he needed, like Musil, to become the blade, in all its cold impartiality.[21] Vivisection becomes a primal scene for the birth of authorship, of thought.[22] For two Viennese modernist authors, however, one canonical, the other peripheral, dissection was more than just a metaphor.

IN THE DISSECTING ROOM: ARTHUR SCHNITZLER AND MARIE PAPPENHEIM

The great pathologist Rudolf Virchow once described Vienna as "the Mecca of medicine."[23] Indeed, under the so-called second Vienna medical school, with physicians and researchers such as Carl von Rokitansky, Josef Škoda, Josef Hyrtl, and Ferdinand Hebra at the forefront in the mid- to late nineteenth century, Vienna became the medical capital of central Europe by 1900. Rokitansky had been named chair of Pathological Anatomy at the university in 1844, and his efforts completely refocused the study of medicine there. Freeing it from its earlier *naturphilosophische* underpinnings, Rokitansky and his colleagues were primarily concerned with establishing a solid, empirical basis for medicine, one which centered on the human body and its pathologies.[24] The body and its pathological conditions henceforth formed the sole, reliable basis for the clinical diagnosis of illness. Viennese medicine from this point on focused on postmortem examination, with the Vienna General Hospital's mortuary and Carl von Rokitansky's autopsy table as its nucleus.[25] Rokitansky is said to have conducted over eighty thousand autopsies over the course of his career in Vienna,[26] and the emphasis on pathological anatomy focused Viennese medicine on the corpse.[27] The dissecting room was, in other words, the center of Viennese medicine for the second Vienna medical school. Arthur Schnitzler took up his medical studies there in 1879, and the prosectorium likewise plays a role in Schnitzler's own literary works.

The medical dimensions of Schnitzler's literary works have been the subject of numerous studies in recent years. Moreover, since the publication of Schnitzler's collected medical writings in 1988, several scholars have turned their attention to these texts, which were directed at an audience of medical specialists.[28] As Hillary Hope Herzog has argued, Schnitzler's medical training schooled him to use a diagnostic lens as he made sense of the world outside the clinic walls. In fact, she identifies medicine as "the primary system of knowledge" framing Schnitzler's perspective on human beings, both as individuals and within society at large.[29] This assertion calls to mind a well-known statement attributed to Schnitzler by his wife, Olga: "Anyone who was ever a doctor can never stop being one. For medicine is a worldview [*Weltanschauung*]."[30]

Even more specifically than medicine as a discipline, however, Schnitzler identified the atmosphere of a concrete medico-institutional site that crucially shaped his worldview: the university's Pathological-Anatomical Institute and, more specifically, the dissecting room.[31] As I will argue, these sites of anatomical study played a role not only in Schnitzler's Weltanschauung as a whole but also in his literary production. It is unsurprising, perhaps, that several early literary texts, composed while he was still a medical student, should reference the dissecting room with a youthful combination of fascination and disgust. What is more revealing, however, is that Schnitzler returned to the dissecting room in one of his most famous works, *Dream Story* (Traumnovelle, 1925–26). For Schnitzler, as well as for other Viennese modernist authors, the dissecting room functions as a locus of the search for truth.

Like Arthur Schnitzler, Bratislava-born Marie Pappenheim (1882–1966) was both a doctor and a writer. Her work caught the eye of Karl Kraus, who published her literary debut, the four poems "Autopsy Room" (Seziersaal), "Separation" (Trennung), "Before the Concert" (Vor dem Konzert), and "First Pregnancy" (Prima Graviditas), in *Die Fackel* in 1906.[32] The notoriously acerbic editor noted Pappenheim's "exceptional talent" and printed her poems under the pseudonym Maria Heim alongside an excerpt from a Strindberg novella while Pappenheim was still a student at the medical faculty.

The University of Vienna's philosophical faculty had only begun admitting women in 1897—comparatively late in the broader European context—and the Medical University followed suit in 1900.[33] A very public debate about the admissibility of women to the medical profession and to medical schooling at all was carried out in Vienna around the turn of the century, and antifeminist sentiment ran rampant throughout the medical community.[34] Male scientists and medical doctors regularly—and successfully—advanced essentialist claims that women were intellectually inferior, emotionally unequipped, and biologically unfit to become doctors, a profession that would purportedly distract women from their roles as mothers and wives.[35] Interestingly, one of the most heated debates surrounding the admissibility of women medical students at the University of Vienna was carried out in precisely the forum that published Pappenheim's medically inflected literary debut: Kraus's *Die Fackel.* Just a year after Pappenheim's poems appeared there, Kraus published a withering position paper, "Female Doctors" (Weibliche Ärzte), by the psychoanalyst and later Freud biographer Fritz Wittels. Working in the vein of Otto Weininger's influential misogynistic theses, Wittels classified women wanting to pursue medical studies as hysterics, "male women" (*Mannweiber*), and their academic pursuits essentially as a sublimation of their sexual energy.[36]

The struggle for equal secondary and postsecondary educational opportunities for women must, of course, be viewed in the wider context of early feminism and the so-called *Frauenfrage*, the "women's question." As elsewhere, in Austria feminism frequently went hand in hand with social reform and political activism, as with the examples of the leading activists Rosa Mayreder (1858–1938), Adelheid Popp (1869–1939), Auguste Fickert (1855–1910), and Marie Lang (1858–1934), to name just a few.[37] In the context of the medical faculty, Berta Szeps-Zuckerkandl (1864–1945), another prominent figure, proudly noted in her autobiography that her husband, the renowned anatomist Emil Zuckerkandl, was among the medical faculty members at the University of Vienna who argued strongly in favor of admitting women.[38]

When Marie Pappenheim received her doctorate in 1909, she was therefore among the first generation of women to complete medical school in Austria. She eventually opened a dermatological private practice with her husband Hermann Frischauf and went on to become active in the Austrian Communist Party. Together with Wilhelm Reich, in the context of the interwar sexual reform movement under the anatomist Julius Tandler, she founded the Socialist Society for Sexual Advice and Sexual Research (Sozialistische Gesellschaft für Sexualberatung und Sexualforschung) in 1928. Despite Pappenheim's early literary successes, which I will look at in detail both here and in chapter 3, she ultimately made the conscious decision to largely turn away from writing around 1910. She later recalled, "I did not want to wander through life as a poet. In my opinion, it was unviable to mix being a doctor—that is, with both feet anchored in reality—with simultaneously publishing poems."[39] Pappenheim's perspective was exactly the opposite of Schnitzler's, who, from early on, felt himself pulled primarily toward the writing life. In a journal entry jotted on October 27, 1879, just one month after beginning medical school, Schnitzler wrote: "I already sense that science will never become for me what art already is."[40]

Pappenheim's early literary production nevertheless reveals a clear connection between medical training and the Viennese literary imagination that came to fruition more famously in the work of Schnitzler. In the same year that Pappenheim received her doctorate, Arnold Schönberg completed his first full-length stage composition, *Expectation* (Erwartung), op. 17, in an atonal expressionist mode—based on a libretto by Pappenheim. Shortly after completing her medical degree, Pappenheim went on *Sommerfrische*, the traditional Austrian summer vacation to the countryside. Schönberg, too, was on holiday with Alban Berg, Anton Webern, Alexander Zemlinsky, and others. During their respective trips, Schönberg asked Pappenheim for an opera libretto, a connection brokered by Karl Kraus and the composer Zemlinsky.[41] Within three weeks, she delivered a monodrama, to which Schönberg made relatively few changes.[42] *Expectation* is a story of one woman's journey of alienation and emotional torment, of love and death. The synopsis of the monodrama reads: "The Woman seeks her lover by night. After terrifying experiences in the forest, she finds his dead body near the house of another woman. The Woman pours out her emotions: horror, sorrow, passion, jealousy, anger, tenderness, compassion, loneliness, fear of the unknown. The sun rises on an uncertain future."[43] Has her lover betrayed her? The answer remains as elusive as the circumstances of his death. What is certain is the embodied fact of his demise, his presence in the dramatic action as a lifeless prop. The unnamed female protagonist turns the table on the conventional narrative of the beautiful female corpse by carrying out her emotional catharsis over *his* dead body.

Conventional interpretations of the work have framed the piece as a Freudian psychoanalytic case study. The year before Schönberg composed *Expectation*, his wife Mathilde's lover, the gifted painter Richard Gerstl (1883–1908), had committed suicide. Some have theorized that Schönberg was working through the ill-fated love affair and its collateral damage in *Expectation*,[44] which tells the story of a love affair ending in the death of one of the triangle's participants. This time the constellation is, however, two women and a man, and it is the man who dies. Others have framed the unnamed Woman as a hysterical protagonist, not least owing to the tantalizing though long-debated family connection between Marie Pappenheim and Bertha Pappenheim (1859–1936), Josef Breuer's famous analysand

Anna O. in *Studies on Hysteria* (1895), copublished with Freud.[45] Yet it has gone largely overlooked that Marie Pappenheim's feminist surroundings and medical training might have played as significant a role in the creation of these early literary efforts.[46] The titles alone of two of the four poems published by Kraus in *Die Fackel*, "Autopsy Room" and "First Pregnancy," reveal the clear link to her medical training—a link reinforced by her abandonment of any early authorial aspirations and subsequent dedication to both her medical career and social-welfare initiatives. In fact, Pappenheim's identity as the author of the monodrama was, until relatively recently, erased almost entirely. This has likewise frequently been the case with interpretations of the work itself and the agency of its sole female character.[47]

If we reframe Pappenheim's poems and the libretto for *Expectation*, however, a new picture emerges. Bringing them into dialogue with early works by Arthur Schnitzler allows us to see the interface between medicine and literature in the youthful writing of two budding doctors, who later chose diverging paths. While Pappenheim would turn away from literature, be forced to leave Austria, and publish again only in 1949, after returning to the country of her birth, Schnitzler became one of the most successful, internationally recognized writers of his generation. Their common experiences as writing medical students spawned a literary engagement with one of the main sites of their training: the prosectorium, or dissecting room. Both writers contemplate the value of life while thematizing a formative experience of any young doctor's training: autopsying human bodies.

Pappenheim's 1906 poem "Autopsy Room" gives the site prominence in the title but registers only the encounter between a first-person female speaker and a corpse—as in *Expectation*—in six rhyming couplets.[48] The position of the speaker in the poem is, however, unclear. The "I" could well be a doctor but could equally be a former lover of the departed man. Perhaps she is both. What is clear from the perspective of the speaker is the depth of the bond that ties the two together, even in death. The speaker gives a clue that might lead us to believe that the man lying on the slab in the autopsy room is a suicide: he is one "whom life broke" (line 2). But the corpse in Pappenheim's rendering has human wants and desires, is still imbued with life. Though "His mouth is pale and his eyes weary, / Like one who stares nightly into the darkness" (lines 3–4), it is "his desire" that "sadly . . . wafts" around the speaker (line 7). It is he who wants her to lay her hand over his eyes (line 6). While the corpse retains traces of life and movement, the speaker's body is a statue-like antipode. Her hand, "slender and cool and still" (line 5), resists the final gesture she imagines him desiring. Her only actions are the abstract, introductory crying that "echoes in [her] soul" (line 1) and her "tortured heart [that] betrays itself" (line 8), that thinks in "life, frenzy, flames" (line 9). This heart—framed in the present tense and possessing its own agency—"gives itself to one weary, wounded, ill" (line 10). The poem's final couplet opens the perspective out to the rest of the autopsy room. The other dead, who surround the encounter between the woman and her beloved, "stare stonily" (line 11). In the concluding line, however, they directly address the speaker in a dark chorus: "Too soon, you, child, must belong to us" (line 12). The personified cadavers provide the speaker with an eerie memento mori, a reminder that the life lived outside the autopsy room is fleeting.

Schnitzler's early poem "Prosector" (Prosektor), dated April 18, 1880, takes a different tack but ends with the same message. Instead of specifying the site, as in Pappenheim's poem, its title marks the speaker's agency. Told from the perspective of the titular figure, the poem opens with a direct address to the cadavers: "Farewell, you corpses, I am leaving you today" (line 1).[49] The prosector proceeds to wash his hands and make his way to the coffeehouse, which serves as a foil for the dissecting room. There, life's pleasures can be savored and enjoyed, "since you only live once" (line 10). The raucous café atmosphere contrasts with the somber academic setting, where the prosector and his colleagues "rummage deliberately in flesh and blood" (line 15). The speaker does not seem entirely displeased with the steady supply of corpses, however, remarking roguishly: "And if no one takes care of his body / Then we have something to do" (lines 13–14). The purposefulness with which the cadavers are treated during the autopsy is contradicted by the irreverence of the doctors once the corpses' scientific usefulness is exhausted: then, the cadavers are simply tossed into the well (line 16). The engagement with the dead allows the speaker to end the poem with a carpe diem message, delivered directly to the reader. Since life is short, and everyone ends as a corpse, it is best to live the present moment to its fullest: "Oh savor as long as you can savor, / And love each other and be happy, / Whether resting in the grave or in the well, / That matters not to the dead" (lines 17–20).

When he wrote "Prosector," Schnitzler was in the second semester of his medical studies and had been attending lectures by the anatomist Carl von Langer, a Viennese pioneer of topographical anatomy.[50] This type of macroscopic anatomical investigation would come to play a key role in later literary texts, as it provided Schnitzler with a methodological template with which to structure the visual regimes of his characters. Ultimately, Schnitzler's characters must concede the shortcomings of this approach to knowledge and subjectivity.

Schnitzler had begun his studies at the University of Vienna in 1879 and received his MD in 1885. After training as a *Sekundararzt* at the Allgemeines Krankenhaus from 1885 to 1888, he worked from 1888 to 1893 at the polyclinic cofounded by his father, Johann Schnitzler (1835–93), a noted laryngologist. Johann Schnitzler founded two influential weekly journals—the *Wiener Medizinische Presse* and the *Internationale Klinische Rundschau*—and his son was a regular reviewer and correspondent for these periodicals, both tailored toward the practicing physician. Arthur Schnitzler went into private practice following his father's death in 1893. Although it was around this time that his literary career began to take off, Schnitzler established a small client base and continued to see patients, even into the 1920s.[51]

Just the day before he penned the poem, Schnitzler had noted in his diary: "med[ical] and poet[ic] worldviews are beating each other up in the most entertaining fashion in my so-c[alled] soul."[52] "Prosector," despite its limited poetic value, gives voice to Schnitzler's "enigmatic, bleak impressions of anatomy," while also clearly articulating the poles between which the young doctor was oscillating in the early years of his studies.[53] Schnitzler's autobiography, *My Youth in Vienna* (Jugend in Wien), gives us insight into how the typical medical student in Vienna learned to come to terms with that fundamental prerequisite of the profession: the dissection. Schnitzler recalls,

> like my colleagues, I too tended to exaggerate to some extent my indifference to the human creature become thing, as if in defense against just such lay sentimentality. But I never went as far in my cynicism as those who considered it something to be proud of when they munched roasted chestnuts with relish at the dissecting table. . . . At the head of the bed on which the dead man lies, even if the man who has just breathed his last is unknown to you, stands Death, still a grandiose ghostly apparition. . . . He stalks like a pedantic schoolmaster whom the student thinks he can mock. And only in infrequent moments, when the corpse apes the living man he once was in some grotesque motion . . . does the composed, even the frivolous man experience a feeling of embarrassment or fear.[54]

Schnitzler's characterizations both of the youthful physician's hubris toward the cadaver as well as of the embodied presence of death at the dissecting table are integral to texts from the earliest and latest phases of his career.

Several months after writing "Prosector," Schnitzler penned another poem, "Spring Night in the Autopsy Room" (Frühlingsnacht im Seziersaal), dated July 18, 1880, which led later that year to a short prose piece by the same title.[55] The "Fantasy," as Schnitzler subtitled it, begins with a young medical student leaving a dance hall by night and feeling strangely drawn to the Anatomical Institute where he spends his days. As in "Prosector," it is the juxtaposition of life and death that entices the first-person protagonist. He is compelled to go to the autopsy room and dissect both "in the service of science" and "to immerse [himself] in the knowledge of death" (7). Schnitzler's narrator sets the scene: "And so I open the door and step into the dark, vaulted room. I take the lamp from a recessed windowsill and light it. I place a green shade over the flame and put it at the head of the dead man. A yellow glow flows over the wan, motionless countenance. Only around the mouth does it seem faintly to twitch. All around, the other cadavers lie in the dark. I toss the black coat over my shoulders, take my knife and the remaining tools to begin my work" (7–8).[56] Before the anatomist commences the dissection, however, he opens the window and lets in the night air. The protagonist describes what streams in and mixes with the atmosphere native to the dissecting room as an "indescribable fairy tale" (8), and it provokes in him a dreamlike state. The boundary between dissecting room and the world outside begins to dissolve, as does that between dream and reality, and it is unclear whether the remainder of the story actually takes place or whether the narrator dreams it.

What follows is the surprising appearance of the narrator's colleague and friend, Stephan Kalman, with Christine, the daughter of the anatomy assistant. The two had come to the prosectorium for a tryst, to which the narrator reacts incredulously. A third figure—a traveling musician, like a figure from a Chagall painting—happens by the open window and springs in over the sill. This curious Pied Piper takes up his fiddle at the head of the dissecting table and incites the couple to dance (10). Stephan and Christine whirl wildly to the jig until the fiddler quits the scene as suddenly as he arrived. The couple collapses, and the narrative resumes in the morning with the protagonist being shaken awake by Christine's father. Apparently the student had blacked out on the threshold between the dissecting room and street. He asks, still sleep-drunk, "What on earth was I dreaming?" (11).

Because of the interplay between dream and wakefulness and the significance of the threshold in the story, a number of scholars have claimed that Schnitzler was anticipating Freudian dream theory.[57] However, while the end of the dream is clearly marked, its beginning is unclear. For this reason, the narrator's state of consciousness must be viewed as liminal, rather than exclusively the domain of dreams. Moreover, his liminal consciousness veers into ever more fantastic territory and is more reminiscent of Franz Grillparzer or E. T. A. Hoffmann than of Freud.[58] The key to the narrator's liminal state as described in "Spring Night in the Autopsy Room" is the setting itself.[59] As Schnitzler wrote in his autobiography, it was not merely his moods but his entire Weltanschauung that were influenced by the atmosphere native to such medico-institutional spaces, sites where life and death meet—and clash.[60] Schnitzler fantastically elevates the dissecting room to dance hall in this early story to drive this point home. It is precisely "the shudder of decay surrounding love" that so unsettles the narrator as he witnesses the couple waltzing in the autopsy room (9). The narrator had headed to the prosectorium after the dance hall to experience the "knowledge of death" that contrasts with life. But by subsequently transforming the dissecting room into a dance hall, Schnitzler allows his protagonist to experience the true nature of that knowledge in a liminal space between life and death.

Nearly half a century later, Schnitzler sends another of his protagonists, Fridolin—the restless doctor and family man of *Dream Story* (Traumnovelle, 1925–26)—into the dissecting room of the University of Vienna's Pathological-Anatomical Institute in a key scene. At the heart of this novella is the question whether partnership and openness about one's deepest desires are mutually exclusive pursuits. Fridolin, like his wife Albertine, experiences the order and security of his bourgeois life as "an illusion and a lie."[61] At the close of the story, Albertine's gesture of placing the mask on her husband's pillow for him to find underscores her awareness of this state of affairs—that their domestic existence is a masquerade full of contradictions, unspoken desires, and unfulfilled dreams. Albertine's pronouncement at the end—"neither the reality of a single night nor even of a person's entire life can be equated with the full truth about his innermost being" (99/503)—shows her to have profited from the unusually frank disclosures she and Fridolin make to one another, a confessional mode that sparks the jealousy and drive for retribution that act as the motor for Fridolin's fitful searching in the bulk of the novella. While Albertine couches her final statement ("Now we're truly awake") with a qualifier ("at least for a good while"), Fridolin's final realization is that "no dream . . . is altogether a dream" (99/503).[62] This pronouncement recalls the liminal state the protagonist of "Spring Night in the Autopsy Room" experiences.

In the key, penultimate chapter of *Dream Story*, Fridolin endeavors to learn the true identity of the mysterious woman from the masked ball of the night before, after reading a newspaper report about the poisoning early that morning of a certain Baronin D. Fridolin is overcome with an intuition that the two women are one and the same and sets out through the city to pursue the inconclusive report. "In any event, dead or alive, he was going to find her. He was going to see her—come hell or high water—whether she were alive or dead. He simply had to see her; nobody on earth could prevent him seeing the woman who had gone to her death for his sake, indeed in place of him! He was to blame for her death—he alone—if she indeed it was. Yes, it was her without a doubt" (87/495). The threefold repetition of "seeing" points already to the mode of perception that will come into play in the dissecting room.[63]

Even before Fridolin goes to the General Hospital and subsequently to the Pathological-Anatomical Institute, where his intuition tells him he will find the corpse in the morgue, he questions his motives, asking himself what he hopes to find there. After all, he knows only the woman's body, not her face, from the masked ball. Fridolin convinces himself that, were he to find her alive, he would certainly have recognized her on the basis of her gait, posture, and voice. "As it was, however, all he would be seeing again was her body, a dead female body—a face he was unfamiliar with except for the eyes—eyes which were now extinguished. Yes—he knew those eyes and that hair too. . . . Would that be enough for him to tell, without the shadow of a doubt, whether or not it was she?" (90/497). The narrator here interjects a question in the subjunctive mood to destabilize the possibility of knowing beyond a shadow of a doubt and, further, to unseat the correlation between seeing and knowing. Indeed, it is the promise of the dissecting room and of the anatomical theater that ocular experience leads to knowledge about the human body. And it is precisely here that Schnitzler introduces doubt, even as Fridolin is making his way to the institute that is supposed to house certainty about such questions.

Fridolin enters the Pathological-Anatomical Institute and is embraced by its pervasive chemical scent, which he experiences as "familiar" and "almost domestic [*heimatlich*]," two properties that stand out in a novella full of strange and unhomely places. The histology lab, across the hall from the prosectorium, is moreover described as an "almost festively illuminated room" (90/497). There he finds his colleague Doctor Adler, now the institute's assistant, whom he has known since his university days. Adler, burning the midnight oil, is surprised to see his colleague at such a late hour. After Fridolin explains the reason for his visit, the two cross the hall to the autopsy room, a bare, clinical space dimly lit by two gas lamps. Less than half of the dissection tables are occupied, and Fridolin and Adler make their way from table to table looking for a possible match for Baronin Dubieski. Fridolin, "as though suddenly and irresistibly drawn there," makes his way to the back of the chamber to a female cadaver that seems to emit a pale glow. The cadaver's head is turned slightly to the side, and the doctor reaches out, again "irresistibly," to straighten it. This poses the question of agency, for Fridolin is compelled "by some unseen power" to touch her and "by some enchantment" to bend down closer to the cadaver. In doing so, he is overcome "with a revulsion normally quite alien to him as a doctor." Regaining his composure so as not to arouse Adler's suspicion, Fridolin elevates the corpse's head with both hands.

The narrator goes on to describe what the protagonist sees: "An ashen face with half-closed lids stared back at him. The jaw hung open loosely, the thin, raised upper lip left the bluish gums and a row of white teeth exposed. Whether this face had ever been beautiful, whether yesterday it had still been so, Fridolin would not have cared to say: now it was a completely null, vacant face, the face of death" (93/499). When Doctor Adler inquires whether this cadaver is in fact that of the woman Fridolin is looking for, Fridolin's reaction is telling. Rather than giving an answer, he bends down even closer to the corpse, again "unconsciously," "as if the intensity of his gaze might wrest an answer from those rigid features" (93/500). Fridolin believes, at least initially, that *seeing* the cadaver of the woman from the previous night will lead to the certainty of identity. Searching for an answer to Adler's question, his penetrating gaze is guided by the glow of a torch, which he allows to pass over the corpse from one anatomical landmark to the next. "He looked at the yellowish, wrinkled neck, noticed the two small girlish, yet slightly sagging breasts, between which the breastbone stood out under the pale skin with gruesome clarity, as if the process of decay already had set in; followed the contours of her lower body, noticing the way the well-formed thighs spread out impassively from shadowy regions that had lost their mystery and meaning; and observed the slight outward curve of the knees, the sharp outline of the shin bones and the slender feet with toes turned inwards" (94/500). The parallelism of the clauses—with "he saw" repeated five times in the original German—and the single long sentence, punctuated by multiple comma splices, have an additive effect, forcing the reader's "gaze" to follow Fridolin's. His is a gaze schooled in descriptive, topographical anatomy, learned from someone like Carl von Langer, yet one which cannot wrest forth a conclusive answer from the immobile topography of the cadaver before him. Ultimately, he cannot truthfully answer the one straightforward question Adler twice repeats: "Is this her?" and "Well—was it her?" (93, 96/499, 501).

Two issues regarding the relationship between sensory perception and epistemology are raised here: that of visual observation and of touch. Both imply acts of transgression vis-à-vis the female body. While the men at the masked ball are forbidden both to touch the enigmatic women's bodies and to see their faces (only their eyes are visible), it is in death alone—in the space of the dissecting room—that the woman's body is made accessible to both the gaze and the touch of the male protagonist. As W. G. Sebald argues, Fridolin's gaze, fixed on the irrevocably lost object of his desire, becomes indistinguishable from that of the anatomist at work: a searching, constantly dissecting gaze, focused on the acquisition of empirical knowledge. In this sense, both gazes are stimulated by a necrophilic desire. That most forbidden desire reveals, Sebald claims, the dark side of the bourgeois ideal of love, a voyeuristic gazing only capable of being exercised undisturbed on a corpse,[64] which threatens neither to return the gaze nor to disrupt the ideal.

Although the gaze—whether scientific or desiring—can be carried out at will on the woman's body (as is the case both in the dissecting room and at the masked ball), it is the forbidden moment of physical contact with the female body that is the true transgressive act. Schnitzler presents this instance too. The necrophilic moment of contact between Fridolin and the woman's cadaver allows the protagonist to play out his power fantasy of possessing her. The narrator describes what happens after Fridolin casts the torchlight across her body: "Fridolin touched the woman's brow, cheeks, arms and shoulders with both hands; then he intertwined his fingers with the dead woman's as if to fondle them, and, stiff as they were, they seemed to be attempting to move and take hold of his; indeed, he thought he could detect a faint and distant gleam in the eyes beneath those half-closed lids, trying to make contact with his own" (94/500). Fridolin's imagining that the corpse is responding to his caress reminds us of the unnerving dissecting-room moments Schnitzler recollects in his autobiography. But rather than the embarrassment or flash of fear the doctor experiences at the dead body's uncanny mimicry of the living, Fridolin finds his desire momentarily actualized, even seemingly mirrored, by the corpse.

Fridolin's reverie is broken by Adler, who catches him in the act. Fridolin wordlessly and seamlessly adopts an appropriately scientific posture, now handling the corpse "even a shade pedantically. . . . He felt as though it were only now, at that very moment, that this woman had died" (94/500).

After sanitizing his hands, Fridolin is beckoned to the microscope by Adler, who is analyzing a culture. The researcher's gaze through the microscope contrasts starkly with the topographic, macroscopic approach to the corpse but serves to legitimize Fridolin's visit. Adler understands this and proposes that Fridolin is thus "satisfy[ing] [his] conscience" (95/501). In contrast to the topography of the woman's corpse, which Fridolin fails to consciously, rationally comprehend, he is perfectly capable of interpreting what he sees through the microscope, despite the newness of Adler's preparation method.

Even before Fridolin answers Adler about the identity of the corpse, even before he inspects the body, he already knows "that even if it were *her* face, *her* eyes, the same eyes that yesterday had gazed into his ablaze with life, he could never know for certain—and perhaps didn't even want to know" (93/500).[65] Like the protagonist of "Spring Night in the Autopsy Room," Fridolin initially goes to the prosectorium in the hopes of garnering some knowledge about death, in this case about a specific death. What he learns, however, on examining the corpse, is that the materiality of the body alone *does not* and *cannot* afford him knowledge about the woman's true identity—and that he does not even want to know whether it is she, even if he could know based on purely scientific, anatomical grounds. What Fridolin believes might have allowed for positive identification—the woman's gait, her posture, her voice—all of these characteristics, her habitus, in short, as well as her soul, died along with her.

Despite this, when Doctor Adler hesitantly inquires one last time whether the woman in the dissecting room is the woman Fridolin was seeking, Fridolin's response is revealing: after a moment's hesitation, he wordlessly nods in the affirmative "and was scarcely conscious that this affirmation might quite possibly be untrue" (96/501). Although Fridolin possibly lies to his colleague about the identity of the cadaver in the dissecting room, he does gain another kind of knowledge, one which extends beyond the threshold of the prosectorium and into his everyday life. Schnitzler closes the chapter, and thus this chapter of Fridolin's life:

> For whether the woman now lying in the mortuary was the one whom twenty-four hours earlier he had held naked in his arms . . . , or whether she was really a complete stranger, of one thing he was absolutely certain. Even if the woman he was looking for, had desired and for an hour perhaps loved were still alive, and regardless of how she continued to conduct her life, what lay behind him in that vaulted room—in the gloom of flickering gas lamps, a shadow among shadows, as dark,

> meaningless and devoid of mystery as they—could now mean nothing to him but the pale corpse of the previous night, destined irrevocably for decay. (96/501–2)

In short, the definitive identification of the corpse via anatomical investigation is not the true knowledge Fridolin achieves in the halls of the Pathological-Anatomical Institute. Rather, the knowledge gained is that the odd and compelling experiences of the night before now belong firmly in the past and are ultimately as lifeless as the soulless body in the morgue.

The dissecting room's liminal space and the encounter with the cadaver serve in *Dream Story* to skeptically frame the conceptual and systemic superstructures of the "truths" of religion and science in general. As Schnitzler wrote in his *Book of Aphorisms and Reflections* (Buch der Sprüche und Bedenken): "We escape from the confusing heterogeneity of isolated phenomena [*Einzelerscheinungen*] into the deceptive uniformity [*Gesetzmäßigkeit*] of scientific systems; from the faintly lit incomprehensibility of human destinies into the shimmering light of philosophical observations . . . and thus we are constantly on the run from the chaotic truth, which we would be incapable of either comprehending or enduring, into the deceptive comfort of an arbitrarily ordered world."[66] This is precisely the illusory orderliness presented by Fridolin's domestic life, which is revealed as the fraudulent bourgeois order that it is.

In the novella's final chapter, Fridolin is armed first with the insight that he will never know about the mysterious woman—insight provoked by the corpse's vacancy—and second with the knowledge that the nighttime experiences at the masked ball are, like the cadaver, dead and gone, also irretrievable. Fridolin is then transformed into a future narrator—a position until this point not afforded him in the narrative by Schnitzler. Among his last words to Albertine are, "I'll tell you everything" (98/503). As with Musil and Freud, for Schnitzler's Fridolin authorship is born in the wake of the encounter with the cadaver in the liminal space of the dissecting room.

VIENNESE SYMPTOMS, HUMAN FRAGMENTS: JOSEPH ROTH'S JOURNALISM

In Joseph Roth's (1894–1939) early journalistic writings and in the visual art of Carry Hauser (1895–1985), the figure of the corpse plays a prominent role. In these works, however, the presence of corpses is bound up with wider questions of the fragmented body, in particular with the omnipresence of the injured war veteran as a new kind of social figure in the interwar years. What links these two iterations of the body-in-pieces is a notion of the sheer corporeal materiality and abjection of the creature, a figure that resides on the margins of society and allows us to map a fundamental value shift in the wake of World War I. Eric Santner has situated the notion of "creaturely life" at the very center of German, and specifically German-Jewish, thought in the twentieth century. The concept of creaturely life, he argues, provides a framework for understanding how social and political "states of exception" manifest in human bodies and minds. In addition to capturing the oscillation between human and nonhuman life-forms, then, creatureliness as a concept also allows for the representation of a modern subjecthood that exists foremost in the force field of competing sociopolitical worldviews.[67] Like the corpse, the creature casts light on "the other side of modern consciousness," as Helmut Lethen asserts.[68] This illuminating function helps explain why the cultural production of the interwar years presents us with a veritable army of corpses and other fragmented bodies.

Like his friend Stefan Zweig, Joseph Roth experienced the First World War as the ultimate collapse of the "Golden Age of Security," as Zweig termed it in *The World of Yesterday*. In the undated manuscript *The White Cities* (Die weißen Städte), Roth describes his generation as "the resurrected dead," born into and having only ever known a buoyant sense of stability and optimistic confidence prior to being thrust into fighting the war and suffering through the resulting cataclysm. In the split second when confronted head-on with death, the whole world "became transformed, disfigured, unrecognizable," he recalls. Delivered from the brink of death, his generation "broke with the whole of tradition, with language, science, literature, art: with the entire cultural consciousness [*Kulturbewußtsein*]. In a single minute, we knew more about the *truth* than all the world's truth-seekers."[69] The violence and the truth of the seismographic, war-induced caesuras Roth describes were played out on the human body, as Walter Benjamin would famously note in his essay "The Storyteller" (Der Erzähler, 1936). Benjamin presents the experience of modern military conflict—and its attendant sociological shifts—as a technologically mediated ruination of the body: "A generation that had gone to school on a horse-drawn streetcar now stood under the open sky in a countryside in which nothing remained unchanged but the clouds, and beneath these clouds, in a field of force of destructive torrents and explosions, was the tiny, fragile human body."[70]

The tenuousness of the corporeal in the face of such radical epochal change, which Benjamin identified in 1936, was already emblematic in Roth's immediate postwar work. Roth's undated, posthumously published story "Sick Humanity" (Kranke Menschheit), for example, finds the protagonist, Heinrich Reinegg, projecting the discourse of an ailing human body onto the whole of society, which is suffering from the symptoms of an ill-defined malady. Reinegg wonders, rhetorically, "Was not the world sick? Its economy, its order? Had not humankind been shaken by fever rigor for twenty years or more? Were not its nerve cords painfully inflamed, overstimulated? Had not a sick brain switched off all inhibitions, so that countless dangerous lunacies were perpetrated, against which no cage bed could offer protection?"[71] Here, the whole world, all of humanity, is reduced to a single symbolic and suffering human body. In his early journalistic work, Roth localized this potent image—localized it to portraits of individual Viennese bodies; localized it to the city itself; and localized it to the vanished empire—employing it as a lens through which to critique Viennese society in the years following World War I.

Between May 1919 and March 1920, Joseph Roth, writing pseudonymously as "Josephus," published a series of articles under the rubric Viennese Symptoms (Wiener Symptome) in the left-leaning daily *Der Neue Tag*.[72] The newspaper, founded by Benno Karpeles (1868–1938), was short-lived (March 1919–April 1920). Modeled on its German counterparts, the *Frankfurter Zeitung* and the *Berliner Tageblatt*, it was conceived as an independent alternative to the politically influenced mass press. The economics of the Austrian press market in the immediate postwar years were not necessarily conducive to new publication ventures—after all, the newly founded state was a fragment of the former monarchy. But the political uncertainty of those early years actually led to a marked uptick for the party-linked, local, and boulevard press branches, as well as to a spate of new, independent periodicals like Karpeles's.[73] Though *Der Neue Tag* never gained as much traction as many of its competitors, it did bring Roth his first real literary notoriety under the formidable feuilleton editor Alfred Polgar (1873–1955), whose tongue-in-cheek style had influenced the rising young journalist.[74]

"Josephus," just one of Roth's pseudonyms, was consciously chosen: Flavius Josephus (37–100 CE), the early Jewish historian, was Roth's role model and ally across the ages.[75] A Jerusalem-born Pharisee, Flavius Josephus was imprisoned by, an envoy to, and eventually a member of the Roman forces during the First Jewish Revolt (66–70 CE). He would later go on to write the history of the war after settling in Rome. Flavius Josephus was an outsider from all sides: he was despised by the Jews who felt he had betrayed the cause and was never fully accepted by the Romans because he was Jewish.[76] Our Viennese Josephus shared several attributes with his historical precursor. Like Flavius Josephus, Joseph Roth was, as the Viennese dialect would call him, a *Zuagroaster*—literally, one who has arrived from elsewhere. Born in Brody, Roth came to Vienna from the far eastern, Galician reaches of the monarchy in late 1913, where he soon continued the university studies in German literature he had begun in Lviv. Both were Jewish, both had experienced a cataclysmic war firsthand, and both had an assimilated emigrant's view of a culture that afforded them a unique perspective from which to chronicle it. With his Viennese Symptoms, Roth took on the role of a physician and with an incisive voice diagnosed—through journalistic dissection—the post–World War I ills of his adopted city.

During the fourteen-month run of *Der Neue Tag*, Roth contributed over one hundred texts. Nearly one-fifth of these ran under Viennese Symptoms.[77] Roth left few stones unturned in his mapping of the daily indignities of immediate postwar life in Vienna, covering topics large, but mostly small, from paper and food scarcity to the political unrest gripping the city, from the finer grammatical points of the Viennese dialect to the degradation of public transportation, from returning war veterans to the crisis of Austrian identity. Roth's assertion in the novel *Zipper and His Father* (Zipper und sein Vater, 1928)—"It is the task of the author to write down what he sees"—provides a concise statement of purpose for his brand of New Objectivity, while also bolstering W. G. Sebald's observation that the single common denominator uniting Roth's aesthetic approach is "fidelity to detail."[78] In Roth's early feuilletons, we find the author sharpening his observational powers by writing small case studies with an often acid tone. These pieces reveal Roth's own increasing politicization and engagement with current events,[79] as well as show him developing what Joan Acocella has fittingly called his characteristic "wised-up, bitter voice."[80] One way Roth achieves this is by attending to the body—the human body, the social body, and the body politic.

The immediate postwar context that inspired Roth's attempts to diagnose Viennese "symptoms" rattled the writer to the core. By the time he arrived back in Vienna after his military service, the city was no longer the imperial capital and seat of a fifty-three-million-strong multinational empire; it was reduced to a shrinking national capital of an unloved rump state.[81] After the armistice of November 1918, the proverbial theater of operations had shifted to the city itself, as the laying down of arms had not ameliorated the home front struggle to survive in the face of malnutrition, poverty, profiteering, epidemics, and material shortages.[82] "This is certainly not the peace they [the Viennese] have waited for," commented Heinrich Leoster in the daily *Die Zeit* on November 30, 1918, shortly after the ceasefire. Correspondents even came to Vienna from overseas, "like gentlemen to tour the quarters of misery."[83] They viewed the city as a kind of "living museum," a contemporary parallel to the wartime exhibitions that had recreated the trenches and battlefield scenes for a wider public.[84] Leoster's front-page feuilleton "Our War Exhibition" (Unsere Kriegsaustellung) is worth quoting at length. Vienna, he remarks,

> again [has] a war exhibition, and this time a bona fide one. Not one that shows how war is waged, but instead what it leads to. . . . Even the long-absent foreign tourists are here again to marvel at what we have to show. There are rarities that have not been on display in such abundance and perfection in central Europe since the Thirty Years' War, perfect, unrivaled miseries. . . . The foreign journalists, who have traveled to [our city] for the express purpose of counting the bones [visible] on [our] bodies, really do stand with wide eyes and mouths agape at that which is presented to them in the gay imperial city on the beautiful blue Danube. . . . Through the poorly lit streets of the "most beautiful city on earth," in which the proud, representative architecture fraudulently shows off, we now lead our guests to the pale, hollow-eyed children, before the gates of clinics closed because of coal and food privation, to the war kitchens, where the middle class is starving on the breadline for municipal leftovers. They take with them flour, which we cannot afford on the black market, as a souvenir to show their triumphing compatriots back home just what has become of [the famous] Viennese pastries.[85]

Leoster's article gives piercing expression to the context that prompted both Hauser's *The Book of the City* and Roth's Viennese Symptoms.

The medical-pathological usage of *symptom* is "a (bodily or mental) phenomenon, circumstance, or change of condition arising from and accompanying a disease or affection, and constituting an indication or evidence of it; a characteristic sign *of* some particular disease."[86] The title of the Viennese Symptoms series positions the author as physician, one who, by adopting a distanced, diagnostic approach, can effectively determine the etiology of the city's suffering.[87] This position contrasts with the "serious doctors" Roth's protagonist Reinegg mentions in "Sick Humanity." Such physicians indeed "saw the signs of illness and wanted to combat them assiduously, but did not find or want to find their causes, because they were afraid of the diagnosis and the conclusions they would be forced to draw from them."[88] In the Viennese Symptoms series and in other related feuilleton texts from the early 1920s, the journalist Roth fearlessly identifies the causes—along with the symptoms—of society's ills, precisely in order to reach verdicts about the state of contemporary Viennese society and to hold accountable those responsible for the present state of affairs. Like Robert Musil's alter ego *monsieur le vivisecteur*, Roth, too, construes himself as an anatomist: "I see through magnifying glasses. I peel the skins from things and people, lay bare their secrets," Roth mused in an undated letter to the German writer Bernard von Brentano. Dissecting his subjects drives home an uncomfortable truth, however; Roth says one loses the ability to believe.[89] The symptoms of the times were legible not only in the material shortages that Roth details but far more as physical traces inscribed visibly on the bodies of the city's residents. It is to these bodies that Roth devotes considerable detail in his satirical, often heartbreaking and grotesque observations of daily life. The bodies—the corpses and "human fragments"—Roth describes do not merely illustrate the city's symptoms and, by extension, the symptoms of postwar society at large. In their evidentiary function, the bodies are themselves symptomatic of the historical traumas that constituted the very essence of postwar Vienna.[90] By attending to the damaged, diseased, and dead bodies of postwar Vienna in his writing, Roth autopsies the city itself.

In the ironically titled "The Resurrection of the Spirit" (Die Auferstehung des Geistes), published on April 11, 1920, Roth identifies three distinct categories of humankind: spiritual man, "alvine" man, and political man. The first, "higher" category, spiritual man, has all but disappeared from modern society, Roth claims.[91] He pinpoints this as the root of the ruination of modern life, "because everything: the hardship and confusion, atrocity and lunacy, wantonness and pusillanimity of our times are . . . the result of being utterly abandoned by spirit [*des völligen Verlassenseins vom Geiste*]" (276). The present sociopolitical environment has actually effected a retrograde biological, "physical development" (*physische Weiterentwicklung*), with humankind's "upper body parts" (*obere Partien*), that is, the spirit, atrophying away (277). What remains is the second category, the *Unterleibsmensch* (lower-body man), as the paradigmatic person of the times—and a grotesque inversion of Nietzsche's ideal Übermensch.[92] A rough English equivalent would be what I will call "alvine man," *alvus* being the Latin term for the abdomen and the viscera it contains. In its adjectival form, the term moreover denotes the excretions from this part of the body. In this sense, *alvine man* is both the literal, fragmented physical body and its figurative, societal excreta. Roth clearly deploys the term in this dual sense. Alvine man, the man of the era, is characterized by an unceasing struggle for physiological survival, his entire existence determined by the constant threat of hunger and malnourishment (277). Physically fragmented, he is narrowed and diminished to a single physical focal point: his lower body. Alvine man is "so wrapped up in the materiality of the present, through and through beggar and fighter for 'naked existence' [*nacktes Dasein*], . . . that the unnaturalness and wrongfulness of the power relations never even enter his consciousness" (276).[93] The precarity of alvine man's existence is so pronounced, his horizons narrowed so exclusively to the search for food and protection, that he becomes ideologically labile. He thus runs the risk of being subjugated by Roth's third category of human, "political man." These people control the power, because they possess the resources (or resourcefulness) to acquire their daily bread and the ammunition to protect their caches of material goods. The contemporary age, according to Roth, is an ongoing tug-of-war between political man and alvine man, a struggle, he implies, that alvine man is destined to lose.

In "Human Fragments" (Menschliche Fragmente), a feuilleton published in the *Prager Tagblatt* (not a part of the Viennese Symptoms series) almost exactly one year prior, on April 17, 1919, Roth provides us with an instantiation of alvine man in the subsection "The Guest" (Der Gast). He describes a soup kitchen and one of its visitors, who each day stops the otherwise lighthearted conversation of the other guests dead in its tracks. This war veteran, identifiable by his tattered uniform, is no longer a human being at all; he is hunger personified. Roth writes, "He is just hungry. He himself is hunger. Hunger in the corpus [*Korpus*] of a human fragment. Big-boned, raw hands with swollen, blue, ropelike veins hang slackly from thin, threadbare uniform sleeves. Hands, whose past was work and attack; their present is begging. Feet swollen red-blue bulge out of the remnants of a torn-up boot. Feet, whose past was moving toward a destination [*Zielschreiten*] and journeying [*Wanderung*]; their present is slinking [*Schleichen*]. He comes every day. Silently and relentlessly he comes, hunger, right when the others are engaged in denying him" (21–22). Two points are worth noting. First, this human fragment's past and the present are inscribed visibly on his body, which has become a legible cipher of the times. And second, Roth performs a double reduction of the human. Both feuilletons frame the human as reduced to a fragment of a former whole, existing now only as a very specific region of the body—the *alvus* and the "corpus," the central part of the stomach, located between the fundus and the antrum. Alvine man and his exemplar, the veteran in the soup kitchen, are moreover diminished to purely physiological, largely unconscious drives to merely exist.[94] Through the *Geist*-less figures of the human fragment and alvine man—both products of wartime horrors and of an utterly unmoored postwar society—Roth thus is able to represent, indeed embody, the destabilization of the very concept of humanity, what it means to be human at all, in the wake of World War I.[95]

Let us step back for a moment to assess the social and scientific context of Roth's human fragments, for Roth's alvine man in "The Guest" is not simply hunger personified: he is a disfigured war veteran. Roth's Viennese Symptoms series and his other contemporaneous feuilletons repeatedly focus on this very specific body-in-pieces. World War I resulted in an unprecedented number of war invalids, by some estimates 2.7 million.[96] Their presence in the visual landscape of European life was undeniable. While they were treated foremost as exemplars of selfless heroism during the war, following it they became indelible reminders of what had been lost. This contrast in perception is reflected in the polarity of wartime and postwar imagery of the injured veteran, which could hardly be starker. Almost immediately upon the end of the war, the wounded veteran devolved from a war hero to an abject creature, a shift revealed clearly by textual and visual representations—both medical and artistic—of the veteran's fragmented body as a paradigmatic body of the times. Carry Hauser's 1922 graphite-and-ink drawing *War Victim* (Kriegsopfer) provides us with a potent example. The soldier has been rendered both blind and altered beyond recognition, his mutilated face reconstructed as a noseless puzzle of skin grafts and suture scars. A nameless creature reduced to his injured organic substance, the disfigured veteran—framed in Hauser's title as a *victim* of the war, rather than as a hero—stands as a visual archetype of the age, an increasingly public return of the repressed traumas of war.[97]

From the outset of World War I, injured soldiers were called *Kriegsbeschädigte* or *Kriegsversehrte*, literally, the "war damaged," and Vienna was the epicenter of treatment for wounded veterans from the whole of the monarchy. They became the objects of multiple, sometimes competing interests: nationalistic-patriotic, medical, and social.[98] Within the first months of the conflict, for example, it became apparent that adequate prostheses were a desideratum. The standard prosthesis was lacking cosmetically as well as in utility.[99] The renowned Viennese engineer and politician Wilhelm Exner (1840–1931) suggested harnessing the expertise of surgeons, orthopedists, and engineers in developing new pros-

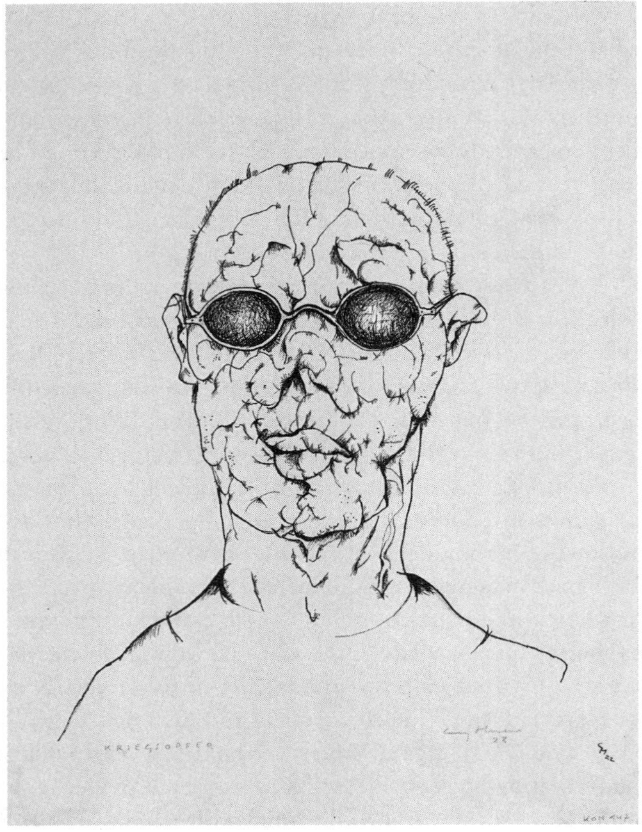

Fig. 16. Carry Hauser, *War Victim* (Kriegsopfer), 1922. Pen and ink, graphite on paper. 43 × 32 cm. Leopold Museum, Vienna. © 2019 Artists Rights Society (ARS), New York / Bildrecht, Vienna.

theses that were both aesthetically and functionally superior. Thus, the Viennese Versuchs- und Lehrwerkstätte für Prothesen, among the first of its kind worldwide, came into being.[100] In the realm of institutionalized medicine, the prominent orthopedist Hans Spitzy (1872–1956) spearheaded the opening of the k.k. Reservespital Number 11 in the Favoriten district of Vienna in 1915, a hospital specifically for orthopedic surgery and therapy, with an affiliated school for war invalids. Under Spitzy's visionary leadership, medical treatment through surgery and orthopedic medicine was combined with physical and occupational therapy, which included mindfulness of the patients' psychological well-being.[101] The capacity for gainful employment and reintegration into the workforce through vocational training and relevant physical accommodations were, Spitzy argued, the key.[102]

Advances in prosthetics manufacturing and medical treatment were reflected in wartime imagery, which tended euphemistically to focus on veterans' abilities, as well as on the functional materiality of their prostheses, which enabled their reemployment.[103] For example, a 1917 advertising poster for the Imperial and Royal Employment Agency for War Invalids (k.k. Arbeitsvermittlung an Kriegsinvalide), created specifically to address veterans' future employability, deployed such imagery.[104] It depicts three amputees and their prosthetic limbs at work, the two arm prostheses tailored to specific tasks that could make skilled and manual labor markets accessible again to wounded veterans. In the popular press, illustrated newspapers such as *Wiener Bilder* published photographic series of returned soldiers fitted with prosthetics and performing everyday tasks, like riding a bicycle—usually in a before-and-after format, and usually in uniform, as in the pictures of a man dancing a "quick six-step" with his nurse. Even the depiction of rudimentary provisional prostheses in the early war years belied their crudeness. Hans Spitzy's *Our War Invalids* (Unsere Kriegsinvaliden, 1915), for example, included a photograph of various kinds of provisional leg prostheses mounted on a series of identical reproductions of kouroi, classical Greek sculptures of idealized male youths. The powerful psychological implication is that the war wounded do not contravene physical ideals. In fact, this combination of the classical ideal with modern prosthetics might even be considered an attempt to advance a quintessentially modern physical ideal in an age characterized by the aftereffects of new forms of massive combatant casualties. This is achieved by employing the fragmentary anatomy of the kouroi—"completed" by the prosthesis—as a way of sanctioning the fragmentation of the modern body, a way of giving this new body a genealogy. In this combined form, the war-damaged and subsequently "repaired" body is codified not only as being squarely within the classical tradition but also as a "natural" extension of this tradition.

After the war, the perspective shifted radically. Whereas during the war the priority had been on maintaining as much useful *Arbeitskraft* (manpower) as possible, the reconstruction of war-torn bodies became a less urgent matter in the postwar period.[105] Roth is critical of the neglect of veterans at the hands of a largely indifferent society. His texts thus mobilize war invalids instead variously as "warning signs," "prophets," and "mirrors" for postwar society, as two final examples of Roth's cavalcade of "human fragments" make clear. "Shoelaces, please!" (Schuhriemen,

Fig. 17. Josef Eberle, poster for the Imperial and Royal Employment Agency for War Invalids, Vienna, 1917. Wienbibliothek im Rathaus, Vienna, Plakatsammlung, PS P-36383.

Fig. 18. Photographic series of a war invalid dancing with his nurse. *Wiener Bilder*, September 5, 1915. Photographer unknown. ANNO/Österreichische Nationalbibliothek, Vienna.

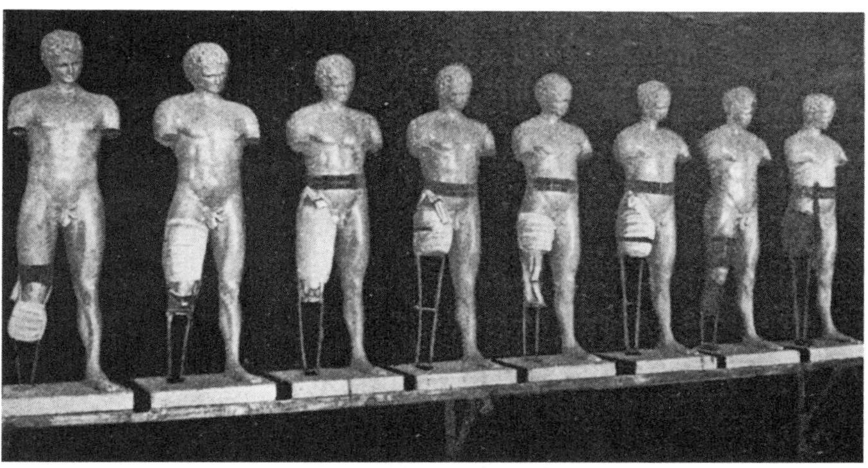

Fig. 19. Photograph of provisional leg prostheses mounted on classical sculptures. Hans Spitzy, *Unsere Kriegsinvaliden: Einrichtungen zur Heilung und Fürsorge* (Vienna: L. W. Seidel & Sohn, 1915), 63. Photographer unknown.

bitte!), part of the Viennese Symptoms series, describes an invalid war veteran turned sidewalk shoelace salesman in postwar Vienna. Roth's snapshot captures the double amputee, "a something of a human" (*ein Etwas von einem Menschen*), propped on "the street corner where war profiteering and the Now meet" (37), unsuccessfully hawking twine made of a cheap, paper-based hemp substitute.[106] The man's timely solution to material scarcity is mirrored his own body, or what remains of it. Roth ironically characterizes him as heroism incarnate, "swiftly produced by the Teisinger method from everyday material, the redesigned and repaired image of God with most modern prosthetic construction" (37).[107] A mash-up, the shoelace salesman embodies the physical traces of the lost war, the third-rate substitute components of economies of scarcity, and the results of capitalist mass production. In this sense, the man—in his physical presence—stands at once as a "symbolic warning" (*Mahnbild*) of the past and "prophet" of the future (38). Roth, the master chronicler of contradictions, finds the ultimate contradiction in this Viennese shoelace salesman, who is both "symbol and remnant of a Great Time" (*Sinnbild und Überrest einer Großen Zeit*) (37)—perhaps a knowing nod to Karl Kraus's "In These Great Times" (In dieser großen Zeit, 1914).[108] Celebrated as heroes during the war, "in that great time," Roth shows us that by mid-1919 disfigured veterans had become hallmarks of defeat and unsettling reminders of the more general urban misery. Roth effectively demonstrates the failure of veterans' social reintegration by presenting the shoelace salesman on the margins of society and as a highly visible collage of the human and the artificial.

Roth takes the juxtaposition of past and present, human and nonhuman, to a final extreme in "Contemporary Man" (Der Zeitgenosse), a subsection of the previously discussed feuilleton "Human Fragments." Here, the broken body of the war veteran functions as a mirror for the whole of postwar society, which has experienced an irremediable caesura in the war. The opening paragraph describes the man's "before" state in the past tense: "That once was a human being. Called himself God's likeness, pinnacle of creation, and walked upright on his feet through the dust from which he was made" (21). Now, however, both the war invalid and the humanity to which he formerly belonged—"a humanity that could celebrate and cry, reign and genuflect, command and plead" (22)—are over and gone. The contemporary "after" side of the image is signaled by the present tense, as Roth describes what the *Zeitgenosse* now looks like: "What is that? Mythical creature, insect, reptile from fabled prehistoric times? The upper body horizontal, the arms bent outward at his sides, in each hand a crutch, face parallel to the sidewalk: a four-footed creature [*Vierfüßler*]" (21). Like alvine man, whom we met earlier, this contemporary figure is still clad in his military uniform, and he is reduced to his bare animal, creaturely essence.

This veteran, moreover, is narrowed to a physical diagnosis. When Roth repeats the question "What is that?" a second time, he offers not merely a description of what he sees, but a scathing indictment of postwar society. This veteran is a "*fragment*, remnant of a humanity" (22; emphasis in original) that, too, has ceased to exist. Moreover, that fragment is no longer even human at all. Posing a series of rhetorical questions to his readers, Roth destabilizes the distinction between animal and human by reversing the two categories of life: "Why is this creature not naked and haired like other animals? Why does it not have a human on a leash? Why does it not wear tags around its neck?" (21). Although outwardly indistinct as a human being, Roth exhorts his readers to acknowledge the veteran for what he truly is: "It is a human! Human with a human face, with a brain that can think, fantasize, invent, dream, work, risk, create! Human, returned to his *Heimat* from the depths of heroism, and cannon-fodder with a broken back and burst nerve fibers" (21). When we regard the war invalid with revulsion or when we avert our eyes, Roth indicates, we abhor or fail to acknowledge our own society. For the veteran's body-in-pieces is the "mirror image" of humanity at large; it represents the broken fragments of a society shattered beyond repair. *Der Zeitgenosse* is the "symbol of a present staggering with a broken back between revolutions, worldviews, and social orders. What are you looking at, Contemporaries? See! It is 'nerve-shock and broken back': your mirror image" (22).[109] The war-wounded veteran is characterized in purely physiological and anatomical terms, reduced to a medical diagnosis, and one which stands representatively for the ills of modern society. This man, and the society in which he lives, have both been diminished to their creaturely essence—to their "naked existence" (*nacktes Dasein*), as Roth phrased it earlier—and he commands us not to look away.

We are reminded here of Rilke's Malte Laurids Brigge, whose encounters with the *Fortgeworfene* (social outcasts) of Paris—its impoverished and homeless—lead him to realize, as Eric Santner has argued, that he is confronting a "new social (or better, *biopolitical*) constellation" of what Santner calls "creaturely life," from which Malte himself is far from immune.[110] Malte constructs a taxonomy, realizing that these individuals are somehow different than mere beggars. Finally, he settles on a designation: the *Fortgeworfene* are "human trash, husks of men that fate has spewed out."[111] They have, very literally, been thrown away by society. Roth's human fragments and war-wounded veterans belong to this social reordering of the creaturely. In his seminal study *Cool Conduct*, Helmut Lethen argued that the literature of the New Objectivity presented a cavalcade of such creatures, including the "war cripple."[112] The creature, Lethen claims, appears in literature and art whenever society feels itself both forsaken by religious certitude and failed by the social institutions designed to provide a safety net.[113] The bare life emphasized in Santner's appeal to Rilke and Lethen's analysis of the creature is realized in the many bodies Roth puts on the examining table in his Viennese Symptoms. Roth's journalism of the body-in-pieces criticizes in the sharpest possible terms the social realities of Vienna in the immediate postwar period that have given rise to this new human type.

THE POLITICS AND POETICS OF VIENNESE CORPSES: CARRY HAUSER AND JOSEPH ROTH

We previously touched on Carry (Carl Maria) Hauser's unsettling image *War Victim* (1922) as a visual counterpart to Joseph Roth's cutting reports about veterans' bodies-in-pieces and their presence in the visual landscape of postwar Vienna. Hauser was among the Viennese visual artists whose work sought to depict graphically the misery Roth described textually. Both Hauser and Roth moreover used the corpse and the dissecting room to thematize wider issues of social injustice and political upheaval in interwar Vienna.

Hauser, a graphic artist, painter, set designer, and writer, was of the same generation as Schiele and Kokoschka but never achieved similar international renown. He was a member of the Viennese Hagenbund, an important artists' organization founded in 1900.[114] Hauser experimented freely with artistic styles, at various points in his career incorporating elements of Futurism, Dadaism, and expressionism.[115] In the early 1920s, his visual idiom evolved from expressionism primarily to a socially critical, Verist New Objectivity (Neue Sachlichkeit) clearly modeled on that of his German colleagues Otto Dix and George Grosz.[116] Hauser's socially conscious work has been called a "panopticon of striking lower-class folk types,"[117] a designation which applies equally well to much of Roth's early journalism. Frequently thematizing the underbelly of city life, in particular the woes of the working poor, Hauser populated his canvases with images of murder, urban overcrowding, illness, and returned war wounded. Commenting on a 1924 exhibition of his works in the Viennese Galerie Würthle, a reviewer for *Der Tag* wrote that the "favored domains of his brush, his style, [are] everything crippled, feeble-minded, morbid."[118] Hauser depicts such bodies, often corpses, as by-products both of their historical moment and of Viennese urban despair. The topographies of ruined bodies are mirrored in the wrecked, wound-like urban landscape that both houses and brings them forth.

Hauser's art book *The Book of the City* (Das Buch von der Stadt, 1921) consists of twenty-seven plates, each of which weaves text and image.[119] Hauser presents the city as a nameless, asphalt urban Moloch, even likening it to a festering wound that threatens to destroy itself and humankind as it heads toward an apocalyptic, "self-rending end [*selbstzerfleischendes ende*]" (24–25). It is an urban jungle of contradictions and chaos, images familiar to us from Roth's bitter feuilletons, as well as from the pens of other interwar authors—Karl Kraus, Felix Dörmann (*Jazz*, 1925), Hugo Bettauer (*Die freudlose Gasse*, 1924), Robert Neumann (*Hochstaplernovelle*, 1930), Rudolf Brunngraber (*Karl and the Twentieth Century*, 1933), to name just a few.[120] Hauser, however, uses image-texts, cleverly wedding content and form to represent the extremes of postwar urban life. While foregrounding New Objectivity's topical social consciousness, *The Book of the City* combines the associative poetics, visual vocabulary, and dramatic coloring of expressionism with a multiperspectival Futurist dynamism à la Umberto Boccioni. Hauser strategically layers geometric forms while fragmenting, multiplying, and overlapping perspectives. The overall effect captures the frenetic pace of the city and rapidly shifting visual impressions. Our guide through the maelstrom, a first-person narrator, is a "wanderer," a flaneur of sorts, and a "guest, wandering away." His "absorbing eye" (*saugendes auge*) turns away from nothing, registers everything (7). This red-rimmed eye is the visual and spatial center of one of the book's plates. While the narrator's eye takes in, he "sing[s] to you in colors, forms, and words" (6)—highlighting the intermediality of *The Book of the City*. Hauser's image-text compositions create a mutually illustrative and disruptive sphere of competing ideologies and discourses in each of the book's striking plates.

The struggle for daily existence played out in the city is one, Hauser writes, of inexorable agony. He represents the collision of worlds both textually and visually: ideas and chatter fluttering around lively café tables contrast starkly with the lust for sale in dark alleys and filthy canals; while profiteers grow rich and corpulent on others' suffering, addicts dull their existential struggles with drugs and drink. The incongruities are reflected in how Hauser structures the city spatially in both image and word. The images' axes are, for the most part, vertical. What ensues on the page is therefore often a visual and textual struggle between the redemption of heaven and the pull of hell, with the city caught between the two and portrayed as an inescapable purgatory of suffering. This strategy allows Hauser to visually represent real social stratification, as well as the figurative underbelly of urban life. The only thing that is certain is the cycle of life: "procreation and death in ceaselessly rolling succession" (8).

Although the city remains nameless, we can identify it as Vienna through a visual and textual clue Hauser includes, and one which Roth, too, would address: the *Leichenbim*, that somber trademark of interwar Vienna with which this chapter began. Alongside the automobiles, subways, and elevated trains, which make up every urban jungle's visual landscape, Hauser writes of "a funeral procession in industrious haste" (11). The juxtaposition of the cortège's solemnity with the businesslike fashion in which the march is conducted implies that there is a backlog waiting to be processed. Hauser paints the incandescent cross that adorns the rear of the *Leichenbim*. The implication of Hauser's image-text is that the streetcar of death—standing ready to convey unclaimed corpses to the dissecting room or ferry them from the Anatomical Institute to the Central Cemetery—is as omnipresent in Vienna as any other mode of transportation.

As we will see in Roth's "The Failed Putsch," the corpse becomes a central symbol of the political unrest of the immediate postwar years in Vienna. Hauser also takes up this theme in *The Book of the City.* One of the book's plates registers calls for revolution, red flags waving everywhere, and sudden shots ringing out. As in Roth's feuilleton, the result is "corpses on asphalt. men women and children" (22). Even before the ideological clashes, though, Hauser introduces the dissecting room, where Schnitzler and Freud first claimed authorship, and gives it a leading position in the kaleidoscope of sites taken in by the narrator's wandering eye. Unlike in the earlier view, however, Hauser describes it in an unflattering light as "the brute's chamber chock-full of savored [*genossen*] corpses. the scholar's closed world. alienated from neighborhood goings-on" (9). Here, the prosector wears a diabolical expression as he roughly saws into the cadaver. The incision is at the center of the plate, forming the focal point of the image, and the prosector is surrounded by a tableau of already anatomized and dismembered bodies. Positioned against dark blue, geometric shapes, they stand like mannequins in shop windows. This visual theme is taken up later in Ödön von Horváth's work. Several plates on, Hauser returns again to the morgue. In the background, two corpses await their turns in the dissecting room. In the foreground, we see a woman's body, her head cast grotesquely to the side, eyes closed in eternal sleep. The pistol that delivered the fatal, self-inflicted shot to her head rests on a table in the lower left. All three figures, Hauser writes, are ones who "escaped" their existential misery through suicide, the only way out (16).

The question whether one was not perhaps better off dead in postwar Vienna—a question clearly posed by Hauser in *The Book of the City*—was also addressed satirically by Joseph Roth in one of his Viennese Symptoms feuilletons for *Der Neue Tag.* The concluding subsection of the buoyantly titled piece "Coffee-House Spring" (Kaffeehausfrühling) carries a darker heading: "Nightlife" (Nachtleben). In it, Roth describes a recurring scene he sees on his nightly walks home through the Mediziner-Viertel in Vienna's Ninth District, Alsergrund: a hearse pulls up in front of the poorhouse at Währinger Straße 45, on the corner of Spitalgasse. The transaction that takes place is "inexorable, dispassionate, businesslike" (33): people who were once cared for by the city administration (*versorgt*) are now carried out in coffins (*versargt*). With an acid tone, the author wonders which of the two states, *versorgt* or *versargt*, is preferable. Roth takes the opportunity to coin the neologism "encoffined" (*versargt*)—noting sarcastically that the single letter separating the two words might be merely a "malicious typo" (33). What his ironic tone points to, however, is the

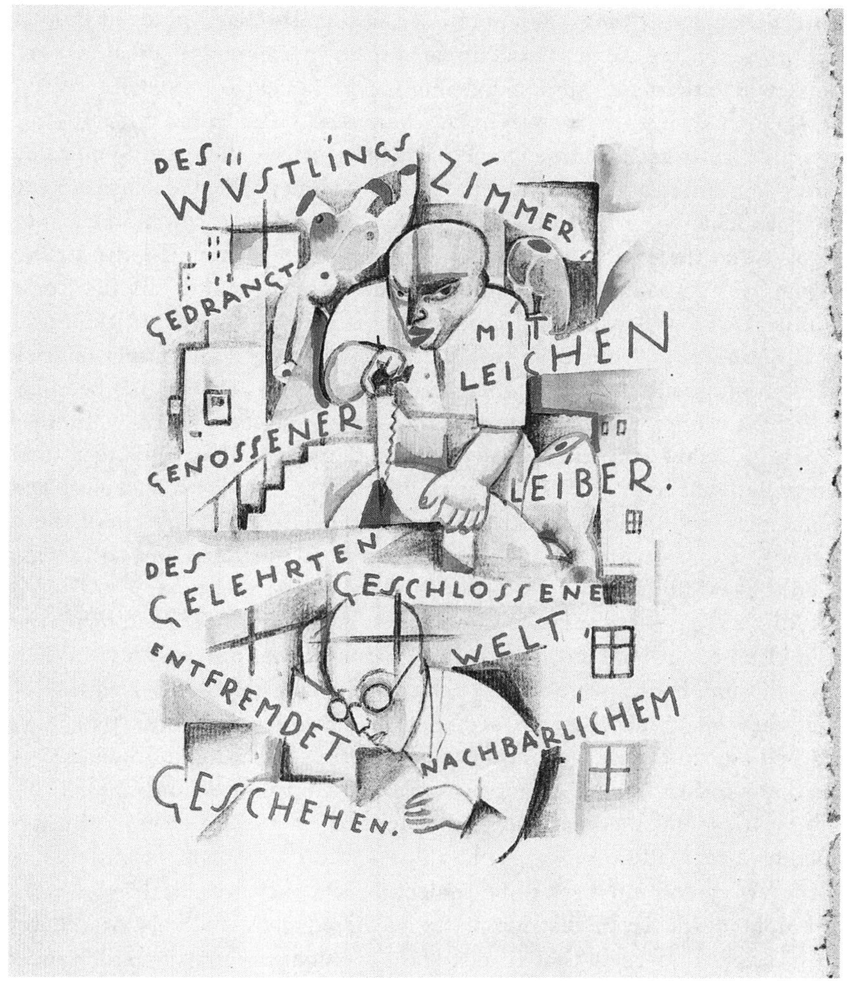

Fig. 20. Plate from Carry Hauser's *The Book of the City* (Das Buch von der Stadt), 1921. Kunsthandel Widder, Vienna. © 2019 Artists Rights Society (ARS), New York / Bildrecht, Vienna.

precariousness of the line between a postwar life of poverty and the proximity of death. The arbitrariness of a typographical error might as well apply to the randomness with which death comes to claim its victims in Vienna. Roth's keen sense for social injustice finds expression in the early journalistic texts, and it is localized, ultimately, at the Anatomical Institute. Like Andreas Pum, the war veteran and protagonist of Roth's third novel, *Rebellion* (1924), many of the socially disadvantaged figures in Roth's reportages end as unclaimed corpses in Vienna's medical institutions, where their subjugation continues, even in death.

Published on June 17, 1919, in *Der Neue Tag*, "The Failed Putsch" (Der missglückte Putsch)—not included as a part of the Viennese Symptoms series—chronicles the violent demonstrations and political clashes of June 15 that rocked Vienna. This feuilleton looks at the political production of corpses and their subsequent co-option by science. It was the third time in just over six months that an attempted violent overthrow by the Communist Party of Austria had failed. This time, more than ten thousand demonstrators attempted to free jailed Communist Party functionaries from the Rossauer barracks where they were being held, having been arrested the night before. The confrontation of the police with the volunteer "People's Guard" militia (*Volkswehr*) and demonstrators resulted in dozens killed and injured.[121] "The Sunday Victims" (Die Sonntagsopfer), the concluding subsection of Roth's essay, considers the aftereffects of these clashes. It takes us to the Institute for Forensic Medicine and Pathology, headed by Albin Haberda (1868–1933) and located in Sensengasse.

Roth's essay pinpoints the intersection between politics and medicine in a blind functionalism, which lays claim to the human body. "When these human bodies were alive," Roth argues, "politics seized them. Now that they are dead, they are occupied by science, as if these two powers had signed a pact, according to which they exchange human beings for one another like piece goods" (77). The common denominator uniting politics and medical science, according to Roth, is their indifference toward the humanity of individuals, their treatment of humans as if they were commodities to be traded. Death, the ultimate leveler, does not uphold the lived distinction between political radicals or moderates. Yet Roth asserts that in death their valuation continues, for their bodies' level of scientific interest as case studies for medical training is paramount. One case in particular, the "instructive headshot" (*der 'lehrreiche Kopfschuß'*)—a cadaver from the Sunday uprising—arouses uncommon interest from the crowd that had gathered in Haberda's dissecting room (77). In a startling allegorization, Roth suggests mobilizing both the corpse and the site to confront those behind the putsch attempt with the bloodguilt of their blind political idealism: "Here lie those dead who died because they believed they could achieve a better existence. And while these people are numbered, autopsied, carved up, and scrutinized, the guilty parties are still concerned with dispatching poor, goaded souls from the tavern table [*Bierbank*] of politics to the autopsy table of science" (77).

In "Nightlife," Roth's daily path also leads him past the Anatomical Institute at Währinger Straße 15, just around the corner from Haberda's institute and down the street from the poorhouse, where he again sees Death, "this time in more modern attire. A streetcar wagon, whose rear bulkhead wears a lighted cross visible from a great distance" (33). Put into service in 1918, the fearsome black *Leichenbim* was a fixture of post–World War I Vienna.[122] Roth describes the institute's main gates standing permanently wide open, ready to discharge at any moment into the specially designed streetcar the endless stream of already dissected corpses. These cadavers are the ironic focus of Vienna's nightlife. Their lot in death represents an advancement over the abjection of their former lives: as cadavers, they have been given a purpose and "promoted to scientific experiments" (*zu wissenschaftlichen Experimenten hinaufavancierten Leichen*) (34). This bitter step up in the social hierarchy contrasts with the seamless

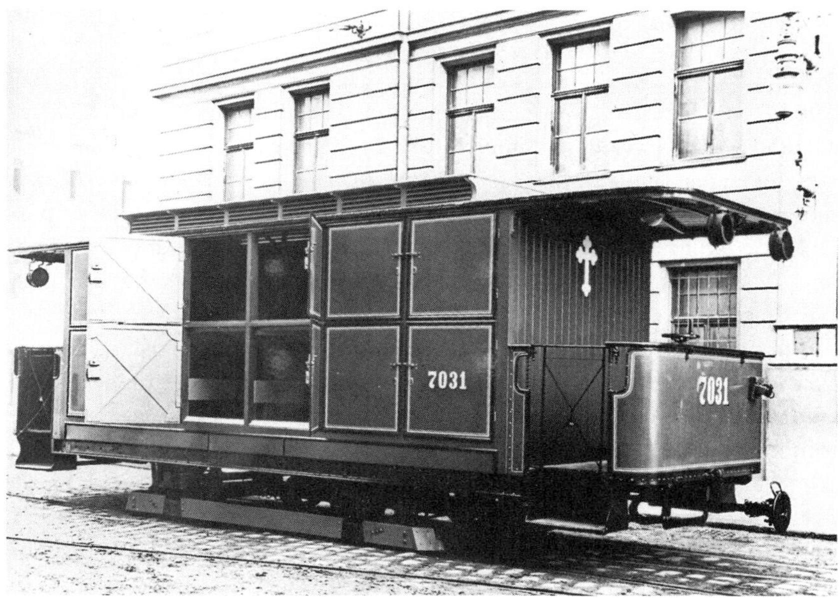

Fig. 21. Photograph of a Viennese corpse tram, after 1945. © Wiener Stadtwerke Bestattungsmuseum, Vienna, B&F Wien—Bestattungen und Friedhöfe GmbH.

shift in ideological occupation of bodies in "The Failed Putsch." The cadaver is thus a material manifestation of social and political struggle.

The true substance of "Nightlife" becomes clear, however, when Roth retools the scene he has just described as a metaphor for the fate both of the Viennese and of the monarchy as a whole. "Such is our 'nightlife,'" Roth concludes. "Like our past, our fellow citizens die and are placed in coffins, their corpses dissected like our homeland" (34). This statement foreshadows Roth's recurrent use of the metaphor of the cadaver in a geopolitical, historical context, as a later letter to Stefan Zweig would again assert. Here, it is not simply Austria-Hungary that was dissected, according to Roth, but all of Europe. He writes, pained, of the collapse: "Europe is committing suicide, and this suicide's slow and gruesome nature comes from the fact that it is a corpse that is committing suicide."[123] Like the double reduction of the human fragment, alvine man, Roth again performs a multiplied annihilation here: not only is Europe voluntarily self-destructing; it was already dead to begin with. The body-in-pieces, the living dead in the form of the war invalid, the corpse—these were the only commensurate figures with which to capture the realities of interwar Vienna.

CORPSE AS CAPITAL: ÖDÖN VON HORVÁTH'S *FAITH, HOPE, AND CHARITY* (1932)

Ödön von Horváth's interwar social drama *Faith, Hope, and Charity* (Glaube Liebe Hoffnung), completed in 1932 and premiered in Vienna in 1936, opens at the Anatomical Institute in Vienna.[124] Horváth mobilizes this site, the figure of the cadaver, and a host of dissectors to address matters of existential survival and to stage what Freud, who published *Civilization and Its Discontents* (1930 [1929]) in the same year that Horváth was drafting *Faith, Hope, and Charity,* called the "pathology of cultural communities."[125] Whereas Schnitzler's and Pappenheim's firsthand experiences of institutional sites as medical students flowed into their literary production, Horváth took a true story as the basis for his play, adapting contemporary courtroom reporting and real inquiries to Vienna's medical school at the turn of the century.[126] This "documentary impulse," as Anton Kaes has termed it, was part of a larger interwar trend under the New Objectivity toward an unvarnished realist-critical literature with the explicit goal of effecting social and political change.[127] Moreover, the centrality of the corpse in Horváth's work anticipates aspects of what the historian and political theorist Achille Mbembe, writing in a contemporary frame, has termed "necropolitics," or "the creation of *death-worlds,* new and unique forms of social existence in which vast populations are subjected to conditions of life conferring upon them the status of the *living dead*."[128]

Born in 1901, Horváth was just six years younger than Joseph Roth and perhaps an even more emblematic son of Austria-Hungary. Horváth once referred to himself in imperial terms as a "typical old-Austrian-Hungarian mixture: Magyar, Croatian, German, Czech," and the stations of his childhood—Fiume, Belgrade, Budapest, Pressburg [Bratislava], Vienna, Munich—encapsulate this fact.[129] Horváth was among the most critical voices of his time, and his works for the theater revolve primarily around sociopolitical themes. He shared with the Austrian novelist Rudolf Brunngraber (whom we will encounter in the epilogue) a preoccupation with the plight of working-class citizens struggling to get by in a time of epochal hardship. To this end, Horváth revived—and sometimes parodied—the Austrian folk theater (*Volksstück*) tradition.[130] Horváth was, as a contemporary critic phrased it, a "resolute realist"; his stable of dramatis personae—similar to those of Roth's journalism and Hauser's images of the early interwar years—represented "the world of the outcasts and the forsaken."[131] Alfred Polgar, Roth's editor at *Der Neue Tag* and one of the sharpest-witted Viennese feuilletonists, linked the universality of Horváth's themes and characters to their creaturely existence. Horváth's particular gift, Polgar remarked, was his attention to the most innate, instinctual physical drives for lust, sustenance, and the avoidance of pain.[132] In the preface to *Faith, Hope, and Charity*, Horváth himself acknowledged that much of his writing was an effort to depict the individual's "animal instinct" fueling the "massive struggle between the individual and society"—a violent, ceaseless, and fundamentally hopeless battle (vii–viii/1:327–28). This is a struggle that Horváth's characters, again and again, are bound to lose, for it is linked to that great human leveler: death. Indeed, in Horváth's works, the struggle is not, as conventionally, between life and death, but "between death and death."[133]

In the opening scene of *Faith, Hope, and Charity*, we find the play's protagonist, Elisabeth, standing before the imposing, locked doors of the university's Anatomical Institute. She is a traveling saleswoman of ladies' foundation garments and will lose her job if she cannot pay off an old fine imposed on her for peddling her wares without the proper permit. Elisabeth, living a precarious existence on the edge of unemployment and poverty, hopes to settle her debts by arranging for the premortem sale of her body to the medical school. The fine and Elisabeth's attempt to commodify her body spark a chain reaction of largely unintentional assumptions, lies, and misunderstandings, which lead not only to another fine and jail term but also, finally, to Elisabeth's death and the premature production of her own corpse.

In act 1, Elisabeth collects her courage and rings the bell to the Anatomical Institute. A dissector opens the door, gives her the once over, and asks her what she wants. She haltingly, yet directly, conveys her business: "I was told quite particularly, you could sell your body here. . . . What I mean is, once I'm dead, the people in there could do what they like with my body in the cause of science . . . but in the meantime I get the fee for it paid out. Right now" (2/1:332). The urgency with which Elisabeth delivers her request conveys the precarity of her situation. Surprised, the dissector denies ever having heard of someone wanting to sell her body. He chalks it up to harebrained ideas spread among the city's working classes. Nevertheless, he asks his superior, the chief dissector, whose reply indicates not only preknowledge of such inquiries but also their frequency.[134] The chief dissector rejoins with palpable exasperation: "What, again? . . . God knows how many times we've had to deny that we buy dead people when they're alive, doesn't anyone ever listen to official announcements? They get some idea, the state's going to pay out something for their body. . . . What makes them think they're that interesting? The state, they think the state should take care of everything" (4/1:334).

Elisabeth's attempt to commodify her body at the Anatomical Institute is part of a wider traffic in the female body around the turn of the century, and Horváth takes up this theme in numerous forms.[135] First, Elisabeth's line of work is the wholesale trade of women's foundations: girdles, corsets, brassieres, and the like. Her field of employ is, in other words, the literal harnessing of the female body. Irene Prantl, the proprietress of the company for which Elisabeth works, explains, "Your job as a saleswoman is to develop the customer's feeling for beauty! The whole country's exercise-mad now, you see naked women everywhere, what could be better publicity for our lines?" (12/1:340). The "new woman" of the interwar years is thus both an active part of the physical culture craze (if we recall chap. 1) while also bound up in the commodification of her own body. Second, this shaped and commodified female body bears an uncanny resemblance to the rigid, fragmented cadavers in the autopsy room, as a stage direction from Horváth's play makes plain. In Prantl's showroom stand "wax dummies wearing corsets, girdles, brassières and so on . . . stacked up in rows, like the heads in the Anatomical Institute" (11/1:339).[136] These wax dummies are reminiscent of Carry Hauser's disturbing scenes from the dissecting room in *The Book of The City*. Third, in the course of the drama, Elisabeth is falsely accused of attempting to exchange her body for money in the more conventional way. At the close of act 4 the vice squad appears at her door because she has been unable to verify the source of her income (34–38/1:362–66). Although Elisabeth has in fact not turned to sex work, the police refuse to believe her. Their intervention sets in motion the chain of events that leads directly to Elisabeth's suicide attempt and subsequent death in act 5. As Helmut Lethen has noted, in *Faith, Hope, and Charity*, Horváth introduces the body—the dead body, specifically—into an exchange economy that treats human remains as a product to be commodified and circulated.[137] Yet the specifics of this trade must be aggregated with reference to the fact that it is the *female* body that is exchanged. It is not simply death that is rationalized but feminine death.

The play concludes with six men encircling Elisabeth's corpse. The assistant dissector remarks coolly that she survived the attempted suicide only to succumb in the end anyway. The true cause of death, he speculates, resulted from extended impoverishment: chronic malnutrition had likely weakened her heart (51/1:379). So while Elisabeth's minor infractions led her to be caught up in the justice system, she fell through the gaps in the social safety net. How the male figures in the play—representing a cross section of the society that preys on and attempts to profit from society's weakest links, poor and working-class women—register Elisabeth's attempts to sell her body in the course of the play and how they react to her death and interact with her corpse reveal their political leanings and class status. Thus, it is the attempted commodification and subsequent production of Elisabeth's corpse—the product of societal injustice and an object of scientific inquiry—that allow Horváth to stage the era's social pathologies.

Horváth's play unmasks the nature of interwar Viennese society, and Elisabeth enacts what amounts to a "little dance of death" (*Ein kleiner Totentanz*), as the play's subtitle reads, a ronde structurally akin to Schnitzler's controversial drama *Reigen*. The cyclical drama has Elisabeth end as a corpse at the very site where she began the play, then very much alive, and still charged with faith, love, and hope, all of which are robbed from her.[138] The repetition of site (Anatomical Institute), figure (corpse), and plot (production of death) demonstrates that the characters are trapped in their earthly, abject existences without hope for resolution or redemption. Horváth's panorama of interwar Viennese social ills is acted out, to speak with Elisabeth Bronfen, "over her dead body." The sacrifice of Horváth's fundamentally virtuous protagonist at the hands of societal injustice serves as a vehicle for social critique.[139] Horváth's drama demonstrates the futility of trying to break out of the patterns of small injustices imposed on the working classes by the welfare and judicial systems. As Hauser's *The Book of the City* makes clear, death is the only way to escape this cycle, and we are reminded of Roth's description in "Nightlife" of the continuous stream of corpses emanating from the poorhouse at the corner of Währinger Straße and Spitalgasse and the ambiguity between *versorgen* and *versargen*.

There is a thread throughout Horváth's work, particularly in his prose texts, of the author integrating medical symptomology and physical revulsion as part of his attempts to thematize the never-ending struggle between the individual and society.[140] In this way, Horváth's Elisabeth calls to mind the other creaturely figures we have encountered—Roth's alvine man and human fragments, Hauser's metropolitan types. All are human detritus, abject beings suspended between life and death, in that they are effectively dead in life and valued, if at all, only in death.[141] Like the others, Elisabeth is the walking dead, a liminal figure, half-dead and half-alive. Her existential battle—"the struggle of drives [*Triebe*] against culture,"[142] Horváth's perpetual theme—is manifested physically by the premature production of a corpse. Whereas Roth's human fragments are clearly the product of both wartime trauma and interwar social misery, Horváth's living corpse, Elisabeth, is perhaps no less indebted to the harrowing yet formative experiential and visual framework of war. Though Horváth was too young to have served in World War I, he reflected in an autobiographical sketch that his "life began with the declaration of war" in 1914. The colorless, mundane images from his childhood were replaced with much more disturbing visual fare, as young people on the home front were confronted with the sight of the broken bodies of war invalids, their fathers foremost among them. Everyday life was transformed, in other words, from a "boring picture book" into an anatomical atlas of the war-torn body.[143] The visual reality of wartime and postwar life was taken up in cadaverous creations in the interwar years, for example, by the painters of the New Objectivity, such as Otto Dix and George Grosz, as well as Carry Hauser in Vienna, and in writing by authors such as Joseph Roth, as we have seen. Such bodies, and those that bore the scars of home front malnutrition, hunger, and disease, were increasingly a part of the public panorama of the interwar years, as in Roth's feuilletons. The inexorable march of death and its native home, the Anatomical Institute, became a fixture of postwar Viennese life, and the traffic in death found its symbol in the *Leichenbim* that emerged from its portals.

If we recall the centrality of the vivisection metaphor for Musil, Nietzsche, and Freud from the beginning of this chapter, it becomes clear that Horváth's pursuit was similar. Alfred Polgar, who noted the universality of Horváth's timely themes, called Horváth's dramas "laboratories," in which the characters are "experimental subjects." In a review essay, Polgar applies the procedural vivisection metaphor to Horváth's trenchant writing style, citing the author as possessing a unique "vivisector dexterity" (*Vivisektor-Geschicklichkeit*) that allows Horváth's fictional figures to embody the universal existential struggles of their era, without, according to Polgar, sacrificing their uniqueness as characters.[144] Horváth's characters, in other words, retain their wholeness—which allows readers and viewers to relate to them—while the vivisection lays bare their motivations and the social conditions that are the motors for their individual actions, that is, provides the fictional framework for social critique. Indeed, in speaking of his intentions for the drama *Faith, Hope, and Charity*, Horváth himself alluded to the old Delphic maxim "Know thyself." That axiom, which provided the foundation for efforts to understand the body at the turn of the century, as chapter 1 details, was also the framework for Horváth's interwar literary efforts. In the preface to *Faith, Hope, and Charity*, he characterized himself as an author "who sometimes imagines his only motive for writing is to allow people to recognize themselves. Please recognize yourself! So that you may acquire that cheerfulness which will alleviate your own life-and-death struggle by virtue of the fact that a dose of honesty places you certainly not above yourself (for that would be conceited) but next to and below yourself, so that in spite of everything you are able to contemplate yourself not from on high, but from in front, behind, sideways and from underneath!" (viii). While Horváth's description references the self as a body-object on an examining table, he likewise felt obliged as a writer to build mirrors, honestly depicted characters, not distortions, in which his audience could plausibly find themselves reflected (viii).[145] In this sense, his efforts correlate with Klimt's allegorical *Nuda Veritas*, holding the mirror up to society to confront it with its own image and likeness, to render visible, in this case, the naked truth of bare, creaturely life.

The encounter with death embodied in the form of the corpse thus allows us to confront and thematize, to speak with Julia Kristeva, the ordering boundaries between the self and the world, between being and otherness. The dissection of the body, forthrightly depicted, of course ultimately effects its fragmentation, its material ruination. The corpse and the body-in-pieces—those anti-ideals of the human form—have the potential to represent, in other words, both a search for the underpinnings of truths about life (as in Pappenheim and Schnitzler) as well as a sense of lost totality and broken epistemic order (as in Roth, Hauser, and Horváth). The shift in the wake of World War I from the body as harboring epistemological potential to the body as a seismograph of elemental considerations of bare life guaranteed that the Viennese could not lay their dead to rest.

CHAPTER THREE

The Patient's Body: Working-Class Women in the Clinic

> The difference between the spiritualists of now and then is that those of today see through their spirits' bones and muscles with X-ray vision. Today's spirits have their scientific accuracy and are hence far more credible than those of a lesser anatomical or optical age.
> —Ludwig Hevesi (1899)

On March 21, 1901, the art of the Vienna Secession became a political matter when fifteen members of the Imperial Council's lower house, the House of Deputies (*Abgeordnetenhaus*), interrupted the order of the day with a formal interpellation. They demanded an explanation from Wilhelm von Hartel (1839–1907), minister of education and cultural affairs, about Gustav Klimt's *Medicine* (1901), one of three large-scale paintings the ministry and the University of Vienna had commissioned from Klimt for the ceiling of the university's Great Ceremonial Hall in 1894. By going forward with the purchase of the painting, the councilors asked, did His Excellency truly intend to give a political, cultural, and financial seal of approval to the Vienna Secession, effectively endorsing it as the "official Austrian art movement"?[1]

Klimt's artistic star had risen along with the historicist façades of the grand Ringstraße buildings of the late *Gründerzeit*, the period of political liberalism and economic expansion that followed the revolution of 1848 and came to an abrupt end with the 1873 stock market crash. *Medicine*, however, with its dense column of suffering, nude figures, marked a departure from the historical tradition to which Klimt's earlier, large-scale paintings for the Imperial Theater (1886–88) and the Museum of Art History (1891) had adhered. Between the commission and the delivery of the first university panel in 1900, Klimt—along with Koloman Moser, Josef

Fig. 22. Gustav Klimt, *Medicine,* 1901 (destroyed in 1945).

Hoffmann, Joseph Maria Olbrich, and others—had founded the Vienna Secession in 1897. The Secession, also known as the Union of Austrian Artists, broke from the conservative, historicist tradition of the *Künstlerhaus,* or Association of Viennese Artists. Already in 1900, *Philosophy,* Klimt's first faculty painting for the university, had sparked outrage, despite garnering Austria-Hungary a gold medal at the Paris World's Fair that year. Almost one hundred university faculty members petitioned the ministry to reject Klimt's rendering of the philosophical "triumph of light over darkness," arguing that *Philosophy* was, among other things, visually unappealing and insufficiently allegorical.[2] But not even the outspoken faculty opposition to *Philosophy* could portend the furor that *Medi-*

cine generated just a year later. *Medicine* was deemed not just ugly and uninterpretable but also obscene.

The key criticism leveled at Klimt's panel centered on the rendering of the human bodies—and on one, in particular: that of a nude pregnant woman in the upper right of the canvas.[3] The press pilloried *Medicine* and the "ghastly anatomy" of its figures.[4] Critics called the column of humanity on the right a "barely disentangleable jumble of dying and birthing figures," a "tangle of naked human bodies," and "a snarl of human limbs . . . , as if a kettle of sausages had been emptied out."[5] To many, Klimt's panel represented, in short, an "apotheosis of the crippled" (*Apotheose der Verkrüppelung*).[6] The district attorney's involvement in the matter only fanned the legislative flames. His office had moved to confiscate and destroy the entire run of the most recent issue of the Secession's periodical, *Ver Sacrum*, which had published sketches of *Medicine*. The draft of the mother-to-be was grounds enough to investigate a charge of offending public morality and modesty. The district court eventually dismissed the charges as baseless, but the firestorm had already been sparked. While even the most critical voices were forced to accept that the "propriety" of the image had been legally upheld, Klimt's "audacity to depict a pregnant woman" appeared inexcusable.[7]

Just two years later, Klimt—perhaps in order to push the controversy even further—brought pregnancy from the margins, as in *Medicine*, to the very center of *Hope I* (1903), a full-length allegorical portrait of an expectant mother. Scandal swirled around this painting too. The remarkably direct image of the artist's mistress in late-term pregnancy was first displayed publicly in 1909 at the second *Kunstschau* in Vienna, where Klimt deployed the image to be a thorn in the side of a bourgeois Viennese society characterized by "weakness and hypocrisy," as Berta Zuckerkandl put it in a feuilleton.[8]

As the example of Klimt's paintings demonstrates, in Vienna during the first decades of the twentieth century, cultural anxieties about women's sexuality were worked out on and through representations of bodies of mothers-to-be. This chapter attends foremost to those bodies that aroused such outcry in the case of Klimt's *Medicine* and *Hope I*: the bodies of expectant mothers. That representations of the pregnant body should be such a flash point is no coincidence, for, as the feminist philosopher Luce Irigaray asserts, pregnancy forces us to contend with the very fact of female sexuality.[9] And while even the most revolutionary thought to emerge from fin-de-siècle Vienna, Freudian psychoanalysis, forever transformed the way we understand human sexuality as such,

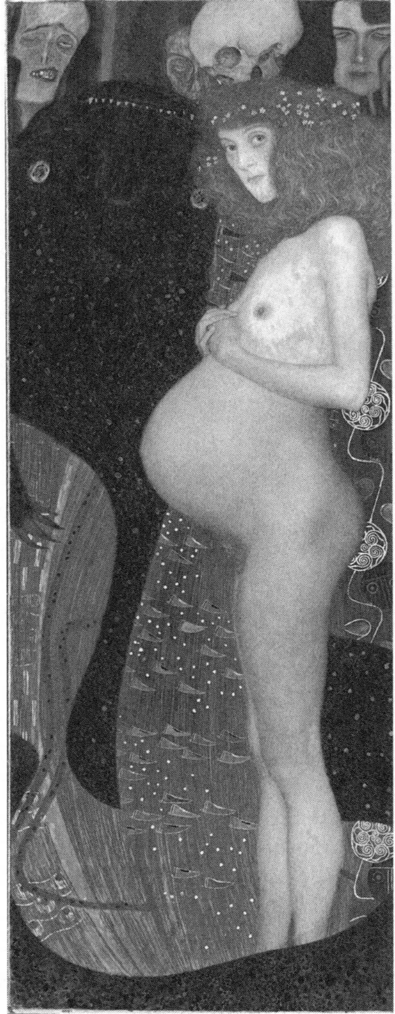

Fig. 23. Gustav Klimt, *Hope I*, 1903. National Gallery of Canada, Ottawa. Oil on canvas. 189.2 × 67 cm. Purchased 1970. Accession number: 16579.

it systematically elides the matter of women's reproductive potential as actual embodied biological experience. The pregnant body is vanished.[10] Yet, as Thomas Laqueur has argued, the cultural construction of gender and the cultural politics of representation—particularly representations of female anatomy—are inextricably linked.[11] In this fashion, depictions of pregnant bodies materialize questions about class and power in addition to those about gender.

Bold women of the Viennese fin de siècle—among them the forgotten authors Ilka Maria Ungar and Marie Pappenheim—developed a poetic mode to give voice for the first time to the authentic experiences of expectant working-class mothers. Meanwhile, changing aesthetic conventions for depicting the female body converged with modern imaging technologies and clinical architecture. These influenced practices of looking but also made the body visible in new ways.[12] Egon Schiele's striking yet understudied series of pregnant nudes from early 1910 depicts working-class obstetrical patients from the Vienna Women's Clinic, where the drawings were executed. Just a decade later, these same patients and clinics assumed a leading role in films crafted not merely for instructional purposes but for public enlightenment and entertainment. Finally, a socially conscious journalism that emerged from the pens of writers such as Else Feldmann and Bruno Frei in the wake of World War I foregrounded expectant mothers—and introduced images of abject bodies in general into the city's textual and visual vernacular. In the case of Jewish writers, the focus on such previously unseen, underserved Viennese populations additionally helped to tacitly thematize the authors' own social marginalization.

By the 1920s, late-imperial bourgeois norms that had previously idealized and sensationalized depictions of women's bodies had yielded to a scientifically informed centrality of working-class bodies—and, specifically, those of mothers and mothers-to-be—a reflection of ascendant Social Democratic biopolitics and public policy in the First Austrian Republic. Interwar Viennese social hygiene initiatives elevated pregnancy and motherhood to conditions requiring political intervention, laying claim to the female body as the site of that intercession. Mothers' bodies thus became a medicalized object of care, prevention, and control in Red Vienna. Julius Tandler, an anatomist and the leading interwar health and welfare policy architect, was part of a largely overlooked network of doctors, artists, and cultural multipliers, through which new significations of the expectant female body could emerge in political, social, and aesthetic discourses. This chapter shows how these diverse registers of cultural production acted on working-class women's bodies at a moment when the societal meaning of motherhood was in flux. Embedding such visual and textual representations in their sociopolitical contexts reintroduces female subjects, many of them from the working classes, into our consideration of modern Viennese culture.

FINDING A VOICE: THE POETICS OF PREGNANCY (MARIE PAPPENHEIM AND ILKA MARIA UNGAR)

Around the same time that Klimt was rankling sensibilities far beyond the art world with his depictions of the female body in all its life stages, the very concept of motherhood was undergoing dramatic transformation. Writing in 1899, the women's rights activist, author, and artist Rosa Mayreder—one of the standard-bearers in first-wave feminist theory—pointed out in no uncertain terms the contradiction between the challenges facing modern mothers-to-be and the traditional bourgeois values of feminine beauty and refinement. In an ironically titled article, "Beautiful Femininity" (Die schöne Weiblichkeit)—published in the influential biweekly feminist journal *Women's Documents* (Dokumente der Frauen), which she coedited with the feminists and social reformers Auguste Fickert and Marie Lang—Mayreder called a spade a spade. She characterized motherhood as "a serious obligation that requires above all the steeling of body and mind, bravery, inner boldness, and a courageous disregard for physical suffering. But we can search for these qualities fruitlessly in the canon of beautiful femininity. The greenhouse culture of good breeding, which makes of the woman a creature of luxury, results in the hypertrophy of precisely those tendencies and instincts that are averse to motherhood; it is a system of cosseting and weakening of body and soul."[13] Most middle- and upper-class mothers, Mayreder argues, are unable to rise to the physical demands of motherhood, let alone childbirth. She urges frank discussions and educational initiatives to close the gap between socially sanctioned, bourgeois feminine ideals and the physiological, psychological realities of motherhood, a divide she had earlier addressed fictionally in her short story "His Ideal" (Sein Ideal, 1897).[14] Two other largely forgotten Viennese writers, Marie Pappenheim and Ilka Maria Ungar, both penned searching, candid verse that gave expectant mothers an authentic voice. That new perspective was commensurate with Mayreder's depiction of the realities of motherhood, which stood in stark contrast to dominant bourgeois cultural paradigms at the fin de siècle.

Marie Pappenheim, whom we already encountered in chapter 2 as the poet and librettist of Arnold Schönberg's *Expectation*, was one of the first women around 1900 to answer the mounting calls for women to study medicine in order to better serve female patients.[15] Women had long remarked on their aversion to seeking treatment from male doctors. This reluctance was in reaction to both a socially engendered sense of shame and a gender bias—compounded for proletarian women by additional discrimination against the working classes—in treatment by bourgeois male doctors.[16] Although Pappenheim ultimately chose dermatology as her specialty, her political engagement for Social Democratic public health initiatives in Red Vienna was pioneering. In the context of the interwar sexual reform movement under the anatomist Julius Tandler, she founded the Socialist Society for Sexual Advice and Sexual Research in 1928 together with Wilhelm Reich (1897–1957), the radical leftist psychoanalyst and sexual evangelist.[17] The society's stated objective was to counter the rising sense of "sexual distress [*Sexualnot*]," particularly among the working classes, by providing free, medically sound counsel about matters of reproductive health and sexual wellness to all Viennese citizens, regardless of means.[18] Pappenheim gave special attention to the neediest cases, who had nowhere else to turn and were otherwise liable to fall prey to back-alley quacks—with often devastating consequences for the women's lives, as we will see in Else Feldmann's novel later in this chapter.

Pappenheim's medical training, as well as her social justice work, clearly informed her literary production from the outset. For as unusual as it was for a woman poet to write about the dissecting room, as we saw with Pappenheim's poem in chapter 2, it was even more revolutionary to write explicitly about pregnancy, and particularly about mothers bearing children out of wedlock. Yet this is exactly what Pappenheim did in another poem, "First Pregnancy." This poem, one of four by Pappenheim published by the tastemaker Karl Kraus in his leading literary journal *Die Fackel* in 1906, acknowledges the existence of single motherhood and begins to demythologize pregnancy.

The poem's speaker directly addresses an unnamed group in the second-person plural, beginning the poem with an image of laborious movement. The anonymous pregnant women walk ponderously with "heavy shoulders" and a "tired, unconscious gait" toward an unknown destination (lines 1–2). In addition to their physical burdens, there is a second, psychic weight the women carry: the shame and dark memories of the past, which accompany the women on their path, casting a pall over their "soul" and "pleasure" (lines 3–4). Self-loathing and longing are personified in these women's listless gazes, which can still spy the halcyon girlhood, now definitively past, which shimmers, "foreign," like a distant shore (lines 13–16). Redolent white lilies, heavy with the weight of their own blooms, issue forth "fever's wish" (lines 17–20). The reference, perhaps to childbed fever, is linked to a kind of natural imagery that is at once associated with chastity, rebirth, and innocence restored, as well as with motherhood. Nevertheless, the poem is by no means dominated by this kind of decadent nature symbolism—unlike that of a poet such as Felix Dörmann, a member of the Young Vienna literary circle, who was well known for his elaborate, dark style, as in *Neurotica* (1891) and *Sensations* (Sensationen, 1892).

In the third stanza, Pappenheim likens the women's smiles to those of fallen soldiers, "without hope and without thanks" (lines 9–10), set in a kind of resigned stoicism. Framing mothers as troops, having only barely survived a battle—both social and physical—is precisely the type of imagery that Rosa Mayreder had in mind in her essay "Beautiful Femininity" from just a few years earlier. The speaker in Pappenheim's poem addresses the nameless women in frank yet empathetic terms—not shying away from the fact that these women might be single mothers-to-be, as is implied by the "shame" that is twice repeated. In the final two lines of the penultimate stanza, the tone shifts measurably. Rather than the weighty burden the expectant mothers have been carrying until this point, the speaker closes with a hopeful turn, indicating that when the child arrives, the mother's "gaze and gesture" turn "childlike" too (lines 23–24)—a re-imbuing of innocence to those society views as having lost their virtue. Pappenheim closes the poem with a final stanza that makes plain the circumstances of these women: it is "As if, that which you receive in ignominy and shame, / When it awakes to life, / Removes the stain from your soul / And restores your purity . . ." (lines 25–28).

It is difficult to overstate the radical modernity of Pappenheim's poem, published in 1906 in the most avant-garde Austrian literary forum of her day, Karl Kraus's *Die Fackel*. In an editorial note that accompanied her work, Kraus described the four poems, published under the pseudonym Maria Heim, as "samplings of first-rate talent."[19] Despite Pappenheim's many gifts as a writer—we need only think of the compelling libretto she composed for Schönberg's opera *Expectation* (1909)—she chose to invest her energies and to deploy her network of influential friends elsewhere: in her medical practice and in her work for social services, focusing on women's sexuality and reproductive rights in the interwar years.[20]

Pappenheim, from a well-situated middle-class family, was not alone in attempting to give a literary voice to those most vulnerable working-class mothers in the first decade of the twentieth century. If Marie Frischauf-Pappenheim's name is one that has largely disappeared from the pages of literary histories, Ilka Maria Ungar's (1879–1911) erasure was even more complete.[21] Without the benefit of a family of means and a strong, upwardly mobile social network, Ungar never made it into literary histories at all. Ungar, however, even more systematically than Pappenheim, made the voices of working-class women and mothers the very heart of her lyric poetry. While many of Pappenheim's patients were socially disadvantaged, Ungar knew personally, intimately, the topics about which she wrote so sensitively. Yet her empathetic poetic approach was paired with a striking frankness, both of tone and subject matter, for Ungar was herself a working-class woman and mother of four who experienced toil, privation, and personal loss in her short, tragic life.

Born Ilka Maria Löwy in Budapest, Ungar moved to Vienna as a child. We know little about her early life, but it is certain that she stemmed from humble circumstances, was probably Jewish, and made her living, likely as a seamstress, working in the imperial dressmaking house Drecoll on Kohlmarkt in Vienna's city center.[22] Widowed at twenty-three, she remarried in 1902 to a merchant from Osijek, a city situated on the Drava River and then the capital, cultural center, and county seat of Virovitica in the Kingdom of Croatia-Slavonia (and Croatia's second-largest city, after Zagreb, in 1910).[23] Ungar lived there with her family from 1904 to 1909. Returning to Vienna after five years, she fell ill and died soon after, but not before seeing her first and only collection of poems in print. *Closing Time* (Feierabend, 1910) was published by the same German press that published *Der Sturm*, the leading expressionist journal of its age. Though not widely reviewed, *Closing Time* is a remarkable document of a working-class woman who was herself writing accomplished lyric poetry about working-class women's issues. Like Pappenheim, whose talent was promoted by Kraus, Ungar, too, found an early supporter who had long since arrived in the upper echelons of fin-de-siècle Viennese literary life: Peter Altenberg.

It is unclear how the two writers became acquainted, but Altenberg published four of Ungar's poems in *Kunst*, the short-lived journal he masterminded in 1903–4. Her poems were subsequently featured in the pages of two leading literary journals in 1905–6: *Österreichische Rundschau* and *Simplicissimus*. The latter ranked among the leading German political-satirical magazines but was initially a forum for the literary and artistic avant-garde. All of the renowned authors of the age published there, from Thomas and Heinrich Mann to Rainer Maria Rilke, Robert Walser, Hermann Hesse, Hugo von Hofmannsthal, Karl Kraus, and many others. Ungar for her part published no fewer than six poems in *Simplicissimus*, some of which would later appear in her collection *Closing Time*. Those in *Simplicissimus* included several from the later poem cycle "Proletarian Songs" (Proletarierlieder), which addresses the tribulations of working-class life, largely from the perspective of women, many of them struggling seamstresses and servants.[24] Even after her death and that of her champion, Altenberg, Ungar was not entirely forgotten, as her poems were published posthumously in *Der Friede* in 1919 and in *Die Muskete* as late as 1934.

If one strand unites the diverse poem cycles contained in *Closing Time*, it is the thematization of the "bitter husks of life," as Ungar phrases it in one verse.[25] The fundamental rift, or "Conflict" (Zwiespalt), as another poem's title suggests, is the discrepancy between the poetic subjects' poverty—many are characterized as "destitute," or *bettelarm*, literally poor enough to beg (37, line 1)—and the life force of their love, empathy, and sensitivity. The volume consists of six poem cycles, three of which are named: "Songs of Death," "Proletarian Songs," and "Drava Idylls." These titles indicate the topics Ungar's poems cover, ranging from death and social iniquity to the natural world. Some of the poems herald a revolutionary voice, championing working-class concerns and denouncing elitist self-interest. The first poem in the "Proletarian Songs" cycle, "To Them" (An sie), opens, for example, with a servant—speaking for others in her line of work—directly addressing the bourgeois family that employs her. "You with the barren hearts," it begins, "Philistines, listen to me" (68, lines 1–2).[26] This urgent plea is characteristic of much of Ungar's verse, as the poet demands acknowledgment and justice.

The unique contribution of Ungar's deeply personal poetry is that, for the first time systematically in the German language, it insistently gives expectant mothers a voice. Though unnamed, the second poem cycle in *Closing Time* can only be characterized as "Songs of the Mother." Thirteen of the fifteen largely anti-idyllic poems in this cycle thematize motherhood, and they are either written from the first-person perspective of a mother or are addressed to a mother or mothers in general. "Mother" (Mutter) and an adjacent poem, "Farmer Mother" (Bauernmutter), share a descriptor of the maternal figure—one poem directed to a universal mother by an unknown speaker, the other to a group of village mothers—as "the Eternal" (*die Ewigkeit*) (42, line 12; 43, line 4).[27] Despite the transcendent imagery, Ungar does not shy away from describing the expectant mother's physical sensations and experiences, as in "Twofold Life" (Zweifach Leben). Reminiscent of Pappenheim's "First Pregnancy," in this poem an expectant first-person speaker walks in the forest with a "heavy gait" (33, line 2). She experiences the world in a hyperaware state, keenly attuned emotionally to all the world's joys and sorrows, while registering the sensation of "a second heart in my body" (33, line 8).

Ungar moreover gives poetic expression to biological processes associated with motherhood, such as birthing and nursing.[28] "After an Arduous

Hour" (Nach schwerer Stunde), for example, opens with a graphic description of a delivery. The speaker, a birthing woman, becomes "an animal in agonizing struggle." Ungar does not spare pain from her portrayal, which references spasming limbs and a final, eviscerating scream (35, lines 1–4). The poem, radical for its time in its explicit description of childbirth, is matched by "Life-Sources" (Lebensquellen), written from the perspective of a nursing mother. Finally, the "after" in the title of "After an Arduous Hour" indicates the hopeful transcendence to which the poet typically appeals. For, beyond the daily sufferings of working-class mothers, the experience of motherhood is, Ungar suggests, a fundamentally transformative experience for a woman. Unwed mothers, too, are elevated in Ungar's vision from socially outcast, seductress "Eves" to emblems of virtue, "Marys," through the "Significant Event" (Bedeutsames Ereignis) of childbirth (31, line 12). In contrast to Pappenheim's poem, which takes on the topic of single motherhood, one of Ungar's poems, "Illegitimate Child" (Unehelich Kind), directly addresses a child born to an unmarried mother (75). While progressively acknowledging the cruel world of contempt, disregard, and alienation the child will encounter as it grows, the speaker's counsel that the child should take comfort in the simple pleasures and beauty of the natural world reads like a bromide against the social reality Ungar knew so well. While still a poet of her time—formally conventional and frequently resorting to euphemism, for example—Ungar nevertheless creates a wholly new poetic vocabulary for describing women's experiences by openly acknowledging the physical realities of motherhood.

The most painful poem in *Closing Time* is surely "Life of the Poor" (Leben der Armen), the penultimate poem in the "Proletarian Songs" cycle. It unites the book's three main themes—working-class poverty, death, and motherhood—in one harrowing opening image: the body of the destitute, expectant mother as a coffin (87, lines 1–2). Even if the child reaches term and is born, it will only accelerate the mother's descent into penury and abjection, the speaker concludes, employing forms of direct address throughout. The poor mother's own body is already a slack-breasted picture of malnourishment, so how is she meant to feed her child? Since certain death lies in wait on the horizon, the mothers may as well just bear their children directly into their own graves, the speaker states outright, with shocking directness (87, lines 5–8). In contrast to other poems in the collection, some of which counter lived misery with a tentative hopefulness, "Life of the Poor" indicates no such possibility. The only promise these lines, these lives, offer is further hardship, misery, sorrow. In the end, and despite some glimmers of optimism, the overarching message of

Ungar's poems is that working-class mothers are "chosen for misery" (as one poem's title has it), shouldering unfathomable burdens that turn them into embodied "chalice[s] of suffering" (42, line 11).

How are we to situate the poetics of pregnancy and of working-class concerns that dominate Pappenheim's poem and Ungar's book of verse? Pappenheim and Ungar are written out of histories of Austrian literature because, poetically, they sit uneasily alongside their predecessors, poets such as Betty Paoli (1814–94) and Marie von Ebner-Eschenbach (1830–1916). Both Pappenheim and Ungar were marginalized because of their sex and their Jewish identity. Ungar, moreover, suffered from additional disenfranchisement because of her class. Having lived her entire life on the invisible fringes of society, she also spent the majority of her authorial existence on the margins of the cultural sphere, indeed of the empire, far removed from the Viennese literary elite. These poets clearly reside on the opposite end of the political and social spectrum from many Austrian women *Heimat* poets.[29]

Despite some key parallels, Ungar and Pappenheim have been cut from literary history in favor of a Zeitgeist dominated by poets such as Rainer Maria Rilke, Georg Trakl, and the expressionists. Ungar, for example, shares thematic and tonal similarities with Rilke, in particular, whose *The Book of Hours* (Das Stunden-Buch, 1905) contains a poem cycle entitled "The Book of Poverty and Death" (Das Buch von der Armut und von dem Tode).[30] Rilke's deep humanism, introspection, devotional tone, and attention to the seemingly quotidian aspects of life are likewise present in Ungar's poetry. Yet the contemporary topical relevance of Ungar's verse, her clarion call of recognition for and ethical solidarity with those whose stories and histories are most frequently erased—the working classes and women, in particular—stand apart. The fact, however, that both Ungar and Pappenheim received contemporary support from the literary establishment reveals an undercurrent of socially engaged writing that prefigured that of the interwar years, which comes into focus later in this chapter.

In *Wiener Mode* in 1911, Paul Wertheimer—a journalist, feuilleton editor at the *Neue Freie Presse*, and writer from the Young Vienna literary circle with Hofmannsthal, Schnitzler, and Bahr—published a review of Ungar's slim volume *Closing Time* just three months before her death. A poet himself, Wertheimer proclaimed that Ungar's collection contained "not a single unessential" poem and that she was an utter unicum, "free from any aesthetic or learned role model."[31] Peter Altenberg concurred. In a sketch dedicated to Ilka Maria Ungar in a revised 1919 version of his book *Märchen des Lebens*, he characteristically effuses, "Never, never has a truer, more exquisite, simpler, nobler book been written."[32] Although Altenberg was the first publisher of Ungar's poems, her thematically unique verse, focused as it is on hardship, particularly on physical suffering, seems to have taken on new resonance for him shortly before his own painful decline and death. For Altenberg, Ungar's poetry consists of "composed, lived pains" (209). Her verses are "truths [*Wahrhaftigkeiten*]," he writes, "paid for with lifeblood, with life-joy." Ilka Maria Ungar, despite her short life and despite being an autodidact, is "not a beginner, but an ender," he asserts (210). In fact, however, Ungar's and Pappenheim's poetics of pregnancy mark the beginning of an increasingly present cultural movement to give authentic voice to overlooked subjects in fin-de-siècle Vienna: working-class women, many of them expectant. The instability of the social signification of this image permeated Viennese modernist cultural production. Among the visual artists, it was Egon Schiele who delivered the images that corresponded to Pappenheim's and Ungar's unflinching poetics of pregnancy. Yet his very access to these models, and how this access was gained, introduces a set of thorny questions about the interface between doctors, artists, and female patients in fin-de-siècle Vienna.

EGON SCHIELE IN THE CLINIC

In Viennese modernist visual art, as perhaps in no other artistic tradition around the turn of the century, the human body was the dominant theme, one that extended from Klimt and the Secessionists to their successors, the expressionists—Richard Gerstl, Egon Schiele, Oskar Kokoschka, Max Oppenheimer, and Herbert Boeckl, among others.[33] The art historian Werner Hofmann has identified "the unequivocal examination of the creaturely"—a kind of "fleshly awareness," in his evocative phrasing—as the defining contribution of Austrian expressionism to the idiom of twentieth-century visual art.[34] The growing public discourse about the tribulations of modern motherhood we saw reflected in the poems of Pappenheim and Ungar called for a commensurate visual representation of mothers-to-be, one that no longer cloaked the female "condition" (*Umstand*) in allegorical visual rhetoric, as with Klimt's two versions of *Hope*.

Egon Schiele (1890–1918), more than any other visual artist of his time, forcefully stripped away the ornamental façade that covered, held in check, the bodies beneath Klimt's shimmering geometry.[35] The radicalism of Schiele's art that caused outrage in his time and has brought him renown today lies in his direct, unabashed representation of the human body.[36] The arresting, understudied series of pregnant nudes he executed in the early months of 1910 are not only a prime example but constitute an unremarked turning point in his aesthetic. Schiele created at least thirteen watercolors of expectant mothers at the University of Vienna's newly opened Women's Clinic for obstetrics and gynecology.[37] The raw, unvarnished corporeality first systematically manifest in this series became Schiele's signature style and defining provocation, and it was a visual starkness that emerged in part from the unusual atelier setting: the medical clinic.[38] The bodies he encountered there, those of working-class women, were subject to the visual regimes of modernity, regimes that were increasingly mediatized and crossed class lines.[39] There is no aesthetic precedent for Schiele's clinic nudes,[40] which lay bare the bodies of expectant mothers, confronting us with the very fact of his sitters' imposing pregnant bodies. His drawings of mothers-to-be exude a candid, radical corporeality, an unaestheticized physicality that sets them apart from even Klimt's paintings of the same theme—*Hope I* and *Hope II*—from around the same time, in addition to the figural elements of *Medicine*, which had sparked such scandal in 1901. Schiele's drawings call attention to questions regarding women's sexuality, social marginality, and the more general problem of scopic power in fin-de-siècle Vienna.[41] Before attending to the intersection between artistic and medical cultures that facilitated this unusual series of drawings, let us first focus on the women.

The patient-subjects of two watercolors, both titled *Pregnant Woman*, look out from the page piercingly, squarely meeting our gaze. The women's postures—heads angled sideways, as if resting on their shoulders—suggest an air of casual indifference, while their eyes tell a different story. One expectant mother peers skeptically through narrowed eyes, assessing with a flinty stare the artist sketching her. The other woman, by contrast, her light, almond-shaped eyes cast with a hint of melancholic clarity, looks out softly at the viewer. Schiele's application of color in these images is especially notable. In contrast to the intense and often rough, red-orange wash that dominates some of the other depictions in the series, Schiele has here carefully outlined the women's bodies in black crayon, paying special attention to their round, protruding bellies. His line is sure, steady, directed; with very few clean strokes, he captures the women's powerful corporeal presence. The unique green wash he applied to the one sitter's countenance, abdomen, and thighs varies in intensity. It is darkest in her face and suggests a sickly pallor, while its gentle translucence on her belly makes her skin almost seem to pulsate. The other woman's emerald abdomen is set apart from the rest of the image, its color contrasting sharply with the ruddy flush of her cheeks and her coppery shock of a bob.

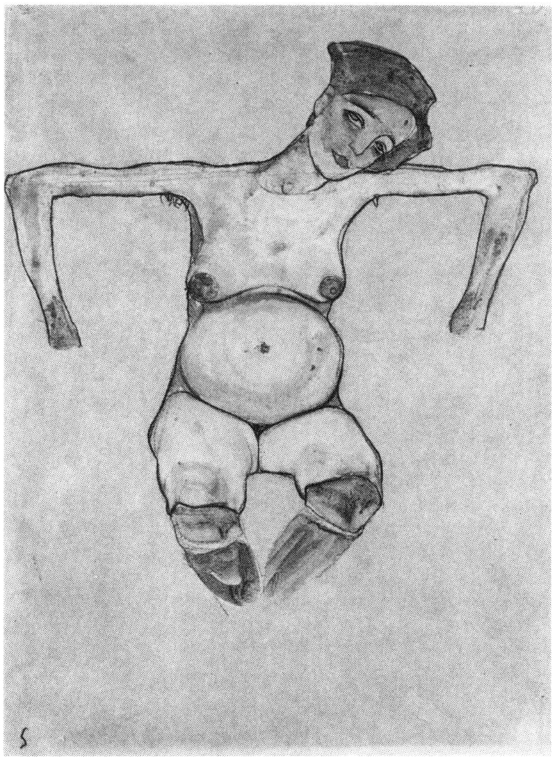

Fig. 24. Egon Schiele, *Pregnant Woman*, 1910. Private collection. Image courtesy of Galerie St. Etienne, New York.

In several more audacious drawings, Schiele extended the linear precision and dramatic coloring of other images from the series but obscured the sitters' identities by leaving their faces incomplete—as if to grant them anonymity. In another image, also entitled *Pregnant Woman*, for example, Schiele has sharply demarcated the contours of the subject's splayed frame with black crayon. The radical red watercolor wash, intense and strategic, emphasizes the convex domes of abdomen and breasts. The tawny paper filtering through visible brushstrokes of monochrome red stain attests to the swift execution of the study. The woman's unfinished face registers as an anonymous mask, detached from the mountainous presence of her pregnant body. The patient in another drawing, *Seated Pregnant Nude, Arms and Legs Outstretched*, is depicted in a similar pose, and the execution of the face is even sketchier, here a blot of rusty ochre. Schiele chose a

Fig. 25. Egon Schiele, *Pregnant Woman*, 1910. Private collection.

more subdued palette: sallow yellows and raw umbers underpainted with green set off the torso from the abdomen and extremities. In both of these faceless drawings, the clear focal points are the ebony triangles of the patients' montes veneris. Perhaps the artist was tacitly nodding to Gustave Courbet's *L'Origine du monde* (The Origin of the World, 1886), which depicts the female anatomy in hyperrealistic detail. Yet Schiele's watercolors do not aspire to such precision, and this is what distinguishes his clinic series from the provocative eroticism of Courbet.[42] Whereas Courbet plays with concealing and revealing by veiling the upper portion of the model's torso, Schiele's sitters, while anonymous, are, for the most part, completely bare, utterly exposed.

A key similarity between Courbet's and Schiele's images—and one that sets them apart from classical nudes, which are most frequently depicted on the diagonal—is the models' lateral, supine position. The viewer is confronted directly with the sitter's genitals. In five of Schiele's series of drawings, the subjects—arms angled uncomfortably and legs spread to varying degrees—are clearly lying on gynecological examination tables, though the tables are, with one exception, absent in the drawings.[43] Around 1900, new designs for operating tables and hospital beds allowed the patient's body to be ever more ideally positioned for medical visualization and examination.[44] As we will see, the new designs for clinical architecture after the turn of the century also served as means to similar ends. In an analysis of how power structures are reflected in human postures, Elias Canetti wrote that lying down is the position of ultimate impotence

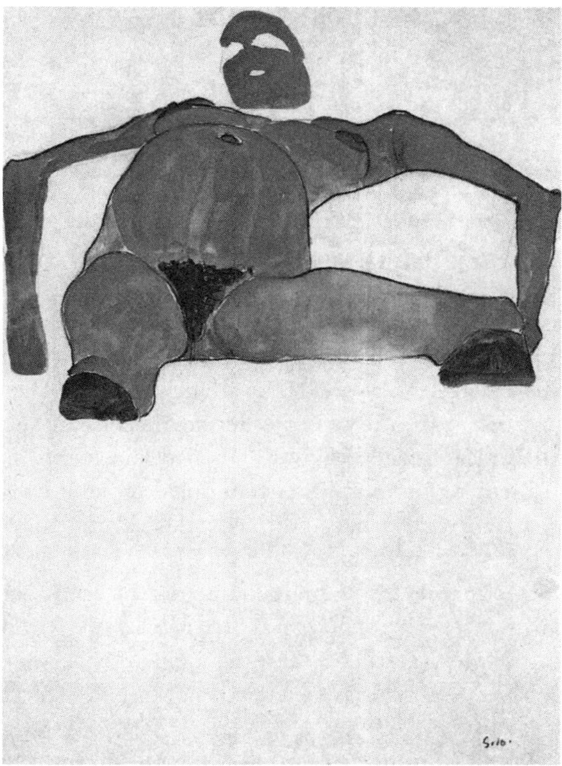

Fig. 26. Egon Schiele, *Pregnant Woman*, 1910.
Leopold Museum—Privatstiftung, Vienna.

and vulnerability.[45] Depicted in the most defenseless imaginable position, the pregnant patients in Schiele's watercolors are deindividuated and optimized as objects of clinical—and in this case also artistic—observation.

Schiele, who was just beginning to experiment with the twisted postures and figural distortion for which his images would soon become known,[46] was surely struck by the geometry of the women's arms on the exam tables. In fact, he carried over the influence of these patients' sharply angled arms and legs into later drawings of men from the same year, most notably in *Seated Male Nude with Lowered Head*.[47] The posture of the limbs of the male subject strikingly mirrors that of several female patients from the clinic series, though the study of the male model is executed from a higher angle. The pregnant figures' left legs in figures 3.4 and 3.5 are angled sharply sideways, exposing the subjects' genitalia, which in both cases is set off by a dark triangle. Schiele left most of the series of drawings unfinished, as the seemingly amputated hands in figures 3.3 and 3.5 indicate. In the case of the *Seated Male Nude*, the right hand is likewise rendered as a disproportionate, perfunctory knob. The incomplete state of many of the drawings from the clinic series of pregnant women further suggests that Schiele executed the sketches hastily, perhaps not wanting to look too long at his subjects.

A very different sense is conveyed by the subject of *Seated Female Nude with Dark Blue Stockings, Facing Front*.[48] The patient sits on the edge of the examination table, cursorily rendered as a flat, one-dimensional block in the lower right quadrant of the sheet. Here, Schiele has captured the awkwardness and self-conscious discomfort of this mother-to-be. The woman's eyes are averted as she leans slightly back on the table, and her body language conveys pure tension: her jaw is set, her shoulders form a firm horizon, and her arms, elbows extended and locked, stretch rigidly downward, squeezing in on the taut roundness of her growing belly. With knees pressed tightly together and hands clasped to a tense knot in her lap, the patient is trying to preserve a modicum of modesty. Her uneasy posture suggests that if this woman could quit the scene, she would. This image alone in the series apprehends the precarious power relations inherent in the clinical setting, where women's bodies were subject to a clinical gaze[49]—one in this case exercised not only by doctors, but also by the artist.

The common denominator in all of Schiele's images from the clinic—and it is the first consistent application of this principle in his work—is that the naked body is all there is. Yet the desire to present the naked truth of his models' corporeality was a decisive stylistic shift for Schiele.

There is precious little in his work through 1909 that would herald the radical breakthrough of 1910, the year in which the body—and the state of the body (*Körperbefindlichkeit*)—became his focus.[50] This was the year in which the nude took center stage in Schiele's drawings and paintings; this was the year in which he completely revolutionized the representation of the human figure, experimenting with rendering exaggerated gestures, awkward postures, and uneasy or defiant facial expressions.[51] Prior to that, his figure studies remain, for the most part, academically inflected. With the clinic series and in its wake, by contrast, Schiele's drawings and paintings are focused almost single-mindedly on his subjects' physical presence, on the contours, angles, and curves of their bodies. The drawings of expectant mothers convey an audacious corporeality, inspired by the sterility of the clinical setting, which thrusts the patients' bodies into the foreground, while the background falls away entirely.

Schiele scholars widely agree that a "break" occurred in his artistic development,[52] yet little consensus reigns as to its source.[53] Both in themes and execution, Schiele's early works—what we might call his pre- or protoexpressionistic phase—bear legible traces of the curriculum of Vienna's Academy of Fine Arts (Akademie der bildenden Künste), where in 1906, at just sixteen years old, Schiele became the youngest student in his class. In 1907, less than a year after beginning his studies, he met Gustav Klimt, who exerted a decisive aesthetic influence on the younger artist and would become a vital advocate for his work. Until late 1909, Schiele's portraiture, in particular, incorporates aspects of Klimt's ornamental, stylized fill[54]—as in the *Portrait of the Painter Hans Massmann* (1909) or the geometric frock in the *Portrait of Gerti Schiele* (1909). Increasingly, however, Schiele began to dispense with ornament. This formal development mapped onto an institutional rebellion against the academy and its conservative old guard, with the historical painter Christian Griepenkerl (1839–1916) as its archetype. Schiele left the school in the summer of 1909 to form the New Art Group (Neukunstgruppe).[55] By early 1910, Schiele had abandoned ornament altogether for a wholly new visual idiom,[56] one perhaps best characterized by what the Schiele scholar Jane Kallir has called "a tensely structured void."[57] This radical stylistic development is evident in the *Portrait of Dr. Erwin von Graff* (1910), for example, which depicts the doctor in a spatial vacuum, utterly detached from any context. Here, it is clear that Schiele has broken free from the decorative influence of Klimt's society portraits by reducing his sitters solely to their physical presence.[58] The play is now between the negative space of the background and the body alone. It was Schiele's direct and immediate firsthand encounters

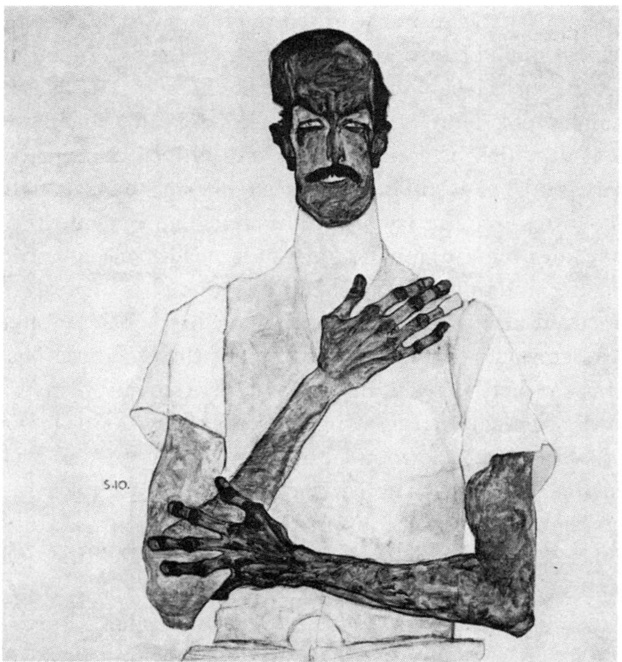

Fig. 27. Egon Schiele, *Portrait of Dr. Erwin von Graff*, 1910. Private collection.

with female patients—and their bodies—in the medical environment at the obstetrics and gynecology clinic in Vienna that decisively prompted Schiele's aesthetic shift in early 1910.[59]

How, exactly, did a young, upstart artist like Schiele gain access to pregnant patients at one of Vienna's gynecological clinics? The answer emerges via an influential network between artists and patrons, many of them physicians, in fin-de-siècle Vienna. Like Berta Zuckerkandl's famous salon, the home of the influential industrialist and art collector Carl Reininghaus (1857–1929) was the site of regular gatherings of the artistic set in Vienna.[60] Arthur Roessler, an art critic, consultant for the Galerie Miethke, and a true cultural multiplier, was among Schiele's earliest supporters.[61] Though Roessler and Schiele had a tempestuous acquaintance, Roessler regularly wrote about Schiele, brokered commissions, and connected the artist with two key patrons: the collectors Dr. Oskar Reichel and Reininghaus.[62] Reininghaus held a small, private exhibition of Schiele's work in early 1910, and it was there that Schiele first met Dr. Erwin von Graff, an obstetrician and gynecologist at the Second Viennese Women's Clinic.[63] Schiele's contact with the Viennese medical community decisively influenced the course of his artistic development, and its influence reverberated in his work until the end of his life.[64]

The Bavarian-born Erwin Graff von Pancsova (1878–1935) split his education between Munich and Graz, where he received his doctorate in 1902. His medical training subsequently took him across Austria, from Graz to Vienna to Innsbruck, and across specializations, including pathological anatomy and general surgery, before he finally settled in Vienna and on obstetrics and gynecology. There, he received his *Habilitation* in 1916 and was awarded the title of professor extraordinarius in 1926. The bulk of his career was spent working at the Second University Gynecological-Obstetrical Clinic.[65] Graff was renowned both as a "true representative of Viennese critical medicine" and as a "master anatomist," a subject he had studied in depth before specializing in obstetrics and gynecology.[66]

When Graff first encountered Schiele at Reininghaus's home, he was a young doctor, not yet thirty-two years old, and moving in Vienna's most influential artistic circles. Although he never became a collector of the likes of his Viennese medical colleagues Oskar Reichel or the dentist Heinrich Rieger, Graff nevertheless extended an invitation that would prove crucial in Schiele's artistic development: Graff offered Schiele access to his female patients in situ at the Women's Clinic in the first months of 1910.[67] Moreover, Graff stepped in just a few months later to provide Schiele with assistance in a thorny personal matter, one also involving the Women's Clinic. Graff adopts a discreet tone in a letter to Schiele from May 18, 1910: "L.A. arrived at the clinic yesterday and was admitted. She is sharing a room with a second woman and seems very unhappy about your disloyalty. It is probably better for you and her this way."[68] Though we do not have Schiele's response, and the woman's identity has never been clarified, the letter implies that the woman in question was admitted to the clinic, perhaps to have an abortion performed under the legal radar. While the letter is cryptic, the timing is provocative. It was common for artists to barter for medical services with paintings and works on paper.[69] Within a few months, Schiele would offer Graff the impressive *Portrait of Dr. Erwin von Graff* and several drawings, including some executed at the clinic in the preceding months. It seems highly probable that the artworks were exchanged for Graff's medical assistance.[70]

When considering who Schiele's subjects were, we must also account for the question of class in the production of artworks, since the models' class in some sense influences how artists portray them, including the liberties artists take in the depiction of their sitters' bodies. While Schiele and Klimt profited from intersecting patronage circles and were often exhibited at the same galleries and shows, their subjects were rarely culled from the same social set. The two painters' increasingly divergent styles reflected an antithetical "social sensibility" that separated mentor and protégé, as Anton Faistauer (1887–1930)—an Austrian expressionist painter-colleague of Schiele's and likewise a member of the Neukunstgruppe—argued. Contemporaries were quick to note that this contrast manifested itself in terms of Klimt's and Schiele's preferred subjects, who split largely along class lines.[71] Writing in 1923, just five years after both Klimt's and Schiele's deaths, Faistauer pegged Klimt as a "painter of high finance," drawn to the well-off urban elite, the Viennese haute bourgeoisie, who, in point of fact, made his career.[72] His innovative society portraits of Adele Bloch-Bauer, Baroness Elisabeth Bachofen-Echt, and Eugenie Primavesi, for example, works executed mostly on commission, document this. Elana Shapira, a historian of art and design, has noted that Klimt's Jewish patrons in particular sought to capitalize on his cachet, supporting his aesthetic modernism and that of the Secession as a kind of acculturation project, in part to self-fashion and position themselves as arbiters of progressive culture and taste in a notoriously anti-Semitic era.[73] Even Klimt's *Hope I*, the earlier referenced full-length portrait of a pregnant nude, which had been barred from public display in 1903, was strategically acquired by the influential Jewish textile industrialist Fritz Waerndorfer. Shapira argues that Waerndorfer theatrically displayed the painting in his home as part of a calculated Gesamtkunstwerk in an effort to reclaim his own body. By staging the transgressive body of the pregnant woman, using Klimt's painting of a woman clearly meant to trouble feminine ideals and flout sexual mores, Waerndorfer aimed both to provoke and to promote Viennese modernism's twin pursuits of style and seduction.[74]

If Klimt was a "painter of high finance," Schiele was riveted above all by the working classes and was a "painter of the proletariat" through and through.[75] Schiele, in contrast to Klimt, selected his models mostly from family, fellow artists, and the working classes.[76] Although this can be attributed to financial considerations as much as to the stylistic radicalism he aspired to, it freed Schiele from a contractual obligation to depict his sitters according to their wishes. He could draw whomever agreed to sit for him, however he wanted. And he was fascinated, as is evident with the drawings of expectant working-class mothers in the clinic, with bodies not conventionally considered beautiful. Faistauer, a sharp observer and friend, noted that residents of Vienna's outer districts—"with their tragic faces, hunger, hatred, and troubling features [*Fratzen*]—weighed heavily on Schiele."[77]

In the first decades of the twentieth century, bourgeois Viennese were just beginning to see what Schiele was already keenly attuned to: the broken, suffering bodies of the working classes. These were becoming, as we will see, an increasing presence in both Viennese art and the city's visual vernacular with the advent of socially conscious photojournalism. Klimt created works that challenged classical notions of aesthetic beauty, as the scandal that engulfed the university faculty paintings demonstrates. His *Nuda Veritas*, if we recall from the introduction, was an early, if allegorical, incarnation of this impulse. But the younger artistic generation that succeeded him—including Schiele, Kokoschka, and Gerstl—cast aside traditional correlations between beauty and truth. Instead, Schiele and his contemporaries increasingly equated truth with the ugliness of very real social conditions.[78] Critics of the time noted this fact as they attempted to articulate what was so radically new about Schiele's work. In a review of the December 1909 Neukunstgruppe exhibition at the Salon Pisko, for example, Arpad Weixlgärtner pinpointed Schiele's primary subject matter as "the abject [*elend*] body of the modern urbanite."[79] Writing retrospectively in 1921, Fritz Karpfen recognized that Schiele had been attempting to depict "the truth" (*das Wahrhaftige*) of his sitters through their bodies. Karpfen observed, "the deformations and pathological gazes [of Schiele's subjects] are really just the faithful representation of the body [*Leib*] and the mind [*Sinn*] of the people of our time."[80] While Schiele may not have intended explicit social commentary through his art—although one of Schiele's contemporaries, the artist Faistauer, did argue precisely this point[81]—the widespread notion that psychosocial experience manifested physically goes some way toward explaining why Schiele focused so single-mindedly on his models' corporeal presences. This is why he often depicted his subjects' bodies mercilessly naked, painfully contorted, seemingly diseased and deformed. As one of Schiele's critics put it in 1917, "he saw the body not merely because he only *wanted* to see the body, but he saw and gave us the body *because the body was all there was*."[82]

The bodies of the working classes, many of them in clinical settings, became specimens for a broad Viennese public to learn about physical health and pathology—to learn about themselves and others. But they first had to gain proficiency in interpreting what they saw. Here, too, Viennese doctors and artists were in league with one another. While Schiele's images of expectant patients, painted in one of Vienna's new maternal health clinics, were not designed for public exhibition, the interface between Viennese modernist artists and the doctors of their generation was not an anomaly. Both live human subjects and representations of patients were put on display before audiences in Viennese lecture halls at the crossroads of visual art, medical science, and pathognomy. A wide Viennese citizenry was taught how to "read" and interpret the human body by experts, such as Julius Tandler, the famous anatomist, who would later become the chief architect of Red Vienna's municipal health and welfare programs. The well-publicized lecture "On Exterior Knowledge" (Über Exterieurkunde), held in 1913 at the Union of Viennese Doctors, was part of a wide-ranging series of lectures, mostly on human anatomy and adjacent topics, that Tandler held at public venues across the city in the first decades of the twentieth century.[83] Like many of his other lectures on medical topics pitched at generalist audiences, "On Exterior Knowledge" was sprinkled with humorous anecdotes and featured demonstrations on live human subjects. Tandler positioned himself as a physiognomist capable of deploying anatomical knowledge to accurately "read" his subjects' professions from their feet, hands, and even their chins—much to the amusement of his audience.[84]

In medical terms, pathognomy refers to the study of characteristic disease markers' symptomatological expression. Patients' bodies call for diagnostic interpretation in the clinical setting. Yet, when publicly presented by medical specialists, they served as institutionally legitimized invitations to correlate surface appearances with the underlying character traits of an individual. Situated firmly in the intellectual tradition of physiognomy, which posits a troubling, quasi-rationalized correlative relationship between external and internal and underlies racist ideologies already being marshaled by nationalist interest groups and protofascist ideologues,[85] audiences were instructed in how to "read" corporeal signs, and patients were often the subjects on which they learned. The mass press advertised and reported on such lectures, designed to appeal to broad audiences. In this fashion, boundaries of the private sphere of the medical clinic were rendered increasingly porous.

A journalist for the *Neue Freie Presse* likened Tandler's lecture to another presentation held just two months earlier[86]—and returns us to Schiele and his clinical portraiture. The Viennese physician Adolf Kronfeld (1861–1938) delivered the lecture "On the Pathology of the Portrait: The Neurological and the Psychiatric (with Demonstrations)" at the 85th

Assembly of German Scientists and Physicians in Vienna in September 1913.[87] Kronfeld, a doctor and journalist whose name has faded into the annals of history, was born on June 3, 1861, in Lviv, Galicia. Like Ernst von Brücke, Freud's revered teacher, and many other doctors of his generation, Kronfeld not only studied medicine but also art history, classics, and philology at the University of Vienna. He worked at the Vienna General Hospital, at the University of Vienna, and as a municipal physician before becoming editor-in-chief of the *Wiener Medizinische Wochenschrift* for close to three decades.[88] The monographs he published in his lifetime show the true thrust of his interests: the intersection of medicine, specifically anatomy, with the fine arts.[89] Schiele's notebooks reveal an acquaintance with Kronfeld, who was part of similar social circles.[90] To illustrate the 1913 lecture on portraiture and pathology, Kronfeld commissioned a series of paintings from Schiele's erstwhile friend, the artist and self-styled confidence man Erwin Dominik Osen.[91] Like Schiele, Osen executed the series of portraits in a clinical setting, at Steinhof, Vienna's psychiatric hospital, with inpatients as his subjects.[92] Kronfeld's lecture deployed the patients' countenances, postures, and gestures—as depicted by Osen—to present pathognomonic interpretations of artworks, to which he applied "the advances of medical knowledge, especially those of modern constitutional pathology."[93] Despite the fact that Osen's execution is amateurish, what sets his portraits of Steinhof patients apart from Schiele's renderings of female patients at the Vienna Women's Clinic are the clinical details Osen incorporates. In contrast to the anonymity of Schiele's women, Osen records the patients' first and last names, patient identification numbers, and admission dates to the hospital, alongside the artist's signature on the paintings. The artist thus embeds each patient's identity in the artwork and acknowledges the individual value of his body, his self, beyond his impersonal status as object of medical study, objectified body.[94] All of these cases, Osen's paintings of Steinhof patients and Schiele's watercolors of obstetrical patients, raise delicate questions about patients' rights and representation.

As Gemma Blackshaw and Leslie Topp have noted with reference to Osen's paintings of Steinhof patients, the access of artists to patients in Viennese clinical settings must be read together with concurrent efforts to put the clinics themselves and their modernity on display to the public. A modern type of medical architecture that emerged around the fin de siècle blurred the boundaries between private and public, while facilitating the production of images that could later be deployed in nonclinical settings. Open houses held at Steinhof, for example, drew visitors who came to the hospital to view the new architecture, see art by patients exhibited, and look at the patients. Such efforts map onto the shift we saw in the context of the human displays in chapter 1 toward semipermeable spaces. The "utopian city" of the modern medical clinic invited the broader public, artists included, to spectate like physicians, similar to the public lectures and exhibitions we have considered. This transformation of the private to the public sphere, along with the clean architectural lines of the new clinic spaces in Vienna, provided—much like Schiele's negative spaces—a neutral backdrop against which the medical conditions of the patients leapt out even more obviously. And it was this visibility of the patients' bodies that was transformative for Viennese modernist artists.[95] It allowed them to develop a clinical gaze.

IN THE WOMEN'S CLINIC: ARCHITECTURE, GAZE, FILM

Just as motherhood was being revalued—alongside, of course, women's roles in society and perspectives about female sexuality more generally—the medical management of childbirth was likewise in flux. In the eighteenth and early nineteenth centuries, birthing had chiefly been a private, domestic event, attended by a midwife and perhaps close female family members. In any case, it was a women's domain, unless problems had presented, and for well-off women, it remained so well into the twentieth century. In the course of the nineteenth century, however, the business of childbirth became progressively more medicalized. Inpatient hospitals were established to provide poverty-stricken women with obstetrical care by doctors and midwives. Increasingly, nineteenth-century claims that childbirth is fundamentally a "pathological" rather than a normal physiological process served to legitimize physicians' calls for clinical obstetrical care and hospital deliveries.[96] Such discourses of pathology underpinned the representation and visualization of pregnancy, which for its part was organized by clinical architecture. In Vienna, this development culminated in the first decade of the twentieth century, with the construction of twin showpiece women's clinics in the Mediziner-Viertel adjacent to the university and a stone's throw from the grandeur of the Ringstraße.

Austria was home to seventeen birthing clinics in 1899, and they had two primary purposes: providing obstetrical care to expectant mothers and supplying live subjects on whom medical students could learn.[97] Often, these aims were at odds. This was a time of massive institutional modernization projects in both public and university hospitals, such as the Second Viennese Women's Clinic where Graff cared for and Schiele drew patients. Mirror images of one another, the two new university women's clinics in Vienna were completed in 1908, less than two years before Schiele's visit. The gynecologists Friedrich Schauta (1849–1919) and Rudolf Chrobak (1843–1910) were the driving forces behind the building projects.[98] The new, pavilion-style architecture of turn-of-the-century hospitals in Vienna and elsewhere spatially reflected the increasing specialization of the medical field, while transferring onto the clinic a differentiated, fragmented anatomical model of the body that had originated in the dissecting room.[99] By investigating the spaces the patients occupied—in essence, by recontextualizing their experiences spatially—it becomes possible to better understand the social dimensions of medical history as a history of the gaze, as Foucault understood it.[100] That gaze, one Schiele was exposed to and adopted, was structured by institutional architecture. If the clinic was an unusual atelier for Schiele in 1910, by 1920 it had become an even more uncommon film set.

Announcing the new women's clinics' impending opening, the *Neue Freie Presse* exclaimed: "How the views about hospital facilities and about individual healthcare have changed in one hundred years!"[101] In stark contrast to the earlier clinics, which had been in service for over a century, the redesigned university clinic Schiele visited and where Graff worked was oriented toward new architectural principles of transparency, light, and air.[102] These tenets emerged in the late nineteenth century as vital to the life reform and hygiene movements, but they were also central considerations in the construction of new clinical architecture in and around Vienna, such as at the famous psychiatric hospital Steinhof.[103] The Women's Clinics exuded "a true luxuriousness of light and air," one emanating from the large windows, south-facing patient rooms, electrical lighting, and whitewashed walls. The grass-planted, flat-roof construction provided an open-air recreational area for convalescents—and a piece of the countryside in the metropolis. In fact, the new clinical architecture was positioned as a link between the natural and the urban environments: "One can see the *Kahlengebirge* [the hills on the outskirts of Vienna]; from a distance, the steeple of St. Stephen greets the new Viennese clinic, which itself should likewise become a proud landmark of the imperial capital."[104] Doctors and architects at the turn of the century viewed the modern clinical spaces both as showpieces for the city and as spatial embodiments of advances in humane patient care.[105]

A commentary by Else Feldmann (1884–1942), a largely forgotten Social Democratic journalist of the interwar years, whom we will encounter in greater detail in what follows, bears witness to the successful implementation of the new clinical architectural principles. In "Pulled from the Water" (Aus dem Wasser gezogen), published in the *Arbeiter-Sonntag* in 1934, Feldmann reflects on a recent hospitalization: "By day, such a hospital ward looks rather lovely, almost cheerful—no bandages, no bloody limbs. Everything here is snow-white, that makes such a sumptuous impression. Like in a sanitarium." More than simply offering an aesthetically pleasing, restful impression, a hospital stay covered the basic existential necessities many of Vienna's neediest lacked. Feldmann explains, "These poor and sick people, many homeless, without proper nourishment, many abandoned and alone, got everything here: food and drink, cleanliness, a bed, medical help, medications, care, charity, bonhomie, comradeship—and tomorrow they will receive all that again; they are content, they are tranquil; here, the persecution ends."[106] Following Feldmann's description, it could be argued that the clinic setting was indeed humane, providing as it did a much-needed respite from the day-to-day existential perils faced by many working poor. For expectant mothers like Schiele's models at the new Women's Clinics, the shared convalescence rooms—with their clean lines, sanitary tile flooring, a modern heating and ventilation system, electric lighting, and tall windows letting in bright sunlight—could seem both hygienic and welcoming.

The "commandment of hygiene" had a concrete, scientific origin in the context of the obstetrical clinic: Ignaz Semmelweis's (1818–65) discovery in Vienna in the 1840s of the source of puerperal, or childbed, fever in physicians' cadaveric contamination. The discourse about hygiene had a flip side, though, and was charged with various symbolic and psychological functions for practitioners as well. The architectural principles of transparency, light, and air served in a sense to spatially sublimate doctors' inarticulable fear of contact with and contamination from their patients. In this regard, hygiene was yet another discursive control mechanism within the clinical complex.[107] Indeed, these buildings were designed foremost with the advancement of clinical study in mind. From its origins in the 1872 *Studienreform*, the Women's Clinic where Schiele painted and Graff worked was conceived of as a teaching hospital. A brief look at two rooms in the new clinics—the operating theater and the lecture hall—reveals how hygienic concepts were translated into dual-purpose pedagogical and therapeutic areas, which spatially structured the medical gaze. In its clear line of sight was the object of observation, study, and procedure: the expectant mother's body.

Gynecological surgeries were carried out in the new clinic's operating theater. What is perhaps most striking about its design is that it is flooded with natural light. The massive, floor-to-ceiling bay window was as wide as the operating room itself, as the floor plans of the clinic reveal.[108] New electric lighting in the form of tubular flood lamps added additional visibility, and operations could now be carried out day or night. State-of-the-art amplification technologies, with speakers mounted in key positions, made the surgeon's commentary audible to onlookers. In the center of the room stood the gynecological operating table with its hydraulic, oil-pump system, which allowed patients' bodies to be optimally positioned. Enabled by superior acoustics and lighting, as well as a by a clearer line of sight and more capacious design, the distance between observers, on the one hand, and the patient, surgeon, and surgical team, on the other, was actually increased in the newly designed operating room. A full-length glass partition now separated students from the procedure. The viewers' gallery was outfitted with support railings, on which observers could lean, not unlike standing-room galleries at the opera or the theater.[109] The sight lines in this thoroughly modern, twentieth-century operating room thus mimicked those of the early-modern anatomical theater, and three levels of agency—observers, doctors and assistants, and patient—were spatially encoded.[110]

Contemporary photographs reveal that the architects applied the same principles to the design of the lecture hall, which a newspaper article from 1908 characterized as making an "imposing" and "exceptionally picturesque [*malerisch*]" impression.[111] There, patients were subject to the probing eyes of up to 250 young, male doctors *in spe*, who were witness to obstetrical demonstrations, gynecological examinations, and live births.[112] The traditional, sloping, semicircular seating gallery in the lecture hall qua anatomical theater was wed with modern design principles and iron construction clearly influenced by contemporary Viennese public works projects by the architect Otto Wagner.[113] The wide gap in the seating gallery was strategically designed to let in increased natural light for the purposes of observation and study. This conscious architectural choice shows the willingness of the clinics' designers to sacrifice capacity for an improved sight line.[114] Here, a hospital bed and its female occupant could be wheeled into the center of the amphitheater for demonstrations. As in traditional anatomical theaters, the axes of the numerous students' and physicians' gazes in the lecture hall of the new Viennese Women's Clinic were directed toward a single focal point: the patient's body, which, given the new design of operating tables and hospital beds, could be ever more optimally positioned. In this fashion, the female body becomes optimized as an object of clinical observation, of study, and—in the best-case scenario—of treatment.[115] We will return to this very lecture hall, as Else

Fig. 28. Vienna Women's Clinic, lecture hall. Rudolf Chrobak and Friedrich Schauta, *Geschichte und Beschreibung des Baues der neuen Frauenkliniken in Wien* (Berlin: Urban & Schwarzenberg, 1911), 65. Photographer unknown.

Feldmann stages a pivotal scene in her novel there. But first we must look to another set of images produced at the clinic: film images. Cinematic representations of expectant mothers catered to interwar audiences eager to enhance their knowledge about the female body, but they also sparked controversy and outrage.

Less than a decade after Schiele drew pregnant subjects at the Second Viennese Women's Clinic where Graff worked, the same site became a film set. The medical cinematography that emanated from the Viennese clinic made pregnant women's bodies objects of an epistemic visualization that extended beyond the clinic.[116] When medical film footage was charged with promoting the interests of public welfare institutions, women not only were objects of medical study but also became subject to public presentation and state censorship. Films of gynecological and obstetrical patients thus became a crossroads where the interests of clinical and popular knowledge intersected—under the direction of state control.

During the First World War, as early as 1917, doctors at the Women's Clinic expressed interest in filming obstetrical and gynecological procedures to supplement clinical instruction. The new clinic, opened in 1908, already housed an institute for X-ray and photography, complete with a photographic atelier, on its top floor.[117] But the equipment and costs for moving film were different and prohibitive, so the plans were initially put on hold. Then, between 1919 and 1924, the newly founded National Film Headquarters (Staatliche Film-Hauptstelle)—a leading producer of both general educational and discipline-specific medical films—commissioned a series of gynecological films for clinical study and provided full financing. By 1920, twelve such films had already been made.[118] The first two films documented "normal" patients: a routine obstetrical examination and *The Normal Birth* (Die normale Geburt, 1919–20).[119] Wilhelm Weibel (1876–1945), later director of the Second Viennese Women's Clinic housed at the Vienna General Hospital (Allgemeines Krankenhaus, or AKH), was among the leading directors of such films. In a summary of his presentation of these films before the Society of Physicians in Vienna in 1920, Weibel found that the examination film held only limited instructional value for doctors. After all, he argued, living subjects are the ideal illustrations for educational demonstrations in the teaching clinic, and they are available anytime.[120] By contrast, he deemed the film of a live birth "substantially more valuable" because—despite the "ample material," that is, the high number of living, birthing subjects—it is not always possible, simply due to timing, to show the final throes of birth "in viva" in the lecture hall.[121]

While several other films focused on operative interventions in gynecological and obstetrical contexts, a number were concerned distinctly with pathological conditions or bodies. Such "anomalies," Weibel contested, "achieve better expression in moving pictures than on simple, dead photographs."[122] *Skeletal Anomalies* (Skelett-Anomalien, 1919–20), known in the 1920s by its original title *Gait of Pregnant Women* (Gangart der Schwangeren), showed a lineup of four pregnant women, one with a "normal" build, three others with various skeletal conditions, including osteomalacia and severe rickets. The patients were made to stride back and forth naked before the camera and were ultimately lined up from tallest to shortest, mimicking "the visual protocol of a clinical demonstration."[123] Another film documents the eclamptic convulsions of three pregnant women. The primary goal had been to capture the pathological obstetrical condition on film so that it could later be employed in instruction.

Weibel's description of the cameramen's attempts to film these patients' seizures—a scene that recalls game hunting—is particularly disturbing. "It cost [us] much work," he writes. "For days, even nights, we lay in wait with the apparatus at the ready before the eclamptic women. But the effort was rewarded with success."[124] Treatment of the patients was clearly secondary in these cases, and the risks to which clinic patients were subjected in the name of medical documentary film eventually caught up with Weibel. In 1935, an incident in his obstetrical-cinematographic practice made international headlines when *Time* magazine reported on the case in an August 1935 issue. The doctor was accused of having caused the death of a woman and child because of a technical glitch with the camera. Apparently, Weibel interrupted the operative birth for mere minutes, his attention captured by the defective film camera.[125]

But what happened when such images crossed the clinic threshold and entered the public sphere? Just two years after these first clinical films, a popular "enlightenment" film that blended fictional and documentary elements also included pregnant women and birth among its subjects. *Marital Hygiene* (Hygiene der Ehe, 1922) brought Viennese biopolitical concerns and efforts to steer women's reproductive choices to mass audiences.[126] The movie, directed by Dr. Erwin Junger and produced by Pan-Film AG, was filmed in conjunction with seven medical advisors, including Julius Tandler, the gynecologist Oskar Frankl, the pediatrician Leopold Moll, and the orthopedist Hans Spitzy (see chap. 2). The hour-long film was a collaborative project by medical clinics and institutes in Prague and Vienna: one orthopedic clinic, three obstetrical clinics—including the Second Women's Clinic in Vienna, where Schiele had drawn—and the Imperial Institute for Maternal Protection and Infant Welfare (Reichsanstalt für Mutterschutz und Säuglingsfürsorge) in Vienna.[127] Tandler's Viennese Municipal Marriage Advice Center (Wiener Städtische Eheberatungsstelle), opened in 1922, was moreover a key site, providing both documentary images as a film set and the driving diegetic impulse.[128] The center was the first such European initiative, and though it was instituted to address the unique health challenges brought on by marriage, it was part of what historian Britta McEwen has called a more widespread "clinic culture" of the interwar years. While some of the problems people brought to the Advice Center were clinical in nature, many of them were social. People had so internalized the municipal health agency's eugenic focus that their concerns were most frequently related to understanding the link between their own bodies as carriers of illness and disease and their potential effects on the social body at large.[129]

In four acts, *Marital Hygiene* tracks fictional couples seeking prenuptial health counseling at the Municipal Marriage Advice Center in city hall. In an attempt to appease the censors, establish the scientific legitimacy of the film, and create a veneer of gentility, the prologue sets the film in a documentary frame. The establishing shot opens in a university lecture hall, where rows of young medical students—several women among them—attend a course by a professor. He shows them a film-within-the-film that advances "the three most important principles for gynecologists: (1) every person should have a medical examination before marrying, (2) sick people should not marry, and (3) healthy people should have children."[130] The film that follows, and which the students are purported to be watching, is *Marital Hygiene*. Fictional interludes of the couples' medical consultations alternate with stop-action animated illustrations of the female reproductive system, menstrual cycle, and pregnancy; impactful three-dimensional anatomical models and pathological preparations; and documentary images of patients, including masked breastfeeding mothers, shot in Viennese medical clinics. The film, it could be argued, constructs the female bodies it represents, as the depicted film still demonstrates. Here, for example, viewed through a circular frame that mimics the camera-eye, we see a man's hands tracing lines of measurement on a two-dimensional image of a woman's torso he might have drawn just moments before.

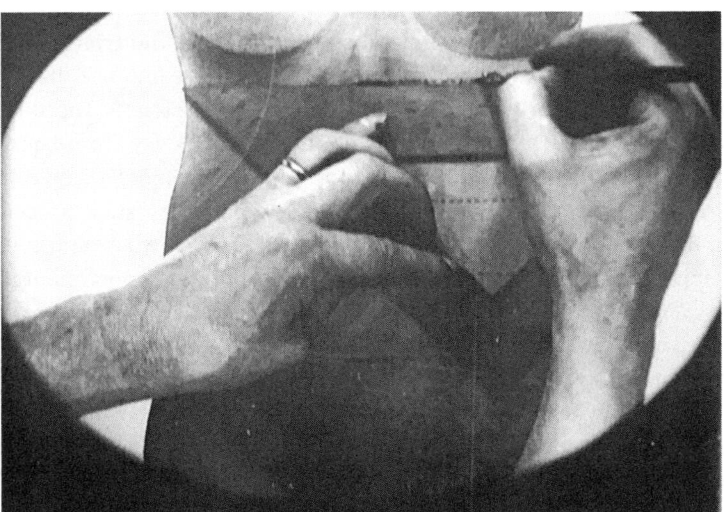

Fig. 29. Film still from *Marital Hygiene* (Hygiene der Ehe), 1922. Courtesy of Filmarchiv Austria.

The film, created in the service of municipal sexual education initiatives, was applauded by the liberal press for its effectiveness in enlightening people about the "mysteries of the body."[131] The Austrian film industry standard, *Kino-Journal*, heaped praise on the film, calling it a "cultural achievement" and predicting that it would "dominate the market." The review added that the film would appeal to all viewers, regardless of gender or class, but would also be of special service to provincial doctors who might have lost touch with the most up-to-date clinical practices in women's health and reproductive matters.[132] The film managed, in other words, to successfully toe the line between clinical implementation and popular appeal.

Predictably, several parts of *Marital Hygiene* riled the censors and the conservative press. But outcry came from doctors too. A report by one of the members of the censorship committee for Lower Austria details a screening in Vienna. The author was Dr. Roland Graßberger, who would soon become director of the University of Vienna's Hygiene Institute, which was founded, like the Women's Clinics, in 1908. Graßberger condemned the film, recommending it be prohibited for public viewing in Lower Austria. His assessment was based on any number of factors, including the mixture of fictional and documentary material; the self-promotion of the sponsoring institutes, including the Viennese Municipal Marriage Advice Center; and an overall lack of thematic clarity and applicability with regard to the "marital hygiene" suggested by the film's title. Graßberger's main criticism, however, was the inclusion of footage taken in and from the clinic, images he deemed unsuitable for presentation in the public sphere. Such footage "belong[s] *exclusively* in instruction for physicians and doctors," Graßberger asserted.[133] In an effort to scare women away from back-alley abortions, the film included, for example, graphic shots of anatomical preparations of female genitalia and fetuses harmed by such procedures. These images were left intact in the censored version, while stark, unaestheticized images of pregnant women in motion and a documentary sequence depicting a live human birth were deemed of particular offense and cut. In his evaluation, Graßberger wrote: "It is utterly superfluous for the enlightenment of the audience when the film presents a naked female person in an advanced stage of pregnancy, who shows her body from all angles while wandering back and forth across the scene."[134] Screening the sequence of a human birth to a coeducational audience of male and female viewers was considered "the pinnacle of crudeness and an offensive breach of public decency."[135] While Graßberger praised the technical facility of the cameraman and the quality of the clinical images, he censured their public presentation in no uncertain terms. The public screening of images from the clinical context transforms them from carriers of knowledge into what Graßberger called mere "crudenesses" (*Krudelitäten*).[136] When medical images of women's bodies leave the clinic, they are transported, in other words, from the scientific realm into one deemed obscene.[137]

Regardless of their intended audiences, films such as *Marital Hygiene* and Schiele's watercolors of patients both abstracted patients' bodies from all context. Viewers are provided with a single focal point: the expectant woman's body as a readily accessible object of (medical) observation.[138] This viewpoint—and these cultural products—were enabled by the new architecture of clinical spaces in Vienna at the fin de siècle. Viennese women, especially those from the working classes, were not only well aware of their vulnerable position; some used that position as a springboard for their own cultural production in texts that laid out the social stakes of their powerlessness. In doing so, they were able to claim a modicum of agency by writing their own stories, while also critiquing the society that gave rise to such conditions.

SPEAKING FOR SUFFERING MOTHERS: ELSE FELDMANN AND CARRY HAUSER

The discrepancy between the pride doctors took in their medical advances—now reflected architectonically by the two new Viennese Women's Clinics built in 1908 and brought into wide circulation by enlightenment films—and working-class female patients' fears of the clinic is striking. Even before the new clinics opened, the women's rights activist and Social Democratic politician Therese Schlesinger-Eckstein (1863–1940) was a member of the Austrian delegation to the International Congress of Women in London in 1899. There she reported on the legal rights of and social ills confronting working-class women in Austria, taking particular care to chronicle the conditions for pregnant women. Schlesinger-Eckstein, who herself had suffered from childbed fever and was afflicted with lifelong aftereffects from the infection, drew attention to the social segregation of patients in the Viennese clinics. In the city's Women's Clinics, there were three classes of care, two of which were reserved for paying patients. In contrast to the paying customers, the third class of patients, those who could contribute little or nothing toward the cost of their care, was pressed into service as "instructional material" (*Unterrichtsmaterial*). This included their prenatal, birthing, and postnatal bodies being the focus of requisite demonstrations, examinations, and, in some cases, operations for student-audiences in the clinics' lecture halls and operating rooms. The result of these circumstances, as Schlesinger-Eckstein noted, was that poor expectant mothers seldom sought care at Viennese clinics, preferring to give birth at home.[139] In the tenement apartment buildings of the outer districts, however, overcrowding and unsanitary conditions—in addition to the lack of readily available medical supplies or care—often resulted in poor birth outcomes.[140] Whether at home in squalor or in the clinic as "instructional material," many Viennese children were born under grim circumstances, Schlesinger-Eckstein lamented to her international audience in England.

Else Feldmann's novel *The Body of the Mother* (Der Leib der Mutter, 1931) describes just how eager women were to avoid going to the teaching clinic and being subjected to the medical gaze. The book paints a contrasting picture to Feldmann's later newspaper article, "Pulled from the Water," published in the *Arbeiter-Sonntag* in 1934, which had presented the hospital as a site of possible respite for the working poor and homeless. In *The Body of the Mother*, Feldmann describes in detail what happens when one of the characters, Marie Miczek, despite her best efforts to steer clear of it, ends up in the Women's Clinic, likely a fictionalized version of the same one where Schiele completed his figure studies. Miczek, an impoverished factory worker, is pregnant with her third child. Due in two months, she has started to look increasingly unwell. Her roomer—the novel's good-hearted protagonist, Absalon Laich—had previously encouraged her to seek medical advice when the time came. Then, her resistance had been as emphatic as it was telling: "I won't go to the hospital. People have told me how badly you're treated there . . . subject to the eyes of all the young students. They study on you at the hospital. . . . No, no, I don't want to suffer like that."[141] The fact that a character in a popular socialist novel, one which had earlier been serialized in forty-one installments in the *Arbeiter-Zeitung* from March 23 to May 5, 1924, knows this information from other women in her milieu demonstrates that such clinical practices were no great secret in Vienna's outer districts. Additionally, it shows that there was a network of grassroots medical knowledge spread by word of mouth between friends, coworkers, and neighbors. Working-class women's widespread fear of becoming objects of medical study at Viennese obstetrical-gynecological clinics, intended to help them in their time of need, stood in stark contrast to the municipal discourse on women's health and welfare, as we will see below.

More than most, Else Feldmann—a committed Social Democrat and a deeply empathetic author and journalist, whose articles were published in the leading newspapers (*Neue Freie Presse, Neues Wiener Journal, Der Abend*, and the *Arbeiter-Zeitung*)—hewed close to the dictum "write what you know." Plagued by illness and hardship throughout her life, she had intimate insight into the city's topography of poverty: its hospitals and dank alleys, its factories and overcrowded tenement homes. Feldmann was born to Jewish parents (her father was Hungarian, her mother Austrian) in Vienna, where the family of nine moved frequently between Vienna's working-class districts: Landstraße, Leopoldstadt, and Brigittenau. The family struggled to make ends meet but was rendered completely destitute when Feldmann's father died in 1913. Feldmann took factory work to help her family but ultimately made her name as a freelance journalist. Her social commentaries appeared in periodicals beginning in 1910, and she saw her play, *The Scream That Nobody Hears: Tragedy from the Ghetto in Four Acts* (Der Schrei, den niemand hört: Tragödie aus dem Ghetto in vier Akten), staged at Vienna's Volksbühne in 1916 with Arthur Schnitzler in attendance. Feldmann's major publications included three novels and one short story collection, and she was active in the establishment of the Austrian Union of Socialist Authors (Vereinigung sozialistischer Schriftsteller), in which she held a supervisory role. After losing her main source of income when the *Arbeiter-Zeitung* was shuttered by the Austrofascists after the Civil War of February 1934, she slipped deeper and deeper into existential and political precarity. The novel considered here, *The Body of the Mother*, was placed on the National Socialists' list of "subversive and undesirable literature" in 1938, and they deported Feldmann from Vienna to Sobibór, where she was murdered in 1942.[142]

In a review of her first novel, *Dandelion* (Löwenzahn, 1921), Felix Salten called Feldmann a chronicler of "lost existences," an advocate for those who, like herself, live their lives on the margins of Viennese society.[143] Feldmann's socially engaged journalism is characterized by an unflinching realism—often giving voice to her subjects in their own words—without sacrificing keen attention to her figures' suffering in favor of sentimentalism or political propaganda. One core concern of much of her writing, *The Body of the Mother* included, was the special consideration she paid to disadvantaged mothers and children. Even early in her journalistic career, Feldmann dedicated a reportage to working-class mothers living in abject poverty in basement tenement apartments of Vienna's outer districts. More than any other Viennese writer of her time, she took literally the injunction of one woman she profiled: "You Have to Descend Down to the Mothers . . ." (*Zu den Müttern müßt ihr hinuntersteigen . . .*)—a quote from her source that Feldmann took as the title of a 1917 article for *Der Abend*. This piece prefigures in nonfictional form the fictional Marie Miczek, around whom Feldmann would later craft an entire novel. Like the novel, the article also calls attention to the suffering of working-class mothers, many of whom considered infanticide the only solution to their insoluble bind of motherhood with absent, often conscripted, fathers (the piece was published during World War I), work obligations, and poverty.[144]

For Marie Miczek, the character in Feldmann's novel, her worst fears become reality when she ends up in the back of an ambulance as the result of a botched abortion. With two children already at home, a punishing work schedule, and an absentee husband, Miczek was confronted with a harrowing choice—at once illegal and threatening to her own health. Miczek had carried two other pregnancies to term and already committed infanticide once. Feldmann's narrator soberly relates the consequences of his landlady's most recent fateful decision: "Now Frau Miczek was destined for the hospital she so feared and hated" (174). Laich, having heard that Miczek is in the obstetrical clinic, goes there as a former orderly to offer his expertise and solidarity. On arrival, however, he immediately recognizes the gravity of the patient's condition. Moreover, he learns that she is to be presented to the students in the lecture hall as a case study in a course. Laich gets an insider's view of one patient's experience as an invalid in "this city of invalids [*Krankenstadt*]," and "He knew what 'course' meant" (175). Laich sneaks into the lecture hall to watch the demonstration:

> He heard a voice behind a brown door. Slowly, he opened it and stood on the stairs of the lecture hall. All the lights were illuminated. The auditors, the young students, sat in the rows. The professor was drawing on the board.
>
> He spoke of the case of the layperson's killing of the germinating fruit. On the rolling bed lay the patient's exposed body. The students filed out of the rows, palpated it. It was Mrs. Miczek who lay there and served science.
>
> "What you see here, gentlemen," explained the professor, "is nothing less than the mother's body [*Leib*]. Here, in this part you see on the drawing, the genesis of human life takes place. Here, we again have the opportunity to observe advanced sepsis in a 34-year-old factory worker. This time we will allow the sepsis to take its lethal course." (176–77)

The professor's observation that the students "again" have the chance to witness a case of advanced sepsis, and his decision that "this time" the septicemia will be allowed to play out without any therapeutic intervention by the doctors attests to the fact that the personnel are more interested in observing the progression of the disease than treating the patient. As Foucault phrased it, "in relation to that which he is suffering from, the patient is only an external fact," an abstracted body.[145] The doctor's remarks further confirm that cases of botched abortions with fatal consequences, such as that of Marie Miczek, were commonplace in interwar Vienna.

While Feldmann describes the medicalization of Marie Miczek's pregnant body textually, one of Carry Hauser's illustrations for the novel depicts the pivotal scene visually. Several of Hauser's portfolio of sixty drawings were included in the serialized version of the novel in the *Arbeiter-Zeitung*. Hauser's socially conscious work often thematized the abjection of city life, in particular the woes of the working poor. His visual art evolved from expressionism to a socially critical, Verist New Objectivity in the early 1920s.[146] Hauser's art—portraying a cross section of working-class misery[147]—is populated with images of *Lustmord*, urban overcrowding, illness, and returned war wounded (see chap. 2). Marie Miczek is very much in line with these other suffering figures. In this pen-and-ink drawing for Feldmann's novel, Miczek's torso is exposed. Her face is not included in the drawing, and her pelvis is draped for decency. The professor, wearing a rather jovial expression, pokes at her pregnant belly with his index finger. Hauser's professor, with both finger and glance striking a single, decisive focal point—the patient's body—represents an epistemological shift in medicine registered by Michel Foucault. After 1800, Foucault argues, the metaphor of touch came to define the clinical eye. Here, with the professor's "index finger palpating the depths," we see that "the tangible space of the body" has become the defining locus of clinical experience.[148] The very site of contact between doctor and patient is, moreover, the focal point of the image and of the clinical eyes. The axis of sight lines in Hauser's illustration replicates both the architecture and the collective yet strictly hierarchical power structures of the clinic's lecture hall.[149] The outsized professor occupies two-thirds of the page, the medical students ring the woman in a semicircle that mirrors the amphitheater, and the faceless patient, objectified, is at the center of the constellation. All the practitioners' eyes are trained on her anonymous body, which is reduced to a medical specimen. Both Hauser's clean line drawing—clearly modeled on the New Objectivity of Otto Dix and George Grosz—and Feldmann's equally sober narrative emphasize the doctors' pitiless materialism, their indifference to the patient as an individual, and their interest in her only as a case study.

Fig. 30. Carry Hauser, illustration for Else Feldmann's *The Body of the Mother* (Der Leib der Mutter), 1923. Wien Museum, Vienna. © 2019 Artists Rights Society (ARS), New York / Bildrecht, Vienna.

Miczek's assertion in *The Body of the Mother*—"Whether sick or healthy, we're nothing but dogs" (82)—is a pointed expression of how working-class women experienced their treatment not only at the hands of society in general but by the Viennese medical establishment in particular.

This perspective likewise marks the beginning of Arthur Schnitzler's *Professor Bernhardi* (1912), a vivid drama about Austrian anti-Semitism, power, and politics. The play opens with a discussion of a specific medical case, an eighteen-year-old woman dying of septic shock after an illegal abortion. The woman remains invisible throughout the play, but her presence behind the closed hospital room door is felt deeply as the spark that sets in motion the remainder of the dramatic action. Despite her function as the hidden driver of the play, the patient in Schnitzler's drama remains a nameless case study—referred to only as "the septicemic" (*die Sepsis*)—similar to the anonymous expectant mothers in Schiele's drawings and the death of Miczek in Feldmann's novel. We learn her name only in the third act of *Professor Bernhardi*, and that comes not from the doctors—a move that would alter the perspective on the patient's treatment as mere material, a case study—but from the press, which has picked up the story. The play addressed not only the anti-Semitic currents of fin-de-siècle Viennese institutions, currents that are expressed on administrative levels throughout society and politics, but also the prevailing medical viewpoint about patients.

In a vigorous defense of the play, which premiered in Germany but had fallen prey to Austrian censors and was not performed there until 1918, the *Arbeiter-Zeitung*'s theater critic, Engelbert Pernerstorfer, wrote that Schnitzler "wants to show us people and conditions, and because he does not live outside of time and space, he thus shows us Austrian people in Austrian conditions. He can do nothing for the fact that the people and the conditions are as they are."[150] The documentary impulse Pernerstorfer ascribes to Schnitzler's play—and the social criticism implied in such an approach—was of course a response to Viennese society at large, and foremost to the prevailing anti-Jewish sentiments. Yet Schnitzler's critique extended to the social conditions that gave rise to the wrongful treatment of women at the hands of the Viennese medical establishment. When women's bodies are relegated to pawns in a larger game, the drama implies, it is a portent of greater social ills. Here, again, we find questions of identity in Viennese society played out "over her dead body."[151]

These specific conditions also mark the end of Feldmann's novel *The Body of the Mother*. Laich returns to the hospital several days after his initial visit, when he witnessed Marie Miczek unconscious before a lecture hall of students. This time, he finds her bed ominously empty, a "dark riddle." The patient chart at the foot of her bed identifies her by name, age, profession, and diagnosis. Laich shudders at the sight of the ciphers on the black chalkboard, which remind him of a gravestone: "one did not see the human being, one read only [her] name and what [she] once was" (181). The patient is dehumanized; in the doctors' eyes she is: Marie Miczek; 34; factory worker; advanced sepsis. She is interesting not as a whole person (*Leib*) but as a moribund biological body (*Körper*), an object of medical study. Here, again, we see the patient merely as an "external fact."[152] The physicians were concerned above all with seeing how her septicemia would play out in order to advance their scientific pursuits. This singular focus on the materiality of the body and its pathology—a kind of therapeutic nihilism—is reminiscent of the doctors' irreverent treatment of patients' mortal remains in both Schnitzler and Horváth that we encountered in chapter 2. In the years between Schnitzler's drama and Feldmann's novel, however, a new kind of socially critical journalism emerged, and its lens was trained on the bodies of working-class Viennese women and children. Else Feldmann was one of the leaders, and she and her fellow journalists set out to weave their own stories and experiences into the fabric of Viennese culture.

THE POLITICS AND PUBLIC VISIBILITY OF WORKERS' BODIES

By the 1920s, at the time of the serialization of Feldmann's novel *The Body of the Mother*, Viennese political efforts to improve social welfare had begun to center on mothers', infants', and children's bodies. At the same time, working-class bodies, in particular those of children, had become increasingly visible carriers of social meaning in art and literature, as well as in investigative journalism and public presentations designed for all classes. Julius Tandler—the renowned professor of anatomy, former assistant to Emil Zuckerkandl, and "the medical pope of [Viennese] Social Democracy"[153]—elevated the mother's body to the key site of political intervention for Viennese social welfare programs.

Tandler became Vienna's municipal councilor for welfare and healthcare (Amtsführender Stadtrat für das Wohlfahrts- und Gesundheitswesen) in November 1920. Together with his Social Democratic allies Hugo Breitner, Otto Glöckel, Karl Seitz, and others, Tandler expended tireless energy on a paternalistic, cradle-to-grave model of social welfare that took as its central tenet care for young people, which he defined as beginning immediately after conception. In a 1925 pamphlet titled *Charity or Welfare?* (Wohltätigkeit oder Fürsorge?), for example, he spelled out the clinical basis of his social initiatives, which created a state-sanctioned institutional framework for the implementation of the latest medical knowledge.[154] Tandler believed that early intervention was the key to cultivating healthy citizens, who could then become sociopolitically engaged once their most basic needs were met. "The more we care for [*befürsorgen*] young people," he wrote, "the less we will need to do for them in old age; this youth will be healthier, more capable of living [*lebenstüchtig*], and more able to withstand the struggle for existence. What we invest in social welfare for expectant mothers and infants, we save on psychiatric facilities. Generous, comprehensive youth welfare is the most economical method in the management of organic capital, that is, of a polity's humankind [*der Menschheit eines Gemeinwesens*]."[155] Expectant mothers could count on financial, material, and medical support from Vienna's welfare office, regardless of their marital status. Above all, Tandler argued, women should be able to rely on the municipal government when all else failed: "Pregnant women . . . should know that even in their darkest hour as mothers, perhaps abandoned by everyone, they have one support under all circumstances: that of the municipality of Vienna."[156]

Interwar efforts to improve the lives of expectant mothers and their children took the form of both large-scale public outreach efforts and individualized intervention. Exhibitions such as the successful *Woman and Child* (Frau und Kind) show were staged to disseminate information to women from all walks of life. Held in Vienna's Messepalast from April to July 1928 by the Austrian Society for People's Health (Österreichische Gesellschaft für Volksgesundheit) in cooperation with the German Hygiene Museum in Dresden, the exhibit combined informational and didactic displays with entertainment to attract the greatest possible audiences. One poster for *Woman and Child*, for example, depicts an angelic-looking young mother holding her infant in a protective embrace. The combination of the woman's modern, bobbed hair and neoclassical, draped garb reveals an attempt to appeal to both more traditional and more modern mothers by combining the visual rhetoric of multiple generations.

Meanwhile, individualized outreach targeted all Viennese mothers and children in an attempt to improve their lives. One of Tandler's flagship initiatives was the introduction of the "layette package" (*Säuglingswäschepaket*) in 1927.[157] The motto of the program, "No Viennese child shall be born on newspaper" (*Kein Wiener Kind darf auf Zeitungspapier geboren werden*), referenced the high number of often life-threatening home births in squalid conditions. Available to every Viennese mother, the parcel contained diapers, clothing, blankets, soap, cream, powder, and useful information about infant care and hygiene. In its initial incarnation, it was personally bestowed on new mothers by a small cadre of social workers.[158] Going door-to-door in Vienna's working-class districts, the staff also took the opportunity to survey the new baby's surroundings and family situation. While humanitarian considerations were certainly one aspect of this initiative, the city government also sought to gain firsthand insight into the destitution that reigned in the tenements of the outer districts. Municipal politics were obviously concerned with poverty because of its possible hygienic, medical, and epidemiological implications. However, the historians Wolfgang Maderthaner and Lutz Musner emphasize that it

Fig. 31. Leaflet for *Woman and Child* exhibition, Vienna, 1928. Atelier Hans Neumann. Printed by Münster & Co. Wienbibliothek im Rathaus, Vienna, Plakatsammlung, P-10927.

was foremost "demographic, industrial, and instrumental [considerations] that led the state administration to describe, measure, and medicalize this misery, and make it the object of a socio-technically motivated discourse of planning."[159] Women's bodies were the sites of such interventions.

Like Marie Miczek in Feldmann's novel, some women caught in this vicious cycle of poverty and exploitation were driven to other choices. *The Body of the Mother*, for example, opens with Absalon Laich, the protagonist, inadvertently witnessing the first of Miczek's infanticides.[160] Miczek's fictional situation and decisions reflect the very real stakes of reproductive choice for working-class women in First Republic Austria.[161] Miczek might not have been forced to this course of action out of sheer desperation had the regulation of women's bodies and reproduction not been such a contentious—and criminalized—sociopolitical matter.[162] In Austria, paragraphs 144–48 of the legal code criminalized voluntary termination of pregnancy with up to five years of jail time.[163] Now, after Miczek's third consecutive pregnancy ends in dubious circumstances,

Fig. 32. "No Viennese Child Shall Be Born on Newspaper" (Kein Wiener Kind darf auf Zeitungspapier geboren werden), advertisement for layette package, 1932. *Der Kuckuck*, March 27, 1932, 3. ANNO/Österreichische Nationalbibliothek, Vienna.

her neighbors catch on to her; one even reports her to the police (174). In the interwar years, as later, the debate about women's right to make decisions about their own bodies was both subject to debate and at the very heart of emancipatory efforts. A front-page article from March 15, 1921, in the Viennese *Arbeiterinnen-Zeitung*, the women's print arm of the Social Democratic Party, clearly articulates the stakes of the debate, as well as the party line on the status of paragraph 144. The anonymous author insists on women's rights "to decide for themselves when, whether, and how often they want to become mothers."[164] For working-class women like Marie Miczek, the situation was often an existential one.

This theme was the subject not only of interwar Austrian literature, as in Feldmann's serialized novel, but also of mass-market Austrian silent films, as in the simply titled *Paragraph 144* (1924).[165] A series of investigative articles in 1924 by Johann Ferch was called "Paragraph 144: The Persecution of Women" (Paragraph 144: Die Hetzenjagd auf Frauen). The series appeared in Hugo Bettauer's influential and controversial *Bettauers Wochenschrift*, subtitled "Life's Problems" (Probleme des Lebens) and founded in 1924. In the series' final installment, printed on August 21, 1924, the author systematically refutes any number of defenses brought by supporters of the law. Arguing for unequivocal repeal, Ferch takes issue foremost with the assertion that "the child and the body of the woman belong to society." He argues for each woman's right to individual self-determination regarding her reproductive decisions and states that the "madness" will end only with the repeal of the law.[166] The issue had gained such urgency by 1926 that *Bettauers Wochenschrift*—just one year after Hugo Bettauer was murdered in an anti-Semitic assassination—dedicated an entire issue to the matter. The special issue, entitled "A Cry for Help" (Ein Notschrei), was advertised with a striking red poster of a wide-eyed, screaming woman's face.[167] While the laws were never reformed in the First Republic, and debates between reformers and opponents within the Austrian Social Democratic Party stymied efforts to achieve decriminalization for women seeking pregnancy termination, the party did ultimately incorporate a compromise position into its party platform in 1926.[168]

In the end, the debate was about far more than the legal status of abortion; it thematized the social circumstances that led women to decide to have abortions in the first place, despite the procedure's legal and mortal risks. Like Wendla Bergmann in Frank Wedekind's earlier drama *Spring Awakening* (Frühlings Erwachen, premiered in 1906) and the nameless case of sepsis in Schnitzler's *Professor Bernhardi*, one of these casualties is Else Feldmann's Marie Miczek, though she's no naïf. The conditions behind women's sometimes fatal choices were often economic, as in Miczek's case, but also frequently a matter of knowledge distribution. Paragraph 144 was hence of central concern to the Socialist Society for Sexual Advice and Sexual Research, cofounded by Marie Frischauf-Pappenheim and Wilhelm Reich in 1928. Pappenheim and Reich's wife, Annie Reich, a leading psychoanalyst, coauthored an important treatise on the topic. *Is Abortion Harmful?* (Ist Abtreibung schädlich?) was published just a year before Feldmann's novel was released in book form.[169]

Decades before such governmentally regulated social programs as the layette package initiative; before large-scale exhibitions began to promote healthy bodies of mothers and their infants; and years before Egon Schiele began using such bodies as subjects for his piercingly observed figure studies, the broken bodies of the working poor had become an increasingly visible part of both art and public discourse in Vienna around 1900. The "other side of fin-de-siècle Vienna," as Maderthaner and Musner have called it in their important corrective social history, was often charged with the discourse of pathology, with the city's administration applying a "medical, coldly distanced, and objectivizing view" to the urban periphery and its inhabitants.[170] That perspective was not only characteristic of a paternalistic city governance, which purported to act in the supposed best interests of all citizens; it was also applied by the clinics' doctors to individual mothers' bodies, as we have seen with regard to both Feldmann's novel and the accounts of institutional clinic architecture after the turn of the century. The bodies of the working classes—and those of poor children, in particular—increasingly became a part of the visual vocabulary of the growing metropolis. This occurred on two fronts: in the realm of visual art and in contemporary photojournalistic reportage.

Among the earliest of such works was a portfolio of algraphs, *The Life of the Poor Is Bitterer Than the Death of the Rich* (Das Leben der Armen ist bittrer als der Reichen Tod, 1900), by the painter and graphic artist Hermine Heller-Ostersetzer (1874–1909).[171] Her socially motivated artwork was something of a less aesthetically modern Austrian cousin to Käthe Kollwitz's, though some of her graphic art bears traces of Alfred Kubin's modernist fantasticality.[172] While still a student, Heller-Ostersetzer was selected to exhibit at the Paris World's Fair in 1900. In Vienna, where she spent most of her years, her prizewinning work was shown in all the major art fora of the time, Secession, *Kunstschau*, and Galerie Miethke included.[173] In a feature essay published in the journal *Erdgeist*, tragically just two days before Heller-Ostersetzer's death in 1909, the art critic and collector Arthur Roessler bemoans her late recognition by the Viennese art establishment and affords her a category all her own among the female painters of her generation.[174] The fact of Heller-Ostersetzer's disappearance from the annals of art history has, perhaps, as much to do with her marginal status as a woman artist in the male-dominated artistic circles of fin-de-siècle Vienna as with the marginal existences of her preferred subjects: the working poor.[175] Her clear-eyed portrayals focused on how existential struggles registered in her subjects' physical comportment: "men depleted by toil [*abgerackert*] and exhausted [*müdgelebt*] women with despondent, sunken countenances," as Roessler put it. Unconcerned with commercial success, Heller-Ostersetzer "steadfastly refused to serve up confections," never wavering from her frank yet empathetic depictions of the working poor. On the occasion of her 1906 exhibition at the Galerie Miethke, however, something notable transpired. As Roessler recounts, well-heeled collectors found themselves drawn to her work despite its subject matter: "wide circles of the 'sophisticated' public, . . . the so-called art-minded Viennese public . . . even resolved to purchase images with 'proletarian' content."[176] That genteel gallerygoers would purchase works thematizing "working-class subject matter" makes the widespread absence of such topics in their own works all the more striking: Vienna's outer districts hardly register in canonical literature of or about the period. This omission is apparent in autobiographies such as Stefan Zweig's *The World of Yesterday* and Arthur Schnitzler's *My Youth in Vienna*.[177]

In the years between the initial publication of Heller-Ostersetzer's portfolio and the 1906 Galerie Miethke group exhibition, social reportage from "the other side of fin-de-siècle Vienna" was evolving into a profitable enterprise.[178] Investigative journalism from Vienna's proletarian quarters attempted to galvanize the working classes politically, while simultaneously offering the middle and upper classes a voyeuristic glimpse from the city's periphery into the lives of the "urban Other."[179] Much of this reporting emerged from social-democratic quarters, penned by socially conscious urban journalists such as Feldmann, Bruno Frei (1897–1988), Emil Kläger (1880–1936), Anitta Müller-Cohen (1890–1962), and Max Winter (1870–1937).[180] These writers, whose vivid renderings of the gritty underbelly of Viennese urban life refused to paper over the complexities and miseries of human experience, were more often than not Jewish. Lisa Silverman argues that Else Feldmann and other Jewish journalists, many of them women and committed Social Democrats, wrote inclusively, unsentimentally, of the rich social and spatial urban landscape of interwar Vienna. Although their writings do not typically focus on specifically Jewish content, they do frequently employ the lenses of gender and class.

Such diversity of perspective "reveals a form of Jewish self-understanding as difference," Silverman maintains, a way of reaching more of the population through humanitarian concerns while also fashioning the self.[181] The question of difference—be it on the basis of sex, ethnicity, religion, or class—was, as we have seen, the defining debate of the age, and it was one people sought to answer by studying their own bodies and those of others.

The breakthrough work in this vein of socially engaged journalism was *Through the Viennese Quarters of Misery and Crime* (Durch die Wiener Quartiere des Elends und Verbrechens, 1908) by Emil Kläger and with images by the jurist and amateur photographer Hermann Drawe (1867–?). Even before the book's publication and subsequent translation into French and Russian, Kläger's research and Drawe's photographs had been the basis for over three hundred public slide lectures between 1905 and 1908 at the Urania, Vienna's premier public educational institution (*Volksbildungshaus*).[182] The lecture drew sixty thousand visitors over the years and caused a political outcry, culminating in a petition submitted to the Viennese City Council (*Gemeinderat*) calling for an immediate halt to the presentations. Even the notoriously anti-Semitic mayor, Karl Lueger, got involved, arguing for the necessity to protect women and children from such shocking imagery.[183] Over a decade later, following the First World War and during a period of seemingly unprecedented economic instability, the subject matter had not lost any of its timeliness: Kläger and Drawe's book served as the basis for a 1920 Austrian "enlightenment" film with a fictional frame narrative but bearing an identical title.[184] In such adaptations and in the journalism from which they derived, Vienna is presented as "a divided urban space, internally cleft and broken."[185] Moreover, the accompanying imagery often depicts the disfigured bodies of workers, children, and the impoverished as the visual sign of this brokenness.

Such broken bodies played an important role in Bruno Frei's works. Frei, an avowed socialist activist, joined Else Feldmann on the staff of *Der Abend* in 1917 and eventually became its editor in the second half of the 1920s.[186] Several books, such as *Viennese Apartment Misery* (Wiener Wohnungs-Elend, 1918) and *Jewish Misery in Vienna* (Jüdisches Elend in Wien, 1920), grew out of his reporting. The cover of *Vienna's Misery* (Das Elend Wiens, 1921), illustrated by Franz Plachy (1896–1968), featured a silhouette of the city's distinctive skyline as a stark backdrop to the family in the foreground: a stoic mother cradling a visibly undernourished infant, her equally emaciated young son holding on to her hand. The book includes a chapter called "The Hell of Misery" (Die Hölle des Elends), which reprinted a number of articles originally published in *Der Abend* between

Fig. 33. Bruno Frei, *Vienna's Misery* (Das Elend Wiens), 1921. Illustration by Franz Plachy. Courtesy Herbert D. Katz Center for Advanced Judaic Studies, University of Pennsylvania.

1917 and 1919. Frei's profiles of individual tenement apartment houses in working-class neighborhoods and the families who live there are illustrated by photographs from Anton and Hans Bock.[187] The article "Help, Not Handouts" (Hilfe, nicht Almosen) illustrates the author's statistics, analysis, and commentary with photographs. They depict four children in obvious ill health: two of the children, Pepi and Anna, smile weakly into the camera; two other anonymous children are identified only by their diagnoses, tuberculosis and rickets. Rickets, caused by an extreme childhood vitamin D deficiency that leads to softening and malformation of

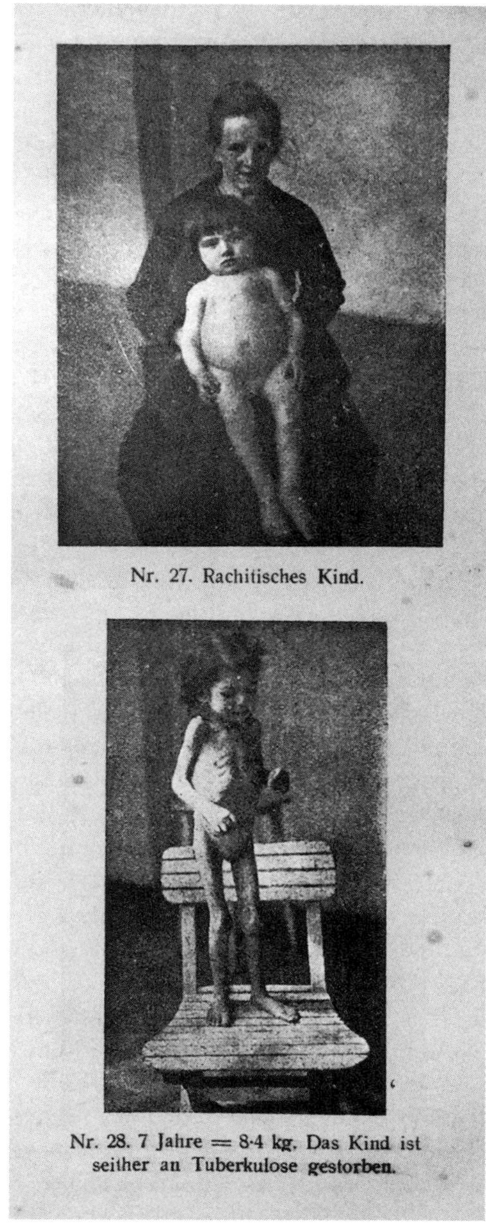

Fig. 34. Mother with child suffering from rickets; child with tuberculosis. Bruno Frei, *Das Elend Wiens* (Vienna: Verlag der Wiener Graphischen Werkstätte, 1921), n.p. Photographs by Anton and Hans Bock.

the bones, was exacerbated by malnourishment and the stricken children's living conditions, often in dank, subterranean quarters entirely devoid of sunlight. The most heartbreaking image is that of an anonymous tubercular girl, who at seven years old weighs only 8.4 kilograms. The caption tersely informs us that she has since succumbed to her disease.[188]

The examples of Heller-Ostersetzer, Frei, and Feldmann, along with a broader trend toward socially conscious journalism from Vienna's working-class periphery, make plain that *Elend* (misery and poverty) had a wide audience,[189] and especially so when the tragedy of life on the margins was manifested in the broken human body. Such reportages fulfilled a sociopolitical function by enlightening all classes to the reality of the Viennese working poor, while also satisfying the voyeurism of well-heeled Viennese society. This is the context in which Schiele's studies of working-class subjects, including the expectant mothers from the clinic, emerged. While his choice of models may indeed have also been motivated by economic considerations, the content of his drawings when hung on gallery walls—as in the posthumous exhibitions in 1919, 1928, and 1929 at the Galerie Würthle, Hagenbund, and Neue Galerie—or published in art journals, such as *Bildende Künstler* in 1911,[190] would have been readily recognizable and, in fact, very legible to an urbane Viennese audience. This audience was, after all, already familiar with the Urania lecture series by Kläger and Drawe, gallery shows displaying Heller-Ostersetzer's work, and ubiquitous, of-the-moment news reporting from Vienna's margins—focusing on working-class people and their bodies.

Schiele, for his part, began drawing working-class children from the streets in 1910, the same year in which he was honing his eye in Graff's clinic. Schiele's depictions of poor boys and girls sought neither—like Bruno Frei or Hermine Heller-Ostersetzer—to make a plea for greater social recognition of underserved and indigent populations nor to activate his viewers' moral consciousness in the style of the *peinture morale* of the preceding centuries.[191] Foremost, Schiele was fascinated, as in so much of his work, by "telling it like it is"—whether the subject of that visual honesty was desire, death, or destitution. The art critic Arthur Roessler, among Schiele's earliest champions, describes in a review essay from 1911 how Schiele had become utterly transfixed by these abject children, drawing them seemingly without pause for months on end. It was, above all, the children's bodies, their external anatomies, that riveted the young artist. Roessler writes, "He was fascinated by the ravages [*Verwüstungen*] of dirty sufferings, to which these intrinsic innocents are exposed. Marveling, he saw the curious changes of the skin, in whose slack vessels thin, watery blood and sour juices sluggishly trickle; amazed, he saw the light-shy, green eyes behind swollen, red lids, the scrofulous bones of their hands, the slimy mouths—and—-the soul in these poor vessels." Schiele "saw with cool, jewellike clarity the pale colors of decay in human faces, the death beneath the skin."[192] Yet this modernist aestheticizing—equating the unadorned figure with truth—reveals a deeper, hitherto unacknowledged discursive shift in the social construction of the body. The straightforwardness with which Schiele registered—and foregrounded—his subjects' bodies was informed by the matter-of-factness of the clinical gaze. It was the gaze of an optical, anatomical age, as the epigraph from Ludwig Hevesi at the outset of this chapter indicates. Roessler draws our attention to the fact that the artist was concerned not only with the bodies-as-matter (*Körper*) of his subjects—the children's "poor vessels"—but far more with the body as a vessel for the soul that resides within (*Leib*). There is a kinship here between Schiele and Laich, the protagonist of Feldmann's novel *The Body of the Mother*. Like Schiele, Laich recognizes and dignifies the soul within the body—in contrast to the medical establishment. Yet in both cases, the aesthetic and the medical, the exposed body has emerged as the figuration of unmediated access to its truth.

Beyond the clinic, in the decades after the turn of the century, the bodies of working-class Viennese—women and children, in particular—came to occupy a central place in the city's visual vernacular. This occurred in the fine arts as well as in medical imagery that was disseminated to wide swaths of the city's populace in films, lectures, and exhibitions. The intersection of new forms of clinical architecture supported the evolution of a medicalized gaze that was schooled in nonspecialist audiences. And that gaze was trained on the bodies of the city's most vulnerable. Yet, ultimately, it was only the women themselves—Marie Pappenheim, Else Feldmann, and Ilka Maria Ungar—who could give voice to their own experiences, on their own terms. In so doing, they inscribed themselves into Viennese culture, reclaiming some small measure of the power the medical establishment and the political and cultural spheres wielded over them.

CHAPTER FOUR

The Body in Motion: Staging Silent Expression

> My gesture: that is who I am—compressed into a moment, it speaks me aloud.
> —Hugo von Hofmannsthal

In a lecture from 1912, the Viennese polymathic wit and cabaret performer Egon Friedell (1878–1938)—whose incisive cultural-philosophical writings would later culminate in the monumental *A Cultural History of the Modern Age* (1927–32)—set out to reflect on the interrelations of silent film and theater. Friedell leveled a counterattack to critics of the cinema, who were in the business of taking film to task for its lack of reliance on language. In fact, Friedell argued that he and many of his contemporaries had lost their conviction in the power of language as such. "I believe that today, we are no longer inclined to cede such absolute hegemony to the word," he asserted. "One might say that for us today, words have something excessively clear [*etwas Überdeutliches*] and for that reason strangely indiscriminate about them. Gradually, the word is losing some of its credit."[1] Friedell's claims neatly encapsulate the centrality within Viennese modernism of Nietzsche's skeptical query from decades before: "Is language the full and adequate expression of all realities?"[2] The notion of a wholesale *Sprachkrise* (crisis of language) has become one of the defining critical commonplaces about the generation of authors and thinkers at work in Vienna around 1900.[3] The language-critical bent of Viennese modernism is manifest perhaps most paradigmatically in Fritz Mauthner's dreams of a "suicide" of language and in Hugo von Hofmannsthal's famous fictional letter from Lord Chandos to Francis Bacon, but it was also central to the thought and practice of figures such as Karl Kraus and Ludwig Wittgenstein. A loss of faith in language's fundamental expressive capacity might even be considered central to literary modernism as a whole.[4]

One response to the perceived modernist crisis of language was a renewed interest in another kind of language—body language, the language of gesture—around the fin de siècle.[5] While the reigning view of Vienna 1900 sees the turn to the language of the unconscious as the era's primary response to this crisis, the unconscious was, in fact, just one among several potential alternatives in the search to secure meaning with a seemingly authentic and reliable referent. In this context, gesture was conceived of as a faithful and soulful expression of the individual—and thus as a counterweight to the rational, impersonal abstraction of language. With its expressive potential, the body was increasingly viewed in utopian terms as a medium for rendering visible and material the innermost stirrings of the subject in a way that words could not.[6] Friedell put a fine point on it in his 1912 essay: "Today, a person's gaze, gestures, or his whole physical bearing can occasionally say more than human speech."[7] That hopeful stance was stimulated, of course, by the birth of cinema. Yet the search for extralinguistic modes of expression had earlier given rise to a revival of pantomime and the emergence of a new kind of modern dance. In pantomime, dance, and early film, it was not language but the silent gestures of the body that transmitted meaning, emotion, and affect. Friedell cautioned his contemporaries, however, not to mistake silence for muteness. Silence, he observed, is "merely another—and perhaps more energetic—form of communication."[8] By looking to gesture—that is, to a language of the body in motion—to supplement, critique, or even to replace linguistic expression, Viennese modernists responded to language's limitations not by resorting to silence but by actively exploring a series of creative possibilities that mobilized the human body as a site of nonverbal expressive capacity. Indeed, even Freud looked to the body to express what words could not, since psychic conflicts often registered first as physical symptoms.

This chapter analyzes the centrality of body language in the cultural production of Viennese modernism and the interwar years. Pantomime, modern dance, and silent film were genres of alterity, safe spaces where matters of difference—medial, of course, but also of gender, class, race, and nation—could be productively addressed by staging the human body. It first looks to Hugo von Hofmannsthal's efforts to rethink the possibilities of literature through a new performative aesthetic of expressive gesture. Read against the backdrop of a crisis of language, the performer's body achieved a new, exalted significance. As authors and directors began to experiment with body-based communicative modes, many—including the writers Hofmannsthal, Arthur Schnitzler, Richard Beer-Hofmann, Hermann Bahr, Max Mell, and Max Reinhardt—turned to pantomime. The revival of pantomime, once exclusively the domain of fairgrounds and variety theater, was now spearheaded by the Viennese cultural elite. This genre allowed the writers of Young Vienna to challenge the divide between high and popular culture, while also providing a semiotically unburdened space for addressing pressing questions of identity. Hofmannsthal's pantomime *The Student* is a prime example. The genesis of free dance in Vienna went hand in hand with the revival of pantomime and likewise offered possibilities for exploring the identity of marginalized segments of society. Vicki Baum's fiction, for example, used dance to explore problematics of Jewish identity and the body. Individual dancers, such as Grete Wiesenthal, were key agents of change, collaborating and cocreating with leading fin-de-siècle authors, such as Hofmannsthal. Wiesenthal challenged the classical ballet establishment, creating a uniquely Viennese style of modern dance. Ultimately, the gestural principles underlying pantomime and modern dance became important templates for silent film actors in the first decades of cinema. Viennese film theories by Béla Balázs and Hofmannsthal from the early 1920s bear witness to a heightened belief in the expressive power of the body in motion. Finally, considering the transformation from free dance to *Ausdruckstanz* (expressive dance) in the interwar years reveals how bodies increasingly became vehicles for political messaging and social critique. The dancers and choreographers Gertrud Bodenwieser and Hilde Holger, leading representatives of Viennese *Ausdruckstanz*, both staged and performed the worker's body. This trend ran parallel to the institutionalization of modern dance in both pedagogical reform and in Social Democratic cultural outreach efforts targeting the working classes.

By considering the interwar years alongside Viennese modernism as it is more strictly defined, this chapter highlights a developmental trajectory in how the expressive, gestural ideal of the performer's body was conceptualized. Whereas it was initially viewed as a tangible alternative to language and as a means to renovate the realism and naturalism of late nineteenth-century stage performance, the body increasingly became a medium for sociopolitical reform. Moreover, this long view demonstrates that the Viennese cultural elite exhibited a profound engagement with popular culture—pantomime, dance, and film. As such, it presents a concrete alternative to the Schorskean notion of a Viennese retreat into the garden of aestheticism. Having engaged both in theory and in practice with pantomime, dance, and film, Hofmannsthal's work is a thread running through the present chapter. Yet, as we will see, his career is also representative of a larger-scale Viennese cultural experimentation with gestural forms of expression, seen across the creative spectrum—and this engagement is obscured if we hew too closely to the Schorskean perspective on Viennese modernism.

BODY LANGUAGE AND CRISIS OF LANGUAGE

The appeal for a language capable of capturing the innermost personal experiences lies at the heart of a thematic strand that runs through much of Hugo von Hofmannsthal's work, from his early essayistic writings to fictional letters and conversations. The anonymous author of the last of Hofmannsthal's invented "Letters of One Returned" (Briefe des Zurückgekehrten, 1907) is paradigmatic for this topos: "If only I possessed a language into which inner, wordless certainties were capable of flowing over!" he exclaims.[9] The central question is how to express the deepest reaches of the self when conceptual language seems hopelessly corrupted. Hofmannsthal's fictional dialogue "On Characters in the Novel and in Drama" (Über Charaktere im Roman und im Drama, 1902) had raised this very issue five years earlier. The exchange is posed as having taken place in 1842 between the French realist novelist Honoré de Balzac (1799–1850) and Joseph Freiherr von Hammer-Purgstall (1774–1856), the influential Viennese Orientalist and diplomat. What Hofmannsthal's fictional Balzac foretells about the cultural production of the final decade of the nineteenth century—excessive emotionalism and sensibility, a morbid tendency toward inward reflection, and language's inability to adequately express emotional experiences—reads like a laundry list for literary aestheticism and decadence. Balzac, however, predicts that these "spiritual sicknesses," limited formerly to poets, will have become "universal" afflictions by 1890 (HGW 7:488). That malady has, moreover, been woven into the fabric of almost every critical narrative on Viennese modernism.[10]

Hofmannsthal had turned twenty-eight in 1902, the year in which he penned the dialogue between Balzac and Hammer-Purgstall and saw his now-canonical "A Letter" (Ein Brief) published. His first poems had appeared under the nom de plume "Loris" when he was just sixteen, and by seventeen the young Loris was already a fixture in the literary circles of fin-de-siècle Vienna. He mingled with such famous (or soon-to-be famous) writers as Richard Beer-Hofmann, Arthur Schnitzler, Hermann Bahr, and Stefan George at Vienna's cafés and literary salons. Earlier in the 1890s, Hofmannsthal had ventured into writing prose and lyric drama, and by the end of the decade he had become a respected cultural critic, whose contributions appeared regularly in all the major Viennese print fora of the time. By around 1900, however, Hofmannsthal had almost entirely ceased writing lyric poetry. Instead, he turned his attention to essays, short fiction (particularly, fictional letters and dialogues), and, above all, dramas.

The familiar line of literary criticism would have us believe that Hofmannsthal's break with lyric poetry was a direct consequence of his critical relationship to language. The "Chandos letter," the oft-cited fictional missive of Philipp Lord Chandos to Francis Bacon, is commonly read historically or biographically to corroborate Hofmannsthal's turn away from lyric poetry. In fact, the letter of Lord Chandos yields more when not read either as the fictitious expression of a personal linguistic or creative crisis or as a final farewell to the lyric poetry of the author's youth cloaked in a seventeenth-century epistle.[11] While "A Letter" represents Hofmannsthal's earliest fiction writing in which language and its perceived inadequacies are the major themes, he had already begun to reflect in nonfictional form on these questions. They were previously present in his essayistic work years before he composed "A Letter" and would remain a leitmotif throughout his career.

The essay "A Monograph" (Eine Monographie, 1895), a review of Eugen Guglia's book on the celebrated *Burgtheater* actor Friedrich Mitterwurzer (1844–97), was Hofmannsthal's first overtly polemical assessment of the state of language in contemporary society. Echoing Nietzsche, it identifies a widespread skepticism about language that Hofmannsthal sees as characteristic of the age. This mistrust stems from a disconnect between conceptual thought and linguistic expression, which has skewed all notions of self, reality, and truth. Hofmannsthal writes that words have taken precedence over everything they are supposed to represent and have become overinflated, overvalued to the extent that they no longer have any direct correlation to that which they describe. The consequence is that "we are in the grip of a terrible process of completely smothering thought with concepts." Rather than having mastery of language as a tool for expression, Hofmannsthal maintains that language now controls us (HGW 8:479–80).

This situation has epistemological and social implications that Hofmannsthal spells out in "A Monograph." On the one hand, language inhibits how we conceive of our feelings, perceptions, and opinions. Hofmannsthal comments, "Hardly anyone is still capable of accounting to himself for what he understands and what he does not understand, of saying what he feels and what he does not feel" (HGW 8:479). On the other hand, language limits our ability to communicate with others. People are only able to converse by assuming roles and speaking of "phantom feelings [*Scheingefühlen*], phantasmic opinions, phantasmic convictions." Because language drives a wedge between what we live and how we recount it, people "quite nearly manage to be continuously absent for their own experiences" (HGW 8:480). The gap between reality and language moreover determines in large measure our relationship with ourselves. Hofmannsthal maintains with conviction that "all deep knowledge about oneself is utterly, utterly beyond words and concepts" (HGW 8:481).[12]

Already in 1895, we find Hofmannsthal concluding that language, in essence, leads not to enlightenment or even to "adequate" expression, in Nietzsche's terms, but to estrangement, both from oneself and others. The reality that confronts a society no longer in command of its own language is the impossibility of articulating knowledge about oneself and the world. The immediacy of emotions, lived experiences, and sensory impressions becomes linguistically incommunicable—a condition Lord Chandos later so poignantly details in "A Letter." This dilemma leaves in its wake "a deep disgust [*Ekel*]" toward language, an "inner fatigue and dull hatred toward words" (HGW 8:479–80), as Hofmannsthal writes in "A Monograph." Such statements presuppose an idealistic, almost mythical faith in an original power of language, which corresponds to the later insight that Hofmannsthal's fictional Chandos gains in "A Letter." Ultimately, Hofmannsthal and others of his generation transferred the belief in the lost expressive power of language onto an ideal of another kind of language: body language. The key can be found in Hofmannsthal's claim in "A Monograph" that the antipathy toward words results in the awakening of "a desperate [*verzweifelte*] love of all arts . . . that are practiced silently: music, dance, and all the artistry of acrobats and jugglers [*Gaukler*]" (HGW 8:479–80).[13]

"A Monograph" and "A Letter"—as well as, of course, the writings of Nietzsche, Mauthner, and Wittgenstein—voiced significant philosophical doubts about the expressive powers of spoken and written language. But the crisis of language was not just carried out on a discursive level, hermetically sealed off from aesthetic production. Hofmannsthal's and other Viennese modernists' attempts to make the experiences of modern life communicable in a new manner led them away from strictly linguistic forms, including Freud and Breuer's famous "talking cure." Rather than turning to language to describe and further encode and obscure the problems with language itself—here we are reminded of Wittgenstein's fundamental problem in the later *Tractatus Logico-Philosophicus*

(1922)—Hofmannsthal and others sought a way through the metalinguistic dilemma not only by writing about their skepticism regarding language but ultimately by experimenting with body language to produce seemingly more authentic, more immediate, more expressive modes of performance. They saw in pantomime, ballet, and film—genres reliant on gesture—a possible solution to the estrangement from language, as "A Monograph" indicates.[14] Hofmannsthal's notes for a 1911 lecture make explicit the link between a language-critical stance and experiments with gestural modes of expression. Referring to the Chandos letter, he directly correlates his "contemporary doubts about language" with "the endeavors with ballet and pantomime." This problematic represents "the utmost in timeliness [*das höchst Zeitgemäße*]," according to Hofmannsthal (HGW 10:510). The belief in communicative possibilities beyond language was initially an idealistic avowal that became a serious programmatic formulation after 1900. In addition to Hofmannsthal, Max Reinhardt, Hermann Bahr, Richard Beer-Hofmann, Arthur Schnitzler, and Max Mell wrote pantomimes that were performed or published with greatly varying degrees of success in the years between 1890 and 1910.[15] This body of work has been little studied in the language-centric critical narratives that have dominated the debates surrounding the era.

Gesture can function in two ways vis-à-vis language in this context. First, it can operate as language's Other, an urlanguage, giving expression to a reality of experience that is not verbally communicable. Second, gesture can serve as a model for an alternate conception of language, capable of overcoming language's arbitrary nature by reconnecting the speech act to the living human body.[16] Georg Braungart has proposed that the latter possibility amounts to nothing less than an "other discourse of modernism," suggesting that—alongside the well-documented tradition of skepticism toward language around 1900—there existed a parallel and concurrent practice of what he calls "incarnate meaning."[17] Hofmannsthal recognized that in order to conceptualize gesture and moreover to transform it into practical, creative action, he would have to go back to the boards—to the theater and to a careful study of acting technique.

Actors "have the language of their body as poets have words," Hofmannsthal noted in 1906 (HGW 10:479).[18] And in fact, the fin-de-siècle search for an aesthetics of gesture to counter a perceived crisis of language mapped onto a reappraisal of the possibilities of theater in the early twentieth century. Directors, authors, and theater theorists such as Hofmannsthal, Georg Fuchs, Edward Gordon Craig, Max Reinhardt, and Vsevolod Meyerhold were searching for new gestural forms of performance to replace the mimetic, declamatory nineteenth-century acting style.[19] Hofmannsthal's contemporary Georg Fuchs, the influential German theater director and founder of the Munich Artists' Theater (Künstlertheater), envisioned a "stage of the future," where actors would be liberated from scripted language, that is from the literary text. Fuchs's revisionist acting technique developed actors' attention to their embodied presence, arguing for the common roots of acting and dancing.[20] Both, he reasons, are "rhythmic motion of the human body in space, performed from the creative impulse to represent an emotion through the expressive means of the human body."[21] While Hofmannsthal did not subscribe completely to Fuchs's Nietzschean concept of Dionysian ecstasy,[22] both dreamed of a reciprocal relationship between stage and society. Body language, gesture, was to replace spoken and written language as a more vital form of communication. For Hofmannsthal, this would ultimately be realized in cinema. First, though, he needed to refine his theory of gesture by studying actors' bodies as a stepping-stone to his work with pantomime and dance, the templates for silent film.

From the very beginnings of his literary career, Hofmannsthal was captivated by the methods of two actors in particular: the Italian actress Eleonora Duse (1858–1924) and the German-born *Burgtheater* actor Friedrich Mitterwurzer, who began performing in Vienna in 1871. Four of Hofmannsthal's early essays, three of them written well before 1900, demonstrate not only his attentiveness to stage technique but also his conviction that well-executed nonverbal, gestural modes of communication can amplify the meaning and expressiveness of spoken language.[23] In the actors Mitterwurzer and Duse, Hofmannsthal found a link between a kind of primal language, dependent on the actor's physical body, and a deeply soulful expressivity. Whereas "pseudo-actors" conceive of gesture merely as "an accompaniment to their words"—an illustrative punctuation contingent on and secondary to the text—"living artists" like Duse and Mitterwurzer deploy a wholly other form of expression (HGW 8:480). Their gestures are true expressions of an inner state of being, conveying what words cannot. Here, Hofmannsthal believed, both the word and the soul are made corporeal, and this corporeality rescues language from its weakened and weakening position in society.

Eleonora Duse has been called the first modern actor.[24] Hugo von Hofmannsthal, in the audience during the Viennese guest performances of Duse's theater company in late February 1892, was among the legion of critics who afforded her universal praise. Her performances mark the beginnings of Hofmannsthal's interest in the role of the gestural within the dramatic form. The similarities between the aesthetic beliefs of the young Italian actress and the young Austrian author center, first, on the problematic nature of language as a communicative medium and, second, on the body and gestures as alternate forms of expression. While Hofmannsthal was still writing lyric poetry early in the 1890s, and while his misgivings about language would only emerge several years later in his review of the Mitterwurzer biography, Duse was already convinced of the ambiguous and contradictory nature of words. She wanted her strongly gestural acting to serve as a new kind of language, defining it as "the outward rendered expressive of the inward; the body instinct with spirit; the soul made incarnate."[25]

Hofmannsthal's first review of Duse's Viennese performances details how the "psycho-physiological event" that precedes the "becoming of a word" is rendered visible through Duse's facial expressions and gestures (HGW 8:471). What resides in the interstices between the actress's lines are, according to Hofmannsthal, the unconscious machinations of the human psyche. Duse renders these unsayable things—"the ripening of a decision, the passing flight of a chain of thought"—visible by the keen sensitivity and power of her gestures. "One reads the unspoken words from her lips. . . . She makes the intangible material" (HGW 8:470–71). The strength of Duse's acting, Hofmannsthal argues, is her body's ability to give expression to the human spirit in a manner more direct and immediate than words. Duse's physical presence and her gestures "reveal the swift, protean movements of the soul." The viewer is thus able to see "the curious catenations of psyche and physis that cannot be painted and cannot be spoken" (HGW 8:477). The only medium that functions as a conduit for the soul is the body; all others fall short. In Hofmannsthal's rendering, Duse's body serves as a converter, transforming the immaterial—words and thoughts—into a legible physical manifestation.

The gestural expressivity of Duse's acting and the ties between body and soul are features Hofmannsthal also recognized in the actor Friedrich Mitterwurzer.[26] As with Duse, Hofmannsthal admired Mitterwurzer's expressive control over his body that allowed his acting to transcend the mere recitation of memorized dramatic text. Mitterwurzer, above all else, conceives of himself as a *Gaukler*, that paradigmatic fairground figure who relies foremost on the body to convey meaning (HGW 8:481). In Mitterwurzer's performances, language regains its lost power by recovering one of its most basic features: the physical fact of its expression. "In his mouth," Hofmannsthal remarks, "the words suddenly become something completely elemental again, [become] the final, most powerful expression of the body." The actor remakes words into weapons here, "like teeth and nails," seductions there, "like smiles and gazes." Embodied language, in the form of the speech act, also renders the intangible concrete. Hofmannsthal writes, "In his eloquence the soul emerges like something physical [*wie ein Leibliches*] and goes through experiences before our eyes" (HGW 8:480–81).

Concomitant with the aesthetics of gesture developed in the essays on Duse and Mitterwurzer, Hofmannsthal began to experiment increasingly with gestural modes of expression, particularly pantomime and dance, in the years around 1900. Beginning in the early 1890s and continuing until his death, he wrote a significant number of libretti exclusively for ballet and pantomime. Many of these experiments remained incomplete and unpublished, but several met with more than a modicum of critical success and paved the way for Hofmannsthal's later experimentation with silent film. More than perhaps any aspect of Viennese modernism, body language evolved into a guiding philosophy for the whole of his career. And Hofmannsthal was not alone. Before turning to one of his crucial pantomimes, we first need to understand both how widespread the engagement with pantomime as an independent form of cultural creation was in Viennese modernism and how a "new" kind of pantomime was conceived of in formal terms.

HUGO VON HOFMANNSTHAL AND THE POWER OF PANTOMIME

Hofmannsthal's fascination with gestural communication was shared by many of his contemporaries. In fact, the revival of pantomime was a centerpiece of Viennese efforts to reconceive modernist literature at the tail end of the nineteenth century.[27] Hermann Bahr, the intrepid networker and programmatic writer, even elevated the pantomime to a critical status in *Overcoming Naturalism* (Die Überwindung des Naturalismus, 1891). For Bahr and his contemporaries, the artistic pantomime—inspired by innovations on Parisian stages—represented the ideal aesthetic antithesis to naturalism's obsession with external reality. Pantomime, Bahr asserts, allows for the reinjection of the fantastic into literature and performance and is the only "handed-down form of old literature" that is commensurate with "modern taste," with the aesthetic demands of the age.[28] Bahr was likely familiar with Stéphane Mallarmé's sketch "Mimique" (The Mime) from the same year, in which Mallarmé exalts the genre as "a pure medium" for its unalloyed fictionality.[29] In Vienna, a city where the folk theater tradition was especially strong, the pantomime was bound to thrive. However, the genre evolved over the decades from a more traditionally oriented "old" form of pantomime to a "new," aesthetically challenging form of modern stage art.

Bahr's circle—the authors who would coalesce as Young Vienna: Hofmannsthal, Richard Beer-Hofmann, Arthur Schnitzler, Felix Salten, and Max Mell, along with the director Max Reinhardt—took up the challenge to renew the ancient folk art of pantomime, largely in the two decades conventionally classified as Viennese modernism, 1890–1910. Beer-Hofmann bookended the efforts with his *Pierrot Hypnotiseur* (1892) and *The Golden Horse* (Das goldene Pferd, 1921).[30] Bahr composed *The Pantomime of the Good Man* (Die Pantomime vom braven Manne, 1893), *The Beautiful Girl* (Das schöne Mädchen, 1902), and *Dear Augustin* (Der liebe Augustin, 1902); Schnitzler penned *The Transformation of Pierrot* (Die Verwandlung des Pierrots, 1908) and *Pierrette's Veil* (Der Schleier der Pierrette, 1910).[31] One of Vienna's leading literary presses, the Wiener Verlag, even published an early anthology of renowned authors' works for so-called small-art stages (*Kleinkunstbühnen*) in 1902, with Hermann Bahr, Felix Salten, Felix Dörmann, Stefan Großmann, and many other current or future leading lights of the cultural scene contributing pantomimes.[32] The experimentation with pantomime did not end with Young Vienna though. Béla Balázs, whose theory of film we will later encounter, wrote a mixed-form ballet-pantomime, *The Shadows: A Pantomimic Stage Trick* (Die Schatten: Ein pantomimischer Bühnentrick, 1920). And Ödön von Horváth, whose play was central in chapter 2, wrote his very first literary work, *The Book of Dances* (Das Buch der Tänze, 1922), as a cycle of seven dance-pantomimes.[33]

Several of the pantomimes were nourished by a Viennese and wider European revival of the commedia dell'arte, the "older" kind of pantomime.[34] The commedia, a largely improvisational theatrical form exemplified by formulaic plotlines, a cast of readily recognizable stock characters, and physical humor, including acrobatic and gymnastic stunts, originated in sixteenth-century Italy. As such, it became a model for many late nineteenth- and early twentieth-century theater practitioners—Edward Gordon Craig, Vsevolod Meyerhold, Antonin Artaud, among them—who were searching for new impulses to move theater away from the naturalism that had dominated European stages through the second half of the nineteenth century.[35] This took the shape of a shift from text-centered to actor-centered theater. Performers' bodies and physical presence were key. Max Reinhardt (1873–1943), born in Baden bei Wien and among the most influential theater directors of his generation, pushed pantomime in yet more novel directions.[36] His stagings of the pantomimes *Sumurûn* (1910) and the monumental *The Miracle* (Das Mirakel, 1911) seemed to herald a new approach to the relationship between text and body language in stagecraft.[37] In 1913, Friedrich Freska, the German libretto author of *Sumurûn*, remarked that, in collaboration with Reinhardt, his pantomime did not aim to mobilize the body in the manner of "old" pantomimes, like the commedia dell'arte, "which substitute stereotypical gestures for words, so that one wonders why the people do not rather just speak."[38] The goal instead was to create stage productions in which language itself was not essential for comprehension at all.[39] In a lecture on dance and pantomime she gave at Hugo Heller's Art Salon (Kunstsalon) in Vienna in 1910, Grete Wiesenthal, the choreographer, dancer, and lead in *Sumurûn*, likewise distinguished between old and new concepts of pantomime. She clarified that the old form of pantomime simply substituted gestural signifiers for language, resulting in a kind of sign language. The new pantomime, by contrast, works with "great mass movements," she argued. Taken together, the characters' "lying, standing, striding, and finally their dancing" must narrate the dramatic action without recourse to language.[40] In Reinhardt's and Wiesenthal's evolving conception of pantomime, then, the characters' gestures were designed to transcend symbolic systems. Although the gestures have no direct linguistic translation, they should still be comprehensible to viewers.

Among the Viennese literati, Hofmannsthal was far and away the most prolific in the pantomimic form. By the mid-1890s, Hofmannsthal had already sketched out three of his own pantomimes in rapid succession: *The Magical Telephone* (Das zauberhafte Telephon, 1893), *Sign of Love* (Liebeszeichen, 1893), and *Viennese Pantomime* (Wiener Pantomime, 1893–94).[41] These first three experiments were mixed forms that combined pantomime with spoken text and musical interludes. Labeled alternately "dance-poems" (*Tanzdichtungen*), "dance-pantomimes" (*Tanzpantomimen*), or "ballet-pantomimes" (*Ballettpantomimen*) by Hofmannsthal himself and scholars,[42] these call to mind classic French vaudeville theater of the late seventeenth and early eighteenth centuries, which later developed into comedic opera.[43] It seems that Hofmannsthal could not settle on a suitable approach to the pantomimic form until several years later. In the meantime, he began experimenting with sketches for dance performances. *Viennese Pantomime*, for example, was originally conceived of as a ballet but had developed into a purer pantomimic form by the time Hofmannsthal abandoned the project in 1894.[44] Interestingly, Hofmannsthal approached these early experiments particularly tentatively: his notes for *The Magical Telephone* clearly state that, should it ever be performed, his name should not be associated with the work.[45] Not a decade later, Hofmannsthal equivocated in a related though much more consequential fashion with what Abigail Gillman has called his "Jewish non-Jewish pantomime" *The Student* (Der Schüler, 1901).[46]

It is significant that Hofmannsthal's first fully realized pieces for dance, pantomime, and a mixed form of the two occurred just before he would compose "A Letter" and several years after the language theme was problematized in "A Monograph." During a stay in Paris in the spring of 1900, he started working in both genres—pantomime and dance—in earnest.[47] Two pantomime sketches, *The Chosen One* (Die Auserwählte, 1900) and *Narcissus and the School of Life* (Narciss und die Schule des Lebens, 1900) preceded his first completed projects in these genres: *Triumph of Time* (Triumph der Zeit, 1900/1901), a ballet, and *The Student*, a pantomime.[48] Hofmannsthal's synchronous work in dance and pantomime, which began in 1900, would continue for the entirety of his career and extend into his efforts with silent film. Moreover, he went beyond merely experimenting with gestural genres to answer misgivings about language as a medium of communication. He used the "liminal form" of pantomime to explore even thornier questions of ethnic, religious, and cultural identity, as Abigail Gillman definitively argues.[49] Both strands are present in *The Student*.

Published in late 1901 in the *Neue Deutsche Rundschau*, one of the leading literary journals of the day, *The Student* has three main characters: the titular student, a scholar/alchemist, and his daughter Taube. Yet the manuscript version of the pantomime casts these characters as eastern European Jews, the alchemist as a rabbi and the student as a bocher, the Yiddish term for a yeshiva student. The pantomime was the subject of a twofold whitewashing of Jewish themes on Hofmannsthal's part: he first changed the two figures' names for the periodical, and he then retracted altogether the book publication that was to accompany *The Student*'s performance. The difference in names is the sole variation between the libretto's manuscript and its published form. Hofmannsthal's editorial intervention, Gillman writes, "quite literally enacts the disappearance of Jewish themes."[50] What remains, though, regardless of the repressed question of Jewish identity, is the critical status of language and the body—not merely as material vehicle for the pantomimic action but also as thematic plot elements. In the original version of the pantomime, Taube's very name—one meaning of which is *deaf*—is an implicit repudiation of spoken language as such. Furthermore, Hofmannsthal's pantomime is acted out over and through the two most socioculturally powerless types of bodies at the fin de siècle: that of the Jewish male and of the daughter.[51]

The plot of *The Student* opens with a rabbi discovering through hermeneutic interpretation a potent correspondence between three texts. Empowered by this revelation and aided by a magic ring, he succeeds in calling to life and triumphantly commanding his own shadow (HGW 6:55–56). The shadow dance ends abruptly when Taube enters the scene. She criticizes her father's "brooding and reading" and professes, in words straight from the mouth of Goethe's Gretchen, "Vater, mir grauts vor dir!"—Father, I am terrified of you (HGW 6:57). Taube is right to be alarmed, as her father begins to admire her beauty and lecherously caress her hair. He is interrupted only by the arrival of the bocher, who has sought out his teacher because he is having difficulty parsing a specific passage of text. Frustrated with the bocher's slow-wittedness, the rabbi commands his daughter to dance. When she protests, her father deploys the power of the magic ring, and Taube begins to sway, spellbound. The bocher, bewitched by Taube's dance, "devours her with his eyes" (HGW 6:59) and begs his mentor in vain to let him use the ring. The rabbi instead quits the scene after commanding his pupil to keep studying.

Left alone, the bocher professes his love for Taube, who, now released from her fugue state, spurns his advances. Why, he asks bitterly, "why not me?" Taube cites his physical appearance—his repulsive hair, red-rimmed eyes, and filthy hands—as the grounds for her repugnance. Laughing spitefully, she cruelly summarizes: "Your body is too ugly to me!" (HGW 6:61). The bocher momentarily appears to abandon his pursuit, and Taube has meanwhile been hatching a plan to escape her father's tyranny by penning a breakout letter destined for a presumptive suitor. When the bocher not only declines to post the missive for her but takes away her paper, Taube disguises herself as her father and escapes. The bocher, for his part, is plotting his own flight: focused on purloining the magic ring, he conscripts a vagrant to murder the rabbi. Fatefully, the coconspirator mistakes the masquerading Taube for her father on her return and inadvertently kills her. The young man's initial celebration yields to fury when he realizes the error. Both the bocher and his accomplice take flight before the rabbi returns. He likewise confuses his daughter's corpse, still costumed as him and now propped at his desk, with someone else: his shadow. He celebrates by dancing circles around the presumed shadow and leaves the scene reverentially (HGW 6:60–66). The pantomime ends as it began: with a lone figure "immersed in the holy book," consumed by assiduous textual study, it would seem. "The mute reader" alone is left to close the pantomimic circle (HGW 6:66).

Hofmannsthal's *The Student*, though long overlooked, encapsulates a number of concerns that occupied Hofmannsthal—and Viennese modernists at large—from the early 1890s well into the twentieth century: a focus on the body, criticism of language, and questions of identity. The bodies of the rabbi and the bocher that Hofmannsthal stages perpetuate quite explicitly the racist typecasting of Jews.[52] The rabbi is the clichéd lame but learned figure. He sits at his desk, poring over his books, and gesticulates in a fashion that stereotypically accompanies Yiddish speech. When he rises, he can only limp along with the help of a walking stick. The bocher is perhaps not enfeebled but is rebuffed by Taube for his homeliness. Taube, for her part, is a physical convention of womanhood: the femme fatale, her body the object of male desire. Two characters in the pantomime undergo physical transformations. The rabbi's triumphant shadow dance, a metamorphosis from lame scholar to celebratory magician, signifies liberation from a body explicitly coded as Jewish.[53] For Taube, too, emancipation from her existence as a female object of desire is achieved only by a transformation. Unlike her father, she ends not as an animated shadow but as a lifeless corpse—a figure redolent with symbolism, as we saw in chapter 2. The bocher is the mirror in both cases, reflecting back to the audience the shortcomings of the body as well as the failures of language. Two of his despairing exclamations encapsulate the play's cynical message. Rebuffed by Taube, he laments: "my whole body a disgrace and a mockery!" (HGW 6:61). When he fails to discern the textual consonance his mentor sees, the bocher realizes with consternation that all of the texts he studies "are dead to the heart, nourish only the brain" (HGW 6:59). The titular student's two assertions stage the discontent with language but far more allow Hofmannsthal "to tell a story that is in the end about bodies attempting to remove themselves from the racist pantomime that is Vienna, 1901. The acts of exorcism and futile escape in *Der Schüler* represent the laughable attempts of stock types to escape the tainted pantomime by discarding their very typehood."[54] What Gillman calls an "allegory of failed acculturation"[55] can only end with the curtain falling on the pantomime, predictably, over the daughter's dead body, mistaken for a shadow.

As Abigail Gillman explains, pantomime—a "liminal form" between stage acting and dance, poetry and drama—is uniquely suited to critical modernist interrogations of identity. Because the genre not only thematizes but also stages the unsayable, it enables the writer to grapple with even the most sensitive of subjects—in Hofmannsthal's case, narratives of cultural, ethnic, and religious identity—with a measure of critical distance. Such questions of belonging can then, in an ideal case, be engaged with consciously through artistic production.[56] Hofmannsthal does this, Gillman convincingly shows, by wedding the "old" Italian pantomimic form, the commedia dell'arte (referenced in the piece's epigraph: "Scaramuccio non parla, et dice gran cose" [Scaramouche does not speak, and says much]), with Germanic intertexts (ranging from Goethe's *Faust* to the golem legend) and, in the pantomime's original version (subsequently retracted by Hofmannsthal), with explicitly Jewish characters. This generic, thematic, and characterological juxtaposition encapsulates Hofmannsthal's own Jewish-Romanic-German/Austrian heritage.[57] In doing so, Gillman argues, Hofmannsthal's pantomime escapes a merely nihilistic reading premised on the racial politics of the Jewish body, for "in turn-of-the-century Vienna, no body was as discursively predetermined as the Jewish body."[58]

A decade after *The Student*, Hofmannsthal's essay "On Pantomime" (Über die Pantomime, 1911) gave theoretical voice to the genre at the time of his most intensive engagement with it. The essay is a formal meditation on the second-century CE text *On the Dance* (De Saltatione) by Lucian of Samosata, an Assyrian satirist and rhetorician, who attempted perhaps for the first time in the history of Western theater to lay out the corporeal and psychological capacities necessary for successful stage performers. Close study of the ancient pantomimic form, according to Hofmannsthal, would offer contemporary theater "a new revival" (HGW 8:502). As in the essays considered previously, Hofmannsthal again questions here whether language is capable of expressing the innermost stirrings of the soul. He contrasts it with body language, positing that the physical body is a more immediate and personal vehicle for expression than words: "The language of words is seemingly individual, in truth generic; [the language] of the body [is] seemingly general, in truth highly personal. The body also does not speak to the body, but the human whole [*das menschliche Ganze*] to the whole" (HGW 8:505).

Hofmannsthal notes the similarities between dance and pantomime and asserts that the two forms share a common expressive basis: gesture, expressed through the body as a rhythmic repetition of physical movements.[59] In contrast to text-based theater, pantomime and dance supply the possibility "to summarize a state of mind in a position [*Haltung*], a rhythmic repetition of movements; therein to express a relation to surrounding people more compressed and more meaningfully than language is capable of; to bring something to light that is too great, too general, too close to be captured in words" (HGW 8:502). Mentioning the dancer Ruth St. Denis and the actress Eleonora Duse in the same breath, Hofmannsthal views the two as belonging to the same category of performer, one possessing the utmost control over the body and capable of expressing the soul beyond words. When we watch a dance or pantomime performance, Hofmannsthal observes, we are aware that the performer "is a human being like us, who moves before our eyes, but freer than we can ever move, and yet the purity and freedom of his gestures says the same thing that we want to say when we, inhibited and quivering, set free [*entladen*] inner fullness" (HGW 8:505). In short, we recognize ourselves, our impulse to express ourselves, in the performers' gestures and are compelled to acknowledge that our conventional modes of expression, language foremost, do not free us but restrict us. Arguing for the primacy of body language, Hofmannsthal compares gesture to words and music at the close of the essay: "But is it only the freedom of the body that buoys us here? Does the soul not reveal itself in a distinctive way here? Does it [the soul] not set free inner fullness here as in sound, but more immediate, more compressed? Words give rise to a keener sympathy, but it is, by the same turn, transmitted, spiritualized [*vergeistigt*], generalized; music [gives rise to] a more intense [sympathy], but it is blunted, yearningly digressive; [the sympathy] called forth by gestures is clearly condensed, present, uplifting [*beglükkend*]" (HGW 8:505).

Hofmannsthal's belief in the potential of physical expressivity of pantomime and dance to overcome the restrictions of language persisted for decades. In this belief, Hofmannsthal was not unique but far more representative of a broad current within Viennese modernism that extended well into the interwar years. This current forms a kind of counternarrative to the well-established psychical turn. In 1925, longtime collaborators and three of the primary players behind the Salzburg Festival[60]—Hofmannsthal, Max Reinhardt, and Richard Strauss—founded the International Pantomime Society (Internationale Pantomimen-Gesellschaft). Though the society was short-lived, lasting little over one year, until the spring of 1926, its founding made the international news.[61] The society's very existence demonstrates just how seriously pantomime was regarded as an artistic form, and this well after the heady Cabaret Fledermaus years in the first decade of the century. While Beer-Hofmann, Schnitzler, Mell, and Bahr all more or less flirted with pantomime, to varying degrees of success and seriousness, Hofmannsthal consistently engaged with the genre and allowed it to reciprocally influence his works for dance—and later silent film. His most intensive creative phase in both genres occurred in the decade between 1910 and 1920 and was sparked by a figure who inspired so many artists of fin-de-siècle Vienna: the dancer Grete Wiesenthal, whose efforts to create a uniquely Viennese form of modern dance we will encounter later in this chapter. Before turning to Wiesenthal and her dance, though, the question of how bodies in motion—in free dance as in pantomime—served as vehicles for exploring questions of identity bears further investigation.

SELF AND OTHER: EXPLORING IDENTITY THROUGH FREE DANCE

Around 1900, at the same time that the dramatic changes associated with literary and theatrical modernism were occurring, the classical aesthetics of dance also underwent thorough reevaluation. Much like the first modernist stirrings in literature, theater, and the visual arts, a radical break with the traditional aesthetic paradigms of classical ballet took place in the final decade of the nineteenth century and the first years of the twentieth century.[62] The beginnings of this so-called free dance in Europe are associated with the reforms of the American modern dance pioneers Loïe Fuller (1862–1928), Isadora Duncan (1877–1927), and Ruth St. Denis (1879–1968) in the 1890s. These women sparked the European developments in dance that occurred somewhat later, in the first decade of the twentieth century.[63] Free dance, however, as received and imagined both in practical and fictional form by Viennese authors such as Hofmannsthal and Vicki Baum served a similar function as pantomime. It was an ideal genre in which to work out questions and ambivalences about identity because it represented a kind of a safe space, a genre in which bodies, as the name implies, were seen as potentially free from their socioculturally determined conventions—whether racial or gestural. Like pantomime, free dance seemed to offer the potential for liberation, even if that liberation—as we saw in the case of Hofmannsthal's *The Student*—is fraught with contradiction. Vicki Baum's short story "The Boy and the Dancer" (Der Knabe und die Tänzerin, 1921) is a yet more explicit articulation of the complexities of identity expressed through dance.

In a letter to Carl J. Burckhardt from 1928, Hofmannsthal outlined his plans for a new comedic drama (which would remain unfinished), in which the main character, a notorious liar, decides to become a dancer and says he chose this profession "because he worships the truth, and dancing is the only profession that contains *only truth*."[64] Hofmannsthal's notion of the dancer as the embodiment of personal freedom and truthful, unmediated expression from the soul overlaps with conceptions that free dancers, such as Fuller and Duncan, had of their own art. In a note from 1911, under the keyword "Inhibition," Hofmannsthal wrote: "Dance frees [you] buoyantly [*Der Tanz macht beglückend frei*]. Unveils freedom, identity. The living person is inhibited compared to the dancer. In contrast the bliss of uninhibited togetherness" (HGW 10:508). Here, as well as elsewhere in Hofmannsthal's work, the dancer is contrasted with a repressed figure, held back by self-consciousness and incapable of free expression. The dancer, by comparison, is idealized, capable of direct physical expression of the self through a dance that at once frees and reveals the bliss that stems from unity with oneself and others.

This conception of the dancer maps neatly onto free dance, which by definition is characterized by "natural" movements, originating in the soul and expressed through movements from the dancer's midsection. From the torso, the motion radiates outward to the extremities in a flowing fashion.[65] Among the modern dancers, two in particular captured Hofmannsthal's imagination: the Viennese dancer Grete Wiesenthal, with whom he would embark on a long, productive artistic collaboration; and, before Wiesenthal, the American Ruth St. Denis. Several years passed between the presence of Fuller, Duncan, and St. Denis on European stages and the emergence of a homegrown Viennese free dance movement. When it did emerge, around 1907, it was largely the work of the Wiesenthal sisters, Grete, Elsa, and Berta—whose uniquely Viennese form of free dance we will encounter in greater detail in the following section.[66]

Ruth Dennis, who called herself Ruth St. Denis, began her career starring in vaudeville productions and musical comedies before turning her attention to free dance. In October 1906, she embarked on her first European tour, which took her to London and Paris, and later to Berlin, Weimar, and Vienna. Hofmannsthal saw St. Denis perform for the first time in early November 1906 on the stage of Max Reinhardt's Kleines Theater in Berlin. With Reinhardt's encouragement, Hofmannsthal adapted the story of Salome into a dance piece with St. Denis in mind. Though Hofmannsthal abandoned the project not long thereafter, St. Denis remained an acquaintance and inspiration, the two having met when St. Denis's tour came to Vienna in January and February 1907.[67] Hofmannsthal's essay about St. Denis, "The Incomparable Dancer" (Die unvergleichliche Tänzerin), appeared in the Viennese newspaper *Die Zeit* on November 25, 1906, shortly after he had seen her perform in Berlin.[68]

The opening of Hofmannsthal's essay shows him convinced of the modernity of St. Denis's art. The dancer and her dances are the "child[ren]

Fig. 35. Ruth St. Denis in *Radha*, 1906. Photographer unknown. Jerome Robbins Dance Division, Denishawn Collection, The New York Public Library. New York Public Library Digital Collections.

of this moment," Hofmannsthal writes, "infused to the utmost with the aroma" of the singular present. He does not believe her dances could possibly have been born of "a less refined, less complex time than ours," even ten short years prior (HGW 8:496–97). The particular currency of these dances is their nonmimetic nature: instead of attempting to faithfully recreate Indian temple rituals, for example, St. Denis *embodies* the goddess Radha, Hofmannsthal argues, dancing from an "inner spiritual imperative" (HGW 8:498).[69] When St. Denis begins to dance, her movements give the impression of wholeness. Hofmannsthal remarks on the effortless, sensual, "intoxicating" flow and authenticity of her gestures. Composed not of individual positions but of a continuum of gestures that build upon one another, St. Denis's dance evokes a naturalness that stands in stark contrast to the conventions, poses, and forced artistry of classical ballet, though it is no less exactingly physical (HGW 8:499). By renouncing language and employing the gestural expressiveness of the human body, dance conveys experience in a seemingly more direct, unmediated manner. St. Denis had mastered this credo, culminating in what Hofmannsthal called a "rigorous, almost dismissive immediacy" that obviates any commentary (HGW 8:501). Immediacy of expression and unity of body and soul are the central convictions at the heart of Hofmannsthal's aesthetics of gesture. St. Denis's performance, Hofmannsthal realized, was dance for dance's sake: "[the] dance, [the] dance in itself, the mute music of the human body" (HGW 8:499). The sheer power of her gestures—silent, yet supremely expressive—is reminiscent of the great Italian actress he so admired, Eleonora Duse, whose stagecraft he had praised more than a decade prior.

Around the same time that Hofmannsthal's acquaintance with St. Denis was intensifying, and just after having met the Viennese dancer Grete Wiesenthal, he published an essay simply titled "Fear" (Furcht, 1907).[70] It thematizes the possibility of expressing lived experience authentically through dance, and Hofmannsthal chose the form of a fictional historical dialogue between two dancers, Hymnis and Laidion. Both are hetaera, educated courtesans and classical dancers in ancient Greece, whose mindsets regarding their shared occupation are at variance. What Gabriele Brandstetter characterizes as an "impaired dialogue" between Hymnis and Laidion is conducted largely in antithetical statements that highlight the irreconcilability of their opposing opinions.[71] While Hymnis takes pleasure in performing traditional dances, Laidion dreams of casting off the fetters of classical dance for an idealized, archaic dance, like that of island women she has heard about from a sailor.[72] The islanders' dance is an annual, communal fertility ritual, in which "their bodies are as one body" (HGW 7:575). Laidion senses that the dance she has only ever heard of is more authentic, closer to the gods and nature, than the nightly dances she and Hymnis perform. Laidion imagines these islanders, whom Hymnis calls "barbarian women" (*Barbarenweiber*), as transcendently, "unspeakably happy" in their dance (HGW 7:577). Pressing Hymnis to reflect on the motivations for their own performance, the skeptic Laidion raises some difficult questions: "Are you running away from yourself? You are hiding:

hiding from the eternal, restless longing in yourself? You ape the gestures of animals and trees: do you become one with them? You strip off your clothes. Do you also strip off your fear?" (HGW 7:574–75). Laidion asserts that it is fear that governs their own nightly dances, making them into nothing more than marionette-like figures steered by a force beyond their control (HGW 7:577).

The titular fear of which Laidion speaks stems from the realization that the traditional dances she and Hymnis perform require the performers to mask their true selves. The mimetic nature of their performances has left Laidion feeling alienated by the false identity in which she must cloak herself. Her body and her soul are not one, and she envisions the islanders' fearless dance as the obverse of the classical dances she performs (HGW 7:575). Laidion imagines, "Everything, the fearing, the yearning, all choice, all insatiable disquiet, everything has been transformed on the border of their body. . . . Everything is unutterable to them" (HGW 7:578). At such cathartic moments when language fails, there is nothing left to do but dance.[73] Laidion ultimately finds herself in the same position, bereft of words, and she can express her experience genuinely only by dancing. Forgetting herself, imagining herself united in thought with the island women she describes, Laidion begins to move, rhythmically, in an oneiric, almost trancelike, amimetic dance, one both of unity and individuality, which continues until she nearly collapses (HGW 7:579).

Laidion's dream of the islanders' dance without fear parallels, not without coincidence, the aims of dancers like Isadora Duncan and Ruth St. Denis, who sought to create a new kind of dance that diverged markedly from the norms and traditions of classical dance forms. Hofmannsthal had, after all, been not only watching these dancers perform but also writing straightforwardly theoretical texts about them. Yet when Hofmannsthal has Laidion raise the issue of identity and masking in dance, he perhaps unwittingly foresaw a problem that would later come to occupy the minds of interwar Viennese writers such as Vicki Baum.

Born Hedwig Baum in Vienna, Vicki Baum (1888–1960) never strove for a career as an author, yet she became one of her era's global best sellers. She trained as a harpist, moved to Germany, and pursued a successful musical career before turning her attention fully to writing. Baum returned again and again to dance in her fiction. There is, of course, the iconic, past-her-prime ballerina Grushinskaya, later immortalized on the screen by Greta Garbo, in Baum's most famous novel *Grand Hotel* (Menschen im Hotel, 1929), the book that secured her reputation.[74] But Baum's third novel, *The Dances of Ina Raffay* (Die Tänze der Ina Raffay), is devoted entirely to the life of a young Viennese dancer who feels drawn away from her schooling in classical ballet and toward free dance and *Ausdruckstanz*. Published by Ullstein in 1921, it paved the way for Baum's commercial success. The theme paralleled that of her contemporary, the painter and writer Albert Paris Gütersloh (1887–1973). Gütersloh, likely paying homage to Ruth St. Denis, whom Hofmannsthal had exalted in his reviews, gives the protagonist of his early expressionist novel *The Dancing Fool* (Die tanzende Törin, 1913) the name Ruth.[75]

"The Boy and the Dancer," a short story from Baum's early collection *Castle Theater* (Schloßtheater, 1921),[76] is of particular interest in the context of our analysis for three reasons. First, it salutes the kind of free dance brought to European stages around the fin de siècle by artists such as Ruth St. Denis, who so captivated the Viennese cultural elite. Second, significantly, it presents the male Jewish body not as a discursively predetermined anti-ideal—as in Hofmannsthal's pantomime *The Student*—but as a paragon of physical beauty. And third, it nevertheless objectifies and exoticizes the body of the cultural Other in a fashion similar to the human displays described in chapter 1.

The story centers on a fictional Australian free dancer, Iszaïl, who arrives with her entourage to great fanfare in an unnamed European city for a series of performances. Her ritual sword dance around a sacrificial fire, like St. Denis's *Radha* that Hofmannsthal commented on so admiringly, was informed by ceremonies of the Indian subcontinent. Like Gütersloh, Baum surely modeled her protagonist on St. Denis. Iszaïl's performance, executed nude, ends in the dancer's staged suicide. Real deaths, however, have haunted her tour. All but one of the eight Indian extras she hired—"these cursed Indians" (119), as she disparagingly terms them—have succumbed to consumption brought on by susceptibility to the unaccustomed European climate. A theater employee is dispatched to find a local replacement to perform as an Indian in brownface. The ideal substitute must conform to Madame Iszaïl's exacting physical requirements: "a boy, slender, slim, with joints the likes of which hardly any European prince possesses, and with unspoiled [*unverbildeten*] feet" (119–20). It is clear, on the basis of the podiatric demands, that the candidate should not be a classically trained ballet dancer; his feet should be natural, undistorted by the physical demands of the danse d'école. Iszaïl's emissary spends a "breathless night" searching the city's cafés, sports clubs, bars, and the streets of the outer districts and Jewish quarter. The next morning, he proudly presents his candidates to Madame in a lineup. Commanding each to strip naked for her evaluating eyes, she is initially dismayed with what she sees. Two rowers are assessed as "healthy, sinewy"; an artist, though uninhibited in his "apathetic and habitual" disrobing, has arms and thighs "unattractively thickened by musculature"; and the most notable feature of two "gaunt" working-class youths are their "money-hungry, shameless eyes." None of the candidates will do. Madame deems them "Very ugly! Very common!"—and utterly unsuited to a nude stage performance (120–21).

The final candidate, however, elicits an entirely different reaction. He undresses and, teary-eyed, lips quivering and hands trembling, encounters a series of rapid-fire questions from Madame Iszaïl: "What is your name? How old are you? Where are you from that you have the body of a god?" (121). She removes her gloves and traces the contours of his body as he answers in a whisper: Raffael Halevy; sixteen; descended from Spanish Jews. Iszaïl, captivated, hires him on the spot. In narrating the master free dancer's positive selection of Raffael on the basis of his physical traits, Baum seems to turn the tables on stereotypically negative representations of Jewish masculinity.[77] Here, the Jewish male body is presented as the quintessence of physical beauty. Raffael's well-developed, limber-jointed, elegant, and ultimately "unspoiled" physis embodies the counterimage of the anti-Semitic corporeal markers typically ascribed to eastern European Jews that Sander L. Gilman has analyzed in depth.[78] Yet Raffael's Jewish body is, like those of the Indians he is to replace and dance alongside, also the object of an exoticizing, objectifying gaze.[79] Raffael, the Sephardic Other, is fascinating to Madame Iszaïl precisely for his difference *within* Jewish difference.

Iszaïl's engagement in the anonymous city lasts for thirteen evenings. On each of those thirteen evenings, Raffael performs alongside her; on each of the thirteen evenings, she takes him home with her and seduces him. Intuiting the impossibility of returning to his old life, he implores the dancer on the last night to make him a permanent member of the traveling company, saying he will die if forced to remain behind. Iszaïl's response presages the story's outcome: "You will die if I take you with me, you child," she says with a dark laugh. "Then you'll die like all of my Indians . . ." (124). Fast-forward to the final performance: Iszaïl's sword dance ends, as each preceding night to passionate applause, in her staged suicide. This final performance, however, harbors a crucial difference: Raffael, whose part was merely to hold Iszaïl's sword, collapses dead alongside her, he in a pool of very real blood. Raffael's onstage suicide follows from his glimpse of a freedom that would remain elusive with Iszaïl's cold refusal. Her inability to perceive Raffael as an individual, her insistent Othering—even if the status of the Other is merely displaced from the Jew onto, or in this case literally fused with, a yet more "exotic" cultural Other through brownface—signals that even Jewish "passing" is ultimately futile. Indeed, Gilman has definitively shown that, by the mid-nineteenth century, the burgeoning discipline of anthropology had, in its study of racial types, conflated blackness and Jewishness.[80] Raffael, having futilely glimpsed another possible lifeworld and cognizant finally of his inability to break Iszaïl's racist frame of reference, sees no way out, save for taking his own life. The cynical message Baum's story advances is that you can take the boy out of the ghetto, but—as far as the prejudicial *Leitkultur* is concerned—you cannot take the ghetto out of the boy. Showing, perhaps, the limits of Hofmannsthal's idealization of body language, "The Boy and the Dancer" stages Raffael as the corporeal ideal yet still subject to a discourse beyond the body.

While, as Lisa Silverman has noted, Jewish women are conspicuously absent in Baum's interwar works, two earlier stories—"In the Old House" (Im alten Haus, 1910) and "Rafael Gutmann" (1911)—depict quite plainly the struggle of European Jews, both women and men, attempting but ultimately failing to escape a ghetto milieu Baum describes in clichéd terms.[81] Right down to the given name, the figure of the innocent youth-turned-artist in Baum's earlier story prefigures Raffael Halevy in "The Boy and the Dancer." The titular protagonist in "Rafael Gutmann," an aspiring young singer from an eastern European, Orthodox Jewish family, sets his sights on a career in the rarefied world of German opera.[82] The dilemma in "The Boy and the Dancer" is similar, yet with a more heterogeneous set of cultural and racial codes. Recruited, perhaps unwittingly, to the stage, Raffael finds in free dance a wholly "new world" (122), a lush dreamscape that stands in stark contrast to his ghetto origins. The reality of his life in the city's Jewish quarter is one of destitution, hunger, and hardship—and rife with negative stereotypes of Ashkenazic Jewish life in western and central Europe. As described by the story's narrator, the ghetto is a dank, "dirty Jewish street [*Judengasse*]," lined with secondhand textile shops and suffused with the acrid smell of onions. More striking is the cast of stock figures who populate the quarter: wig-clad, "scolding, yellow women"; wailing children; a "mother with hungry eyes," who pickpockets from her own son; a "sickly brother"; a rag-picking father with a persistent cough (124). Baum, herself a Jewish writer, serves up the full panoply of anti-Semitic representations of eastern European Jews. She brands her ghetto figures with stereotypical markers of Jewish "difference"—disease, infirmity, and indigence—that would have been readily legible to any reader in 1921, given the pervasiveness of such imagery in popular culture.[83] Yet she consciously frames the young dancer Raffael Halevy as the physical antithesis to these, his relatives. He, by contrast, can pass: his ethnic identity is undetectable, his Jewishness invisible.[84]

What are we to make of the conflicting messages and seemingly incompatible identities—Ashkenazic, Sephardic, Indian—Baum inscribes on to her characters' bodies in "The Boy and the Dancer"? On the one hand, the narrative presents the Jewish male body as a sexually desirable paragon of beauty.[85] The story also appears to widen the frame of typical cultural representations of Jewish life in Europe by making one of the title characters Sephardic.[86] On the other hand, these notable shifts take place at the expense of two other groups: eastern European Jews and South Asians. Here, conventional rhetoric about Jewish "difference" is simultaneously upheld in the anti-Semitic depiction of ghetto residents and displaced onto, in fact replicated in, the representation of a different cultural Other, the Indian male. Like the eastern European Jews who live in the ghetto, the Indians are caricatured as physically weak, sickly, and fundamentally unable to assimilate to a European climate. The story's triple Othering is striking: Raffael Halevy, the other Jewish Other, whose twofold difference is initially invisible to Madame Iszaïl, is pressed into masquerading as the Other—a different Other—through brownface in the free dance. The brownface performance in effect merges Raffael's actual Jewish body with the imagined body of the Indian. Absent any culturally sanctioned sense of self, Raffael Halevy is forced to literally embody the Other by performing in brownface. The contradictory simultaneous presence and absence of the Jewish body in Baum's story predated Hugo Bettauer's nearly contemporaneous *The City without Jews* (Die Stadt ohne Juden, 1922), a chillingly prophetic novel of Vienna's anti-Semitism and expulsion of its Jewish residents.[87] Baum's story indicates that, as Gilman has pointedly asserted, "one cannot hide from the lessons of race."[88] Constructed difference is inescapable, for racism and representation always go hand in hand. Thus, in the context of the narrative, the invisibility of Raffael's Jewish difference is inadmissible; his Otherness needs to be rendered visible. The uncomfortable copresence of Jewish anti-Semitism and European orientalist cultural imperialism in Baum's story demonstrates the tenaciousness of Otherness, the impossibility of being regarded as an individual.

The problem outlined here is not merely a racial one; it is also a question of gender and class. Might Baum be attempting, as David A. Brenner and Lisa Silverman propose with regard to her other works, to navigate her own doubly, even triply, disadvantaged sociocultural status as an Ashkenazic Jewish woman of modest origins by laying out a narrative of striving, acculturation, and escape parallel to her own?[89] If so, then the struggle for sociocultural transformation and legitimization is one, "The Boy and the Dancer" suggests, that is bound to fail. Even if one possesses, like Raffael Halevy, the "body of a god," there is no escaping one's roots—let alone the rampant racism of Austrian (and German, European) culture in the long fin de siècle. And racism always requires an Other, legible as such. This is why Raffael is forced to perform in brownface. In an ironic twist, one of which Baum herself seems unaware, her fiction modeled for readers the admissibility of constructing narratives of self-empowerment (in this case, the Jewish body as physical ideal) by "graft[ing] negative self-images onto a perceived 'Other.'"[90] In Baum's story—and in the human displays detailed in chapter 1—it is an Other perceived, whether consciously or not, as sufficiently foreign and distant to absorb the force of the sublimated prejudice Jews and women confronted daily, and clearly not just in Vienna. As we witnessed with Hofmannsthal's pantomime *The Student* and here with Baum's fictional story about free dance, the staging of the wordless body in motion opened up a safe space in which to explore the most vexed questions about Austrian identity, though, crucially, at the expense of others'—and Others'—bodies. In the interim between these two works, professional dancers in Vienna were considering what it meant to be Austrian, as they strove to create a form of free dance that was to be "authentically Viennese."

MAKING MODERN DANCE VIENNESE

Just months before "Fear" appeared in October 1907, Hofmannsthal saw the Viennese dancer Grete Wiesenthal (1885–1970) perform for the first time in Max Mell's pantomime *The Dancer and the Marionette* (Die Tänzerin und die Marionette). The pantomime, which Wiesenthal had choreographed and in which she appeared as the lead, was staged in early June 1907 at a garden party organized by Gustav Klimt, Koloman Moser, and Josef Hoffmann. The gathering was designed to showcase the work of these artists' students at the School of Applied Arts, with its links to the *Wiener Werkstätte*.[91] The real felicitous event, however, was Wiesenthal's public appearance with her new style of free dance, which would ripple through the Viennese cultural scene and influence many of its leading figures.

Grete Wiesenthal was trained in classical ballet and was a soloist with the Viennese Imperial Opera Ballet (Hofopernballett), the pinnacle of any prima ballerina's career. But frictions between Wiesenthal and the ballet master, Josef Haßreiter, over stylistic matters led her and her sister Elsa to leave the corps de ballet in May 1907. The subsequent experiments with free dance carried out by Grete, together with her sisters Elsa and Berta, would make "the Wiesenthals" a household name. As Grete Wiesenthal reflected in her autobiography, a large part of her dissatisfaction with classical ballet stemmed from what she perceived as a lack of soulful unity between dance and music. She felt that the lifeless, drill-like precision of ballet steps was in the best case merely an accompaniment to the music; in the worst case the two domains lacked correspondence entirely.[92] What it was surely not: a deeply felt and directly danced expression of the music. "No one knew anything about the growing together of music and movement," she remembers thinking. As her cognizance of the disconnect grew, so too did her desire to create a more "truthful" form of dance. While still in the opera company, she recalls consciously measuring her imagined dance against the classical ballet and learning "how one should *not* do it."[93] In her lecture "Dance and Pantomime" (Tanz und Pantomime), Wiesenthal detailed her conception of a new kind of free dance as originating in a finer understanding of music and centered on the idea that the dancer's movements should be an organic physical extension and manifestation of sound.[94]

On January 14, 1908, Grete, Elsa, and their younger sister Berta made their solo debut, rehearsing self-choreographed pieces before an esteemed audience at the Cabaret Fledermaus. Hugo von Hofmannsthal, Richard Beer-Hofmann, Max Mell, Josef Hoffmann, Gustav Klimt, Koloman Moser, Otto Wagner, and even the famed American dancer Ruth St. Denis were among the invited circle of illustrious guests at the rehearsal.[95] The small variety theater had opened just months before and had quickly become one of Vienna's premier creative wellsprings.[96] This performance would be the Wiesenthal sisters' watershed and would catapult Grete, in particular, overnight to the forefront of the dance world, both in Vienna and, soon, abroad. Helga Malmberg, later Peter Altenberg's biographer, was in the audience that night, and she describes the small performance space as filled to overflowing. Nearly every member of the Viennese cultural elite had turned out. With the opening bars of music, a Chopin waltz, and from the first graceful motions of the dancers, "[one] sensed immediately that something completely new was being tried here: a spiritual-rapturous naturalness of dancing. Any reliance on the ballet's artistic routine was avoided. Nevertheless, one saw that the young artists had supple and powerful [*leistungsfähige*] bodies. Nothing was reminiscent of dilettantism. There were no artificial poses whatsoever; everything was dissolved in motion."[97] After a two-hour-long program, group dances interspersed with two solo numbers by Elsa and three by Grete, it was clear that a new star had been born. The audience's enthusiasm was unprecedented, and from that evening on, Johannesgasse, the side street of Kärntner Straße where the cabaret's entrance was located, was jammed with waiting carriages. Every seat and standing room spot was taken, filled by the Viennese artistic glitterati, students, and white-collar workers: everyone wanted to say they had seen the Wiesenthals dance.[98] In short, Malmberg recalls, "the Wiesenthals had triumphed, they had danced their way into the hearts of the Viennese."[99] The Viennese St. Denis was born.

The Cabaret Fledermaus has been called a Gesamtkunstwerk of the *Wiener Werkstätte*, owing to the comprehensiveness of its aesthetic realization.[100] In this basement cabaret, architecture, interior design, and stagecraft functioned as a single unit. Its tiny stage quickly became synonymous with the diversity of Viennese modernism in all its guises: prose declamation, avant-garde theater, musical recitals, and modern dance came together in the variety theater tradition. The "small-art stage" (*Kleinkunstbühne*) did not merely reflect the political and intellectual climate of its cultural context.[101] Far more, it was a crucial site where, as Elana Shapira has pointed out, questions of identity—both of Jewish identity and of womanhood—could be negotiated via the staging of the body.[102] It was the support of modern dance by key financial and artistic benefactors, including the industrialist and arts patron Fritz Waerndorfer, that, Shapira argues, allowed cultural insiders, many of them Jews, to enact a "fantasy of male bodily reclamation," one staged, not coincidentally, by female performers such as Wiesenthal.[103] Whereas female avant-garde dancers often bared their bodies onstage, mobilizing their nudity as a programmatic statement of feminist liberation at the fin de siècle, male Jewish patrons such as Waerndorfer and writers such as Peter Altenberg served more traditionally as financial and intellectual underwriters of modernist cultural creation. They deployed their names and cachet to support female performers, thereby vicariously fashioning a space of belonging for themselves in a sociocultural sphere as anti-Semitic as it was innovative. (These were, after all, the later years of Karl Lueger's mayorship [1897–1910].) Both the dancers and the patrons sought to position themselves not only as "modern" but as specifically "Viennese." These two terms took on special meaning in Wiesenthal's efforts to position herself within the world of dance.

The particularly Viennese qualities of Wiesenthal's free dance style are a recurring theme throughout contemporary reviews of the dancer's performances and technique. Hugo von Hofmannsthal, for example, remarked that the Viennese were eager to claim her dancing as their own. It seemed to them a kind of national treasure, "our very own possession." Characterized by "a *Heimat*-like quality [*das Heimatliche*]" and a kind of "folkish [*volkshafte*] mystery," there was, Hofmannsthal remarked unironically, "nothing foreign" about Wiesenthal's dances.[104] What commentators identify as specifically Viennese are above all Wiesenthal's symbolism of the natural world, which links her to the Viennese fine and applied arts of Jugendstil, and her musical sensibility, drawing on Austrian composers such as Schubert and Strauss. Homegrown points of reference, it seemed, allowed for a sense of "authenticity" that sidestepped the relational questions raised by the orientalism of, for example, Ruth St. Denis's dances.

Wiesenthal's style of free dance was a coalescence of music and movement inspired by that quintessentially Viennese nineteenth-century musical form and social dance: the waltz. The three-quarter-time composition of Johann Strauss the Younger's "On the Beautiful Blue Danube" (An der schönen blauen Donau) is the unofficial Austrian national anthem, and the exhilarating, liberating rhythmic circling of dance partners gliding across the parquet is a popular paragon of Vienna to this day. Anton Kuh, the sharp-tongued Viennese journalist and essayist, saw the waltz,

Fig. 36. Grete Wiesenthal in *Donauwalzer*, demonstrating horizontal extension, ca. 1907. Photograph by Rudolf Jobst, Vienna. Genthe photograph collection, Library of Congress, Prints and Photographs Division

not uncritically, as the consummate encapsulation of the Viennese "persuasion [*Gesinnung*]."[105] A scandalous, revolutionary dance in its origination,[106] the Viennese waltz was adapted by Wiesenthal as the basis for a new, natural musicality of flowing physical movement.[107] Wiesenthal saw her dance as the embodiment—and logical, modern evolution—of a specifically Viennese form. The waltz as a "work of dance art [*Tanzkunstwerk*]" was, in her view, Austria's primary contribution to world culture.[108] Writers such as Oscar Bie, the German art historian and dance critic, concurred. Wiesenthal's movement was "a breath of Vienna" because she "gave . . . waltzes a body"[109]—in essence by imparting soulful content to an otherwise decorative, if socially radical, form.

Wiesenthal also looked beyond music to the natural world, gathering inspiration from the movement of the elements, plants, and animals. Her choreography in *The Wind* (Der Wind, 1910) demonstrates this, even earning her the name "bride of the wind."[110] By carefully studying nature and then "rhythmizing" it, Wiesenthal's dance was a kindred spirit to Klimt's paintings.[111] Both artist and dancer share a common bond, Bie recognized: the predisposition of Jugendstil to look to nature for inspiration and then stylize its patterns to decorative effect. In this way, Wiesenthal's dance was identifiable as the newest iteration of a long Viennese aesthetic tradition. She represented, Bie reasoned, "the decorative instincts that laid in Vienna's buildings and people, plays and arts, from back in the age of the margravate to the Secession." Yet Wiesenthal's dance was not merely ornamental and static; it was applied and dynamic. It "liberated motion from Minne, Mackintosh, and Moser."[112] With new choreography to a Viennese musical form, and taking its cues from the Austrian landscape and the Secession's homegrown Jugendstil tradition, Wiesenthal's dance was deemed a specifically Viennese incarnation of modern dance.

When the Wiesenthal sisters performed abroad in Berlin—a staging made possible by their connection to the network around Hofmannsthal and Reinhardt—reviewers there remarked on the sisters as the embodiment of Viennese culture. The art historian Max Lehrs, for example, singled out the naturalness and simplicity of the Wiesenthals' dance, which seemed to provide a direct bodily conduit for the expression of the soul. Such choreography was bound to be misunderstood in Berlin, that "city of pure reason."[113] Vienna, by contrast, was imagined as closer to the natural and the intuitive, the home of the "sensual-instinctual," the "unconscious," the "improvisational." "All of that is to a certain extent native to the specifically Austrian expression of art [*Kunstäußerung*]," commented the Viennese critic and musicologist Alfred Rosenzweig.[114]

Fig. 37. Grete Wiesenthal in *The Wind.* Oskar Bie and Erwin Lang, *Grete Wiesenthal* (Berlin: Erich Riess, 1910), n.p. Woodcut by Erwin Lang.

Wiesenthal represented the essence of Vienna in a new style of free dance, filling each gesture with "a world of physicality [*Körperlichkeit*]."[115]

That physicality was manifest in a technique Wiesenthal dubbed "spherical dance" (*sphärischer Tanz*). Contemporary photographs depict the dancer in flowing dresses, a veritable dervish of circular motion. The momentum and seemingly antigravitational quality of the leaps and spins, the spatial physicality and powerfully expressive motions of Wiesenthal's dancing, her swirling circles, were not only revolutions in the literal sense but also revolutionary contributions to free dance in Vienna. And it is the adapted waltz's concentric circles of Wiesenthal's dance that most captured critics' imaginations at the turn of the century.[116] In his book *The Modern Dance* (Der moderne Tanz, 1921), Hans Brandenburg, a leading contemporary dance critic, provided a description of Wiesenthal's dancing: "One movement follows from another harmonically, and Grete Wiesenthal seems to concentrically draw into herself all circles that live in the space. The circle, the consummate geometric figure—and the one which governs the waltz's choreographic design, be it social dance or artistic dance—is presented here in the most varied form and formally perfect variations."[117] Brandenburg's commentary makes note of the unity between music and motion that Wiesenthal strove for: as the music intensifies, so too does the pace of the dancer's gestures and movements. Moreover, he also describes the unique geometry of her dance, based on the Viennese waltz's perpetual revolutions.

Wiesenthal conceived of the spherical dance in spatial terms along both horizontal and vertical axes. In an undated lecture, Wiesenthal described how her spherical technique required a wholly different sense of physical balance and stability than traditional dance. Spherical dance, she explained, is a series of movements "that poses the greatest challenge to balance, namely: to achieve the most stability possible in the body's greatest possible extension and reach to all sides, in the horizontal, in difficult positions bent backwards." With its wide swinging arm and leg motions, spherical dance presented a marked contrast to classical ballet, in which the pirouetting motions are executed tightly along a primarily vertical axis.[118] Whereas balletic pirouettes strive for an ideal of stability, vertical control, and spatial alignment, "whirling expressionistic dance," as Gabriele Brandstetter calls it, thematizes loss of control and spatial orientation—that is, intoxicating freedom—even while being carefully choreographed, as in Wiesenthal's spherical dance. Spherical dance, according to Brandstetter, reveals the tightly controlled vertical virtuosity of classical ballet to be pure physical effect, empty of soulful content.[119] Many wanted to learn the Wiesenthal technique, and Wiesenthal opened a successful dance school, the School for Artistic Dance and Rhythmic Gymnastics (Schule für künstlerischen Tanz und rhythmische Gymnastik), in Vienna in 1927, before going on to teach in the dance division of the Academy for Music and the Performing Arts in 1934.[120]

Like perhaps no other dancer of her time, Wiesenthal was influential for prominent figures in the Viennese literary circles. Among those she inspired were Peter Altenberg, Oskar Kokoschka, Franz Blei, Alfred Polgar, and Rainer Maria Rilke, to name just a few. It is then unsurprising that she also became not only a good friend of but also an inspiring artistic ally to Hofmannsthal. Driven by a common belief in the greater expressivity of body language over words,[121] the artistic partnership between Wiesenthal and Hofmannsthal began almost immediately after their first meeting and continued with varying intensity for years. For Hofmannsthal, Wiesenthal's dancing became the fulfillment of his artistic quest for an expressive medium beyond language. It was "not word, . . . but more than word, it spoke the intrinsically unutterable, the mysterious formula of individual longing and its fulfillment."[122] It was Wiesenthal who inspired Hofmannsthal to write more sketches for dance and pantomime after the turn of the century, and it was with her as his leading lady that he wrote his first silent film.

Although Wiesenthal was a dancer foremost, the physicality of her performances energized Hofmannsthal to create pantomimes with her in mind. In a letter to Clemens von Franckenstein, Hofmannsthal would later write that he held her "formidable gift for mimic invention" in far higher regard than her "actual gift for dance."[123] Though the author and the dancer had been acquainted since 1907, Wiesenthal had been actively developing her solo career since her departure from the Imperial Opera Ballet. Among her successes was the title role in Reinhardt's *Sumurûn*, which she performed to great acclaim in April 1910 and after in Berlin. Hofmannsthal appears to have been directly influenced by Reinhardt's production, which included dance elements and called to mind the "mixed form" of dance-pantomime with which Hofmannsthal had earlier experimented.[124] He actively recruited Wiesenthal to collaborate that summer, enticing her with ideas for two pantomimes: *Amor and Psyche* (Amor und Psyche, 1910–11) and *The Foreign Girl* (Das fremde Mädchen, 1910–11), the latter of which Hofmannsthal would later realize in film form.[125] The two spent an intensely creative time developing the scenes at Hofmannsthal's summer home in Aussee in August 1911, and both premiered together on September 15, 1911, in Berlin. While working with Wiesenthal, Hofmannsthal also wrote the theoretical text "On Pantomime," which he completed at approximately the same time as the two pantomime libretti, in August and September 1911. After the successes of the performances in Berlin, Hofmannsthal would go on to conceptualize four more dance and pantomime pieces with Wiesenthal in mind.[126]

In the summer of 1911, right around Hofmannsthal's most intensive collaboration with Wiesenthal, Harry Graf Kessler—the writer, diplomat, and great patron of the arts, who had been sending Hofmannsthal regular reports about the dance scene in Paris since 1909 and raving, in particular, about the guest performances of Sergei Diaghilev's *Ballets Russes* (with its star dancers Vaslav Nijinsky and Anna Pavlova)—wrote to Hofmannsthal at Diaghilev's behest. The ballet impresario had requested that Hofmannsthal compose a ballet, with a score by Strauss, in which Nijinsky was to star.[127] Kessler had been trying to broker the connection for two years, urging Hofmannsthal to visit Paris, see the *Ballets Russes* perform, and set to writing. "It is truly a new art that is being born there," Kessler declared.[128] The count suggested *Amor and Psyche* as suitable material, but Hofmannsthal was already in the process of finalizing it as a pantomime with Wiesenthal and so did not pursue it as a ballet libretto. While Hofmannsthal did not go to Paris to see Kessler and meet Diaghilev, he was able to attend the *Ballets Russes*'s Vienna performance in March 1912. Kessler had been right: Hofmannsthal was so inspired by the dancers that he sketched, in rapid succession, the "tragic ballet" *The Furies* (Die Furien, 1912) and *La mort du jeune homme voluptueux* (1912), both of which remained unfinished. *The Legend of Joseph* (Josephslegende), which he had begun around the same time as the two fragments, was ultimately completed for Diaghilev in 1914, after nearly two years of collaboration with Kessler and with a score by Richard Strauss.[129] It premiered in Paris on May 14, 1914—without Nijinsky, who had fallen out with Diaghilev shortly before—and in London one month later. Though the press reacted largely ambivalently shortly before the outbreak of the First World War, the piece was taken up again and performed after the war in 1921 (Berlin and Munich), 1922 (Bern, Vienna, and Prague), and 1924 (Zurich), a fact that attests to its lasting appeal.[130]

The exceptionally fruitful creative partnership between Hofmannsthal and Wiesenthal resulted from kindred ideas about the limits of language and the seemingly unlimited expressive potential of the human body. As Mary Fleischer has noted, the collaboration between the author and the dancer was an attempt to forge, practically, a "hieroglyphics of the body" through a nonmimetic language of the body, gesture, and motion.[131] Wiesenthal's dance style was particularly suited to this task because, as the Viennese journalist Alfred Polgar wrote, "with [Wiesenthal] like no other the body speaks the dance so convincingly as its own essential idiom, speaks in it [the dance] as if in its mother tongue, completely free, light, self-evident, immediate, in a language, that is, with which it is one, in which it is protected, and which allows it to say the most tender and passionate things it has to say."[132] By renouncing the traditional notion of pantomime and rejecting the formal strictures of classical ballet in search of a "new" pantomime and a "free" dance, both Hofmannsthal and Wiesenthal sought to mobilize the human body in their striving for a more direct, immediate, unmediated, and pure form of expression that would overcome the division between performer and audience and between performer and expression. In these ways, Hofmannsthal's continued engagements with dance and pantomime are clearly the attempts of an author firmly rooted in a late nineteenth-century sensibility to expand his reach into the modernism of the twentieth century. The new century brought with it a revolutionary new medium that both encompassed Hofmannsthal's work with dance and pantomime and gave the ideal of a gestural language an incalculably wider horizon. Cinema allowed Hofmannsthal to reach a mass audience—and to theorize the social potency of body language.

CELLULOID GESTURES AND THE CINEMATIC BODY

Hofmannsthal's critical assertions about language in the Mitterwurzer essay "A Monograph" were written in 1895, the same year in which the Lumière brothers first publicly screened silent films with their patented *Cinématographe*.[133] It seemed possible that the language Hofmannsthal's Chandos longs for in "A Letter"—a language that would make possible thought "in a medium more direct, fluid, and passionate than words"[134]—had surfaced with the advent of film. It is common in criticism to conceive of cinema as a language of images. It is, however, equally, if not more so, body language, a language of gesture. In the context of the modernists' search for unmediated expression, cinema appeared to be the logical extension of the preoccupation with a new kind of pantomime and a freer, more expressive form of dance at the fin de siècle and beyond. As Giorgio Agamben asserts, "Gesture rather than image is the cinematic element."[135] Cinema screens flickered with alluring dreamscapes and leading ladies, grotesque fantasies and historical illusions, newsreels and propaganda, all mediated largely in the absence of language, all conveyed primarily through the body. The sense of the modern metropolis as a soulless prison house was offset by the seductive movie house gloaming, as Georg Lukács observes in an early essay, "Thoughts toward an Aesthetic of the Cinema" (1913). Lukács argues that the modern city dweller may have lost his soul on the featureless factory floors and city streets, teeming with faceless masses. At the movies, however, "he gains in exchange his *body*."[136]

The desire to recapture the body was already manifest in the various facets of the life reform movement (considered in chap. 1), and modern dance was a significant aspect of this drive. The innovations in dance and pantomime played out on stages in Vienna and across Europe and America were already underway as cinema began its rise. Because of their training in physical expression, many mimes and dancers became the leading ladies and men in film's early years. This tendency was further shored up in

Vienna, in particular, by restrictions placed on *Burgtheater* actors limiting their professional involvement with the film industry.[137] A closer look at Béla Balázs's *The Visible Man* (Der sichtbare Mensch, 1924), a pioneering work of early film theory written in interwar Vienna, reveals how theories of cinema acting derived from Vienna's strong focus on pantomime at the fin de siècle and the wider developments within modern dance charted previously in this chapter. The central tenet of all three genres was the body as a crucible of expressive potential, with gesture as its native medium.

Yet, as with the "authentic" Viennese dance, this new medium brought with it inherent paradoxes that would complicate its role as an expressive ideal. Hofmannsthal—who also reflected on cinema in theoretical form and, like many other Viennese artists (Schnitzler, Reinhardt, Horváth, and Balázs among them), realized projects for silent film—points out the equivocality of the new medium in the context of cultural production. The *Kino-Debatte* (cinema debate), which raged on well into the 1920s, was carried out between apologists, who emphasized the medium's modernity, legitimacy, and democratizing potential, and detractors, who dismissed movies as worthless rubbish.[138] Many authors working in cinema, Hofmannsthal included, were caught in the middle, torn between the desire to probe cinema's artistic potential and the lure of a lucrative enterprise. Balázs put a fine point on the situation at the outset of *The Visible Man*, urging the cultural and intellectual elite to action:

> Now, I say to the philosophers, we must make haste, for time is pressing. Film has now become a fact, a fact that is producing such profound universal, social and psychic effects that we must engage with it, whether we will or no. For film is *the popular art* of our century. Not, unfortunately, in the sense that it arises from the spirit of the people, but in the sense that it is out of film that the spirit of the people arises. . . . The aesthetes can be as sniffy as they like; there is nothing we can do to change that. The imagination and emotional life of the people are inspired and given shape in the cinema. It is pointless to discuss whether this is good or bad. In Vienna alone, for example, films are shown every evening in almost 200, and I mean *two hundred* cinemas, each with an average of 450 seats. They provide three or four showings a day. So if we assume that the cinemas are three-quarters full, that comes to around 300,000 (*three hundred thousand!*) people in a not very large city.[139]

With a single barefaced pronouncement, Balázs sought summarily to dispense with the debate about cinema. Turning a blind eye to a medium that exercised such a magnetic pull was no longer an option for the cultural elite, so what was to be done? Both Balázs and Hofmannsthal offer concrete suggestions in their programmatic texts on film, written in the first half of the 1920s.

Born Herbert Bauer in Szeged, Austria-Hungary, Béla Balázs (1884–1949) was a successful writer and journalist, known today foremost as the librettist of Béla Bartók's *Bluebeard's Castle* (1912). Balázs moved to Budapest in 1902, where he become closely allied with the composers Bartók and Zoltán Kodály, as well as with Georg Lukács and the famous Budapest Sunday Circle of leftist intellectuals.[140] As a result of the political unrest in Hungary that ensued after the fall of the Austro-Hungarian Empire, and in particular following the collapse of the short-lived Hungarian Council (Soviet) Republic in 1919, Balázs, like many other Hungarian Marxists, fled the country and went into exile in Vienna from 1919 to 1926. The Viennese years would be among the most formative for Balázs, and it was during this time that he first fully formulated his thoughts on film. His first two years were spent translating his own literary works into German, and one of his plays was staged in 1920. In 1921, he began his direct involvement with the film industry, writing scripts for the successful Viennese director and producer Hans Otto Löwenstein.[141] Hired as the film critic for the newly founded Viennese liberal daily newspaper *Der Tag* in late 1922, Balázs's column was called "The Film Reporter." Balázs was extremely prolific, publishing over two hundred film reviews and commentaries on cinema in the roughly two and a half years he wrote for *Der Tag*.[142] Finally, in 1924, *The Visible Man* was published in Vienna.

The Visible Man was the first theoretical monograph in German that contributed directly to the cinema debate that had been raging for well over fifteen years by that time.[143] A compendium of reflections on silent film, and a theoretical extension of Balázs's journalistic work, *The Visible Man* strengthened his reputation as a film theorist in the German-speaking world and beyond. It was translated into eleven languages in its first years of publication but was, until recently, unpublished in English. Perhaps most significantly, Balázs's monograph anticipated notable aspects of later film theory, including that of Siegfried Kracauer, Rudolf Arnheim, and Walter Benjamin.[144] Dubbed an attempt at the "philosophy of the art of film" (3), Balázs viewed his book as a programmatic contribution to an aesthetics of a new kind of visual culture, one marked by a shift from the "abstract mind" to the "visible body" (13). Conscious knowledge, Balázs argued, needs to be reincorporated, "materialized as culture in the body" (13). The new kind of visual culture Balázs proclaims is thus a distinctly physical culture, and one that is deeply utopian in its inflection.[145]

In *The Visible Man*, Balázs details how the forces of modernity have affected humans' relationship to their bodies and to their ways of seeing. The rise of the printing press—what would later come to be known as Marshall McLuhan's "Gutenberg galaxy"—led to a dominance of language and the printed word as expressive media. Expression had become a "culture of words," a culture Balázs characterizes as "dematerialized, abstract and over-intellectualized," one which "degrades the human body to the status of a biological organism" (11). In the culture of words, Balázs argues, modern Europeans have lost the ability to mobilize their bodies as a holistic, soulful expressive medium. Neglected, the body has atrophied, becoming essentially functionless (11–12). "The soul has migrated into the word and become crystallized there. The body, however, has been stripped of soul and emptied" (10). People have realized this, Balázs writes, but their efforts to recover their bodies have been expended on the wrong target: athletics.[146] "While sport can make the body healthy and beautiful," Balázs counters that "it cannot make it [the body] eloquent, since it strengthens only the animal qualities. Sport cannot make of the body a sensitive medium of the soul, capable of registering its slightest motion" (12). Physical activity might indeed serve a practical purpose, but it does not get at the heart of the core problem Balázs associates with the dominance of a culture of words: the loss of the body as a communicative medium.

In the modern age, Balázs argues, people are no longer equipped with the ability to express themselves, their innermost experiences and emotions, through their bodies. Malcolm Turvey relates Balázs's cynicism regarding what had become the dominant mode of human vision—one retrenched by the rule of the word—to what he calls modern consciousness theory, rooted in Romanticism. Human cognition—the way people think and perceive, acquire and process knowledge—is decisively shaped by the increasing pervasiveness of science, technology, and reason in modernity, a development that dramatically accelerated around the turn of the century. Modern consciousness is thus effectively detached from sensory and physical experience, from the natural world. This led to a widespread sense that modern consciousness was too "rational," not "immediate" enough.[147] In response, Balázs develops a kind of typology of expression and believes that each medium has the potential to express something specific that other media cannot express, much like Hofmannsthal's earlier claims. Balázs's typology is, as Gertrud Koch has described it, an "anthropometric poetics" strongly influenced by *Lebensphilosophie* and the phenomenology of Balázs's two early mentors, Georg Simmel and Henri Bergson.[148] In short, the dominance of a culture of words and the corollary atrophying of the body has provoked a twofold loss: the mode of expression has been lost, and, moreover, access to that which is exclusively expressible through the body is restricted. The loss of corporeal expressivity has resulted in a spiritual impoverishment characteristic of humans in the modern age: while the rationalism and conceptualism of the word remain, the nonrational is unexpressed, irretrievable.

Balázs thought that silent film offered new possibilities for expression and believed in the power of film to induce a realignment in humankind's perception and cognition—through gesture. The body should become a channel for the direct and immediate expression of the soul, a possibility not afforded by language, which is too indirect, too mediated. Similar to Hofmannsthal, Balázs believed that "the language of gestures is far more individual and personal than the language of words" (13). Like the printing press, Balázs anticipated that silent film was poised to trigger a radical shift in expression and perception by introducing "the *first international language,* the language of gestures and facial expressions," with the possibility "of redemption from the curse of Babel" (14; emphasis in original). That international language, one of gestures, necessitates a steep learning curve on the part of both actors and audiences. Reminiscent of Hofmannsthal's essays on Mitterwurzer and Duse, Balázs writes that actors must relearn how to use their bodies as expressive vehicles. Here, dance, pantomime, and the theater can provide models, but, ultimately, a wholly new language of gesture must be developed for film, because the close-up—"the technical precondition" for both film art and modern acting theory—allows audiences to see in far greater detail than they can in traditional stage performances (37). As such, film directors must master the effective use of the close-up, but audiences must relearn—through silent film—how to see, how to "read" the body, and they must grasp that the physical can express that which lies beyond words, since body language is "the true mother tongue of mankind" (11), a kind of gestural Esperanto.[149]

Balázs differentiates between three distinct kinds of gesture in the arts, one each for theater, dance, and film. Each type of gesture not only has its own function but also a different origin. Balázs calls theatrical gestures "linguistic" because they illustrate, supplement an excess of meaning that language cannot contain. "They express only what's left over. *Whatever has to be said,* but won't go into words" (24; emphasis in original). The "expressive" gestures implemented in dance, Balázs argues, are, by contrast, too specific and individual, too artful and "decorative" to speak to a broad audience (24). Moreover, their reach is limited by the fact that modern dance is "a concert-hall experience for the few," so dancerly gestures fail to connect to most people's lifeworlds (13). The "gestural language of film," as Balázs terms it, is of a different nature entirely (25). In his ideal conception of cinematic gesture, the gesture is more than signifier, more than signified; it goes far beyond an ersatz language for the hearing impaired and mute. The "man of visual culture" mobilizes gesture in a fundamentally different manner. His gestures are freed from the burden of signification. They are instead "the direct expression of his own non-rational self, and whatever is expressed in his face and his movements arises from a stratum of the soul that can never be brought to the light of day by words. Here, the body becomes unmediated spirit, spirit rendered visible, wordless" (9). The cinematic gesture is, in short, "the visual corollary of human souls immediately made flesh" (10). Balázs's film theory is argued physiologically and physiognomically, positing a direct correlation between body and soul. In this way, it is in many senses an extension of Hofmannsthal's earlier theories about dance, pantomime, and stage acting.

Hofmannsthal's own film theory predated Balázs's *The Visible Man* and is differently oriented, though no less idealistic in its vision. The Viennese daily *Neue Freie Presse* published Hofmannsthal's "Three Small Observations" (Drei kleine Betrachtungen) on March 27, 1921. The second of these essays, "The Substitute for Dreams" (Der Ersatz für die Träume), is, like Balázs's monograph, a defense of cinema, but it is also a theory of the psychological effects of film. In addition, Hofmannsthal's decades-long critical relationship with language again figures prominently, set this time in the context of contemporary mass culture. The article is framed as a report of a discussion Hofmannsthal had with a friend about the reasons for the vast appeal of film. Cinema-going audiences largely consisted of the urban working classes, whose daily sufferings and routinized lives were forced on them by social and financial necessity. Whether on the assembly line or the construction site, workers repeat an unending, tedious series of often mechanically mediated motions. Ultimately, Hofmannsthal argues, echoing Marx, that the worker "becomes a machine himself, a tool among tools." People seek refuge from this plight, relief from "the barrenness of existence," at the movies.[150]

Alternatives to the cinema abound, Hofmannsthal concedes, but the siren song of film images is stronger than the desire for edification or political engagement. No other medium—not literature or newspapers, not lecture halls, political assemblies, or theaters—exerts the same pull on the masses because they fail to provide transcendence from everyday life. The old adage "knowledge is power" has ceased to apply in modern society, Hofmannsthal explains, for people mistrust knowledge as yet another mechanism of social control, only extending the sense of servitude they feel in the workplace. Just as knowledge has become suspect as a tool of potential manipulation, so too has the language used to transmit it become dubious: "in their depths, without knowing it, these people fear language; they fear in language the instrument of society."[151] Like Balázs, Hofmannsthal claims that language essentially hinders representation of the most essential aspects of human experience. Most people feel language, whether literary or colloquial, spoken or written, to be "something foreign." Likening language to algebraic formulas, in which every letter stands in for a numeral, Hofmannsthal argues that the end result is nothing more than "the abbreviation of a reality."[152] The connections to reality brokered by language are tenuous, "too indirect," "too abstract." Language "does not really lift up the spirit, does not carry it off anywhere." Instead of expressing the intricacies of inner experiences, language only "ripples the surface, but it does not awaken what sleeps in the depths." The result is that the attempt to adequately express oneself in linguistic terms "leaves behind something more like renunciation and again this feeling of being a powerless part of a machine" (114–15/HGW 9:142–43).

People's aversion to language, Hofmannsthal writes, is counterbalanced by "another power, a real one, the only real one: the power of dreams" (115/HGW 9:143). Whereas language fails to grasp what lives in our souls, dreams afford us access to "the dark ground of life, the region where the individual ceases to be, this dark ground which he so rarely reaches with a word, hardly even a word of prayer or the stammer of love" (116/HGW 9:145). Dreams help us cope with the routine aspects of daily living because of their synthesizing character; they resurrect an individual totality, a sense of wholeness lost to the fragmenting effects of language and modern urban existence. Though the details of dreams may fade from memory upon waking, Hofmannsthal asserts that it is only an illusion of having forgotten. What actually remains is a sort of dream-residuum, which—though amorphous and indeterminate—carries over into our waking state as "a faint but decisive coloring of our affect" (115/HGW 9:144). Children, those "powerful beings" with their perpetual wonder at life's smallest joys, understand this intuitively, leading an existence in which the boundaries between dreams and reality remain unmarked. Because children's dreams are the stuff of everyday life, they stumble on magic everywhere, a state of being that stands in stark contrast to the powerlessness of adult existence in mass society. Hofmannsthal interprets silent film as a variant of the same dreamworld life experience, but for grown-ups: "and now there is once again a box with enchanted junk that opens up: the movie theater" (115/HGW 9:143). This veneration of the childlike, the archaic, the dreamworld—and their accessibility through cinema—points the way to a utopian social reordering, one which anticipates key aspects of Walter Benjamin's later thoughts on film.[153]

In this, his final move of the essay, Hofmannsthal asserts that cinema and dreams are analogous, both reactivating our access to small wonders of daily existence. Like dreams, Hofmannsthal argues, film can access the deepest recesses of the psyche "into which no written or spoken word reaches" (115/HGW 9:144). Both films and dreams allow for the transcendence of everyday life because they replace language's "number"—which only serves to remind people of their workaday struggles—with "vision," relying on images, rather than on the spoken or written word, to transmit meaning (116/HGW 9:145). Moreover, the effect of film on the individual is even more decisive than that of dreams because viewers are conscious of their wakeful state while in the cinema: "The dreamer knows that he is awake; he does not need to leave anything outside him; with everything that is in him, down to the most secret fold, he stares at this flickering wheel of life that turns eternally. It is the whole person who gives himself up to this spectacle" (115/HGW 9:144).

Critically, the synthesis afforded by film extends beyond the individual to the communal. Cinema has a totalizing effect that allows people to come together in a transitory community that transcends the individual. While both films and dreams grant admittance to the "dark ground of life," film can access "the region where the individual ceases to be [an individual]." Hofmannsthal argues that from this deepest core of being streams forth "the most secret and deepest of all life-feelings," namely, "the presentiment of indestructibility, the belief in necessity, and the disdain for the merely real that is only accidentally there" (116/HGW 9:145). Film, in other words, makes people cognizant of the fact that the social conditions of their daily lives—the toil and drudgery spoken of at the essay's outset—are mere trivialities. Instead, viewers are reminded of their uniqueness, both as individuals and as communal beings, a feeling absent in modern mass society, where one perceives of oneself as nothing more than a cog in the machinery. Hofmannsthal has his friend conclude, "to me the atmosphere of the movie theater is the only atmosphere in which the human beings of our time—those who constitute the mass—come into a tremendous, even though peculiarly arranged spiritual inheritance in a quite immediate, quite uninhibited relationship, life to life." What emerges in the minds of Hofmannsthal's cinemagoers is a form of "spiritual truth" beyond the realities of everyday life. This truth, "inaccessible to reason," this most elemental of all human feelings, for Hofmannsthal, comes to light only in the quickening darkness of movie theaters (116/HGW 9:145). In this manner, film functions as a more effective substitute for dreams in shaping our awareness of self and the world. Adopting a confessional tone, Hofmannsthal writes, "the crowded, half-dark room, with the images flickering past, is to me, I cannot say it any other way, almost holy, as the place to which the souls flee in a dark drive to self-preservation" (116/HGW 9:145). Hofmannsthal thus sees in cinema a critical, if utopian, social function, one with the potential to reach and impact a word-weary and world-weary audience mistrustful of politics, literature, and theater.[154]

In addition to ascribing a crucial, and positive, social purpose to film, Hofmannsthal also saw in it the potential for the renewal of literature through gesture, anticipating Balázs's notion of cinema's "international language." The narrator's friend in the frame story addresses criticisms frequently leveled against cinema in its early years. Cultural conservatives see in film, he reports, a technologically mediated, "wretched tangle of industrial desires," leading not only to diminished spiritual and intellectual faculties but also opening audiences to manipulation (116/HGW 9:145). Much of the *Kino-Debatte* was carried out along precisely these lines, with many authors and publishers additionally concerned that cinema would threaten literature and, in particular, theater. Perhaps surprisingly, Hofmannsthal's essay reveals a rather progressive stance toward film. Film does not threaten literature but rather promotes it—beyond any divide between "high" and "popular" culture—in an age of increasing indifference toward literary language. "In the film an entire literature flies by in torn fragments, no, a whole chaos of literatures," he writes. Snippets of narratives, from the high to the low, detective and adventure stories, novels and historical dramas, are all found in the movie theater, alongside "beautiful beings and transparent gestures, expressions and glances, from which the whole soul bursts forth" (115/HGW 9:144). Silent film has the ability to encapsulate the whole of world literatures, entire novels and dramas, without relying on words, drawing instead on the alternate communicative capacity of gesture. Because audiences can see the expressions and gestures it would take hundreds of words to convey, the transmission of meaning is more immediate, more penetrating, than language. In addition, ranks of people who would never otherwise read a book or could never afford to attend the theater are given access to a world beyond their social reach.[155] Hofmannsthal saw the inherent democratizing potential of cinema, with its power to inspire, inform, and transform life not only for the consumers but also for the creators of culture.[156] How that played out in Hofmannsthal's own works for film is central to an understanding of Hofmannsthal's creative production—and of Viennese modernism in general.

Over the course of his career Hofmannsthal saw two film ideas he developed realized on the big screen: *The Foreign Girl* (Das fremde Mädchen, 1911–13) and *Der Rosenkavalier* (1923–26), directed by Robert Wiene of *The Cabinet of Dr. Caligari* (1920) fame.[157] In a letter to Richard Strauss, addressing some of the composer's concerns about their filmic version of the opera *Der Rosenkavalier*, Hofmannsthal asserted that he viewed the emergence of cinema as "a powerful demand for the continued existence and renewal of the stage."[158] The notion that traditional stage productions could garner new impulses from silent film presents a parallel to Hofmannsthal's view of the advantages dance and pantomime could offer theater. Grete Wiesenthal, who inspired some of Hofmannsthal's most fully realized pantomimes and ballets, likewise sparked his first attempts at screenwriting: a film version of the pantomime *The Foreign Girl*.[159]

Just one year after the pantomime's stage premiere in Berlin in 1911, Hofmannsthal and Wiesenthal secured a contract with the Danish Nordisk Film Kompagni to script it as a film. The movie, now lost, was shot under Mauritz Stiller's direction, as the Stockholm production firm Svenska Biografteatern ultimately took over the contract.[160] The film premiered on the big screen in Vienna in August 1913, several weeks later in Berlin, and soon thereafter in Sweden and the United States. Both the staged pantomime and the silent film share the same basic plot: a wealthy young man is enraptured by the dance of a beautiful young stranger, who is desperately poor. The man becomes entangled in a robbery plot and is unwittingly used as an innocent decoy by shady characters from the dancer's social milieu. While the man escapes relatively unscathed, the attempt on her suitor's life proves too overwhelming for the emotionally fragile young dancer, and she collapses, dead, at the close of the film.[161]

One reviewer, Ludwig Klinenberger, wrote that the marked lack of intertitling set Hofmannsthal's film apart from others, which relied much more heavily on words. *The Foreign Girl* was "simply a cinematographically recorded pantomime" that did not forfeit comprehension along with language.[162] Hofmannsthal had clearly learned much about the effective use of body language from his earlier, extensive work in pantomime and dance—especially with Wiesenthal. While the technique was successful, the plot was another matter. Many reviewers condemned the movie harshly, calling it "a travesty from the very beginning" and lambasting it as "a series of atrocious images, trivial in conception and impact, full of fatuous romanticism." One even derided the author personally, writing, "Hofmannsthal has sinned against his good name."[163] Karl Kraus, in typically trenchant fashion, concurred, calling Hofmannsthal "A Lost One" (Ein Verlorener) in *Die Fackel.* Hofmannsthal's engagement with film says everything about the author's "commercial ambition" and nothing about cinema's inherent artistic potential, Kraus proclaimed.[164] A film critic for the *Neue Freie Presse* wonders, by contrast, whether the willingness of one of the generation's leading authors to write for film is not argument enough for the medium's aspiration to high art.[165] The Viennese viewpoints of Kraus and the *Neue Freie Presse* reviewer encompass, in a nutshell, the two prevailing poles of the *Kino-Debatte.* The reality was likely something of both extremes: *The Foreign Girl* was certainly not a masterpiece, but Hofmannsthal was not just in it for the money. As his later essay "The Substitute for Dreams" shows, he held a deep belief that gesture, body language, had the ability to widen the possible audience for cultural creation, while also affecting all social classes with the kind of transcendence through art that he strove for his entire career.

An interview Hofmannsthal gave to the *Münchner Telegrammzeitung* eighteen years after *The Foreign Girl* hit the theaters, and in the year before his death, reveals his conviction about the power of the body in motion to be as strong as ever, regardless of his disappointments with the film industry's realities. "Film is first and foremost a mimic art," he said, "and therein lie its limitless possibilities. In any case it is strange enough to think that, by virtue of such a mimic instrument, one can relay the frissons [*Erschütterungen*] of a legend rooted here in our homeland to even the most remote Japanese village. Language is incapable of such transmission."[166] Hofmannsthal maintained, unbroken, his assertions about the power of physical expression, from the early essays on and experiments with dance and pantomime to the very year in which talkies came on the market. Here, he again emphasizes, like Balázs, the universal comprehensibility of gesture as an expressive form. It was a progressive, media-positive sentiment from a writer known better for his culturally and politically conservative views. It moreover reveals a dimension of his cultural production and of Viennese modernist epistemology obscured by previous critical engagements.

If we recall Egon Friedell's assertion from the beginning of this chapter that the human body is capable of communicating more than language and view it in tandem with his Viennese contemporaries' creations for pantomime, dance, and silent film in the long fin de siècle, the human body in motion—its gaze, posture, and gestures, to which Friedell referred—seemed to fulfill the promise of an other, more potent form of expression than language. The engagement with film, dance, and pantomime in late nineteenth- and early twentieth-century Vienna was more than isolated experimentation on the part of a few outliers. Rather, as we have seen, the attempts to harness and employ something of the body's animated vitality in the service of expressing authenticity, immediacy, and truth permeated even the Viennese cultural elite to a remarkable extent. The social function Hofmannsthal ascribed to gestural expression in film took on increasing significance in the interwar years, as a new form of modern dance, *Ausdruckstanz*, was both institutionalized and assumed a decisive role in Vienna's sociopolitical fabric.

THE WORKER'S BODY: MODERN DANCE, MACHINE CULTURE, AND SOCIAL DEMOCRACY

Just one month before Hofmannsthal died in 1929, the headlines of London's illustrated paper *World's Pictorial News* blazoned: "TOUCHES OF TRUE BEAUTY. Seven Guarded Girls Captivate West End with New Style of Dance. Machine-Like Movements and Mystery—from Vienna."[167] Gertrud Bodenwieser's Viennese troupe had just danced to great acclaim at the London Coliseum and in cities all over Europe, while Mary Wigman, the grande dame of German expressionist dance, or *Ausdruckstanz*, would embark with her group on their first American tour the next year.[168] While the names of Wigman and her German dance colleagues—Clotilde von Derp, Gret Palucca, Valeska Gert, Kurt Jooss, and others—are familiar to dance scholars, their Austrian counterparts, including Bodenwieser, Hilde Holger, Gertrud Kraus, Hanna Berger, Rosalia Chladek, Hedy Pfundmayr, Tilly Losch, Gisa Geert, Cilli Wang, and many others, have largely disappeared from the annals of history. German and Austrian dance of the 1920s and 1930s shared common roots though. Around 1900 the American dancers Loïe Fuller, Isadora Duncan, and Ruth St. Denis began touring Europe, often meeting with more notoriety on the Continent than at home. Alongside the fiction by Baum, Gütersloh, and others, Hofmannsthal's essays on St. Denis, which we encountered earlier in this chapter, are a product of this engagement. Fuller's, Duncan's, and St. Denis's free dance proved liberating for many of the prima ballerinas trained in the danse d'école of the Imperial Opera Ballet, the premier Viennese dance institution of the time, where Grete Wiesenthal had her start. Free dance loosed classical ballet's formal strictures—boned corsetry, torturous pointe shoes, limbs arched with uncanny precision, and muscles taut with superhuman tension—one by one. Fuller engulfed in a swirl of fabric; Duncan barefoot and tunic-clad; St. Denis an Indian princess with bells on her ankles: free dance scandalized—and thrilled—bourgeois audiences in Vienna and all over Europe while providing a generation of young dancers with impulses that would revolutionize the dance establishment.

As Gabriele Brandstetter has emphasized, it is necessary to distinguish between free dance and *Ausdruckstanz*. Although both challenged institutionalized classical ballet, the difference in their aesthetic conventions could hardly be starker: one sought "truth" through graceful and natural bodily motions; the other through defamiliarization of those movements, by staging the body in abstracted and often grotesque forms. Free dance emerged before and around 1900 with individual dancers, including Fuller, Duncan, and St. Denis, thus predating *Ausdruckstanz*. Their style highlighted the connection between body and soul while emphasizing simple, "natural" movements emanating from the body's core. The dominant aesthetic ideal was one of physical naturalness and grace, which fused with emergent notions of the "new woman." *Ausdruckstanz*, by contrast, was more institutionalized and had a different aesthetic focus. It was affiliated with, though did not run exactly parallel to, expressionism in literature and the visual arts. Like those forms of expressionist cultural production (and here we might be reminded of Egon Schiele's drawings), *Ausdruckstanz* consciously experimented with representing ugliness in dance for the first time. It centered on the Bratislava-born dancer and choreographer Rudolf von Laban's movement theory teachings and began to emerge in the 1910s, gaining strength in the 1920s and into the 1930s.[169] Laban had established a summer school for movement theory (*Bewegungslehre*) during World War I at Monte Verità—not Thomas Mann's magic mountain, but rather the "mountain of truth"—the artists' colony and countercultural stronghold in Ascona, Switzerland. Laban's primary influences were the nineteenth-century French pedagogue François Delsarte and the Vienna-born Émile Jaques-Dalcroze. Delsarte, concerned foremost with the functional transfer between affect and bodily expression, taught expressivity through gesture and voice, later influencing Vsevolod Meyerhold's ideas about biomechanics. Dalcroze built on Delsarte's teachings and devised a system of rhythmic gymnastics in the first years of the twentieth century. To establish an institutional framework for

Fig. 38. Postcard of rhythmic gymnastic exercises from the New Hellerau School for Rhythm, Music, and Physical Training, Laxenburg bei Wien, 1920s. Author's collection.

his method, Dalcroze cofounded the School for Music and Rhythm (Bildungsanstalt für Musik und Rhythmus) in 1910 in Hellerau, near Dresden. Whereas Laban focused on dance, Delsarte and Dalcroze were concerned more generally with movement as such.[170] In 1925, Dalcroze's Hellerau school, later called the School for Rhythm, Music, and Physical Training (Schule für Rhythmus, Musik und Körperbildung) and without Dalcroze at the helm, resettled to Laxenburg, in Lower Austria, less than twenty kilometers south of Vienna.

In the annals of modern dance, German cities such as Berlin and Munich are remembered as centers of the central European dance avant-garde. Vienna, if considered at all, is known foremost for the Wiesenthal sisters, who, as was previously discussed, in a bold move challenged the city's dance status quo by leaving the Imperial Opera Ballet to found their own school for modern dance. The Wiesenthals were advocates of free dance, striving for naturalness, grace, and harmony of movement, and this strain became the dominant paradigm of modern dance in Vienna. However, as in so many other regards, Vienna's dance scene was a unique amalgam of influences, a melting pot. By the mid-1920s, Vienna was home to nearly forty private modern dance schools following the principles of Delsarte to Wigman and everyone in between—including Laban and Dalcroze.[171] In point of fact, Vienna had its own strain of *Ausdruckstanz* strongly influenced by its neighbor to the north but with its own distinct twist. It combined free dance's emphasis on the naturalness of the body and its motions with strong links to musicality and a defining feature of *Ausdruckstanz*: the abstracted, and sometimes grotesque, human body.[172] Additionally, the Austrian tradition gave special importance to pedagogical reform through physical education. Two dancers and choreographers, Gertrud Bodenwieser and Hilde Holger, embodied the pedagogical, thematic, and stylistic distinctiveness of Viennese *Ausdruckstanz*. For them, social reform and social critique—through the human body in motion—went hand in hand. In this way, they sought to solve the paradox of "authenticity" that arose with Wiesenthal.

Born Gertrud Bondi, Bodenwieser (1890–1959) received her early dance training from Carl Godlewski, an Imperial Opera Ballet dancer and teacher. Bodenwieser learned about more contemporary dance movements on her own, though, through experimentation and self-study, foremost of the Wiesenthal sisters' dances and the methods of Delsarte, Dalcroze, and Laban.[173] Inspired to perform her own pieces, Bodenwieser made her solo debut in 1919 at the Vienna Concert House (Konzerthaus) as part of an exhibition by the New Union for Painting, Graphic Arts, and Sculpture (Neue Vereinigung für Malerei, Graphik und Plastik). Her performance was met with rave reviews. One commentator called her "a wholly modern dancer of most striking individuality," describing her dance as "unconditionally new," an "unconditional renunciation" of all traditions.[174] That performance and subsequent solo dance evenings catapulted her to the forefront of the burgeoning modern dance movement in Vienna. She was soon offered a position as docent at the New Viennese Conservatory (Neues Wiener Konservatorium) and by 1921 was teaching dance and mimic art at the State Academy for Music and Performing Arts (Staatsakademie für Musik und darstellende Kunst). She opened her own school of dance in 1922, in the Konzerthaus itself, and the "Gertrud Bodenwieser Dance Group" made its debut performance in 1923. By 1927, she had collaborated with Max Reinhardt on a monumental Viennese production of *The Miracle* at the Circus Renz.[175] Free dance and *Ausdruckstanz* had achieved such a high level of estimation in Viennese cultural life that official (often political) ceremonies and celebrations in the late 1920s and early 1930s frequently included a requisite modern dance performance by Bodenwieser and others.[176] In 1928, she was awarded the academic title of State Professor of Dance, the first such appointment anywhere in the world. Austria was a global vanguard in this regard, which attested as much to Bodenwieser's reputation as to the institutional legitimacy that *Ausdruckstanz*—now placed on par with music, theater, and painting—had achieved in Vienna.[177]

Unlike classically trained ballerinas such as the Wiesenthal sisters and Bodenwieser, Hilde Holger (1905–2001) was an autodidact who began her formal training quite late for a dancer, enrolling at Bodenwieser's dance school in 1919 at age fourteen. After a punishing first year under the regimented yet stimulating tutelage of "Frau Gerty," as Bodenwieser had come to be known, Holger was selected as one of the founding dancers in Bodenwieser's hand-picked dance troupe in 1921.[178] Her solo debut took place in 1923 at the Vienna Secession, where, over twenty years prior, in 1902, Isadora Duncan had performed for the Viennese artistic royalty.[179] While Holger continued her parallel work as a soloist and as a member of Bodenwieser's troupe, the desire to develop her own pedagogical methods and work more closely with children and youth ultimately led her to part ways with the Bodenwieser group in 1926 and found her own dance school.

The New School for Movement Art (Neue Schule für Bewegungskunst), which Holger cofounded with her friend and colleague Lizzi (later known as Litz or Liz) Pisk, a talented dancer, costume designer, and painter, was housed in the Ratibor Palace at Singerstraße 16 in the city center. As a newspaper ad from the time reveals, the curriculum at the school consisted of two components, one practical, the other theoretical. The first track included rhythmic gymnastics and calisthenics, dance, ballet technique, and acrobatics; the second was representative of a broad humanistic education and included anatomy and physiology, pedagogy and psychology, instruction in form and harmony, the history of art, music, dance, and gymnastics, costume art, and figural and ornamental drawing.[180] Holger's first class comprised fifty students, which she divided into two groups, the "Hilde Holger Dance Group" with older students and a children's dance group. A commentator for the *Wiener Neueste Nachrichten* remarked on the significance of Holger's work with children and physical education, placing her curriculum in the context of contemporary thought about

Fig. 39. Advertisement for Hilde Holger's New School for Movement Art, 1920s. Image courtesy of the Hilde Holger Archive and Primavera Boman-Behram. © Primavera Boman-Behram, 2001. All rights reserved.

pedagogy and the importance of physical education in particular: "In general, psychologists, pedagogues, and artists are of one mind about the value of the physical and spiritual [*seelische*] education of youth through dance, but they disagree about the method. It was time, then, to venture an attempt to solve this problem and to suggest an appropriate path for the modern, gymnastic training of the youngest."[181] Holger's method filled this gap, and by 1928 her students' "rhythmic-gymnastic performances" were featured on important Viennese stages, such as the grand auditorium of the Urania public educational institute.[182]

The integrative approach of Holger's New School for Movement Art became a paradigm for politically inflected physical training. Indeed, the

Austrian Social Democratic Party seized on the chance to cooperate with the dancer both to widen the reach of and to capitalize on her technique. In 1919, the party had founded a dedicated Arts Bureau (Kunststelle) under the direction of David Joseph Bach, the influential culture editor of the *Arbeiter-Zeitung*. Ten years later, the Arts Bureau partnered with Holger's school to offer formal training in modern dance to all Viennese. The evening courses, available for a reduced fee to white-collar workers, students, and the working classes, were designed with special consideration for participants' professional lives and organized by trade. By "supplying the fatigued body new energies in the evening hours," the goal was to encourage "a new pleasure for life [*Lebensfreude*] [to] blossom."[183] The principles of the life reform movement, on which so much of modern dance had been based, had migrated into elite performance culture, and now—through efforts such as those of the Kunststelle—these principles were again being offered to those who most needed the physical respite: the working classes.[184] In practical and theoretical terms, the body was the medium to heal modern alienation.

Holger no doubt learned much about how to structure a curriculum from her time at Bodenwieser's dance school, which likewise followed a two-pronged practical and theoretical approach.[185] Like Holger, Bodenwieser was regarded as an expert in the field, contributing several articles on the significance of dance, rhythmic gymnastics, and physical education for primary and secondary education to prominent dance publications at home and abroad.[186] But the emphasis on physical education and gymnastic training in both Bodenwieser's and Holger's curricula was shared by the preeminent pedagogue and progressive educational reformer of the day: Eugenie Schwarzwald. Holger's New School for Movement Art was actually just a stone's throw from both St. Stephen's Cathedral and Schwarzwald's esteemed girls' school. In addition to instruction by the likes of Oskar Kokoschka, Adolf Loos, and Arnold Schönberg, dance and physical education were also orders of the day at Schwarzwald's lyceum.[187] Photographs from the time show students performing gymnastic exercises and dancing on the roof with a view over central Vienna.

Schwarzwald, Holger, and Bodenwieser shared the idea that dance, rhythmic training, and movement should be integral components in schools' accredited curricula. The contribution of physical culture to such curricula followed from a holistic approach to education, one stemming from the belief, in Holger's words, that "dance fulfills the whole person. . . . Everything is connected in dance: the intellectual, the spiritual, and the physical."[188] Such pedagogical practice of physical culture was more-

Fig. 40. Gymnastic exercises on the rooftop of the Schwarzwald School, Vienna, 1915. Advertising brochure of the "Schwarzwald'schen Schulanstalten." Wiener Stadt- und Landesarchiv, Vienna.

over integrated into the programs of such renowned organizations as the Union of Austrian Women Artists. By 1917, the union had its very own "gymnastic atelier," home to the Institute for Hygienic-Harmonious Body Culture for Women. As an informational pamphlet reveals, it took an integrative approach to address body, mind, and soul.[189] The more the body, like the mind, came to be seen as something to be nurtured, cultivated, strengthened, and trained, something that could positively influence the psyche, the more credibility and currency pedagogical reform through physical culture gained in the first decades of the twentieth century. Appraising the changing educational landscape, Bodenwieser wrote, "The same spirit which has thrown open the windows of the nurseries to let in light, air, and sunshine, is opening the windows of the child's soul, drawing out the spectres of old-time standard dicta of education and flooding it with new light and happiness." What she calls "the wide field of artistic dancing" is part and parcel of a more general resurgence of interest in all sports, and both, she argues, must be integral components of educational reform.[190] Bodenwieser's rationale centered on the link between body and mind, namely, "that the body's tautness and repose reflect onto [one's] inner life [*Innenleben*], that a fortified, healthy, and freely mobile body is of the utmost influence on the psychic life [*Seelenleben*] of a growing individual." Were a new approach to pedagogy that integrated physical training through dance to become standard educational practice, Bodenwieser declared, "we would not have any more unshapely people dissatisfied with their bodies." Buoyantly, rhetorically, she asks, "Is this not a beautiful prospect?"[191] Notwithstanding the visionary optimism afforded to the role of dance in education for children and the working classes in Vienna, choreographers were considerably less sanguine in their view of the effects of modernization and urbanization on the human body—which they took up as key themes for their dance beginning in the 1920s.

As the titles of their dances indicate, Bodenwieser's *Demon Machine* (Dämon Maschine, 1924) and *Mechanization (Ford System)* (Mechanisierung [Ford-System], 1928) and Holger's *Mechanical Ballet* (Mechanisches Ballett, 1926) sought new ways to depict—and critique—industrial processes through the human body. Scenes akin to those that would eventually become familiar to moviegoers were present on Vienna's stages before film images from Fritz Lang's *Metropolis* (1927) were common currency. The key in these choreographies was to mobilize the corporeal in abstract, rhythmic gestures and motions. Despite the heaviness of the topic, the aesthetic effect was compelling, as the headlines from the *World's Pictorial News* about Bodenwieser's dance cited at the outset of this section document. Audiences were captivated by the dancers' "machine-like movements," which—in spite of the risk of estranging viewers—managed to retain an air of mystery and beauty.[192] Though critical reflections about the effects of mechanization and industrialization on society, the human spirit, and the human body were a shared concern for German and Austrian dancers, the Viennese style of *Ausdruckstanz* was aesthetically distinct from the German. In short, Viennese *Ausdruckstanz* combined the lyricism, musicality, and naturalness of free dance with the physical abstraction, geometry, and defamiliarization of German expressionist dance—all without the overall impression alienating the audience.[193] In this way, Viennese choreographers and dancers such as Bodenwieser and Holger attempted to transcend the social and cultural paradoxes raised by both modernity and modernism in many of their pieces.

Bodenwieser's choreography *Demon Machine* was the second in a cycle of four dances performed together under the title *Forces of Life* (Gewalten des Lebens). Before its debut in Vienna in 1924, Hede Juer, one of Bodenwieser's first students, recalls that Bodenwieser was consumed with "the idea of translating into movement the frightening aspects of mechanization" and its deleterious consequences for humankind. At the rehearsals, the energy in the air crackled with possibility, excitement, and physical and mental exhaustion, as the members of the troupe (Holger included) "felt instinctively that we were about to create under Bodenwieser a kinetic masterpiece, the relevance of which concerned the whole world, and which the whole world would understand." Juer depicts the two-part performance in detail:

> In the first part the dancers moved weightlessly, untroubled by any problems, in paradisal [*sic*] innocence, through space, while Bodenwieser, as the evil spirit of the machine, kept in the background squatting, staring, rigid. Suddenly a crashing chord and Bodenwieser's first abrupt, thumping movement shattered the innocence and peace. Now with ever-increasing force the demon drew the people closer, gradually overpowering their resistance, until they suddenly became grouped in front of the demon as parts of a dehumanised, soulless mechanism, completely under the demonic compulsion. Now the machine began to work, with presses, pistons, wheels, and seemingly all the reciprocating motions that the observer sees who looks into the heart of moving machinery. Gathering speed as it worked, it exerted its unrelenting force and momentum. Music and movement stopped together abruptly, the power switched off. No trace of humanity is left.[194]

Reviewers were impressed with the power of Bodenwieser's choreography, noting that the dancers fully embodied the machinery they danced without losing their beauty. Writing for a British dance publication in 1929, Arnold L. Haskell remarked, "These beautiful girls became a great, powerful, efficient machine, and the effect was inspiring and terrifying as a visit to the engine room of some great works. A truly remarkable achievement."[195] Similarly, a German critic mentioned the transcendent effect of the performance. Six dancers "lost soul and consciousness. They became gearwheels of the mechanical construction: crank, transmission, safety valve, and who knows what else, their limbs whirled like pistons, hummed like wheels, roared like hammer mills; joints creak; sparks spring." Audience members lost their sense of place, the commentator remarked, forgetting they were in a concert hall and wondering whether they were not instead

Fig. 41. Gertrud Bodenwieser, *Demon Machine,* 1939. The demon machine in action, as produced in New York, London, and Australia. Papers of Gertrud Bodenwieser, National Library of Australia, Class MS 9263/Series 2/Piece 31.

in a machine room. It was irrelevant in the end, for the only feeling that remained was "the power of the everything-crusher [*Alleszermalmerin*]," the machine.[196] Bodenwieser again took up the theme of the machine as "everything-crusher" in a later choreography, *Mechanization (Ford System),* which she performed with an enlarged troupe.[197] Part of the *Current and Countercurrent* (Strömung und Gegenströmung) cycle from 1928, the dance, like *Demon Machine,* was a critical commentary on the dehumanizing power of industrial mechanization. *Demon Machine* would become a cornerstone of Bodenwieser's repertoire and was performed well into the 1930s, both in Vienna and abroad, to critical and popular acclaim.

Even a cursory glance at photographs and eyewitness accounts of Bodenwieser's and Holger's dances makes plain that their strain of Viennese *Ausdruckstanz* was thematically and stylistically linked not only to German *Ausdruckstanz* but also to the Bauhaus.[198] The similarities are striking, right down to the title of Holger's solo choreography, *Mechanical Ballet*. Holger's piece, which debuted at Vienna's Modernes Theater in 1926, shares its title with a 1923 performance choreographed by the Bauhaus students Kurt Schmidt and Georg Teltscher, as well as with an essay by Oskar Schlemmer, published in 1927.[199] Schlemmer's pathbreaking *Triadic Ballet* (Triadisches Ballett, 1915/1922) attempted to realize onstage the new performative possibilities afforded by the technological optimization of the machine age, along with its effect on the human body. Instead of seeking authenticity in the "natural" body, as had been the case in the late nineteenth century, by the second decade of the twentieth century choreographers were exploring the potential of melding human and machine bodies. Schlemmer, for example, reflected that the goal of the *Triadic Ballet* was, ultimately, the "dematerialization" of the body.[200] This was to be achieved by successively abstracting and obscuring the natural human form. Masks and structural, geometric costumes were meant to evoke architecture, robots, puppets, and machine components—staging the possibility of an intersection of the human and the "'un'human."[201] The costumes' effect was further underscored by the dancers' denaturalized, mechanical movements that took their cue from automatons, dolls, marionettes, and machines.[202] Schlemmer saw the potential such figures represented for humans, "the attempt to release man from his constraints and to heighten his freedom of movement above the natural measure."[203] Bodenwieser's design for *Demon Machine* is reminiscent of the structured geometry employed by the Bauhaus artists, and Holger's *Mechanical Ballet* defamiliarized the human body with costumes that bore a notable likeness to the Bauhaus's robot-like "artificial figures" (*Kunstfiguren*), as Schlemmer called them.

Despite the stylistic similarities, the underlying philosophies differed. While Schlemmer (and the Bauhaus at large) had a predominantly favorable relationship to mechanical reproduction and believed that the controlled application of systems of machine technology could, in principle, benefit society and stimulate cultural production, Bodenwieser's choreographies take a fundamentally oppositional, critical stance more in line with Hofmannsthal's idealism. Her dances explicitly thematize the negative effects of mechanization on the body and soul. As we have seen, Social Democratic cultural policy was likewise concerned with the ramifications of modernization and urbanization on the Viennese, advocating body-based movement, and dance in particular, to improve the physical and mental well-being of the working classes. Austrian *Ausdruckstanz* may well have originated in the Konzerthaus with Bodenwieser and been formally institutionalized with her professorship. Yet the shift away from a modern dance that was the exclusive domain of a cultured elite was realized in interwar Vienna through its inclusion in pedagogical reform and politically sanctioned working-class educational and leisure programs.

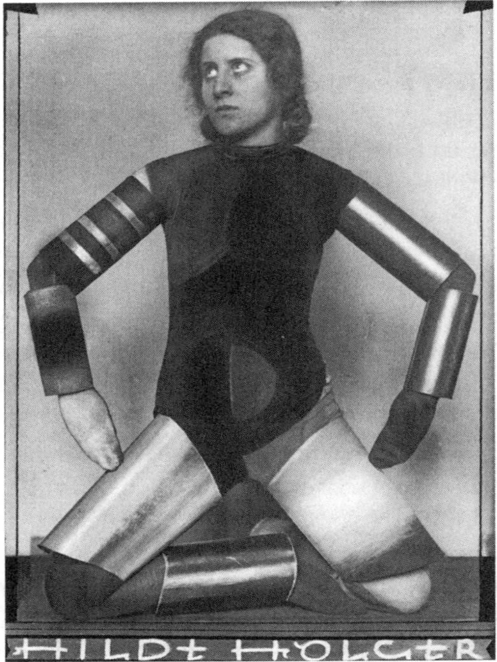

Fig. 42. Hilde Holger, *Mechanical Ballet*, 1926. Photograph by Anton Josef Trčka (Antios). Image courtesy of the Hilde Holger Archive and Primavera Boman-Behram.

Regardless of context, however, the belief remained consistent that "the body"—conceived as an ideal topos of expression—held the potential to heal the civilizational and social damage wrought by modernization.

⁂

If we return to Egon Friedell, the influential cultural critic with whom we began this chapter, it becomes clear that by the 1930s—with the advent of talkies, which robbed film of its silence and re-rendered gesture as merely an accompaniment to the spoken word—the circle had closed. For many, the utopian potential of body language was lost, threatened by the dual encroachment of mechanization (thematized, e.g., in Bodenwieser's dance) and mediatization. Friedell, who had seen such promise in cinema early on, if we recall his 1912 lecture, had by the late 1920s transformed into a cine-pessimist—befitting his essayistic, historiographical project to document the "crisis of the European soul," as the subtitle of his monumental, three-volume *A Cultural History of the Modern Age* read. Cinema had become, for Friedell, an encapsulation of the technologized nightmare that was the modern world, and he now counted film alongside air travel and gas warfare as its negative apotheosis. Again, we encounter here the disillusionment with literary language: "the finest and deepest verse" is still incapable of expressing the ineffability of experience.[204] The mute gestures of the body in motion—on silent celluloid and in pantomime and dance—had seemed to hold the promise of a new kind of expressivity, one rooted in the body and independent of language's conceptual deception. With "talking pictures," however, the scales had fallen from Friedell's eyes. The word was again part of the picture, but, in the late 1920s, word and picture were both mediated so comprehensively as to strip away all uniqueness of experience. The transformation in Friedell's perspective is remarkable. He writes:

> As long as the cinema was [mute], it had other than [purely] film[ic] possibilities: namely, spiritual ones. But the sound-film has unmasked it, and the fact is patent to all eyes and ears that we are dealing with a brutish dead machine. The bioscope kills the human gesture only, but the sound-film the human voice as well. Radio does the same. . . . Both cinema and radio eliminate that mysterious fluid which emanates from artist and public alike, making of every concert, every lecture, a unique spiritual experience. The human voice has achieved omnipresence, the human gesture eternity, but at the cost of the soul. It is the Tower of Babel. . . . Here indeed is the "Decline of the West." There are no realities any more, there is only apparatus. It is a world of automata, conceived in the brain of a malicious and crazy Doctor Miracle.[205]

Friedell nods here quite openly to that other voluminous work of cultural pessimism from the interwar years, Oswald Spengler's *The Decline of the West* (1918–22), as well as, perhaps, to Béla Balázs's reflections on language and cinema. But what Friedell's simultaneously cynical and disenchanted vision gestures toward is a return of the fear Hofmannsthal, Wiesenthal, Reinhardt, and others responded to decades earlier—namely, that the soul and the body, the spiritual and the physical, had become detached from one another. Unlike these earlier theorists, however, Friedell ends his cultural history of the modern age not with the blaze of hope that the body had offered at the fin de siècle proper but merely with a glimmer of promise that it might yet rise again. For Freud and psychoanalysis, Friedell writes, stand "at the end of the Modern Age." The power afforded the word, the Logos, in psychoanalysis, Friedell argues, forces "an unequivocal admission of the supremacy of the spiritual over the physical."[206] It would seem that *homo psychologicus* had triumphed in Friedell's estimation, and this is the view that would define later critical descriptions of the entire era. In the meantime, all that remains is the fully functionalized, soulless body—and the "faint gleam of light," a "light from the other side," that might yet foretell an era when the body again could harbor utopian potential by being reunited with the soul. "The history of this light," Friedell writes—the history of *homo physiologicus,* in other words—will be "the next chapter of European cultural history."[207] Yet, as we have seen, that history of the body was an integral part of Vienna's cultural history from the 1870s to the 1930s, rather than its next chapter. It was, far more, both the prologue and all the preceding chapters. Friedell, now staring down the rise of fascism across Europe, might be forgiven for forgetting—or, perhaps more accurately, reframing—his own prognostic recognition from two decades prior. Whereas in 1912 "a person's gaze, gestures, or his whole physical bearing,"[208] one's body, in short, offered the promise of a new day, it would soon be deployed to unspeakable ends—in the name of fashioning a National Socialist *Volkskörper.* This subsequent history so overshadowed the utopian moment that permeated Viennese modernism that later critical gazes have since failed to see it at all. Friedell, reading the writing on the wall, knew that the story of the body was far from over.

EPILOGUE

In the relationship of individuals to the body, their own and that of others, is reenacted the irrationality and injustice of power as cruelty.
—Max Horkheimer and Theodor W. Adorno, *Dialectic of Enlightenment*

If, as this study has argued, the discourses surrounding the body in late imperial and interwar Viennese culture had their roots in the socio-scientific and medical cultures of the liberal era, we must look forward and ask what happened to the body at the intersection of culture, medicine, society, and politics under the totalitarian regime that superseded the empire and the First Republic. How, in other words, was the body marshaled in the fascist body politic?

Rudolf Brunngraber's (1901–60) panoramic interwar novel *Karl and the Twentieth Century* (Karl und das zwanzigste Jahrhundert, 1933) allows us to approach this question laterally.[1] The life of Brunngraber's titular Viennese protagonist, Karl Lakner, is a paradigmatic embodiment of the struggle to survive in an era of epochal change and upheaval. Although the political and economic developments detailed in the novel are of a global scale, they nevertheless directly steer the course and outcome of Karl Lakner's dismal existence. Karl is subject to intractable political and economic forces, as indicated by the two epigraphs Brunngraber chose for his novel. One is a statement attributed to Napoleon around 1800: "Politics is destiny"; the other is Walther Rathenau's assertion, over a century later, that "the economy is destiny."[2] Brunngraber's inclusion of the first aperçu calls to mind a famous—and heatedly debated—assertion of Freud's, one Freud explicitly acknowledges is a twist on Napoleon's "well-known" remark: "Anatomy is destiny."[3] Understood contextually, Freud's statement suggests that the very fact of having a human body leads unavoidably to psychic conflict. While this is not the biologically deterministic perspective it is often made out to be, it is a deeply pessimistic take on the potential for human happiness.[4] The link between the body and subjectivity is, for Freud, contingent on other agents and other forces—"civilization" chief among them.[5] The cynicism inherent in these formulations of human existence as subject to political, economic, and psychophysical forces beyond our control is spelled out in Brunngraber's interwar novel. And it centers on the human body as the site where that control is exerted.

Writing in a "poetic-sociological" mode,[6] Brunngraber opens and closes his novel with the Taylorist principles of scientific management—a theme taken up in modern dance by Gertrud Bodenwieser and Hilde Holger just years before (see chap. 4). Taylorism reorganized industrial production processes to maximize human efficiency in a fashion commensurate with the demands of an increasingly global capitalist market economy. It also, however, resulted in a fully rationalized human subject as by-product, and the trickle-down effects through all social strata allow Brunngraber's protagonist Karl Lakner to be counted among them, though he does not labor in a factory. The worker is quantified, functionalized, anatomized—and ultimately dehumanized—a situation Karl Marx's economic theory had long since registered critically.[7] When Lakner, unemployed and impoverished, commits suicide in 1931, the reader learns of it only indirectly, via one of three newspaper clippings that compose the final chapter of Brunngraber's "newsreel novel."[8] This report is juxtaposed with another journalistic account, whose eerie description presents the human as nothing more than a source of raw materials to be extracted and subsequently commodified:

> According to statements made by Dr. Charles H. Mayo of Rochester, a human being is worth exactly half a dollar, this estimate being based upon the market value of the elements and compounds of which the human body is made up. There is, for instance, enough fat to make seven pieces of soap. The iron could be forged into a fairly large nail. The sugar would suffice to sweeten half a dozen apple-fritters. There is enough lime to whitewash a hencoop. The phosphorous would provide the heads of twenty-two hundred matches. The magnesium is equal to that contained in an ordinary dose of Epsom salts. There is enough sulphur to rid a dog of its fleas. As for the potassium, that would supply the niter needed for one discharge from a toy-cannon.[9]

Whereas in earlier generations the worker's body was understood as a "human motor," whose energy could be channeled into industrial production processes,[10] the socially critical literature of the interwar years presents the body merely as a degraded by-product of those processes, a by-product like any other: completely objectified and disposable, save the use value of its elemental parts. The kind of quantification, anatomization, and dehumanization of the human body Brunngraber ascribes to the perpetual tug-of-war between politics and economics in modernity—and which we saw reflected in the Viennese bodies-in-pieces in chapter 2—foretells the sinister years to come. With genocidal literalness, the National Socialists would adopt a similarly functionalizing and reductive-destructive stance toward the bodies of the victims of its persecution and extermination machinery.

As chapter 1 detailed, the notion of the body in the outgoing nineteenth century in the contexts of human exhibitions and certain strands of the life reform movement already harbored a clear bent toward ideas about purity and naturalness. Even Julius Tandler's theories of hygiene and eugenics, though directed toward a paternalistic betterment of the social body under the comprehensive interwar, state-sanctioned welfare system, clearly tread treacherous ground.[11] Rooted in medical knowledge about the body, such ideologies necessarily presuppose a spectrum ranging from pathological and weakened at the one extreme to healthy and robust at the other. As we saw in chapter 3, these discourses were also applied to cultural production. The body of the cultural Other—whether African, Native American, or Jewish—was most often placed at the unfavorable extreme.[12] It was mobilized as a metaphorical manifestation for social ills while also as a negative foil in attempts to define national and individual identity. In the Viennese context, for example, the popular daily newspaper *Kikeriki* never tired of deriding the city's Jewish population, often caricaturing the Jewish body to purportedly correlate with larger-scale Viennese and Austrian sociopolitical ills. That is to say, a counterimage of the "diseased" Jewish body had already evolved from the idealized portrayal of the healthy, robust Germanic body long before the National Socialists adopted this imagery and sought to eliminate it in the Holocaust.

The late nineteenth century privileged museums and live displays to document, represent, measure, and compare bodies of all sorts (chap. 1), and institutional medical architecture structured and created a clinical gaze in the first decade of the twentieth century (chap. 3). But by the late 1930s, film had long since become the great visual leveler (chap. 4). It was no great stretch from Wilhelm Prager's *Ways to Strength and Beauty* (Wege zu Kraft und Schönheit, 1925) to Leni Riefenstahl's *Olympia* (1938), both with their images of gleaming Germanic bodies enhanced by routinized athletic training and fortified by nature's bounties. Much of the pomp and pageantry of fascist mass spectacles like those depicted in Riefenstahl's earlier *Triumph of the Will* (1934) lay in their subjugation of the individual to the whole. These were, quite literally, mass movements—the synchronized, choreographed motion of thousands of bodies in unison—intended to amaze and awe. As Horkheimer and Adorno argued in "Interest in the Body," included in their notes and sketches for *Dialectic of Enlightenment*, fascism takes a detached, rationalized view of "the body as a mobile mechanism," subject to optimization and regulation.[13] The totalitarian mass spectacle emphasized regimented physical fitness and the mechanistic efficiency of military platoons. With the individual body subsumed into the whole, the mass body became a highly visible, material incarnation of National Socialist political ideology. In a perverse sense, this was no less a realization of a somatic utopia than the ideals of earlier generations.

These strands come together in a chilling fashion if we return to the site where we began this journey: the Prater park. Just a stone's throw from the zoological garden where human displays were held and from the amusement zone, which housed Präuscher's Anatomical Museum, a stadium was erected in the interwar years. July 1931 marked the celebratory inauguration of the structure, as well as the Second International Workers' Olympics, for which it had been built. The stadium was an infrastructural manifestation of interwar Vienna's communal politics and reflected the central position of physical culture within that political vision. The Social Democrats extolled workers' sport—a politicized cousin of the largely apolitical physical culture movement around 1900 (chap. 1)—as a corrective to the ills of modern civilization and the physical toll paid by working-class citizens. The Workers' Olympics included a staged mass celebration alongside sporting events.[14] Both sports and this festival—a series of theatrical performances exulting the triumphs of socialism over the perceived evils of industrial capitalism—took place in the stadium.

The stadium, that utopian, social-democratic space, had already become a site for stagings of competing ideological visions before the "Anschluss." In a cruel twist of history, eight short years after the arena's completion it was repurposed by the National Socialists. It became not a staging ground for fascist pageantry, as we might expect from Riefenstahl's films, but, first, a casern for Wehrmacht soldiers briefly in 1938, and then a detainment camp for Jewish men. Just days after the German invasion of Poland on September 1, 1939, the Gestapo violently rounded up over one thousand Viennese, mostly Jewish men of Polish descent or otherwise stateless, on September 10 and 11.[15] They were initially held in district prisons, such as in the Rossauer (ninth district, Alsergrund) and

Hermanngasse (seventh district, Neubau) prisons, but were soon moved to the Prater stadium, where the spaces beneath the tribunes had been transformed into makeshift holding pens. Under the seating areas—from which rapt viewers had watched the bodies of athletes and performers on the field in the preceding years, months, and even weeks before—the prisoners now became "scientific" material, their bodies subjected to medical-anthropological studies. The forced studies, ordered and organized by Josef Wastl, the director of the Natural History Museum's anthropological division, took place over the course of six days in late September and were carried out on nearly half of the one thousand prisoners. In the course of the "research," the men's bodies were systematically measured and photographed. They were required to fill out extensive, standardized surveys. Wastl and his eight-person committee collected hair samples from some and took plaster of Paris face masks of others.[16] The information and specimens were intended for use in a planned exhibition, "The Physical and Mental Constitution of the Jews," at the Natural History Museum. Designed to present the purportedly "scientific," biological foundations of the Nuremberg race laws, the exhibition was to rely heavily on quantitative data that illustrated supposedly "characteristic" physical and psychological traits of Jewish individuals.[17] In the stadium, the men's bodies were used as objects of scientific, medical studies one final time before being deported to Buchenwald. There, the last physical energy of many was extracted in labor, and almost none escaped the ultimate destruction of the body. Rudolf Brunngraber's cynical vision of the body in modernity had become heinous reality.

Even as knowledge about the body was harvested under National Socialism, it was simultaneously suppressed. The dubious interaction between political ideology and scientific opportunism—with the human body as their object—is made clear by the Prater stadium example from 1938. But the anatomical knowledge about the body contained in Präuscher's Anatomical Museum, also in the Prater, became a target of National Socialist purges before it burned down in the final months of the war in 1945. A copy of the museum guide to the anatomical collection at Präuscher's from the early 1940s—today held at the library of the University of Vienna—contains inserted leaflets with Nazi insignia. The city administration had ordered the removal of large portions of Präuscher's anatomical displays that it found offensive, in particular those thematizing female anatomy and preparations of venereal diseases, supposedly in the interest of public morality and decency. Scientific knowledge about the human body, and about anatomy in particular, presented for all to see at Präuscher's popular museum was too great a threat for the regime.[18] While fabricating and instrumentalizing knowledge about bodies to support their ideology—and then subsequently exterminating the human beings who had yielded that information—the National Socialists also sought in the end to censor popular, public scientific knowledge about the body.[19] Knowledge about the human body, the knowledge on which so much of interwar Social Democratic biopolitics was built, continued to be the prerogative of the state under National Socialism, but to a diametrically opposed end: the suppression of precisely that enlightenment about the body that the fascist regime's ideological predecessors espoused.

In light of the unfathomable and so fundamental destruction of bodies under National Socialism, we must further ask what became of the Austrian bodies that remained in postwar Vienna. The egregious fascist cooption of all aspects of life—the body included—and the continuity of ideological complacency in the early decades of the Second Republic sparked a furious backlash from the post–World War II Austrian avant-garde. Many artists and intellectuals expressed fierce opposition to the founding myths and Austrian identity politics professed by the Second Republic. In this view of the events of World War II, enshrined in the Moscow Declarations of 1943, the so-called Anschluss of 1938 was an unlawful occupation by an unwelcome, foreign fascist regime—and Austria Hitler's first victim. Such an interpretation of history allowed Austria to absolve itself of culpability for the Holocaust.[20] The defiance and open scorn of the Austrian avant-garde toward this historical distortion was an unabashed rejection both of these founding myths and of a perceived totalitarian institutional continuity. The outrage became a springboard for a new aesthetic radicalism in the postwar years.

In this context, it would be interesting to link the centrality of the body in Viennese modernism that this study has advanced to the postwar Viennese avant-garde. While Werner Hofmann had remarked on the connection in passing in the mid-1980s,[21] it was three decades later, as I was drafting the final lines of this manuscript in Vienna, that posters for an exhibition at the mumok, the Viennese Museum of Modern Art, went up around the city.[22] "Body, Psyche, and Taboo" posited, for the first time in depth, the genealogy toward which Hofmann gestured and the present study has elaborated: namely, that there is a hidden history of Viennese modernism that foregrounded the body and not just the psyche. Moreover, the exhibition furthers a position first suggested by Hofmann, a perspective this book necessarily opens out onto: that it is possible to trace a direct trajectory from the corporeal history of Viennese modernism to the postwar cultural production of the Wiener Gruppe (Vienna Group) and Wiener Aktionismus (Viennese Actionism), which were likewise uniquely focused on body-based art.

For example, the Wiener Gruppe of the mid-1950s to mid-1960s—Konrad Bayer, H. C. Artmann, Gerhard Rühm, and Peter Handke—put forth a concept of explicitly deinstitutionalized theater. Breaking open the bourgeois *Burgtheater* tradition, the Wiener Gruppe in many ways brought the genre back closer, in a radical fashion, to the gesture-laden folk-theater (*Volkstheater*) tradition that was so strong in Vienna until the mid-nineteenth century. That meant bringing their work to the streets, warehouses, and basements of the city, situating their art in contexts familiar to us from the cabaret, fairground, and popular culture performance traditions cited in this study. Furthermore, much of the writing of the Wiener Gruppe carried forward the tradition of language criticism, albeit in a revolutionary, politicized version that was such a part of fin-de-siècle Austrian culture from Mauthner to Wittgenstein, Hofmannsthal to Kraus, as discussed in chapter 4. Potential links between Viennese modernism and Viennese Actionism of the 1960s and early 1970s and beyond also bear further consideration. The often severe and grotesque body art and aggressively physical performance art of Günter Brus, Hermann Nitsch, Otto Mühl, Rudolf Schwarzkogler, and others emphasize the materiality of the body by using it as a site of aesthetic and physiological production—in essence, as raw material (or as a source of raw materials)—and as a canvas. The Actionists' radical use of the body has both informed and in some cases sparked fierce reactions in the work of artists, such as Maria Lassnig, VALIE EXPORT, and Elke Krystufek, whose work in turn has centered on the female body.

The trajectories for further research noted above hint at the imperative of breaking through the ramparts surrounding the fin-de-siècle Vienna myth of an exclusively inward-oriented, psychologized withdrawal into aestheticism, as Schorske influentially argued. This paradigm, so widely propagated in the academy, museology, and tourism, simplifies and distorts the city's cultural field, emphasizing only a handful of usual suspects and a narrow range of cultural products while neatly packaging the era and the city for maximum appeal and marketability. In this view, foundational elements of Viennese modernism are obscured. While Schorske's *homo psychologicus* was a central figure of Viennese modernism, *homo physiologicus* was an equally present paradigm and in fact predated psychological man. Examining a common engagement with the body within Viennese culture of the long fin de siècle has shown the canon of Viennese modernism as previously imagined to be unnecessarily, even tendentiously, restrictive. To begin to grasp the true richness and complexity of Vienna's cultural production at the fin de siècle and beyond, it is necessary to embrace the unmistakable interactions between the full spectrum of cultural production and its social, medial, philosophical, and technoscientific surroundings. This approach allows us to take leave of a myopic form of historiography in favor of a matrix of Viennese modernisms, one which can accommodate all of the parts and voices in Karl Kraus's "perpetually tuning" orchestra of Viennese culture and disposition.[23] The Young Vienna member Friedrich Michael Fels wrote in 1891, "the decisive hallmark of the modern is that it is not a one-sided trend, that in it the most varied and divergent ideas and endeavors find a place."[24] The features of what would come to be known as modernism that Fels names—its inclusivity, its multifariousness, its plurality—were all dynamics at work in the fin-de-siècle Viennese cultural milieu. The body was their common point of engagement.

Just as there is space for a multiplicity of modernisms, there is also room for a phalanx of bodies. It has become clear that the body is what we make it—and make with it. The human body, Norman O. Brown once asserted, is not simply physical matter, the biological facticity of our existence. Far more, it is "a continuous creation," polyvalent, chameleon-like.[25] Throughout history, people have looked to the body—the body of the self and the body of the other—for solutions to their eras' most pressing social, artistic, and existential questions: Who am I? Who are we? What is "authentic," "natural," "normal," "real," "immediate," "healthy," "ideal"? In the end, it is not the solutions the body seems to offer that matter. What is of far more consequence is the asking of the questions, the exploration and experimentation—the continuous creation—*of* and above all *with* our bodies.

ACKNOWLEDGMENTS

A project so long in the works owes debts of gratitude to multitudes, some institutional, others personal. I gratefully acknowledge the following institutions and organizations, which provided material support at various stages: the US Fulbright Commission—together with the Austrian-American Educational Commission and the IFK International Research Center for Cultural Studies in Vienna—enabled much of my earliest research; Stanford University's Department of German Studies and School of Humanities and Sciences; New York University's Department of German and Faculty of Arts and Science; and the Austrian Federal Ministry for Science, Research, and Economy (BMWFW), whose Richard Plaschka Fellowship, administered by the Austrian Agency for International Cooperation in Education and Research, Centre for International Cooperation and Mobility, made possible the completion of this manuscript.

Special thanks are due to my graduate and undergraduate students at NYU. In seminars that have so often developed into conversations beyond the classroom, we have tested ideas and built connections that have immeasurably enriched my thinking. Your curiosity and challenges, comments and questions inspire me each day.

At Stanford, Russell Berman was the first to help me begin to see "the Vienna forest for the trees," as he once quipped. Elizabeth Bernhardt, Eavan Boland, and Amir Eshel reminded me of the place of pragmatism, poetry, and voice, respectively. My colleagues, current and former, in the Department of German at NYU—especially Ulrich Baer, Robert Cohen, Eckart Goebel, Avital Ronell, Friedrich Ulfers, Leif Weatherby, and Christopher Wood—have contributed to a thought-provoking environment in which to teach and write. Andrea Dortmann is both a treasured, like-minded colleague and a dear friend. In matters large and small, Elisabeth

Bronfen has been an invaluable mentor. Lindsay O'Connor, with her wry insight and good humor, has made the very day-to-day possible at all. Within the wider NYU community, Ruth Ben-Ghiat, Emanuela Bianchi, Juliane Camfield, Patrick Deer, Jay Garcia, Stefanos Geroulanos, Sarah Girner, Jordana Mendelson, Ara Merjian, Christopher Schlottmann, Liana Theodoratou, Cristina Vatulescu, and Larry Wolff have provided feedback and support that have made a difference. Aaron Gray was instrumental in preparing the manuscript, notes, and bibliography. The solidarity and *Sitzfleisch* of Elizabeth Benninger and Lauren Wolfe, unparalleled, mean the world.

Portions of this work have been presented at national and international conferences and workshops, as well as in invited lectures. I have profited immensely from colleagues' questions and remarks at these events over the years. Wendelin Schmidt-Dengler shaped much of my early thinking in and about Vienna, and many conversations that began with him have continued even in his absence. For their intellectual engagement and generosity, my deepest gratitude is owed Leslie Adelson, Susan Bernofsky, Tobias Boes, Deborah Coen, John Deak, Paul Fleming, Deborah Holmes, Anton Holzer, Dania Hückmann, Andreas Huyssen, Christine Ivanovic, Katja Kaluga, Teresa Kovacs, Leo Lensing, Helmut Lethen, Venkat Mani, Simon May, Werner Michler, Dorothea von Mücke, Martin Anton Müller, Lutz Musner, Fatima Naqvi, Martin Rauchbauer, Lisa Silverman, Ingrid Söllner-Pötz and the entire IFK team, Lauren Shizuko Stone, Janek Wasserman, Erica Weitzman, and Ingo Zechner. I am honored that Robert Hass granted permission to quote from his poem.

The staffs of many libraries and archives have not merely facilitated my research but have, more times than I can count, led me to hidden treasures it sometimes took me years to fully appreciate. Special thanks are due to the Österreichische Nationalbibliothek, the Filmarchiv Austria, the Museum für angewandte Kunst, the Albertina, the Leopold Museum and its Egon Schiele Dokumentationszentrum, the Josephinum, the Österreichisches Theatermuseum, and the Wien Museum. Particular appreciation is reserved for the Wienbibliothek im Rathaus, my scholarly home, and to all the amazing librarians and archivists there, as well as to its former director, Sylvia Mattl-Wurm.

Priya Nelson at the University of Chicago Press could not possibly have been a more skilled or generous editor. I am grateful to her for believing in this project—and in me. The same could be said for Dylan Montanari, editorial associate, who likewise provided unparalleled expertise and professionalism. Elizabeth Ellingboe's eagle eye and precise pen spared me many embarrassments. Thanks are owed to the two anonymous readers who evaluated the manuscript for the press. Their astute readings and vital criticisms helped to shape the final contours of this project. Shannon Li prepared a detailed index with skill.

I am profoundly indebted to my friends and family, who are my home, my heart, my center. Anastasia Arabatzi, Siarhei Biareishyk, Hana Blahová and Kurt Ifkovits, Claire Blake, Pia Clodi, Janice Gitterman and Steve Kirschner, Elisabeth Hargassner, Sophie Hochhäusl, Armin Loacker, Lee Pinkas, Romana and Philipp Sammern, Tatjana Schimkat, Walter Schübler, Jill Shaw, Paige Sweet, Cornelia Untersberger, Jorge Daniel Veneciano, Nina Wenko, and Kelly Whitman have provided boundless encouragement, confidence, laughter, and benevolent care that have bolstered me, even in the most challenging times. Long before I knew her personally, Rhonda Garelick was a role model—and has continued to be in friendship. Nitzan Lebovic delivered inspiration at an especially crucial point in the project by reminding me to use the present tense. When I seemed to have forgotten the steps, Sonia Werner has led me in the dance. Though chance may have brought us together, the home Franziska Schenker, Franziska Liepe, and I created in the legendary Hahngasse has lived on. Together with Maxi Lengger, they are my *Seelenverwandten*. After all these years, they have continued to open their subsequent homes and their always-loving hearts to me, embracing me only as chosen sisters can. Words cannot begin to express my gratitude.

My great fortune is to have inherited—by some cosmic stroke of luck—a tribe I could not have better chosen had I been given the chance. Barbara and Chris Brassill, Carmen and Bruce Davis, Ray Iannetta, Sharon Iannetta, Frances X. Lopes and Austin Cave, and Heidi and Steve Pollack have shaped immeasurably the way I think, live, and love. Without Irmgard and Gert Künzel, my second parents, I would not speak German at all, let alone have visited Vienna in the first place. The Kurtz family and its extensions, including Toby Hobish, have been supportive beyond measure. Krysten George and Zach Reed-Harris, together with Owen, are the lights of my life. Finally, Glenn Kurtz has been there since before this book was even a glimmer in my mind's eye. At every step of the way, he has lived with me living with it—and lovingly accepted and encouraged, nourished and sustained me in more ways than I could possibly name. This book is dedicated to my mother, Kledus George, and to the memory of my father, Charles George—both health-care providers who, through their work, embodied commitment, service, and the power of a humane touch.

NOTES

INTRODUCTION

1. The Austrian Theater Museum's exhibition "Gegen Klimt: Die 'Nuda Veritas' und ihr Verteidiger Hermann Bahr" (May 10–November 26, 2012) contextualized the painting. No catalog was published. For a satirical take on the building project and its widespread press coverage, see Karl Kraus, "Villa Bahr," *Die Fackel* 2, no. 50 (August 1900): 23–24.

2. The painting was a reworking of a motif Klimt published in the Vienna Secession's art journal *Ver Sacrum* the year prior, in March 1898. The composition is essentially the same, but Klimt chose two different aphorisms for the images. In the painting, Klimt plays on Schiller and Goethe's polemical, two-line *Xenien* (1795–96), penned in answer to their critics. The painting was taken as the centerpiece for a wonderful exhibition at the Leopold Museum, Vienna, in 2005. See the catalog by Tobias G. Natter and Max Hollein, eds., *The Naked Truth: Klimt, Schiele, Kokoschka and Other Scandals*, trans. Elizabeth Clegg (Munich: Prestel, 2005). Though the title of the exhibition is the same as that of this book, the focus is different.

3. Michel Foucault, "Utopian Body," in *Sensorium: Embodied Experience, Technology, and Contemporary Art*, ed. Caroline A. Jones, trans. Lucia Allais, with Caroline A. Jones and Arnold Davidson (Cambridge, MA: MIT Press, 2006), 233. The reference is clearly to Jacques Lacan, *Écrits*, trans. Bruce Fink (New York: W. W. Norton, 2002).

4. "Ein Mensch *ist* immer zugleich Leib . . . und *hat* diesen Leib als diesen Körper." Helmut Plessner, "Lachen und Weinen," in *Philosophische Anthropologie*, ed. Helmut Plessner (Frankfurt: Fischer, 1970), 43. Originally published in 1941. For the terminological distinction, see Dietmar Kamper, "Körper," in *Ästhetische Grundbegriffe*, ed. Karlheinz Barck et al. (Stuttgart: Metzler, 2001), 3:426–50. It is also worth noting the centrality of the "naked" truth in Hans Blumenberg's metaphorology in *Paradigms for a Metaphorology*, trans. Robert Savage (Ithaca, NY: Cornell University Press, 2010), 40–51.

5. Hermann Bahr, "Die Moderne," in *Die Wiener Moderne: Literatur, Kunst und Musik zwischen 1980 und 1910*, ed. Gotthart Wunberg (Stuttgart: Reclam, 1981), 189–91.

6. Carl E. Schorske, *Fin-de-Siècle Vienna: Politics and Culture* (New York: Vintage, 1980), 4.

7. Schorske, *Fin-de-Siècle Vienna*, 280. For a crucial rereading of this aspect of Schorske's work, see Scott Spector, "Beyond the Aesthetic Garden: Politics and Culture on the Margins of Fin-de-Siècle Vienna," *Journal of the History of Ideas* 59, no. 4 (1998): 691–710.

8. Recent examples of how this inward turn has been applied to Viennese modernist portraiture and literature can be found, respectively, in Eric R. Kandel, *The Age of Insight: The Quest to Understand the Unconscious in Art, Mind, and Brain, from Vienna 1900 to the Present* (New York: Random House, 2012), and David S. Luft, *Eros and Inwardness in Vienna: Weininger, Musil, Doderer* (Chicago: University of Chicago Press, 2003).

9. Bahr, "Die Moderne," 190.

10. See Monika Sommer, Marcus Gräser, and Ursula Prutsch, eds., *Imaging Vienna: Innenansichten, Außenansichten, Stadterzählungen* (Vienna: Turia + Kant, 2006).

11. Karl Toepfer, *Empire of Ecstasy: Nudity and Movement in German Culture, 1910–1935* (Berkeley: University of California Press, 1997), 6. See also Harold B. Segel, *Body Ascendant: Modernism and the Physical Imperative* (Baltimore: Johns Hopkins University Press, 1998), who emphasizes the existence of a "physical imperative" within modernism more broadly. Additional works about the German and Austrian historical contexts include Michael Cowan and Kai Marcel Sicks, eds., *Leibhaftige Moderne: Körper in Kunst und Massenmedien 1918 bis 1933* (Bielefeld: transcript, 2005); Christiane Arndt and Silke Brodersen, eds., *Organismus und Gesellschaft: Der Körper in der deutschsprachigen Literatur des Realismus (1830–1930)* (Bielefeld: transcript, 2011); Siegfried Mattl, "Beiträge zu einer Geschichte des Körpers" (Habilitationsschrift, University of Vienna, 1994); Anne Fleig, *Körperkultur und Moderne: Robert Musils Ästhetik des Sports* (Berlin: de Gruyter, 2008); Claudia Benthien and Christoph Wulf, eds., *Körperteile: Eine kulturelle Anatomie* (Reinbek bei Hamburg: Rowohlt, 2001); Annette Keck, *Buchstäbliche Anatomien: Vom Lesen und Schreiben des Menschen—Literaturgeschichten der Moderne* (Würzburg: Königshausen & Neumann, 2007); Michael Hau, *The Cult of Health and Beauty in Germany: A Social History, 1890–1930* (Chicago: University of Chicago Press, 2003); and Erik N. Jensen, *Body by Weimar: Athletes, Gender, and German Modernity* (New York: Oxford University Press, 2010).

12. Toepfer, *Empire of Ecstasy*, 7.

13. Toepfer, *Empire of Ecstasy*, 7.

14. George L. Mosse, *Nationalism and Sexuality: Middle-Class Morality and Sexual Norms in Modern Europe* (Madison: University of Wisconsin Press, 1985), 48–65. For a more recent take on the effects of World War I on medical science and the understanding of the human body in a trans-European context, see Stefanos Geroulanos and Todd Meyers, *The Human Body in the Age of Catastrophe: Brittleness, Integration, Science, and the Great War* (Chicago: University of Chicago Press, 2018).

15. Hubert Christian Ehalt, "Die Neuerfindung Wiens—Carl E. Schorske," in *Schorskes Wien: Eine Neuerfindung*, Wiener Vorlesungen im Rathaus 167 (Vienna: Picus, 2012), 18. See also Nathan J. Timpano, *Constructing the Viennese Modern Body: Art, Hysteria, and the Puppet* (New York: Routledge, 2017). Timpano has positioned

what he calls the "non-abstracted body" as the hallmark of fin-de-siècle Viennese visual art, a type of figuration no less radical, he argues, than other iterations of European modernist art, such as cubism (3). His thesis that "hystero-theatrical gestures" were a defining feature of Viennese modernist cultural production draws heavily on and extends previous scholarship in art history that makes largely speculative connections between Viennese modernist portraiture and photographs of hysteria patients from Jean-Martin Charcot's work at the Salpêtrière hospital in Paris. See Gemma Blackshaw and Leslie Topp, eds., *Madness and Modernity: Mental Illness and the Visual Arts in Vienna 1900* (Farnham: Lund Humphries, 2009), and Gemma Blackshaw, "The Pathological Body: Modernist Strategising in Egon Schiele's Self-Portraiture," *Oxford Art Journal* 30, no. 3 (2007): 377–401.

16. Werner Hofmann, "Das Fleisch erkennen," in *Ornament und Askese im Zeitgeist des Wien der Jahrhundertwende*, ed. Alfred Pfabigan (Vienna: Brandstätter, 1985), 120–29; Hilde Spiel, *Vienna's Golden Autumn 1866–1938* (London: Weidenfeld and Nicolson, 1987), 79–82.

17. Hofmann, "Das Fleisch erkennen," 125. Eric L. Santner, *On Creaturely Life: Rilke, Benjamin, Sebald* (Chicago: University of Chicago Press, 2006), xviii–xix, has argued in a different context that attention to creaturely life can show how extraordinary sociopolitical circumstances are manifested through and on the body.

18. It is designated the "second Vienna medical school" to distinguish it from Gerard van Swieten's "first Vienna medical school," backed by Joseph II's reformist, enlightened absolutism of the second half of the eighteenth century. Van Swieten's innovations included a focus on hygiene, the introduction of bedside clinical training, and, not least, the founding of the Vienna General Hospital in 1784.

19. Sigmund Freud, *The Standard Edition of the Complete Psychological Works of Sigmund Freud*, ed. and trans. James Strachey, 24 vols. (London: Hogarth Press, 1953–74), 19:191. The list of scholars who have followed Freud's directive is too long to list here. The philosophical and scientific legacies of positivism, German idealism, and neo-Kantianism for psychoanalysis have been demonstrated, e.g., by Paul Ricoeur, *Freud and Philosophy: An Essay on Interpretation* (New Haven, CT: Yale University Press, 1970); Frank Sulloway, *Freud, Biologist of the Mind: Beyond the Psychoanalytic Legend* (New York: Basic Books, 1979); Peter Gay, *Freud: A Life for Our Time* (New York: W. W. Norton, 1988).

20. William M. Johnston, *The Austrian Mind: An Intellectual and Social History, 1848–1938* (Berkeley: University of California Press, 1972), 229.

21. W. F. Bynum, *Science and the Practice of Medicine in the Nineteenth Century* (Cambridge: Cambridge University Press, 1994), 97.

22. Luft, *Eros and Inwardness in Vienna*, 22. See also Erna Lesky, *The Vienna Medical School of the 19th Century*, trans. L. Williams and I. S. Levij (Baltimore: Johns Hopkins University Press, 1976), 7.

23. On Freud's "radical materialist" phase, see Ernest Jones, *Sigmund Freud: Life and Work*, vol. 1, *The Young Freud, 1856–1900* (London: Hogarth Press, 1956), 47–50; and Sulloway, *Freud, Biologist of the Mind*.

24. In Vienna, Rokitansky became chair of the first independent department of pathological anatomy in the German-speaking world.

25. Johnston, *The Austrian Mind*, 223. Fritz Wittels, *Freud and the Child Woman: The Memoirs of Fritz Wittels*, ed. Edward Timms (New Haven, CT: Yale University Press, 1995), writing from a firsthand perspective, was perhaps the first to employ this term.

26. Philipp Sarasin, *Reizbare Maschinen: Eine Geschichte des Körpers 1765–1914* (Frankfurt: Suhrkamp, 2001), 96.

27. Within Austrian culture, this tenet makes its presence felt in everything from the detailed rules governing the treatment of mortal remains in the elaborate Habsburg burial practices to Hermann Nitsch's *Orgien Mysterien Theater*, a series of ongoing action-performances first conceived as a Gesamtkunstwerk in the 1950s. Hofmann, "Das Fleisch erkennen," 126.

28. David Luft, "Modernism, Postmodernism and the Human Sciences," in *Metropole Wien: Texturen der Moderne*, 2 vols., ed. Roman Horak et al., Wiener Vorlesungen 9 (Vienna: WUV-Universitätsverlag, 2000), 2:36–37. See also Luft, *Eros and Inwardness in Vienna*.

29. Friedrich Nietzsche, *Thus Spoke Zarathustra: A Book for All and None*, ed. Adrian Del Caro and Robert Pippin, trans. Adrian Del Caro (Cambridge: Cambridge University Press, 2006), 23.

30. See Maxine Sheets-Johnstone, *The Corporeal Turn: An Interdisciplinary Reader* (Exeter, UK: Imprint Academic, 2009); John Tamborino, *The Corporeal Turn: Passion, Necessity, Politics* (Lanham, MD: Rowman & Littlefield, 2002); and Barbara Kirshenblatt-Gimblett, "The Corporeal Turn," *Jewish Quarterly Review* 95, no. 3 (2005): 447–61.

31. Norbert Elias, *Über den Prozeß der Zivilisation: Soziogenetische und psychogenetische Untersuchungen*, 17th ed., 2 vols. (Frankfurt: Suhrkamp, 1992); Michel Foucault's four-volume *History of Sexuality*, the first three of which have been translated in English by Robert Hurley (New York: Pantheon Books, 1978–86); Michel Foucault, *The Birth of the Clinic: An Archaeology of Medical Perception*, trans. A. M. Sheridan Smith (New York: Vintage, 1994); Michel Foucault, *Discipline and Punish: The Birth of the Prison*, trans. Alan Sheridan, 2nd ed. (New York: Vintage, 1995).

32. A brief bibliography of the field would begin with four key edited projects: Michel Feher, Ramona Naddaff, and Nadia Tazi, eds., *Fragments for a History of the Human Body*, 3 vols. (New York: Zone Books, 1989); Alain Corbin, Jean-Jacques Courtine, and Georges Vigarello, eds., *Histoire du corps*, 3 vols. (Paris: Seuil, 2004); Linda Kalof and William Bynum, eds., *A Cultural History of the Human Body*, 6 vols. (London: Bloomsbury, 2010–12); Sarah Toulalan and Kate Fisher, eds., *The Routledge History of Sex and the Body, 1500 to the Present* (London: Routledge, 2013); as well as Maren Lorenz, *Leibhaftige Vergangenheit: Einführung in die Körpergeschichte* (Tübingen: edition diskord, 2000). All contain comprehensive bibliographies for body studies at large. Other significant works, and this list is by no means exhaustive, include Dietmar Kamper and Christoph Wulf, *Die Wiederkehr des Körpers* (Frankfurt/Main: Suhrkamp, 1982); Roy Porter, "History of the Body," in *New Perspectives on Historical Writing*, ed. Peter Burke (Cambridge: Polity Press, 1991), 206–32; Catherine Gallagher and Thomas Laqueur, eds., *The Making of the Modern Body: Sexuality and Society in the*

Nineteenth Century (Berkeley: University of California Press, 1987); Thomas Laqueur, *Making Sex: Body and Gender from the Greeks to Freud* (Cambridge, MA: Harvard University Press, 1990); Caroline Bynum, "Why All the Fuss about the Body? A Medievalist's Perspective," *Critical Inquiry* 22, no. 1 (1995): 1–33; Kathleen Canning, "The Body as Method? Reflections on the Place of the Body in Gender History," *Gender & History* 11, no. 3 (1999): 499–513; Anson Rabinbach, *The Human Motor: Energy, Fatigue, and the Origins of Modernity* (New York: Basic Books, 1990); Mike Featherstone, Mike Hepworth, and Bryan S. Turner, eds., *The Body: Social Process and Cultural Theory* (London: SAGE, 1991); Richard Sennett, *Flesh and Stone: The Body and the City in Western Civilization* (New York: Knopf, 1994); Philipp Sarasin and Jakob Tanner, eds., *Physiologie und industrielle Gesellschaft: Studien zur Verwissenschaftlichung des Körpers im 19. und 20. Jahrhundert* (Frankfurt: Suhrkamp, 1998); Tim Armstrong, *Modernism, Technology, and the Body: A Cultural Study* (Cambridge: Cambridge University Press, 1998); Ivan Crozier, "Introduction: Bodies in History—The Task of the Historian," in *A Cultural History of the Human Body in the Modern Age*, ed. Ivan Crozier, A Cultural History of the Human Body 6 (London: Bloomsbury, 2010), 1–22; and Sarasin, *Reizbare Maschinen*.

33. Bynum, "Why All the Fuss."

34. Judith Butler, *Gender Trouble: Feminism and the Subversion of Identity* (New York: Routledge, 1990); Judith Butler, *Bodies That Matter: On the Discursive Limits of "Sex"* (New York: Routledge, 1993); Susan Bordo, *Unbearable Weight: Feminism, Western Culture, and the Body* (Berkeley: University of California Press, 1993); Susan Bordo, *The Male Body: A New Look at Men in Public and in Private* (New York: Farrar, Straus and Giroux, 1999); Elizabeth Grosz, *Volatile Bodies: Toward a Corporeal Feminism* (Indianapolis: Indiana University Press, 1994).

35. Bordo, *Unbearable Weight*, 26–28.

36. See Sander L. Gilman, *Difference and Pathology: Stereotypes of Sexuality, Race, and Madness* (Ithaca, NY: Cornell University Press, 1985); Sander L. Gilman, *The Jew's Body* (New York: Routledge, 1991); Sander L. Gilman, *Freud, Race, and Gender* (Princeton, NJ: Princeton University Press, 1993); Sander L. Gilman, "Der jüdische Körper: Gedanken zum physischen Anderssein der Juden," in *Die Macht der Bilder: Antisemitische Vorurteile und Mythen*, ed. Jüdisches Museum der Stadt Wien (Vienna: Picus Verlag, 1995), 168–79.

37. Gilman, *Freud, Race, and Gender*, 5–6; Klaus Hödl, *Die Pathologisierung des jüdischen Körpers: Antisemitismus, Geschlecht und Medizin im Fin de Siècle* (Vienna: Picus, 1997). For more on the corporeal turn in Jewish studies, specifically, see Kirshenblatt-Gimblett, "The Corporeal Turn."

38. Bynum, "Why All the Fuss," 7.

39. Lynda Nead, *The Female Nude: Art, Obscenity, and Sexuality* (London: Routledge, 1992), 16.

40. For the intersection of these domains in what is termed *new cultural history*, see Peter Burke, *What Is Cultural History?*, 2nd ed. (Cambridge: Polity, 2008), 51–76.

41. Marshall Berman, *All That Is Solid Melts into Air: The Experience of Modernity* (New York: Penguin, 1988). See in particular the introduction "Modernity: Yester-

day, Today and Tomorrow" (15–36), in which he lays out the terminological distinctions between "modernity," "modernization," and "modernism" (15–16)—definitions to which I adhere.

42. Schorske, *Fin-de-Siècle Vienna*, 4–5, 226; Jacques Le Rider, *Modernity and Crises of Identity: Culture and Society in Fin-de-Siècle Vienna*, trans. Rosemary Morris (New York: Continuum, 1993); John W. Boyer, *Culture and Political Crisis in Vienna: Christian Socialism in Power, 1897–1918* (Chicago: University of Chicago Press, 1995).

43. Sara Danius, *The Senses of Modernism: Technology, Perception, and Aesthetics* (Ithaca, NY: Cornell University Press, 2002), 7, 54.

44. W. H. Auden, sonnet XXV from "In Time of War," in W. H. Auden and Christopher Isherwood, *Journey to a War* (London: Faber and Faber, 1939), 283.

45. Robert Musil, *The Man without Qualities*, trans. Sophie Wilkins and Burton Pike (New York: Vintage, 1996), 1:412.

46. Elaine Scarry, *The Body in Pain: The Making and Unmaking of the World* (New York: Oxford University Press, 1985), 14.

47. Michael Sappol, "Introduction: Empires in Bodies; Bodies in Empires," in *A Cultural History of the Human Body in the Age of Empire*, ed. Michael Sappol and Stephen P. Rice, A Cultural History of the Human Body 5 (London: Bloomsbury, 2012), 28.

48. Hermann Bahr, *Tagebuch* (Berlin: Cassirer, 1909), 67.

49. The most important studies on the history of the body for the period I consider treat specific national contexts in Europe, with Germany a particular focus. See Mark M. Anderson, *Kafka's Clothes: Ornament and Aestheticism in the Habsburg Fin de Siècle* (Oxford: Clarendon Press, 1992); Paul Weindling, *Health, Race and German Politics between National Unification and Nazism, 1870–1945* (Cambridge: Cambridge University Press, 1989); Hau, *Cult of Health and Beauty*; Jensen, *Body by Weimar*; Chad Ross, *Naked Germany: Health, Race and the Nation* (New York: Berg Publishers, 2005); Cornelie Usborne, *The Politics of the Body in Weimar Germany: Women's Reproductive Rights and Duties* (Ann Arbor: University of Michigan Press, 1992); Alfred Thomas, *The Bohemian Body: Gender and Sexuality in Modern Czech Culture* (Madison: University of Wisconsin Press, 2007); Armstrong, *Modernism, Technology, and the Body*; Cowan and Sicks, *Leibhaftige Moderne*; Mattl, "Beiträge zu einer Geschichte." Three foundational edited volumes look at the cultural history of the body transnationally, yet the individual contributions often adhere to national boundaries: Feher, Naddaff, and Tazi, *Fragments for a History of the Human Body*; Crozier, *A Cultural History of the Human Body in the Modern Age*; Sappol and Rice, *A Cultural History of the Human Body in the Age of Empire*.

50. Scott Spector, "Marginalizations: Politics and Culture beyond *Fin-de-Siècle* Vienna," in *Rethinking Vienna 1900*, ed. Steven Beller (New York: Berghahn, 2001), 137.

51. Two masterful examples of the revelations afforded by an approach that transcends conventional chronologies are Britta McEwen, *Sexual Knowledge: Feeling, Fact, and Social Reform in Vienna, 1900–1934* (New York: Berghahn, 2012), and Marci Shore, *Caviar and Ashes: A Warsaw Generation's Life and Death in Marxism, 1918–1968* (New Haven, CT: Yale University Press, 2006).

52. McEwen, *Sexual Knowledge*; Weindling, *Health, Race and German Politics*; Hau, *Cult of Health and Beauty*; and Edward Ross Dickinson, "Biopolitics, Fascism,

Democracy: Some Reflections on Our Discourse about 'Modernity,'" *Central European History* 37, no. 1 (2004): 1–48, as well as the following studies on eugenics: Gerhard Baader, Veronika Hofer, and Thomas Mayer, eds., *Eugenik in Österreich: Biopolitische Strukturen von 1900–1945* (Vienna: Czernin, 2007); Gudrun Exner, Josef Kytir, and Alexander Pinwinkler, *Bevölkerungswissenschaft in Österreich in der Zwischenkriegszeit: Personen, Institutionen, Diskurse* (Vienna: Böhlau, 2004); Marius Turda, ed., *The History of East-Central European Eugenics, 1900–1945: Sources and Commentaries* (London: Bloomsbury, 2015); Marius Turda, *Modernism and Eugenics* (Basingstoke: Palgrave Macmillan, 2010).

53. Geoff Eley, "Introduction 1: Is There a History of the *Kaiserreich*?," in *Society, Culture, and the State in Germany, 1870–1930*, ed. Geoff Eley (Ann Arbor: University of Michigan Press, 1996), 31. See also Zygmunt Bauman, *Modernity and Ambivalence* (Ithaca, NY: Cornell University Press, 1991), 29, and Dickinson's excellent "Biopolitics, Fascism, Democracy," 6. Eley contests that "the ground for the Final Solution was being discursively laid" even prior to World War I (28).

54. Steven Beller, ed., *Rethinking Vienna 1900* (New York: Berghahn, 2001); Wendelin Schmidt-Dengler, *Ohne Nostalgie: Zur österreichischen Literatur der Zwischenkriegszeit* (Vienna: Böhlau, 2002); Ehalt, "Die Neuerfindung Wiens," 13–35; Evelyne Polt-Heinzl, *Ringstraßenzeit und Wiener Moderne: Porträt einer literarischen Epoche des Übergangs* (Vienna: Sonderzahl, 2015); Moritz Czáky, *Ideologie der Operette und Wiener Moderne: Ein kulturhistorischer Essay zur österreichischen Identität* (Vienna: Böhlau, 1996).

55. The framework I suggest moreover answers to historian Pieter Judson's call for new, large-scale narratives that suggest alternative ordering structures for historical research on Austria. Pieter M. Judson, *The Habsburg Empire: A New History* (Cambridge, MA: Belknap Press of Harvard University Press, 2016), 15.

56. Gotthart Wunberg, ed., *Die Wiener Moderne: Literatur, Kunst und Musik zwischen 1890 und 1910* (Stuttgart: Reclam, 1981).

57. Ehalt, "Die Neuerfindung Wiens," 15.

58. Roman Horak et al., eds., *Metropole Wien: Texturen der Moderne*, 2 vols., Wiener Vorlesungen 9 (Vienna: WUV-Universitätsverlag, 2000), 2:11. Many of the editors are or were affiliated with the Society for the History of the Workers' Movement in Vienna (Verein für die Geschichte der Arbeiterbewegung) and its important mythbusting work.

59. *Traum und Wirklichkeit: Wien 1870–1930* (Vienna: Eigenverlag der Museen der Stadt Wien, 1985); Johnston, *The Austrian Mind*. See Peter Nicholls, *Modernisms: A Literary Guide* (Berkeley: University of California Press, 1995), for a wider perspective.

60. Helmut Gruber, *Red Vienna: Experiment in Working-Class Culture, 1919–1934* (New York: Oxford University Press, 1991); Deborah Holmes and Lisa Silverman, eds., *Interwar Vienna: Culture between Tradition and Modernity* (Rochester, NY: Camden House, 2009); Wolfgang Kos, ed., *Kampf um die Stadt: Politik, Kunst und Alltag um 1930* (Vienna: Czernin, 2009). See also Heidemarie Uhl, "Carl E. Schorske und die Erfindung von 'Wien um 1900,'" in *Schorskes Wien: Eine Neuerfindung*, Wiener Vorlesungen im Rathaus 167 (Vienna: Picus, 2012), 37–42.

61. Schorske, *Fin-de-Siècle Vienna*; Johnston, *The Austrian Mind*; Allan Janik and

Stephen Toulmin, *Wittgenstein's Vienna* (New York: Simon and Schuster, 1973); Kandel, *The Age of Insight*; Wunberg, *Die Wiener Moderne*; Le Rider, *Modernity and Crises of Identity.*

62. In other national traditions, Vanessa R. Schwartz, *Spectacular Realities: Early Mass Culture in Fin-de-Siècle Paris* (Berkeley: University of California Press, 1999); Janet Ward, *Weimar Surfaces: Urban Visual Culture in 1920s Germany* (Berkeley: University of California Press, 2001); Andreas Huyssen, *After the Great Divide: Modernism, Mass Culture, Postmodernism* (Bloomington: Indiana University Press, 1986); and Andreas Huyssen, *Miniature Metropolis: Literature in an Age of Photography and Film* (Cambridge, MA: Harvard University Press, 2015), have demonstrated the imperative of integrating popular culture into our work on modernism. Two newer, internationally oriented surveys of modernism—Daniel Albright, *Putting Modernism Together: Literature, Music, and Painting, 1872–1927* (Baltimore: Johns Hopkins University Press, 2015), and Peter Gay, *Modernism: The Lure of Heresy* (New York: W. W. Norton, 2007)—show just how enriching such an approach can be.

63. Huyssen, *After the Great Divide.*

64. Mary Gluck, "Afterthoughts about Fin-de-Siècle Vienna: The Problem of Aesthetic Culture in Central Europe," in *Rethinking Vienna 1900*, ed. Steven Beller (New York: Berghahn, 2001), 268–69.

65. See especially Steven Beller, introduction to *Rethinking Vienna 1900*, ed. Steven Beller (New York: Berghahn, 2001), 11–18, and Horak et al., *Metropole Wien*, 1:7, 2:7–12.

66. Lisa Silverman, *Becoming Austrians: Jews and Culture between the World Wars* (New York: Oxford University Press, 2012); Julie M. Johnson, *The Memory Factory: The Forgotten Women Artists of Vienna 1900* (West Lafayette, IN: Purdue University Press, 2012); Harriet Anderson, *Utopian Feminism: Women's Movements in Fin-de-Siècle Vienna* (New Haven, CT: Yale University Press, 1992). See also Polt-Heinzl, *Ringstraßenzeit und Wiener Moderne*; Lisa Fischer and Emil Brix, eds., *Die Frauen der Wiener Moderne* (Vienna: Verlag für Geschichte und Politik, 1997); David F. Good, Margarete Grandner, and Mary Jo Maynes, eds., *Austrian Women in the Nineteenth and Twentieth Centuries: Cross-Disciplinary Perspectives* (Providence: Berghahn, 1996); Brigitte Spreitzer, *Texturen: Die österreichische Moderne der Frauen*, Studien zur Moderne 8 (Vienna: Passagen Verlag, 1999); Megan Brandow-Faller, "An Art of Their Own: Reinventing *Frauenkunst* in the Female Academies and Artist Leagues of Late-Imperial and First Republic Austria, 1900–1930" (PhD diss., Georgetown University, 2010); and Deborah Holmes, *Langeweile ist Gift: Das Leben der Eugenie Schwarzwald*, trans. Esther Marian and Fanny Esterházy (Salzburg: Residenz Verlag, 2012).

67. Stefan Zweig, *The World of Yesterday*, trans. Anthea Bell (Lincoln: University of Nebraska Press, 2009), 43–44.

68. Steven Beller, *Vienna and the Jews, 1867–1938: A Cultural History* (Cambridge: Cambridge University Press, 1989); Silverman, *Becoming Austrians*; Marsha L. Rozenblit, *The Jews of Vienna, 1867-1914: Assimilation and Identity* (Albany: State University of New York Press, 1983); Marsha L. Rozenblit, *Reconstructing a National Identity: The Jews of Habsburg Austria during World War I* (New York: Oxford University Press, 2001); Abigail Gillman, *Viennese Jewish Modernism: Freud, Hofmannsthal,*

Beer-Hofmann, and Schnitzler (University Park: Pennsylvania State University Press, 2009); Elana Shapira, *Style and Seduction: Jewish Patrons, Architecture, and Design in Fin-de-Siècle Vienna* (Waltham: Brandeis University Press, 2016); Alison Rose, *Jewish Women in Fin-de-Siècle Vienna* (Austin: University of Texas Press, 2008); Elisabeth Malleier, *Jüdische Frauen in Wien, 1816–1938* (Vienna: Mandelbaum, 2003); Klaus Hödl, *Wiener Juden—jüdische Wiener: Identität, Gedächtnis und Performanz im 19. Jahrhundert* (Innsbruck: Studien-Verlag, 2006); and Hillary Hope Herzog, *Vienna Is Different: Jewish Writers in Austria from the Fin de Siècle to the Present* (New York: Berghahn, 2011), have all documented the central contributions of Jewish writers and intellectuals to the Viennese modernist cultural field.

69. Scott Spector, *Violent Sensations: Sex, Crime, and Utopia in Vienna and Berlin, 1860–1914* (Chicago: University of Chicago Press, 2016); Spector, "Beyond the Aesthetic Garden"; Wolfgang Maderthaner and Lutz Musner, *Die Anarchie der Vorstadt: Das andere Wien um 1900* (Frankfurt: Campus Verlag, 1999), translated by David Fernbach and Michael Huffmaster as *Unruly Masses: The Other Side of Fin-de-Siècle Vienna* (New York: Berghahn, 2008).

70. "Klimt und die Frauen," Belvedere, Vienna, 2000–2001; "Egon Schiele's Women," Galerie St. Etienne, New York, 2012; "The Women of Klimt, Schiele, and Kokoschka," Belvedere, Vienna, 2015–16.

71. Friedrich Stadler, *Vom Positivismus zur "wissenschaftlichen Weltauffassung": Am Beispiel der Wirkungsgeschichte von Ernst Mach in Österreich von 1895 bis 1934* (Vienna: Löcker, 1982), was the first to mark this omission by Schorske. Deborah R. Coen, *Vienna in the Age of Uncertainty: Science, Liberalism, and Private Life* (Chicago: University of Chicago Press, 2007), charts the development of the sciences in Vienna through the microhistory of a single family. Kandel, *The Age of Insight*, framed fin-de-siècle Viennese portraiture as the starting point for modern neuroscience, while sexual science in Vienna was the focus of Luft, *Eros and Inwardness in Vienna*, and McEwen, *Sexual Knowledge*. Laura Otis, *Membranes: Metaphors of Invasion in Nineteenth-Century Literature, Science, and Politics* (Baltimore: Johns Hopkins University Press, 2000), shows how advances in cell biology dovetailed with social anxieties about contamination and were manifested metaphorically in late nineteenth-century literature. The intersection between turn-of-the-century psychiatry, the visual arts, and architecture was the focus of a 2009 exhibition and catalog, Blackshaw and Topp, *Madness and Modernity*. Finally, Markus Oppenauer, *Der Salon Zuckerkandl im Kontext von Wissenschaft, Politik und Öffentlichkeit: Populärwissenschaftliche Aspekte der Wiener Salonkultur um 1900* (Weitra: Bibliothek der Provinz, 2012), highlighted Berta Zuckerkandl's salon as an intellectual matrix of influencers that reached into nearly every aspect of Viennese life around 1900.

72. Edward Timms, *Karl Kraus, Apocalyptic Satirist: Culture and Catastrophe in Habsburg Vienna* (New Haven, CT: Yale University Press, 1986); Edward Timms, *Karl Kraus, Apocalyptic Satirist: The Post-War Crisis and the Rise of the Swastika* (New Haven, CT: Yale University Press, 2005); Edward Timms, *Dynamik der Kreise, Resonanz der Räume: Die schöpferischen Impulse der Wiener Moderne* (Weitra: Bibliothek der Provinz, 2013).

73. Janek Wasserman, *Black Vienna: The Radical Right in the Red City, 1918–1938*

(Ithaca, NY: Cornell University Press, 2014), has followed a similar tack for interwar intellectual culture and politics, while Tobias Natter, ed., *Die Galerie Miethke: Eine Kunsthandlung im Zentrum der Moderne* (Vienna: Jüdisches Museum der Stadt Wien, 2003), highlights the social networks and patronage webs in which leading artists were enmeshed.

74. Robert Musil, *Precision and Soul: Essays and Addresses*, ed. and trans. Burton Pike and David S. Luft (Chicago: University of Chicago Press, 1990), 6.

75. Paul Valéry, "Some Simple Reflections on the Body," in *The Collected Works of Paul Valéry*, vol. 13, *Aesthetics*, trans. Ralph Mannheim (London: Pantheon, 1964), 31–40.

CHAPTER ONE

1. "Aschanti-Neger in Wien," *Neues Wiener Tagblatt*, July 11, 1896, 5.

2. "Ankunft der Aschanti-Neger," *Illustrirtes Wiener Extrablatt*, July 11, 1896, 4.

3. R[obert] F[ranceschini], "Das Aschanti-Fieber," *Neues Wiener Tagblatt*, October 7, 1896.

4. "Im Aschantidorf: Exotische Gäste im Wiener Thiergarten," *Neues Wiener Tagblatt*, July 16, 1896, 3.

5. See Sadiah Qureshi, *Peoples on Parade: Exhibitions, Empire, and Anthropology in Nineteenth-Century Britain* (Chicago: University of Chicago Press, 2011).

6. Werner Michael Schwarz, *Anthropologische Spektakel: Zur Schaustellung "exotischer" Menschen, Wien 1870–1910* (Vienna: Turia + Kant, 2001), 16. Schwarz's book includes an appendix detailing the individual exhibitions. All further information about specific exhibitions in Vienna—including dates, locations, organizers, number of participants, etc.—is culled from his documentation unless otherwise noted. Schwarz, *Anthropologische Spektakel*, 223–44.

7. See Nicola Lepp, Martin Roth, and Klaus Vogel, eds., *Der Neue Mensch: Obsessionen des 20. Jahrhunderts* (Ostfildern-Ruit: Hatje Cantz, 1999).

8. Of the more than fifty *Völkerschauen* Vienna hosted between 1870 and 1910, the Ashanti village of 1896 was the first large-scale exhibit of its kind in the zoological garden. Schwarz, *Anthropologische Spektakel*, 148.

9. "Im Aschantidorf," 3. Organized by Bouvier and Bamberger, the display was mounted from July 10 to October 20, 1896.

10. "Aschanti-Neger in Wien," 5; "Bei den Aschanti-Negern," *Neues Wiener Tagblatt*, August 9, 1896, 6. The exhibition was so consistently popular that Bamberger brought a second exhibit, the "Grand Ethnographic Exhibition: The African Gold Coast," with approximately 120 natives to Vienna just six months later (April 18 to October 24, 1897).

11. F[ranceschini], "Aschanti-Fieber," 1.

12. Else Feldmann, "Aschanti und Buren," *Arbeiter-Zeitung*, January 15, 1928, sec. Sonntagsbeilage der Arbeiter-Zeitung.

13. Quoted in Werner Michler, *Darwinismus und Literatur: Naturwissenschaftliche und literarische Intelligenz in Österreich, 1859–1914* (Vienna: Böhlau, 1999), 356.

14. Qureshi, *Peoples on Parade*, 2–4.

15. Vanessa R. Schwartz, *Spectacular Realities: Early Mass Culture in Fin-de-Siècle Paris* (Berkeley: University of California Press, 1999), 2.

16. Felix Salten, *Wurstelprater* (Vienna: Rosenbaum, 1911). See also the reprint of Salten's text and accompanying essays in Siegfried Mattl, Klaus Müller-Richter, and Werner Michael Schwarz, eds., *Felix Salten: Wurstelprater. Ein Schlüsseltext zur Wiener Moderne* (Vienna: Promedia, 2004).

17. Schwarz, *Anthropologische Spektakel*, 35.

18. "Aschanti-Lotterie," *Neue Freie Presse*, October 11, 1896, Morgenblatt edition, 7; Arthur Schnitzler, *Tagebuch 1879–1892* (Vienna: Verlag der Österreichischen Akademie der Wissenschaften, 1987), 2, 218; Arthur Schnitzler and Richard Beer-Hofmann, *Briefwechsel 1891–1931*, ed. Konstanze Fliedl (Vienna: Europaverlag, 1992), 106. Schnitzler's curious story "Andreas Thameyer's Last Letter" (Andreas Thameyers letzter Brief, 1902) relates the story of a cuckolded Viennese husband in denial, whose wife bears a black child after visiting the human display in the Prater.

19. Theodor Herzl, "Der Menschengarten," in *Feuilletons I*, ed. Theodor Herzl (Berlin: Singer, 1911), 153. For more on Herzl's reception of the Ashanti displays of 1896 and 1897, see Michler, *Darwinismus und Literatur*, 351–95.

20. Heinrich Leutemann, *Lebensbeschreibung des Thierhändlers Carl Hagenbeck* (Hamburg: Hagenbeck, 1887), 48; quoted and translated in Eric Ames, "From the Exotic to the Everyday: The Ethnographic Exhibition in Germany," in *The Nineteenth-Century Visual Culture Reader*, ed. Vanessa R. Schwartz and Jeannene M. Przyblyski (New York: Routledge, 2004), 314.

21. Susan Stewart, *On Longing: Narratives of the Miniature, the Gigantic, the Souvenir, the Collection* (Durham: Duke University Press, 1993), xii, 136.

22. Translated by and quoted in Ames, "From the Exotic to the Everyday," 313.

23. Schwartz, *Spectacular Realities*, 128–30; Siegfried Mattl, "Körperspektakel: Ein anatomisch-pathologisches und ethnologisches Museum im *fin-de-siècle* Wien," *Wiener Zeitschrift zur Geschichte der Neuzeit* 4, no. 2 (2004): 61.

24. Alys X. George, "Anatomy for All: Medical Knowledge on the Fairground in *Fin-de-Siècle* Vienna," *Central European History* 51, no. 4 (2018): 535–62; Mattl, "Körperspektakel," 61; Schwartz, *Spectacular Realities*, 131.

25. Human displays grew out of an earlier, but related, kind of commercialization of the body, that of the circus and its adjacent freak show, in the mid-nineteenth century. See Robert Bogdan, *Freak Show: Presenting Human Oddities for Amusement and Profit* (Chicago: University of Chicago Press, 1990), and Rosemarie Garland Thomson, ed., *Freakery: Cultural Spectacles of the Extraordinary Body* (New York: New York University Press, 1996).

26. For more on this interface with specific attention to displays of human anatomy, see George, "Anatomy for All."

27. "Zwischenfälle im Aschantidorf," *Neues Wiener Tagblatt*, October 12, 1896, 3.

28. "Gerichtssaal: Die Gattin des Aschanti-Häuptlings," *Neues Wiener Tagblatt*, October 15, 1896, Abendblatt edition, 2; "Gerichtssaal: Die Gattin des Aschanti-Häuptlings vor dem Bezirksgericht," *Neues Wiener Tagblatt*, October 13, 1896, Abendblatt edition, 2.

29. Volker Mergenthaler, *Völkerschau—Kannibalismus—Fremdenlegion. Zur Ästhetik der Transgression (1897–1936)* (Tübingen: Niemeyer, 2005), 30.

30. Mark B. Sandberg, *Living Picture, Missing Persons: Mannequins, Museums, and Modernity* (Princeton, NJ: Princeton University Press, 2003), 95–97. See also Tony Bennett, *The Birth of the Museum: History, Theory, Politics* (London: Routledge, 1995).

31. The history of the world's oldest zoo, at the Schönbrunn palace in Vienna, nicely illustrates this transformation. Founded in 1752 as a royal menagerie and initially closed to the public, it was renovated and retrofitted with new, partially open-air enclosures at the end of the nineteenth century under the directorship of Alois Kraus. These enclosures included moats and trenches separating animals and viewers, as well as diaphanous netted enclosures in which birds flew freely. The changes at the Schönbrunn zoo also characterized a wave of new zoo foundings in other European cities.

32. Mergenthaler, *Völkerschau*, 30.

33. Schwarz, *Anthropologische Spektakel*, 96. Schwarz notes that these qualities replaced earlier publicity strategies that emphasized the native people's "exoticism" and "wildness." These two attributes would have created a different kind of transgression, imbuing viewers with a sense of danger and threat. Meant to discourage interaction between foreigners and viewers, it encouraged a more straightforwardly spectatorial gawking.

34. Ames, "From the Exotic to the Everyday," 314. In a related vein, Schwarz argues, "Regardless of however wild the 'exotic' people were presented to be, the narrative and constellation were always directed at key European values. These made the presentation relatable and comprehensible and thus created the mirroring effect that made the shows attractive and into projection screens in the first place." Schwarz, *Anthropologische Spektakel*, 150–51.

35. Schwarz, *Anthropologische Spektakel*, 152–54. Schwarz suggests that the impresarios, Hagenbeck among them, even used physical appeal as a selection criterion when choosing exhibition participants.

36. "Ankunft der Aschanti-Neger," 4; "Aschanti-Neger in Wien," 5.

37. See George L. Mosse, *Nationalism and Sexuality: Middle-Class Morality and Sexual Norms in Modern Europe* (Madison: University of Wisconsin Press, 1985), and Sander L. Gilman, *The Jew's Body* (New York: Routledge, 1991), 234–43.

38. Karl Kraus, "Antworten des Herausgebers," *Die Fackel* 1, no. 4 (1899): 26.

39. Andrew Zimmerman, *Anthropology and Antihumanism in Imperial Germany* (Chicago: University of Chicago Press, 2001), 4.

40. In the wake of Cesare Lombroso, this kind of positivistic profiling was often used in criminal anthropology to identify possible felons and petty criminals. It was also influential for the work of Max Nordau.

41. Schiele's drawings are accompanied by photographic documentation of skulls in Erwin Hanslik, *Wesen der Menschheit*, Schriften des Instituts für Kulturforschung 5 (Vienna: Verlag Institut für Kulturforschung, 1917), n.p. Schiele would likely have learned such drawing techniques from his teacher at the Academy of Fine Arts: Hermann Vincenz Heller, *Grundformen der Mimik des Antlitzes: Im freiem Anschlusse an Piderits "Mimik und Physiognomik"; mit besonderer Berücksichtigung der bildenden Kunst* (Vienna: Schroll, 1902); Hermann Vincenz Heller, *Proportionstafeln der*

menschlichen Gestalt, 2nd ed. (Vienna: Schroll, 1919 [1913]). See Franz Smola, "Vom 'Menschenbewusstsein' zum neuen Menschenbild—Egon Schiele und der Anthropogeograph Erwin Hanslik," in *Die ästhetische Gnosis der Moderne*, ed. Leander Kaiser and Michael Ley (Vienna: Passagen Verlag, 2008), 123–46.

42. Schwarz, *Anthropologische Spektakel*, 39.

43. Then still housed in the Hofburg imperial palace, it was the foundational collection for the Natural History Museum, now on Maria-Theresien-Platz, which would not open its doors to the public until 1889. The Hofburg anthropological-ethnographic holdings were accessible only to royalty and their guests, experts, and academics.

44. Committee meeting minutes, June 11, 1878. AGW Archive, Naturhistorisches Museum (NHM), Vienna. Quoted in Irene Ranzmaier, *Die Anthropologische Gesellschaft in Wien und die akademische Etablierung anthropologischer Disziplinen an der Universität Wien 1870–1930* (Vienna: Böhlau, 2013), 58.

45. Mergenthaler, *Völkerschau*, 23. Mergenthaler also details how Germany's colonial history intersected with the phenomenon of human displays. Though Austria-Hungary had no colonies of its own, it did harbor colonial aspirations in the late nineteenth century. Closer to home, however, within the Habsburg empire, the anthropological and ethnological expeditions into the farthest corners of Austria-Hungary that were undertaken had a tenor not unlike that of the German, French, or British colonial expeditions to Africa and elsewhere. Members of various ethnic groups within the monarchy were subject to similar anthropometrical batteries for documentary, scientific, and statistical purposes. See Janos Frecot, "Das Volksgesicht," in *Portrait im Aufbruch: Photographie in Deutschland und Österreich 1900–1938*, ed. Monika Faber and Janos Frecot (Ostfildern-Ruit: Hatje Cantz, 2005), 78–89.

46. Mergenthaler, *Völkerschau*, 24. Like the encyclopedic form he developed, Luschan is remembered today foremost for having devised a chromatic scale widely used in the early twentieth century to classify skin color. By the time the Ashanti troupe arrived in Vienna and the German "Colonial Exhibition" took place, Luschan had assumed a position as assistant director at Berlin's Museum für Völkerkunde, the present-day Ethnological Museum. See Peter Ruggendorfer and Hubert D. Szemethy, eds., *Felix von Luschan (1854–1924): Leben und Wirken eines Universalgelehrten* (Vienna: Böhlau, 2009).

47. For an account of the debate surrounding Luschan's approbation and, more generally, the establishment of anthropological disciplines at the University of Vienna, see Ranzmaier, *Die Anthropologische Gesellschaft in Wien*, 179–216, esp. 182–83. The medical faculty's commission tasked with deciding the admissibility of Luschan's petition in 1881–82 consisted of several of the most prominent names in Viennese medicine: the anatomist Carl von Langer, the physiologist Ernst von Brücke, and the psychiatrist Theodor Meynert. All three were members of (and Langer and Meynert even held rank in) the AGW, and all three had themselves conducted research in physical anthropology. Luschan was allowed to proceed with his *Habilitation* at the medical faculty, although the commission expressed uncertainty about the future place of anthropology within the university. They recommended that anthropology would perhaps find a more logical home in the humanities, rather than in the natural sciences.

48. Ranzmaier, *Die Anthropologische Gesellschaft in Wien*, 24. For more on an-

thropology in the Austro-Hungarian context, see Brigitte Fuchs, *"Rasse", "Volk", Geschlecht: Anthropologische Diskurse in Österreich* (Frankfurt: Campus Verlag, 2003).

49. Tatjana Buklijas, "The Politics of *Fin-de-Siècle* Anatomy," in *The Nationalization of Scientific Knowledge in the Habsburg Empire, 1848–1918*, ed. Mitchell G. Ash and Jan Surman (London: Palgrave Macmillan, 2012), 211.

50. See Ranzmaier, *Die Anthropologische Gesellschaft in Wien*, 34–43, for the influence of key anatomists and pathologists in the AGW's early years.

51. Felix von Luschan, quoted in Mergenthaler, *Völkerschau*, 21–22.

52. Schwarz, *Anthropologische Spektakel*, 100.

53. Schwarz, *Anthropologische Spektakel*, 41–42. Researchers and scientists often photographed the subjects for further visual study, as in fig. 1.3.

54. Schwarz, *Anthropologische Spektakel*, 96–99.

55. These developments were underscored by the founding of national anthropological and ethnological museums, with similar agendas, which occurred in Europe in the last few decades of the nineteenth century. Vienna's Natural History Museum was opened to the public in 1889. Mattl, "Körperspektakel," 49, 57.

56. Schwarz, *Anthropologische Spektakel*, 15. Emphasis in original.

57. Peter Altenberg to Gretl Engländer, August 22, 1896. Altenberg's letters from August and September 1896, which I will cite, are housed in the Teilnachlass Peter Altenberg at Handschriftensammlung of the Wienbibliothek im Rathaus, inventory number ZPH 973. This archive will henceforth be cited as ZPH 973.

58. Peter Altenberg, *Ashantee* (Berlin: Fischer, 1897), 5. This text will henceforth be cited parenthetically with page number.

59. Evelyne Polt-Heinzl has urged scholars to approach Altenberg's life and work, and particularly his fascination with underage girls, more critically. Evelyne Polt-Heinzl, *Ringstraßenzeit und Wiener Moderne: Porträt einer literarischen Epoche des Übergangs* (Vienna: Sonderzahl, 2015), 42. See also Evelyne Polt-Heinzl, "Peter Altenberg und die zeitgenössische Bildproduktion—Mythen, Legenden und blinde Flecke," in *Peter Altenberg—prophetischer Asket mit bedenklichen Neigungen*, Wiener Vorlesungen im Rathaus 155 (Vienna: Picus, 2011), 43–71, and Larry Wolff, *Child Abuse in Freud's Vienna: Postcards from the End of the World* (New York: New York University Press, 1995).

60. Ulrich Baer, *The Rilke Alphabet*, trans. Andrew Hamilton (New York: Fordham University Press, 2014), 4. See also Baer's sensitive reading (pp. 1–9) of Rilke's poem "The Ashanti," published in *The Book of Images* (1902).

61. A comparative analysis of Altenberg's text and the original encyclopedia entry, which was reduced to one-tenth its original length, as well as the implications are in Ian Foster, "Altenberg's African Spectacle: *Ashantee* in Context," in *Theatre and Performance in Austria: From Mozart to Jelinek*, ed. Ritchie Robertson and Edward Timms (Edinburgh: Edinburgh University Press, 1993), 47–49.

62. Sander L. Gilman, *Difference and Pathology: Stereotypes of Sexuality, Race, and Madness* (Ithaca, NY: Cornell University Press, 1985), 111.

63. Foster, "Altenberg's African Spectacle," 49.

64. Peter Altenberg to Ännie Holitscher, August 11, 1896, ZPH 973.

65. Peter Altenberg, "Abschied der Aschanti," *Wiener Allgemeine Zeitung*, October 26, 1897, 2.

66. Altenberg, "Abschied der Aschanti," 2.

67. Altenberg, "Abschied der Aschanti," 2.

68. Peter Altenberg to Gretl Engländer, August 5, 1896, ZPH 973. In a similar vein, early on in *Ashantee*, the tutor, speaking about Tíoko, exclaims to Fortunatina: "This purity, this wonderful, smooth, cool skin, the ivory teeth, the delicate hands and feet, the aristocracy of the joints!" (10).

69. Another sketch, "Le Cœur," takes up the same theme, with the narrator there criticizing in indignant terms the popular press, which sought to gloss over the natives' discomfort (60).

70. What is lost in the translation of this quote is the simultaneous presence of three different languages: German, English, and "Odji," as Altenberg calls the Ashantis' native tongue. French is also used at some length in the book. For more about the use of multiple languages in *Ashantee*, see David D. Kim, "The Task of the Loving Translator: Translation, Völkerschauen, and Colonial Ambivalence in Peter Altenberg's *Ashantee* (1897)," *TRANSIT* 2, no. 1 (2006): 1–21.

71. Sabrina K. Rahman, "'Die Aschanti' von Peter Altenberg und 'Der Neger' von Karl Kraus: Die Frage schwarzer Präsenz im spätkaiserlichen Wien," in *Ashantee: Afrika und Wien um 1900*, ed. Kristin Kopp and Werner Michael Schwarz (Vienna: Löcker, 2008), 152.

72. Gilman, *Difference and Pathology*, 111–27.

73. Foster, "Altenberg's African Spectacle," 45.

74. Peter Altenberg to Ännie Holitscher, August 11, 1896, ZPH 973.

75. Peter Altenberg to Ännie Holitscher, August 22, 1896, ZPH 973.

76. W. G. Sebald, "Peter Altenberg—Le Paysan de Vienne," in *Unheimliche Heimat: Essays zur österreichischen Literatur* (Frankfurt: Fischer, 1995), 68, 75, 69.

77. Altenberg, "Abschied der Aschanti," 2.

78. The Rotunde was the architectonic embodiment of the heady economic boom of the *Gründerzeit*. Until being consumed by a devastating fire in 1937, it was the world's largest cupola construction, far larger even than the Pantheon in Rome.

79. Josef Gally, ed., *Offizieller Katalog der unter dem höchsten Protektorate Sr. k. u. k. Hoheit des Durchlauchtigsten Herrn Erzherzogs Leopold Salvator stehenden Allgemeinen Hygienischen Ausstellung Wien-Rotunde 1906*, 2nd ed. (Vienna: Ausstellungsdirektion, 1906), 47–58.

80. Gally, *Offizieller Katalog*, 4.

81. Direktions-Komitee der Ausstellung, ed., *Schlussbericht über die unter dem höchsten Protektorate Seiner kaiserlichen und königlichen Hoheit, des Durchlauchtigsten Herrn Erzherzogs Leopold Salvator stattgehabte Allgemeine Hygienische Ausstellung in Wien-Rotunde 1906* (Vienna: Reisser, 1906), 21–22, 32.

82. The photograph was taken in Venice, where Altenberg spent several months (May–October 1913) with Adolf Loos and others, who had picked him up from Steinhof, the Viennese psychiatric hospital, where he was undergoing treatment from December 1912 to May 1913. Hans Bisanz, *Peter Altenberg: Mein äußerstes Ideal. Altenbergs Pho-*

tosammlung von geliebten Frauen, Freunden und Orten, ed. Historisches Museum der Stadt Wien (Vienna: Verlag Christian Brandstätter, 1987), 82.

83. See Michael Hau, *The Cult of Health and Beauty in Germany: A Social History, 1890–1930* (Chicago: University of Chicago Press, 2003).

84. There existed a strong Viennese and Austrian life reform movement independent of that in Germany, which has received a great deal of scholarly study. In addition to the sources cited in what follows, see Kai Buchholz et al., eds., *Die Lebensreform: Entwürfe zur Neugestaltung von Leben und Kunst um 1900*, 2 vols. (Darmstadt: Häusser, 2001), Chad Ross, *Naked Germany: Health, Race and the Nation* (New York: Berg Publishers, 2005), and Bernd Wedemeyer-Kolwe, *"Der neue Mensch": Körperkultur im Kaiserreich und in der Weimarer Republik* (Würzburg: Königshausen & Neumann, 2004), for the German context. For the specifically Austrian history, the defining source is Gerald Wintersberger, "Lebensreformer, Anarchisten, Freisozialisten: Reformer und Revolutionäre in Österreich von der Jahrhundertwende bis zum ersten Weltkrieg" (PhD diss., University of Vienna, 1986), while Siegfried Mattl, "Beiträge zu einer Geschichte des Körpers" (Habilitationsschrift, University of Vienna, 1994), also contains important information.

85. Wolfgang R. Krabbe, "Die Lebensreformbewegung," in *Die Lebensreform*, ed. Kai Buchholz et al., 1:25.

86. Reinhard Farkas, "Lebensreform in der Donaumonarchie: Personen, Vereine und Netzwerke," in *Pädagogische und kulturelle Strömungen in der k. u. k. Monarchie: Lebensreform, Herbartianismus und reformpädagogische Bewegungen*, ed. Johanna Hopfner and András Németh (Frankfurt: Peter Lang, 2008), 11.

87. Hau, *Cult of Health and Beauty*, 10.

88. Farkas, "Lebensreform in der Donaumonarchie," 12. See also Alfred Pfabigan, "Proletarische Badekultur in der austromarxistischen Gegenwelt," in *Das Bad: Körperkultur und Hygiene im 19. und 20. Jahrhundert*, ed. Sylvia Mattl-Wurm and Ursula Storch (Vienna: Eigenverlag der Museen der Stadt Wien, 1991), 158–66.

89. Philipp Sarasin, "Der öffentlich sichtbare Körper: Vom Spektakel der Anatomie zu den 'curiosités physiologiques,'" in *Physiologie und industrielle Gesellschaft: Studien zur Verwissenschaftlichung des Körpers im 19. und 20. Jahrhundert*, ed. Philipp Sarasin and Jakob Tanner (Frankfurt: Suhrkamp, 1998), 450.

90. Direktions-Komitee der Ausstellung, *Schlussbericht*, 32.

91. "Hygiene-Ausstellung.—Der Mensch.—Der Neue Haushalt. (Ein Rundgang)," *Rohö-Flugblatt*, May 15, 1925, 1.

92. Alfred Polgar, "'Der Mensch,'" in *Kleine Schriften*, ed. Marcel Reich-Ranicki and Ulrich Weinzierl, vol. 2, *Kreislauf* (Reinbek bei Hamburg: Rowohlt, 1983), 301.

93. Polgar, "'Der Mensch,'" 299.

94. For the history of the various German "Transparent Man" models, see Klaus Vogel, "The Transparent Man: Some Comments on the History of a Symbol," in *Manifesting Medicine: Bodies and Machines*, ed. Robert Bud, Bernard Finn, and Helmuth Trischler (Amsterdam: Harwood Academic, 1999), 31–61. For the prehistory of these twentieth-century anatomical modeling techniques in the Viennese context, see George, "Anatomy for All."

95. *Offizieller Führer durch die Hygiene Ausstellung Wien 1925* (Vienna: Verlag der Hygiene-Ausstellung, 1925), 18–19.

96. *Offizieller Führer durch die Hygiene Ausstellung Wien 1925*, 10. For more on the evolution of discourses about hygiene in the Viennese context—beginning from Johann Peter Frank's (1745–1821) inauguration of a concept of "Medizinische Polizei" at the turn of the eighteenth to the nineteenth centuries—see Erna Lesky, "Von der Staatsarzneikunde zur Hygiene," *Wiener klinische Wochenschrift* 71, no. 10 (1959): 168–71.

97. See Michael Sappol, *Body Modern: Fritz Kahn, Scientific Illustration, and the Homuncular Subject* (Minneapolis: University of Minnesota Press, 2017).

98. Corinna Treitel, "Gesundheit! Globalizing German Epistemologies of Health" (paper presented at the German Studies Association Conference seminar "Fragments of the German Body, 1600–2000," Pittsburgh, PA, September 28, 2018). Treitel is embarking on a project to chart the dissemination of knowledge about health and hygiene through the translation and publication histories of German-language books.

99. Simon Weber-Unger, ed., *Der naturwissenschaftliche Blick: Fotografie, Zeichnung und Modell im 19. Jahrhundert* (Vienna: Wissenschaftliches Kabinett, 2009), 5–11.

100. "Führer durch die Ausstellung 'Turnen—Sport—Spiel,'" 1931, 1–2. Ausstellungen I 1262/Hk.103, MAK–Museum für angewandte Künst, Vienna.

101. The weekly—published by Benno Karpeles, who also founded the daily *Der Neue Tag*, in which Joseph Roth's Viennese Symptoms series appeared (see chap. 2)—included contributions by the sharpest journalistic voices of the time, including Egon Erwin Kisch, Anton Kuh, Robert Musil, Alfred Polgar, and many others. Loos was responsible for the concept of the "Guidelines" and wrote the preface, as well as the sections on visual art and theater. But he contracted specialists for some portions of the text. Arnold Schönberg contributed the section on music, for example. For more on the context of the publication, see Klaus Amann, "Staatsfiktionen: Bilder eines künftigen Österreich in der Wiener Wochenschrift *Der Friede* (1918/1919)," in *Die Dichter und die Politik: Essays zur österreichischen Literatur nach 1918* (Vienna: Deuticke, 1992), 15–30.

102. Adolf Loos, *Richtlinien für ein Kunstamt*, ed. Adolf Loos (Vienna: Lanyi, 1919), 3.

103. Loos, *Richtlinien*, 4.

104. Among the other instructors were Arnold Schönberg for composition and music theory and Oskar Kokoschka for painting. Famous Schwarzwald students were Vicki Baum, Trude Fleischmann, Marie Jahoda, Else Pappenheim, Hilde Spiel, and Helene Weigel. The most comprehensive biography of Schwarzwald's influential life is Deborah Holmes, *Langeweile ist Gift: Das Leben der Eugenie Schwarzwald*, trans. Esther Marian and Fanny Esterházy (Salzburg: Residenz Verlag, 2012).

105. Adolf Loos, *Sämtliche Schriften in zwei Bänden*, ed. Franz Glück, vol. 2, *Trotzdem 1900–1930* (Vienna: Herold, 1962), 454. For more detail on Loos's cultural-political activities, see Inge Podbrecky and Hermann Czech, eds., *Leben mit Loos* (Vienna: Böhlau, 2008).

106. Marcel Mauss, "Techniques of the Body," trans. Ben Brewster, *Economy and Society* 2, no. 1 (1973): 70–88.

107. Adolf Loos, "Vom Stehen, Gehen, Sitzen, Schlafen, Essen und Trinken: Vortrag des Architekten Adolf Loos [1911]," in *Gesammelte Schriften*, ed. Adolf Opel (Vienna: Lesethek Verlag, 2010), 406. Adolf Loos, "Ornament and Crime," in *Ornament and Crime: Selected Essays*, ed. Adolf Opel, trans. Michael Mitchell (Riverside, CA: Ariadne Press, 1998), 167–76. See also Christopher Long, "The Origins and Context of Adolf Loos's 'Ornament and Crime,'" *Journal of the Society of Architectural Historians* 68, no. 2 (June 2009): 200–223.

108. Emphasis in original. See Leo A. Lensing's thorough and insightful work on Altenberg's collection of photographs: Leo A. Lensing, "Peter Altenberg's Fabricated Photographs: Literature and Photography in Fin-de-Siècle Vienna," in *Vienna 1900: From Altenberg to Wittgenstein* (Edinburgh: Edinburgh University Press, 1990), 47–72; Leo A. Lensing, "Peter Altenbergs 'beschriebene Fotografien': Ein zweites Oeuvre?," *Fotogeschichte* 15, no. 57 (1995): 3–33; Andrew Barker and Leo A. Lensing, *Peter Altenberg: Rezept die Welt zu sehen* (Vienna: Braumüller, 1995), 133–67.

109. Peter Altenberg, *Pròdrŏmŏs* (Berlin: Fischer, 1906), 110, emphasis in original. This text will henceforth be cited parenthetically with page number.

110. Kurt Pinthus, review of *Semmering 1912*, by Peter Altenberg, *März* 7, no. 19 (1913): 213; quoted in Barker and Lensing, *Peter Altenberg*, 122. The book was actually published in late 1905, but postdated to 1906.

111. Though often dismissed as trivial blather, *Pròdrŏmŏs* has attracted scholarly attention. See Burkhard Spinnen, "Idyllen in der Warenwelt: Peter Altenbergs *Pròdrŏmŏs* und die Sprache der Werbung," *Zeitschrift für Literaturwissenschaft und Linguistik* 22, nos. 87/88 (1992): 133–50; Viktor Žmegač, *Tradition und Innovation: Studien zur deutschsprachigen Literatur seit der Jahrhundertwende* (Vienna: Böhlau, 1993), 119–51; Andrew Barker, *Telegrams from the Soul: Peter Altenberg and the Culture of Fin-de-Siècle Vienna* (Columbia: Camden House, 1996), 107–18; Petra Leutner, "Über den Körper der Künstler und Schriftsteller: Eine aktuelle Ökonomie des Körperlichen in den diätetischen und die Hygiene betreffenden Notizen von Pontormo, Charles Baudelaire und Peter Altenberg," in *Macht Text Geschichte. Lektüren am Rande der Akademie*, ed. Markus Heilmann and Thomas Wägenbaur (Würzburg: Königshausen & Neumann, 1997), 60–71; Heinz Lunzer and Victoria Lunzer-Talos, *Peter Altenberg: Extracte des Lebens* (Salzburg: Residenz, 2003), 114–15; Roland Innerhofer, "'Aus den facheusen Complicationen herauskommen': Peter Altenbergs diätetische Lebensrezepte," in *Peter Altenberg—prophetischer Asket mit bedenklichen Neigungen*, Wiener Vorlesungen im Rathaus 155 (Vienna: Picus, 2011), 11–42; Simon Ganahl, *Karl Kraus und Peter Altenberg: Eine Typologie moderner Haltungen* (Konstanz: Konstanz University Press, 2015), 119–212.

112. The residential colonies at Monte Verità in Switzerland and Worpswede in Germany drew artists, writers, and notables in the first decades of the twentieth century. Rainer Maria Rilke, for example, lived at Worpswede for a time and was committed to vegetarianism, abstinence, and physical culture. See Thorsten Carstensen and Marcel Schmid, eds., *Die Literatur der Lebensreform: Kulturkritik und Aufbruchstimmung um 1900* (Bielefeld: transcript, 2016).

113. See Barker, *Telegrams from the Soul*, 108; Spinnen, "Idyllen in der Warenwelt," 133–50; Žmegač, *Tradition und Innovation*, 135. Despite the stylistic difference from

his earlier works and the seemingly indiscriminate order of the texts, Andrew Barker has noted that Altenberg's methodology throughout his career remained the same: a "kaleidoscopic" vision that was already evident in his first book. Barker, *Telegrams from the Soul*, 111.

114. Žmegač, *Tradition und Innovation*, 126.

115. Žmegač, *Tradition und Innovation*, 123.

116. Ganahl, *Karl Kraus und Peter Altenberg*, 145.

117. Rolf Winau, "Die Entdeckung des menschlichen Körpers in der neuzeitlichen Medizin," in *Der Mensch und seinen Körper: Von der Antike bis heute*, ed. Arthur E. Imhof (Munich: C. H. Beck, 1983), 212.

118. Philipp Sarasin, *Reizbare Maschinen: Eine Geschichte des Körpers 1765–1914* (Frankfurt: Suhrkamp, 2001), 96–99.

119. Simon Ganahl, "'Markt der Lebensweisen' oder Diätetik und Reklame in Peter Altenbergs *Pròdrŏmŏs*," *Deutsche Vierteljahresschrift für Literaturwissenschaft und Geistesgeschichte* 90, no. 3 (2016): 382; Anson Rabinbach, *The Human Motor: Energy, Fatigue, and the Origins of Modernity* (New York: Basic Books, 1990).

120. Barker, *Telegrams from the Soul*, 112.

121. Žmegač, *Tradition und Innovation*, 119.

122. Similar formulations and recommendations are found throughout the text, as well as in a supplement to the book he published in a Munich-based cultural journal in 1914—alongside articles by Heinrich Mann, Dostoevsky, and Georges Clémenceau. See Peter Altenberg, "Nachtrag zu Prodromos," *Das Forum* 1, no. 2 (May 1914): 89, 93.

123. Ganahl, *Karl Kraus und Peter Altenberg*, 115.

124. Spinnen, "Idyllen in der Warenwelt," 133–50.

125. Leo A. Lensing, "Peter Altenberg's Fabricated Photographs: Literature and Photography in Fin-de-Siècle Vienna," in *Vienna 1900: From Altenberg to Wittgenstein* (Edinburgh: Edinburgh University Press, 1990), 47–72, and Lensing, "Altenbergs 'Beschriebene Fotografien,'" 3–33. The terminology stems from art historian Anne Hoy.

126. See, e.g., Adolf Loos, "Die Herrenmode [1898]," "Das Luxusfuhrwerk [1898]," "Die Herrenhüte [1898]," "Wäsche [1898]," "Buchdrucker [1898]," in *Gesammelte Schriften*, ed. Adolf Opel, 58, 96–103, 117, 145–52, and 168–69, resp.

127. Janet Stewart, *Fashioning Vienna: Adolf Loos's Cultural Criticism* (London: Routledge, 2000), 98–130.

128. Žmegač, *Tradition und Innovation*, 127.

129. Thomas Mann, "Brief über Peter Altenberg," in *Das Altenbergbuch*, ed. Egon Friedell (Leipzig: Verlag der Wiener Graphischen Werkstätte, 1921), 71–72.

130. Barker, *Telegrams from the Soul*, 177.

131. Žmegač, *Tradition und Innovation*, 124.

132. See Rabinbach, *Human Motor*.

133. Altenberg, "Nachtrag zu Prodromos," 95.

134. Altenberg, "Nachtrag zu Prodromos," 91.

135. Friedrich Nietzsche, *The Gay Science*, ed. Bernard Williams, trans. Josefine Nauckhoff (Cambridge: Cambridge University Press, 2001), 247.

136. Ganahl, *Karl Kraus und Peter Altenberg*, 145. See also Leutner, "Über den Körper der Künstler und Schriftsteller," 60–71.

137. Barker, *Telegrams from the Soul*, 115.

138. Mann, "Brief über Peter Altenberg," 69–70. Emphasis in original.

139. Bahr praised *Pròdrŏmŏs* in his journal; see Hermann Bahr, *Tagebuch* (Berlin: Cassirer, 1909), 66. Adorno also published an article about Altenberg in the *Frankfurter Zeitung*; see Theodor W. Adorno, "Physiologische Romantik [1932]," in *Gesammelte Schriften*, ed. Rolf Tiedemann, vol. 11, *Noten zur Literatur* (Frankfurt: Suhrkamp, 1974), 634–36. Together with the latter two, Altenberg formed an informal triumvirate Karl Kraus once called the "superior triple alliance" (*besserer Dreibund*). Barker, *Telegrams from the Soul*, 98.

140. Karl Kraus, "Satiriker," *Die Fackel* 8, no. 213 (December 11, 1906): 24.

141. Karl Kraus, "Warnung vor der Unsterblichkeit (zu einer Peter Altenberg-Vorlesung)," *Die Fackel* 15, nos. 374/375 (May 8, 1913): 15.

142. Hugo von Hofmannsthal, "Das Buch von Peter Altenberg," in *Das Altenbergbuch*, ed. Egon Friedell (Leipzig: Verlag der Wiener Graphischen Werkstätte, 1921), 150.

143. Bahr, *Tagebuch*, 67.

144. The design was never realized, but the architect's plans are housed in the Adolf Loos Archive at the Albertina, Vienna, along with two photographs of a model of the Baker House taken by Martin Gerlach. See Anne Anlin Cheng's fascinating *Second Skin: Josephine Baker and the Modern Surface* (New York: Oxford University Press, 2011), esp. 49–79.

145. "Josephine Baker-Bulletin," *Wiener Allgemeine Zeitung*, February 3, 1928.

146. Mine is a composite account that draws on several sources: "To 'Atone' for Nude Dancer," *New York Times*, March 12, 1928, 4; Robert Scheu, "Oster-Chronik der Weltereignisse," *Prager Tagblatt*, April 8, 1928, 3; "Guard Josephine Baker," *New York Times*, February 2, 1928, 23. Contemporary Viennese news reporting from the months before and after Baker's performances is covered in Roman Horak, "'We Have Become Niggers!' Josephine Baker as a Threat to Viennese Culture," *Culture Unbound* 5 (2013): 515–30. See also Bennetta Jules-Rosette, *Josephine Baker in Art and Life: The Icon and the Image* (Urbana: University of Illinois Press, 2007); Kira Thurman, "Dancing in a Banana Skirt in the City of Music: Josephine Baker in 1920s Vienna" (paper presented at the American Historical Association Annual Meeting, Atlanta, GA, January 7, 2016); Roman Horak, "Josephine Baker in Vienna: Blackness, Art, and Americanization," in Horak et al., *Metropole Wien*, 2:197–203; and Phyllis Rose, *Jazz Cleopatra: Josephine Baker in Her Time* (New York: Doubleday, 1989), 127–30.

147. This account largely follows the reporting of Eugen Hajnal, "Die Affen des Dr. Thun-Hohenstein," *Arbeiter-Zeitung*, March 4, 1928, 8, and Otto Hollborn, "Biologische Gymnastik," *Arbeiter-Zeitung*, March 11, 1928, 14.

148. "Die badenden Affen und die Bewegungskultur," *Neue Freie Presse*, February 28, 1928, 6.

149. The focus on efficiency bears more than a passing resemblance to the American, Europe-based physician Bess (Elizabeth Marguerite de Varel) Mensendieck's (ca. 1866–1959) popular movement system, which emphasized everyday, domestic actions, particularly for women. See Bess M. Mensendieck, *Körperkultur der Frau: Praktisch hygienische und praktisch ästhetische Winke* (Munich: Bruckmann, 1906).

150. Hajnal, "Die Affen des Dr. Thun-Hohenstein," 8. See also Hofrat Dr. Habison,

"Die Schule des Körpers nach dem System des Grafen Thun," *Die Bühne* 187 (1928): 35, 46; Hollborn, "Biologische Gymnastik," 14.

151. Stefan Größling, "Max Graf von Thun und Hohenstein," *Österreichisches Biographisches Lexikon 1815–1950*, vol. 14 (Vienna: Verlag der Österreichischen Akademie der Wissenschaften, 2014), 328–29.

152. Hajnal, "Die Affen des Dr. Thun-Hohenstein," 8.

153. Cheng, *Second Skin*, esp. 1–15.

154. See Cheng, *Second Skin*, 49–79, and Beatriz Colomina, *Privacy and Publicity: Modern Architecture as Mass Media* (Cambridge, MA: MIT Press, 1994). For a differing perspective, see Elana Shapira, "Dressing a Celebrity: Adolf Loos's House for Josephine Baker," *Studies in the Decorative Arts* 11, no. 2 (Spring–Summer 2004): 2–24.

155. To the point of the powerful male gaze, it bears mention that Loos was convicted of child molestation in 1928 and served several months in jail. While his friend Altenberg, who constantly crossed lines with young girls, was never formally accused, Egon Schiele, too, was imprisoned for similar charges, sexual misconduct and kidnapping of a minor, as well as the display of pornographic images, in 1912. He was imprisoned in Neulengbach for twenty-four days.

156. Baker likewise had completely retooled her Broadway performances for Parisian audiences in 1925, in that instance to make them more "African." Henry Louis Gates Jr. and Karen C. C. Dalton, introduction to *Josephine Baker and La Revue Nègre: Paul Colin's Lithographs of "Le Tumulte Noir" in Paris, 1927* (New York: Abrams, 1998), 6–7.

157. *Arbeiter-Zeitung*, March 1928. Quoted and translated in Horak, "Josephine Baker as a Threat," 521.

158. *Wiener Allgemeine Zeitung*, March 1928. Quoted and translated in Horak, "Josephine Baker as a Threat," 522.

CHAPTER TWO

1. Arguing on the basis of efficiency and hygiene, the engineer, industrialist, and painter Franz Ritter von Felbinger (1844–1906) and the architect Josef Hudetz (1842–1909) had conceived the idea in anticipation of the cemetery's opening. The project was met with approving assessments by various city commissions but was ultimately defeated in the municipal council, which cited concerns over the project's projected costs, particularly in the wake of the 1873 financial crisis. The basis of Felbinger and Hudetz's idea was, however, soon realized as a pneumatic postal transport system that operated in Vienna from 1875 to 1956. Florian Bettel, "Technik, Kommerz und Totenkult: Die technische Vision der pneumatischen Leichenbeförderung zum Wiener Zentralfriedhof von 1874," in *Technology Fiction: Technische Visionen und Utopien in der Hochmoderne*, ed. Uwe Fraunholz and Anke Woschech (Bielefeld: transcript, 2012), 43–64.

2. Matsch (1861–1942) and Klimt—classmates at the *Kunstgewerbeschule* who, together with Klimt's brother Ernst, had founded the Künstler-Compagnie (1883–92)—received the joint commission for the university paintings in 1894. Both artists were each to deliver six allegorical spandrel panels representing various branches of knowledge. Matsch was to execute the monumental central panel and one faculty

painting (theology), while Klimt was tasked with depictions of the three other faculties (philosophy, medicine, and jurisprudence). A scandal about the faculty paintings erupted as soon as Klimt presented his drafts for *Philosophy* in 1898 and only intensified with his rendering of *Medicine* in 1901. The brouhaha about Klimt's rendering of the human form, as we will see in the next chapter, ultimately resulted in his wholesale withdrawal from the project.

3. We need only consider a long tradition that most prominently includes Rembrandt's *The Anatomy Lesson of Dr. Nicolaes Tulp* (1632). In the more modern Austrian tradition, it is worth noting *The Anatomist* (Der Anatom, 1869) by the Prague-born, Austro-Hungarian allegorical painter Gabriel von Max, as well as the Viennese art critic and academic painter Adalbert Franz Seligmann's *Billroth's Lecture Hall at the Vienna General Hospital* (Der Billroth'sche Hörsaal im Wiener Allgemeinen Krankenhaus, 1888/1889).

4. Viennese doctors and art critics praised Matsch's painting for its realistic rendering of the cadaver. See, e.g., Adolf Kronfeld, *Die Entwicklung des Anatomiebildes seit 1632*, Beiträge zur Geschichte der Medizin 2 (Vienna: Moritz Perles, 1912), 28. Herbert Boeckl's series of paintings and drawings of corpses from the early 1930s were the aesthetic antithesis to Matsch's elegant cadaver.

5. Thomas W. Laqueur, *The Work of the Dead: A Cultural History of Mortal Remains* (Princeton, NJ: Princeton University Press, 2015), 11, 18.

6. Michel Foucault, *The Birth of the Clinic: An Archaeology of Medical Perception*, trans. A. M. Sheridan Smith (New York: Vintage, 1994), 146.

7. See Erin E. Edwards, *The Modernist Corpse: Posthumanism and the Posthumous* (Minneapolis: University of Minnesota Press, 2018), for the role of the corpse in American literary modernism.

8. Elisabeth Bronfen, *Over Her Dead Body: Death, Femininity and the Aesthetic* (New York: Routledge, 1992), xi, 181.

9. Bronfen, *Over Her Dead Body*, xi.

10. Julia Kristeva, *Powers of Horror: An Essay on Abjection*, trans. Leon S. Roudiez (New York: Columbia University Press, 1982), 4.

11. Robert Musil, *Diaries, 1899–1942*, ed. Mark Mirsky, trans. Philip Payne (New York: Basic Books, 1999), 3. This source will henceforth be cited parenthetically with page number.

12. Carl E. Schorske, *Fin-de-Siècle Vienna: Politics and Culture* (New York: Vintage, 1980), 345; William M. Johnston, *The Austrian Mind: An Intellectual and Social History, 1848–1938* (Berkeley: University of California Press, 1972), 181–86; Allan Janik and Stephen Toulmin, *Wittgenstein's Vienna* (New York: Simon and Schuster, 1973), 133–38.

13. Jean-François Lyotard, *The Postmodern Condition: A Report on Knowledge*, trans. Geoff Bennington and Brian Massumi (Manchester: Manchester University Press, 1984), 41.

14. Mark Mirsky, the editor of the diaries, notes this connection (508).

15. Friedrich Nietzsche, *Sämtliche Werke: Kritische Studienausgabe*, ed. Giorgio Colli and Mazzino Montinari, 15 vols. (Berlin: de Gruyter, 1967–88), 7/2:133.

16. Friedrich Nietzsche, *The Case of Wagner: A Musician's Problem*, in *The*

Anti-Christ, Ecce Homo, Twilight of the Idols, and Other Writings, ed. Aaron Ridley and Judith Norman, trans. Judith Norman (Cambridge: Cambridge University Press, 2005), 262.

17. Friedrich Nietzsche, *On the Genealogy of Morality*, ed. Keith Ansell-Pearson, trans. Carol Diethe (Cambridge: Cambridge University Press, 1994), 75.

18. Nietzsche, *Genealogy of Morality*, 70.

19. Friedrich Nietzsche, *The Gay Science*, ed. Bernard Williams, trans. Josefine Nauckhoff (Cambridge: Cambridge University Press, 2001), 180.

20. Sigmund Freud, *The Standard Edition of the Complete Psychological Works of Sigmund Freud*, ed. and trans. James Strachey, 24 vols. (London: Hogarth Press, 1953–74), 5:413, 5:452–55, 5:477–78. This source will henceforth be cited parenthetically with volume and page number.

21. Freud would of course go on to deploy the procedural metaphor any number of times, most prominently in the title of the thirty-first of his *New Introductory Lectures on Psycho-Analysis* (1933 [1932]), "The Dissection of the Psychical Personality." Freud, *Standard Edition*, 22:57–80.

22. A related claim is convincingly made for Kafka in Winfried Menninghaus, *Disgust: The Theory and History of a Strong Sensation*, trans. Howard Eiland and Joel Golb (Albany: State University of New York Press, 2003), 298–307.

23. Johnston, *The Austrian Mind*, 227; Eric R. Kandel, *The Age of Insight: The Quest to Understand the Unconscious in Art, Mind, and Brain, from Vienna 1900 to the Present* (New York: Random House, 2012), 23.

24. Johnston, *The Austrian Mind*, 227; Erna Lesky, *The Vienna Medical School of the 19th Century*, trans. L. Williams and I. S. Levij (Baltimore: Johns Hopkins University Press, 1976), 107; Isabelle Percebois, "Medical Developments in the Nineteenth Century: The Vienna Clinical School," *Medicographia* 35, no. 5 (2013): 354.

25. Lesky, *Vienna Medical School*, 106.

26. Johnston, *The Austrian Mind*, 224; Percebois, "Medical Developments," 355; Kandel, *The Age of Insight*, 24.

27. Percebois, "Medical Developments," 355.

28. See Horst Thomé, "Vorwort: Arthur Schnitzlers Anfänge und die Grundlagenkrise der Medizin," in *Medizinische Schriften*, by Arthur Schnitzler, ed. Horst Thomé (Vienna: Zsolnay, 1988), 11–59; Laura Otis, "The Language of Infection: Disease and Identity in Schnitzler's *Reigen*," *The Germanic Review* 70, no. 2 (1995): 65–75; Laura Otis, *Membranes: Metaphors of Invasion in Nineteenth-Century Literature, Science, and Politics* (Baltimore: Johns Hopkins University Press, 2000); Hillary Hope Herzog, "'Medizin ist eine Weltanschauung': On Schnitzler's Medical Writings," in *A Companion to the Works of Arthur Schnitzler*, ed. Dagmar C. G. Lorenz (Rochester: Camden House, 2003), 227–41; Dirk von Boetticher, *Meine Werke sind lauter Diagnosen: Über die ärztliche Dimension im Werk Arthur Schnitzlers* (Heidelberg: Winter, 1999); Eva Kuttenberg, "Soma, Psyche, Corpse, and Gaze: Perception and Vision in Arthur Schnitzler's Early Prose Fiction," *Modern Austrian Literature* 40, no. 2 (2007): 21–42.

29. Herzog, "'Medizin ist eine Weltanschauung,'" 229. See also Boetticher, *Meine Werke sind lauter Diagnosen*.

30. Olga Schnitzler, *Spiegelbild der Freundschaft* (Salzburg: Residenz, 1962), 53.

31. Arthur Schnitzler, *Jugend in Wien: Eine Autobiographie* (Vienna: Molden, 1968), 104; Arthur Schnitzler, *My Youth in Vienna*, trans. Catherine Hutter (New York: Holt, Rinhart and Winston, 1970), 126–27. He characterizes the relationship between the two spaces as analogous to sacristy and church.

32. Maria Heim [Marie Pappenheim], "Gedichte ['Seziersaal,' 'Trennung,' 'Vor dem Konzert,' 'Prima Graviditas']," ed. Karl Kraus, *Die Fackel* 8, no. 202 (April 30, 1906): 23–25.

33. Birgit Bolognese-Leuchtenmüller and Sonia Horn, eds., *Töchter des Hippokrates: 100 Jahre akademische Ärztinnen in Österreich* (Vienna: Verlag der Österreichischen Ärztekammer, 2000); Felicitas Seebacher, *Das Fremde im "deutschen" Tempel der Wissenschaften: Brüche in der Wissenschaftskultur der Medizinischen Fakultät der Universität Wien* (Vienna: Verlag der Österreichischen Akademie der Wissenschaften, 2011), 383–409.

34. Among the most prominent opponents was the surgeon Eduard Albert, *Die Frauen und das Studium der Medicin* (Vienna: Hölder, 1895). His screed arguing against women in medicine triggered challenges from, among others, Emanuel Hannak, *Prof. E. Alberts Essay "Die Frauen und das Studium der Medicin" kritisch beleuchtet* (Vienna: Hölder, 1895); and [Ernst] M[oriz] Kronfeld, *Die Frauen und die Medicin: Professor Albert zur Antwort. Zugleich eine Darstellung der ganzen Frage* (Vienna: Konegen, 1895).

35. Londa Schiebinger, *The Mind Has No Sex? Women in the Origins of Modern Science* (Cambridge, MA: Harvard University Press, 1989).

36. [Fritz] Avicenna [Wittels], "Weibliche Ärzte," *Die Fackel* 9, no. 225 (May 3, 1907): 11–12. For Wittels's usage of the term "male woman" (*Mannweib*), see the later essay, [Fritz] Avicenna [Wittels], "Das Kindweib," *Die Fackel* 9, no. 230–31 (July 15, 1907): 14–33.

37. Reingard Witzmann, ed., *Aufbruch in das Jahrhundert der Frau? Rosa Mayreder und der Feminismus in Wien um 1900* (Vienna: Eigenverlag der Museen der Stadt Wien, 1989). Rosa Mayreder's foundational *Zur Kritik der Weiblichkeit* is a key text, in which she takes on Cesare Lombroso, Richard von Krafft-Ebing, Otto Weininger, and other then-influential proponents of theories of sexual difference. Rosa Mayreder and Herman Scheffauer, *A Survey of the Woman Problem* (New York: G. H. Doran, 1913); Rosa Mayreder, *Zur Kritik der Weiblichkeit* (Jena: Diederichs, 1905).

38. Berta Szeps-Zuckerkandl, *My Life and History*, trans. John Sommerfield (New York: Knopf, 1939), 166–67.

39. Pappenheim, cited in Karl Fallend, "Marie Frischauf-Pappenheim," *Literatur und Kritik* 31, nos. 305/306 (1996): 105. For more on Pappenheim's biography, see Karl Fallend, *Wilhelm Reich in Wien: Psychoanalyse und Politik*, Veröffentlichungen des Ludwig-Boltzmann-Institutes für Geschichte der Gesellschaftswissenschaften 17 (Vienna: Geyer-Edition, 1988), 95–106; Marcus G. Patka, "Nachwort: Literatur versus Medizin—Marie Frischauf, geborene Pappenheim," in *Der graue Mann: Roman und Gedichte für Arnold Schönberg*, by Marie Frischauf, ed. Marcus G. Patka (Vienna: Theodor Kramer Gesellschaft, 2000), 109–39; and the newspaper clipping archive "Frischauf-Pappenheim, Marie" at the Tagblattarchiv of the Wienbibliothek im Rathaus, inventory number TP 013815.

40. Arthur Schnitzler, *Tagebuch 1879–1892* (Vienna: Verlag der Österreichischen Akademie der Wissenschaften, 1987), 12.

41. Fallend, "Marie Frischauf-Pappenheim," 105.

42. Fallend, "Marie Frischauf-Pappenheim," 105.

43. Cited in and translated by Elizabeth L. Keathley, "'Die Frauenfrage' in *Erwartung*: Schoenberg's Collaboration with Marie Pappenheim," in *Schoenberg and Words: The Modernist Years*, ed. Charlotte M. Cross and Russell A. Berman (New York: Garland, 2000), 139.

44. Fallend, "Marie Frischauf-Pappenheim," 103–4.

45. E.g., Bryan R. Simms, "Whose Idea Was *Erwartung*?," in *Constructive Dissonance: Arnold Schoenberg and the Transformations of Twentieth-Century Culture*, ed. Juliane Brand and Christopher Hailey (Berkeley: University of California Press, 1997), 100–108; Laura A. McLary, "The Dead Lover's Body and the Woman's Rage: Marie Pappenheim's 'Erwartung,'" *Colloquia Germanica* 34, nos. 3/4 (2001): 257–69; Alexander Carpenter, "Schoenberg's Vienna, Freud's Vienna: Re-Examining the Connections between the Monodrama *Erwartung* and the Early History of Psychoanalysis," *The Musical Quarterly* 93, no. 1 (2010): 144–81. Drawing on reliable genealogical research, Carpenter appears to have settled conflicting accounts of the women's kinship, "Schoenberg's Vienna," 152–53, 168–70. They were apparently second cousins once removed. Nevertheless, Frischauf-Pappenheim's biographer disagrees. See Fallend, "Marie Frischauf-Pappenheim," and Fallend, *Wilhelm Reich in Wien*. Bertha Pappenheim was herself an influential writer and women's rights and social activist, who founded the League of Jewish Women (Jüdischer Frauenbund) in 1904.

46. The one exception to this is Keathley, "'Die Frauenfrage,'" 149. She reads *Expectation* as akin to a "feminist *Bildungsroman*," though her larger point is to redress the dearth of attention to women's roles in musical modernism.

47. McLary, "Dead Lover's Body," 257.

48. Heim [Pappenheim], "Gedichte," 23. "Autopsy Room" was part of a planned poem cycle by the same title, as a handwritten archival note indicates. Inventory number IN 164.529, Karl Kraus-Archiv, Wienbibliothek im Rathaus.

49. Arthur Schnitzler, *Frühe Gedichte*, ed. Herbert Lederer (Berlin: Propyläen Verlag, 1969), 18.

50. Schnitzler's early diaries comment on how insufferable he found Langer's lectures. See, e.g., Schnitzler, *Tagebuch*, 55. Indeed, Langer was known for his straightforward and unadorned teaching style, one which stood in stark contrast to Langer's own famous showman-like anatomy professor, Josef Hyrtl. Lesky, *Vienna Medical School*, 218. Langer had literally written the textbook on anatomy: his *Lehrbuch der Anatomie des Menschen* (1865) was the standard work of the time, replacing that of his teacher Hyrtl, whose *Lehrbuch der Anatomie des Menschen* (1846) had been the standard work of the previous generation.

51. Thomé, "Vorwort," 15–16; Herzog, "'Medizin ist eine Weltanschauung,'" 229; Otis, *Membranes*, 125.

52. Schnitzler, *Tagebuch*, 42.

53. Schnitzler, *My Youth*, 105; Schnitzler, *Jugend*, 128. A diary entry from Febru-

ary 24, 1881, reads, e.g.: "Early mass. Home at 6. Then paged through the papers. Dissected a young woman shortly thereafter. Muddled [*Confus*]." Schnitzler, *Tagebuch*, 98. It was Langer's assistant, the anatomist Emil Zuckerkandl, who exerted a particular fascination on the young Schnitzler. Schnitzler describes Zuckerkandl in his robes looking as if straight out of Rembrandt's 1632 painting *The Anatomy Lesson of Dr. Nicolaes Tulp*. Schnitzler modeled himself on Zuckerkandl, going from coffeehouses to his studies and back, but in contrast to his teacher with the emphasis on the extracurricular. By his own admission, Schnitzler was, from early in his medical studies, at best a "desultory" pupil, lacking the clear purpose, focus, and enthusiasm of his fellow students. Schnitzler, *My Youth*, 103–5; Schnitzler, *Jugend*, 126–28.

54. Schnitzler, *My Youth*, 104; Schnitzler, *Jugend*, 127.

55. Schnitzler, *Frühe Gedichte*, 20–21. The prose sketch was not published during Schnitzler's lifetime. Arthur Schnitzler, "Frühlingsnacht im Seziersaal," in *Entworfenes und Verworfenes: Aus dem Nachlaß*, ed. Reinhard Urbach (Frankfurt: Fischer, 1977), 7–11. All subsequent references to the prose text will henceforth be cited parenthetically with page number.

56. This passage's similarity to the middle three stanzas (lines 13–24) of the earlier lyric version is striking.

57. The earliest mention is Frederick J. Beharriell, "Schnitzler's Anticipation of Freud's Dream Theory," *Monatshefte* 45, no. 2 (1953): 81–89. See also Michaela L. Perlmann, *Der Traum in der literarischen Moderne: Untersuchungen zum Werk Arthur Schnitzlers* (Munich: Fink, 1987).

58. Lorna Martens, *Shadow Lines: Austrian Literature from Freud to Kafka* (Lincoln: University of Nebraska Press, 1996), 257n29.

59. For a brief interpretation, see Filippo Smerilli's summary in Christoph Jürgensen, Wolfgang Lukas, and Michael Scheffel, eds., *Schnitzler-Handbuch: Leben—Werk—Wirkung* (Stuttgart: Metzler, 2014), 239.

60. Schnitzler, *My Youth*, 104; Schnitzler, *Jugend*, 126.

61. Arthur Schnitzler, *Dream Story*, trans. J. M. Q. Davies (London: Penguin, 1999), 79; Arthur Schnitzler, *Traumnovelle*, in *Gesammelte Werke: Die erzählenden Schriften*, vol. 2 (Frankfurt: Fischer, 1961), 434–504, here 488. These texts will henceforth be cited parenthetically together with page numbers, with the English translation preceding the corresponding passage from the German edition.

62. For an overview of the many interpretations applied to this aspect of the novella, see Michael Scheffel's analysis in Jürgensen, Lukas, and Scheffel, *Schnitzler-Handbuch*, 228–32.

63. On the centrality of vision in the literature of Viennese modernism, see Andreas Huyssen, "The Disturbance of Vision in Vienna Modernism," *Modernism/Modernity* 5, no. 3 (1998): 33–47.

64. W. G. Sebald, *Die Beschreibung des Unglücks: Zur österreichischen Literatur von Stifter bis Handke* (Frankfurt: Fischer, 1994), 60.

65. The German does not hedge the statement. It reads, "he would not and could not know—and in the end did not want to know" (500; my translation).

66. Arthur Schnitzler, *Aphorismen und Betrachtungen*, ed. Robert O. Weiss (Frankfurt: Fischer, 1967), 26.

67. Eric L. Santner, *On Creaturely Life: Rilke, Benjamin, Sebald* (Chicago: University of Chicago Press, 2006), xviii–xix.

68. Helmut Lethen, *Verhaltenlehren der Kälte: Lebensversuche zwischen den Kriegen* (Frankfurt: Suhrkamp, 1994), 244; Helmut Lethen, *Cool Conduct: The Culture of Distance in Weimar Germany*, trans. Don Reneau (Berkeley: University of California Press, 2002). Along with the *creature*, Lethen pinpoints the *cool persona* and the *radar type* as three characteristic figures manifest in the cultural production and philosophical anthropology of the interwar years.

69. Joseph Roth, *Werke*, ed. Hermann Kesten, vol. 3, *Erzählungen* (Cologne: Kiepenheuer & Witsch, 1976), 884, 881, 884. Emphasis in original.

70. Walter Benjamin, *Illuminations*, ed. Hannah Arendt, trans. Harry Zohn (New York: Schocken, 1968), 84. In *The Sleepwalkers* trilogy (1931–32), Hermann Broch describes how the fragility of the human body was offered scant protection by the psychological and material encasement of the military uniform. The uniform, elevated to a "cult" in a secular age, serves as an ordering principle between self and world in Broch's rendering. It is designed to "arrest the confusion and flux of life, just as it conceals whatever in the human body is soft and flowing." Hermann Broch, *The Sleepwalkers*, trans. Willa and Edwin Muir (New York: Vintage, 2000), 15.

71. Joseph Roth, "Kranke Menschheit," in *Werke*, ed. Fritz Hackert, vol. 4, *Romane und Erzählungen 1916–1929* (Cologne: Kiepenheuer & Witsch, 1989), 43.

72. Richard A. Bermann [pseud. Arnold Höllriegel] and Rudolf Olden [pseud. Renatus Oltschi] also contributed short texts under this rubric. For details about Roth's early publications, in particular his work for *Der Neue Tag*, see Deborah Holmes, "Joseph Roth's Feuilleton Journalism as Social History in Vienna, 1919–20," *Austrian History Yearbook* 48 (2017): 255–65; Irmgard Wirtz, *Joseph Roths Fiktionen des Faktischen: Das Feuilleton der Zwanziger Jahre und "Die Geschichte von der 1002. Nacht" im historischen Kontext* (Berlin: Erich Schmidt, 1997), 31–65; Ingeborg Sültemeyer, *Das Frühwerk Joseph Roths 1915–1926: Studien und Texte* (Vienna: Herder, 1976), 46–63; and Gabriella Pelloni, "Spazieren in Nachkriegswirren: Joseph Roth als Chronist des Wiener Lebens 1919/20 (in vergleichender Perspektive zu Francis Wolf-Cirian)," in *"Baustelle Kultur": Diskurslagen in der österreichischen Literatur 1918–1933/38*, ed. Primus-Heinz Kucher and Julia Bertschik (Bielefeld: Aisthesis, 2011).

73. Kurt Paupié, *Handbuch der österreichischen Pressegeschichte 1848–1959*, vol. 1, *Wien* (Vienna: Braumüller, 1960), 40–44.

74. See David Bronsen, *Joseph Roth: Eine Biographie* (Cologne: Kiepenheuer & Witsch, 1974), for biographical information on Roth's years in Vienna (185–207) and a discussion of Polgar's influence (189–91). Other notable contributors to the newspaper included Egon Erwin Kisch, Richard A. Bermann (Arnold Höllriegel), Leo Perutz, and Eugenie Schwarzwald.

75. Another nom de plume Roth employed was "the red Joseph" (*der rote Joseph*)—a simple homonymic reversal of his first and last names—indicative of his political leanings at this time and especially well-suited to his writings for the Social Democratic newspaper *Vorwärts*.

76. See Frederic Raphael, *A Jew among Romans: The Life and Legacy of Flavius Josephus* (New York: Pantheon, 2013).

77. Bronsen, *Joseph Roth*, 192.

78. Joseph Roth, *Werke*, ed. Fritz Hackert, vol. 4, *Romane und Erzählungen 1916–1929* (Cologne: Kiepenheuer & Witsch, 1989), 601; W. G. Sebald, "Ein Kaddisch für Österreich—Über Joseph Roth," in *Unheimliche Heimat: Essays zur österreichischen Literatur* (Frankfurt: Fischer, 1995), 116.

79. Sültemeyer, *Frühwerk*, 52.

80. Joan Acocella, "European Dreams: Rediscovering Joseph Roth," *New Yorker* 79, no. 43 (January 19, 2004): 80.

81. The population declined from well over 2 million to approximately 1.8 million.

82. Maureen Healy, *Vienna and the Fall of the Habsburg Empire: Total War and Everyday Life in World War I* (Cambridge: Cambridge University Press, 2004), 300–313, and David F. Strong, *Austria (October 1918–March 1919): Transition from Empire to Republic* (New York: Columbia University Press, 1939).

83. H[einrich] Leoster, "Unsere Kriegsaustellung," *Die Zeit*, November 30, 1918, Morgenblatt edition, sec. Feuilleton, 1.

84. Alfred Pfoser, "Wohin der Krieg führt: Eine Chronologie des Zusammenbruchs," in *Im Epizentrum des Zusammenbruchs: Wien im Ersten Weltkrieg*, ed. Alfred Pfoser and Andreas Weigl (Vienna: Metroverlag, 2013), 686. See Healy, *Vienna and the Fall*, 87–121.

85. Leoster, "Unsere Kriegsaustellung," 1.

86. *Oxford English Dictionary*, s.v. "symptom, *n*.," accessed February 20, 2016, https://www.oed.com/view/Entry/196320.

87. Helen Chambers, "Signs of the Times: Joseph Roth's Weimar Journalism," in *German Novelists of the Weimar Republic: Intersections of Literature and Politics*, ed. Karl Leydecker (Rochester: Camden House, 2006), 103; Klaus Amann, *Die Dichter und die Politik: Essays zur österreichischen Literatur nach 1918* (Vienna: Deuticke, 1992), 50.

88. Roth, "Kranke Menschheit," 44.

89. Joseph Roth to Bernard von Brentano, undated: "Ich sehe durch Lupen. Ich schäle die Häute von den Dingen und Menschen, lege ihre Geheimnisse bloß—dann kann man freilich nicht mehr glauben." Joseph Roth, *Briefe 1911–1939*, ed. Hermann Kesten (Cologne: Kiepenheuer & Witsch, 1970), 75.

90. Pelloni, "Spazieren in Nachkriegswirren," 119; Amann, *Dichter und die Politik*, 52. Jon Hughes has offered a differently inflected reading. He notes the significance of the fragmentation of narrative in Roth's work and links it in particular to concurrent developments in the visual arts (Futurism, cubism), which resisted a totalizing wholeness, preferring instead "self-conscious incompleteness." Hughes applies this insight to issues of (masculine) identity and the self in Roth's characters. Jon Hughes, *Facing Modernity: Fragmentation, Culture, and Identity in Joseph Roth's Writing in the 1920s* (London: Maney, 2006), 66.

91. Joseph Roth, *Werke*, ed. Klaus Westermann and Fritz Hackert, vol. 3, *Das journalistische Werk 1915–1923* (Cologne: Kiepenheuer & Witsch, 1989), 277–78. All subsequent references to Roth's essays cited parenthetically with page number in-text refer to this edition and volume.

92. Erica Weitzman, "Human Fragments: Plastic Surgery and Bare Life in Joseph Roth's Feuilletons," *Journal of Austrian Studies* 46, no. 4 (2013): 95.

93. Weitzman, "Human Fragments," 95–96, reads this reduction to "bare existence" productively with Walter Benjamin's nearly contemporaneous "Critique of Violence" (1921) and relates both texts to Giorgio Agamben's revision of biopolitics through the notion of "bare life."

94. Weitzman, "Human Fragments," 94–95.

95. This question, "Was für ein Naturding ist der Mensch?," is, as Helmut Lethen argues, the central question that occupied philosophical anthropology in the 1920s. Lethen, *Verhaltenlehren der Kälte*, 52, 255.

96. Lethen, *Verhaltenlehren der Kälte*, 246; Lethen, *Cool Conduct*, 196.

97. Lethen, *Verhaltenlehren der Kälte*, 255–56; Lethen, *Cool Conduct*, 204–5.

98. Verena Pawlowsky and Harald Wendelin, "Der Krieg und seine Opfer: Kriegsbeschädigte in Wien," in *Im Epizentrum des Zusammenbruchs*, ed. Pfoser and Weigl, 311.

99. "Die österreichische Prothesen-Aktion," *Wiener Bilder*, September 5, 1915, 11.

100. "Österreichische Prothesen-Aktion," 11.

101. Felix Czeike, *Historisches Lexikon Wien*, 6 vols. (Vienna: Kremayr & Scheriau, 1992). After the war, Spitzy transitioned the institution to a civil hospital and remained its director.

102. Heather R. Perry, "Brave Old World: Recycling der Kriegskrüppel während des Ersten Weltkrieges," in *Artifizielle Körper—Lebendige Technik: Technische Modellierungen des Körpers in historischer Perspektive*, ed. Barbara Orland (Zurich: Chronos-Verlag, 2005); Hans Spitzy, *Unsere Kriegsinvaliden: Einrichtungen zur Heilung und Fürsorge* (Vienna: L. W. Seidel & Sohn, 1915). Prostheses were central in helping veterans to reintegrate into their premilitary professions, but Spitzy's training programs also allowed them to transition to new professions, including everything from basket weavers and barbers to musicians and bookkeepers—and, of course, prosthetics makers.

103. Thomas Rohringer, "Kriegsbeschädigte und Kriegsfolgenbewältigung," in *Im Epizentrum des Zusammenbruchs*, ed. Pfoser and Weigl, 320; Healy, *Vienna and the Fall*, 114–15.

104. A poster designed by Paul Suján for the regional war welfare exhibition (Landes-Kriegsfürsorge-Ausstellung) in Bratislava in 1917 likewise depicts a farmworker with a prosthetic arm performing manual labor. Inventory number P-35379, Paul Suján, Wienbibliothek im Rathaus.

105. Pawlowsky and Wendelin, "Der Krieg und seine Opfer," 316; Perry, "Brave Old World." Roth's essay "The Reconstruction of Man" (Der Wiederaufbau des Menschen), e.g., published in the *Neue Berliner Zeitung* in June 1921, documents the declining interest in reconstructive medical procedures. It concerns the German plastic surgeon Jacques Joseph's (1865–1934) facial plastic and reconstructive surgery ward at Berlin's Charité hospital. The department was facing a merger or closure, but Roth argues for the continued imperative of its existence. See Weitzman, "Human Fragments." The emergence of a "psychophysical indication"—linking patients' psychological well-being to their external adherence to sociophysical norms—gave plastic and reconstructive surgery new relevance with the societal reintegration of war veterans. Annelie Rams-

brock, *The Science of Beauty: Culture and Cosmetics in Modern Germany, 1750–1930*, trans. David Burnett (New York: Palgrave Macmillan, 2015), 90–108.

106. The material is *Papierspagat*, a wartime solution to inflationary hemp pricing and material shortages. See "Der Papierspagat," *Die Zeit*, August 15, 1915; and Hubert Weitensfelder, "'Kriegsware': Ersatzstoffe in Produktion und Alltag," in *Im Epizentrum des Zusammenbruchs*, ed. Pfoser and Weigl, 172–79.

107. Field marshal lieutenant during World War I, Heinrich Teisinger was made to stand before a commission investigating war crimes in 1920 because he was accused of having declared 200,000 infirm veterans fit for military service. He was posthumously acquitted, but the case was widely covered in the press. "Der Fall Teisinger," *Arbeiter-Zeitung*, March 9, 1920, Morgenblatt edition, sec. Beilage, and "Generalmajor Teisinger gestorben," *Arbeiter-Zeitung*, February 3, 1920, Morgenblatt edition, sec. Tagesneuigkeiten. Roth, too, covered the end of the story in a feuilleton for *Der Neue Tag* on January 21, 1920 (227–29), as did Alfred Polgar in "Der Teisinger."

108. Karl Kraus, *In These Great Times: A Karl Kraus Reader*, ed. Harry Zohn (Chicago: University of Chicago Press, 1990), 70–83.

109. In German, the idiom "jemandem das Rückgrat brechen" also carries the figurative meaning to ruin or break someone or something.

110. Santner, *On Creaturely Life*, xvi. Emphasis in original.

111. Rainer Maria Rilke, *The Notebooks of Malte Laurids Brigge*, trans. Stephen Mitchell (New York: Vintage, 1990), 40.

112. Lethen, *Verhaltenlehren der Kälte*, 245–47; Lethen, *Cool Conduct*, 196–97.

113. Lethen, *Verhaltenlehren der Kälte*, 256; Lethen, *Cool Conduct*, 205.

114. Hauser served as the organization's president in 1927–28. In 1938, the National Socialists placed him under *Berufsverbot* because of his political orientation and his marriage to a Jewish woman, and he went into exile in Switzerland. After the war he returned to Vienna and became an important public figure in the postwar arts scene. Czeike, *Historisches Lexikon Wien*, 3:88–89. Cornelia Cabuk, *Carry Hauser: Monografie und Werkverzeichnis*, Belvedere Werkverzeichnisse 2 (Weitra: Bibliothek der Provinz, 2012).

115. Much like his contemporary Otto Rudolf Schatz (1900–1961). A recent exhibition at the Wien Museum paired the two artists.

116. See Cabuk, *Carry Hauser*, 111–17.

117. Cabuk, *Carry Hauser*, 138.

118. Cited in Cabuk, *Carry Hauser*, 141.

119. It was one of five such limited-edition art books Hauser made in the early 1920s. *The Book of the City* was displayed at the Hagenbund in 1928 and subsequently in 1931 at the International Salon of Contemporary Book Art in the Petit Palais des Beaux Arts de la Ville de Paris. The facsimile edition referenced here is Carry Hauser, *Das Buch von der Stadt*, ed. Roland Widder (Weitra: Bibliothek der Provinz, 2016). This text will henceforth be cited parenthetically with page number.

120. See Evelyne Polt-Heinzl, *Österreichische Literatur zwischen den Kriegen: Plädoyer für eine Kanonrevision* (Vienna: Sonderzahl, 2012).

121. "Arbeiter und Arbeiterinnen! Soldaten! Mahnruf!," *Arbeiter-Zeitung*, June 15, 1919, Morgenblatt edition.

122. Roth calls it "the only Viennese electric [tram], whose guests, in silent kindliness, do not step on [each other's] long since dissected toes" (34). In another of the Viennese Symptoms essays, "Modern Vehicles" (Moderne Vehikel) (September 23, 1919), Roth suggests several new "Fahr*un*gelegenheiten"—the clever antonym of "transportation options." His ironic proposals include a "Pendelleichenwagen," or corpse shuttle service, from Schottentor to the Central Cemetery. For just sixty *Heller*, Roth suggests, people could voluntarily ride to the Central Cemetery and be buried only half dead, i.e., in their current state, thus allowing them to "easily and painlessly" avoid the coming Viennese winter (145). Roth is clearly anticipating another devastating winter like the one prior, in which bitter cold, food shortages, and the global influenza pandemic claimed tens of thousands of lives in Austria alone.

123. Joseph Roth to Stefan Zweig, October 23, 1930. Joseph Roth and Stefan Zweig, *"Jede Freundschaft mit mir ist verderblich": Joseph Roth und Stefan Zweig. Briefwechsel 1927–1938*, ed. Madeleine Rietra and Rainer Joachim Siegel (Göttingen: Wallstein, 2011), 53.

124. Horváth remarked on the universality of the title and subject matter in the "Author's Aside" to the play: "Any one of my plays could be called 'Faith, Hope, and Charity.'" Ödön von Horváth, *Faith, Hope, and Charity: A Little Dance of Death in Five Acts*, trans. Christopher Hampton (London: Faber and Faber, 1989), viii; Ödön von Horváth, *Glaube Liebe Hoffnung*, in *Gesammelte Werke*, ed. Dieter Hildebrandt, Walter Huder, and Traugott Krischke, 4 vols. (Frankfurt: Suhrkamp, 1970), 1:325–80; here 1:328. The text will henceforth be cited parenthetically, with the English translation preceding the corresponding passage from the German edition. The first drafts of *Faith, Hope, and Charity* were written in 1930, and its premiere had originally been planned for January 1933 at the Deutsches Theater in Berlin. The plans of director Heinz Hilpert, whom Max Reinhardt had hired in 1926, were dashed by the volatile German political climate, though Hilpert had successfully premiered Horváth's *Geschichten aus dem Wiener Wald* there in 1931. Elias Jubal finally staged the play in 1936 in Vienna at his basement theater, the Theater für 49—referring to the number of seats in the venue—in the souterrain of the Hôtel de France. The Theater für 49 was among the most politically critical theaters under Austrofascism. Hilde Haider-Pregler and Beate Reiterer, eds., *Verspielte Zeit: Österreichisches Theater der dreißiger Jahre* (Vienna: Picus, 1997).

125. Freud, *Standard Edition*, 21:144. The connection is made with respect to another of Horváth's texts by Andreas Ehrenreich, "Die Symptomatik der Wundkultur: Tod und Sterben bei Ödön von Horváth," *Maske und Kothurn* 59, no. 3 (2013): 120.

126. The inspiration for Horváth's play came from an acquaintance, Lukas Kristl, a Munich court reporter, who published an article in the *Münchener Post* in July 1929 detailing a recent case. The defendant was a saleswoman for women's undergarments. The details of her case revolved around accusations of fraud, false identity, and nonpayment—in short, petty offences, not capital crimes. In the end, the woman was sentenced to three months in jail. Horváth, *Gesammelte Werke*, 1:69–70. Horváth took these basic contours of the case to thematize how both the fictional and the real-life accused are unable to extricate themselves from the vagaries of a legal system that penalizes petty crimes with outsized sentencing.

127. This is a chapter title in Anton Kaes, ed., *Weimarer Republik: Manifeste und*

Dokumente zur deutschen Literatur, 1918–1933 (Stuttgart: Metzler, 1983), 319–45. See also David Midgley, *Writing Weimer: Critical Realism in German Literature, 1918–1933* (Oxford: Oxford University Press, 2000); Sabine Becker, *Neue Sachlichkeit*, vol. 1, *Die Ästhetik der neusachlichen Literatur 1920–1933* (Cologne: Böhlau, 2000); and Helmut Lethen, *Neue Sachlichkeit 1924–1932: Studien zur Literatur des "weißen Sozialismus"* (Stuttgart: Metzler, 1970).

128. Achille Mbembe, "Necropolitics," trans. Libby Meintjes, *Public Culture* 15, no. 1 (2003): 40. Mbembe's focus is on neocolonialism and its "repressed topographies of cruelty," including plantations and colonies.

129. The list of cities is the title of an autobiographical sketch by Horváth from 1929. Horváth, *Gesammelte Werke*, 3:9–10.

130. For the history and aesthetics of the *Volksstück*, see Hugo Aust, Peter Haida, and Jürgen Hein, *Volksstück: Vom Hanswurstspiel zum sozialen Drama der Gegenwart*, ed. Jürgen Hein (Munich: Beck, 1989).

131. nn. [pseud. for Jura Soyfer?], "Theater für 49," *Neues Wiener Tagblatt*, November 15, 1936, sec. Theater und Kunst, 15.

132. Alfred Polgar, "Ödön von Horváth: Kasimir und Karoline," in *Alfred Polgar: Kleine Schriften*, ed. Marcel Reich-Ranicki and Ulrich Weinzierl, vol. 5, *Theater I* (Reinbek: Rowohlt, 1985), 547.

133. Herbert Gamper, "Todesbilder in Horváths Werk," in *Horváth-Diskussion*, ed. Kurt Bartsch, Uwe Baur, and Dietmar Goltschnigg (Kronberg: Scriptor, 1976), 81. For parallel perspectives on the role of death in Horváth's work, see Ehrenreich, "Symptomatik der Wundkultur," 113–24, and Karl Müller, "'Wo ganz plötzlich ein Mensch sichtbar wird': Lebens- und Todeskämpfe," in *Ödön von Horváth: Unendliche Dummheit—dumme Unendlichkeit*, ed. Klaus Kastberger (Vienna: Zsolnay, 2001), 19–34.

134. The rumor that the Anatomical Institute was trafficking in corpses was persistent. As Tatjana Buklijas has shown based on archival materials from the Medical University of Vienna from the decade between 1898 and 1908, the institute received several letters per year with offers similar to Elisabeth's. Most came from working-class Viennese, who wanted to profit in life from the sale of their physical remains on death. The real-life letter writers often played up their extraordinary physical characteristics and anomalies, while referencing prior contact with other physicians prepared to give attestations about the scientific value of the applicants' bodies. The source of the rumor is unknown, but it has been speculated that it was linked to Viennese anatomists' efforts around 1900 to increase the supply of corpses for anatomical study. Tatjana Buklijas, "Public Anatomies in Fin-de-Siècle Vienna," *Medicine Studies* 2 (2010): 84–85.

135. It is a leitmotif Horváth embedded into the very title of one of his plays, *A Girl Is Sold*. Ödön von Horváth, *Ein Fräulein wird verkauft und andere Stücke aus dem Nachlaß*, ed. Klaus Kastberger, Supplementband II zur Kommentierten Werkausgabe in Einzelbänden (Frankfurt: Suhrkamp, 2005), 125–39.

136. This stage direction links to a policeman's warning to Elisabeth in the opening scene as they stand in front of the Anatomical Institute: "You take care, miss," he says, "there's heads in there, stacked up in rows" (1/1:331).

137. Helmut Lethen, "Horváths Biotope und die 'Weltoffenheit' in der Anthropolo-

DEPRESSION

Darkness visited me when I least expected it. It crept up in the form of sudden, indefinable health issues. No one was able to locate their cause. No medical treatment was effective. I remained helpless. Darkness spread, and without light, everything looked different. The world I thought was my life looked very different. Insidiously, the physical suffering began to manifest itself in my psyche. Out of the suffering I developed a depression. It was an unusual affliction, as I had always known how to pull myself out of darkness. But not this time. This time, confusion and emptiness took over. This time, everything fell apart.

DEPRESSION is #2 of a series of thirty artworks presented in the book "1111". Illustrated and narrated by NYCHOS, published by Rabbit Eye Movement in 2020.

gie der Zwischenkriegszeit," in *Ödön von Horváth: Unendliche Dummheit—dumme Unendlichkeit*, ed. Klaus Kastberger (Vienna: Zsolnay, 2001), 8.

138. For a structural analysis of the play's sites, including the Anatomical Institute, see Ingrid Haag, *Ödön von Horváth: Fassaden-Dramaturgie. Beschreibung einer theatralischen Form* (Frankfurt: Peter Lang, 1995).

139. See Bronfen, *Over Her Dead Body*, 181.

140. Müller, "'Wo ganz plötzlich ein Mensch sichtbar wird,'" 32–33.

141. The protagonist of Horváth's posthumously published prose fragment "Marianne, or The Decay" (Marianne oder: Das Verwesen) is another example of a living cadaver; here the theme of psychic disintegration manifests physically. Ödön von Horváth, *Himmelwärts und andere Prosa aus dem Nachlaß: Supplementband I zur kommentierten Werkausgabe in Einzelbänden*, ed. Klaus Kastberger (Frankfurt: Suhrkamp, 2001), 16.

142. Horváth, *Himmelwärts*, 16.

143. Horváth, *Gesammelte Werke*, 3:8. See Ehrenreich, "Symptomatik der Wundkultur," 121.

144. Polgar, "Ödön von Horváth," 547.

145. There is a neat parallel between Horváth's depiction of his methodology and what Roy Porter has called "doing medical history from below." Roy Porter, "The Patient's View: Doing Medical History from Below," *Theory and Society* 14, no. 2 (1985): 175–98.

CHAPTER THREE

1. Quoted in Hermann Bahr, ed., *Gegen Klimt* (Vienna: J. Eisenstein, 1903), 47.

2. See Bahr, *Gegen Klimt*, 13–37, and Carl E. Schorske, *Fin-de-Siècle Vienna: Politics and Culture* (New York: Vintage, 1980), 227–31.

3. Schorske speaks of the "naturalistic concreteness" of the corporeal in Klimt's paintings of this era. Schorske, *Fin-de-Siècle Vienna*, 242. Two classic studies in the vast literature on the nude in visual art are Kenneth Clark, *The Nude: A Study in Ideal Form* (New York: Pantheon, 1956), and Lynda Nead, *The Female Nude: Art, Obscenity, and Sexuality* (London: Routledge, 1992).

4. Anonymous, quoted in Bahr, *Gegen Klimt*, 55.

5. Plein-Air [pseud. Adalbert Franz Seligmann], Eduard Pötzl, and anonymous, quoted in Bahr, *Gegen Klimt*, 52, 41, 55, respectively.

6. Quoted in Bahr, *Gegen Klimt*, 51. Another ground for the condemnation of *Medicine* was that it was purportedly inappropriate for its commissioned setting. The legislative motion in the Imperial Council found the naked figures better suited to an anatomical museum than to the interior design of a representative public hall at the University of Vienna. Quoted in Bahr, *Gegen Klimt*, 46.

7. Quoted in Bahr, *Gegen Klimt*, 47; Plein-Air [pseud. of Adalbert Franz Seligmann], quoted in Bahr, *Gegen Klimt*, 53.

8. B[erta] Z[uckerkandl], "Die Hoffnung," *Wiener Allgemeine Zeitung*, April 26, 1909, 6 Uhr-Blatt edition, sec. Kunst und Kultur, 2. Zuckerkandl gives a brief history

of the traditional religious iconography of pregnant women. See also a contemporary work, A[nton] M[aximilian] Pachinger, *Die Mutterschaft in der Malerei und Graphik* (Munich: Georg Müller, 1906), which Zuckerkandl references.

9. Luce Irigaray, *This Sex Which Is Not One*, trans. Catherine Porter and Carolyn Burke (Ithaca, NY: Cornell University Press, 1985), 23–33. The most salient historiography on sexuality in Austria includes Britta McEwen, *Sexual Knowledge: Feeling, Fact, and Social Reform in Vienna, 1900–1934* (New York: Berghahn, 2012), and Günter Bischof, Anton Pelinka, and Dagmar Herzog, eds., *Sexuality in Austria*, Contemporary Austrian Studies 15 (New Brunswick: Transaction, 2007), especially the following chapters: Dagmar Herzog, "Sexuality in Twentieth-Century Austria," 7–20, and David S. Luft, "Thinking about Sexuality and Gender in Vienna," 21–30. The literature for the German context is vast, but two studies bear explicit mention: Atina Grossmann, *Reforming Sex: The German Movement for Birth Control and Abortion Reform 1920–1950* (New York: Oxford University Press, 1995), and Scott Spector, Helmut Puff, and Dagmar Herzog, eds., *After "The History of Sexuality": German Genealogies with and beyond Foucault* (New York: Berghahn, 2012).

10. Rosemary M. Balsam, *Women's Bodies in Psychoanalysis* (New York: Routledge, 2012), 31–54; Rosemary H. Balsam, "Freud, the Birthing Body, and Modern Life," *Journal of the American Psychoanalytic Association* 65, no. 1 (2017): 63–64. Margarethe Hilferding (1871–1942), the first woman to receive a medical degree from the University of Vienna (in 1903) and the first woman admitted to the Vienna Psychoanalytic Society (in 1909), was perhaps the first to theorize the sexuality of pregnancy and motherhood, specifically with regard to psychoanalysis. Predictably, her ideas caused much consternation among her male colleagues in the society. She eventually withdrew from the society in 1911, in the wake of Alfred Adler's (1870–1937) break with Freud. Eveline List, *Mutterliebe und Geburtenkontrolle—zwischen Psychoanalyse und Sozialismus: Die Geschichte der Margarethe Hilferding-Hönigsberg* (Vienna: Mandelbaum, 2006), 134–46.

11. Thomas Laqueur, *Making Sex: Body and Gender from the Greeks to Freud* (Cambridge, MA: Harvard University Press, 1990).

12. Lisa Cartwright, *Screening the Body: Tracing Medicine's Visual Culture* (Minneapolis: University of Minnesota Press, 1995); Paula Treichler, Lisa Cartwright, and Constance Penley, eds., *The Visible Woman: Imaging Technologies, Gender, and Science* (New York: New York University Press, 1998); Sandra Matthews and Laura Wexler, *Pregnant Pictures* (New York: Routledge, 2000).

13. Rosa Mayreder, "Die schöne Weiblichkeit," ed. Auguste Fickert, Marie Lang, and Rosa Mayreder, *Dokumente der Frauen* 1, no. 5 (May 15, 1899): 124. Interestingly, this more modern habitus was later applied to doctors as well. Dr. Adolf Kronfeld, for example, writes in 1927, "the modern gynecologist is simple, straightforward, without excessive sentimentality, also without too many words—just as the modern, simple, courageous woman and expectant mother should be." A[dolf] Kronfeld, "Universitätsprofessor Doktor Erwin Graff: Ein Porträt," *Neues Wiener Journal*, February 13, 1927, 17. A draft of this article is "Kronfeld, A.: Universitätsprofessor Doktor Erwin Graff, ein Porträt," undated typescript, SA 3.603, Archive of the Medical University of Vienna.

14. Rosa Mayreder-Obermayer, "Sein Ideal," in *Übergänge* (Dresden: Pierson, 1897), 197–217.

15. In 1903, Margarethe Hilferding became the first woman to receive a medical degree from the University of Vienna. Important parallels exist between her career path and that of Pappenheim. See List, *Mutterliebe und Geburtenkontrolle*.

16. This subject is addressed, e.g., in the Austrian Women's Club position about the scandal surrounding the possible admission of women to medical studies at the University of Vienna in "Der österreichische Frauenverein," *Arbeiterinnen-Zeitung*, November 7, 1895, sec. Vermischtes, 7.

17. See McEwen, *Sexual Knowledge*, 133–36; Karl Fallend, *Wilhelm Reich in Wien: Psychoanalyse und Politik*, Veröffentlichungen des Ludwig-Boltzmann-Institutes für Geschichte der Gesellschaftswissenschaften 17 (Vienna: Geyer-Edition, 1988), 122–27; and Maria Mesner, "Educating Reasonable Lovers: Sex Counseling in Austria in the First Half of the Twentieth Century," in *Sexuality in Austria*, ed. Bischof, Pelinka, and Herzog, 48–64.

18. As advertised in a communist periodical: "Proletarische Sexualberatungsstellen in Wien," *Die Rote Fahne*, January 27, 1929, 4. Predictably, hostility from the Catholic-conservative political right toward such initiatives increased into the 1930s, as the fascist threat grew. Writing in 1933, one journalist for the conservative *Reichspost*—directly addressing Pappenheim, Reich, and the society by name—subtitled an article "Keep Your Hands Off Austria!" O. N., "Wien die neue Zentrale der kommunistischen 'Sexualreformbewegung'?," *Reichspost*, May 5, 1933, 7.

19. Editorial note to Maria [Marie] Heim [Pappenheim], "Gedichte ['Seziersaal,' 'Trennung,' 'Vor Dem Konzert,' 'Prima Graviditas']," ed. Karl Kraus, *Die Fackel* 8, no. 202 (April 30, 1906): 23.

20. As Pappenheim once remarked in an interview, "I did not want to wander through life as a poet. In my view, it was incompatible to be a doctor, i.e., to stand with both feet in reality, and to simultaneously publish lyric poetry." Interview with Marie Frischauf, 1949, quoted in Marcus G. Patka, "Nachwort: Literatur versus Medizin—Marie Frischauf, geborene Pappenheim," in *Der graue Mann: Roman und Gedichte für Arnold Schönberg*, by Marie Frischauf, ed. Marcus G. Patka (Vienna: Theodor Kramer Gesellschaft, 2000), 109. Pappenheim's choice to lead a life of social engagement in the interwar years was followed by persecution and exile under Austrofascism and National Socialism. After surviving in Paris and Mexico, Pappenheim returned to Austria after World War II—and renewed her literary efforts, publishing a critical social novel, *The Grey Man* (Der graue Mann) in 1949.

21. I am grateful to Philipp Ramer (University of Geneva) who, in a long-ago conversation about Peter Altenberg and *Kunst*, mentioned Ungar's name.

22. The scant extant biographical information about Ungar was painstakingly researched by Vlado Obad, "Ilka Maria Ungar: Ein Kampf um die dichterische Selbstverwirklichung," in *"Wir wollen der Gerechtigkeit und Menschenliebe dienen . . .": Frauenbildung und Emanzipation in der Habsburgermonarchie—der südslawische Raum und seine Wechselwirkung mit Wien, Prag und Budapest*, ed. Vesela Tutavac and Ilse Korotin (Vienna: Praesens Verlag, 2016), 80–93. The lack of clarity about Ungar's denomination stems from conflicting documentary evidence. However, her sons and

husband were all murdered in the Jasenovac concentration camp. See Obad, "Ilka Maria Ungar," 82, 84. Ungar's employment was the topic of several poems, including "Tailor's Shop" (Schneiderei), "Überstunden" (Overtime), and "Closing Time" (Feierabend).

23. Carl Bethke, *(K)eine gemeinsame Sprache? Aspekte deutsch-jüdischer Beziehungsgeschichte in Slawonien, 1900–1945*, Studien zur Geschichte, Kultur und Gesellschaft Südosteuropas 12 (Berlin: Lit Verlag, 2013), 70–77.

24. The poems published in *Simplicissimus* included "Tailor's Shop" (Schneiderei), "Working Hands" (Arbeitshände), "Soul of Women Workers" (Arbeiterinnenseele), and "Illegitimate Child" (Unehelich Kind)."

25. "O sehet nicht mein Kleid," line 24. Ilka Maria Ung[a]r, *Feierabend: Gesammelte Gedichte* (Berlin: Julius Bard, 1910), 89. Individual poems from this volume will henceforth be cited parenthetically with page number and line.

26. Another poem from the same cycle, "The Plebeian Woman" (Die Plebejerin), commences with a roar: "I who must serve you—I hate you!" (73, line 1).

27. In one case, "you" is the Eternal, in the other, "I am the Eternal."

28. See Obad, "Ilka Maria Ungar," 88–89.

29. See Obad, "Ilka Maria Ungar," 92–93. Obad problematically references Paula Grogger and Enrica von Handel-Mazzetti, both of whom wrote provincial verse and were, to varying degrees, *völkisch* in their views and aligned with the National Socialists.

30. Obad, "Ilka Maria Ungar," 92, 90.

31. Paul Wertheimer, "Eine österreichische Poetin: Ilka Maria Ungar," *Wiener Mode* 25, no. 10 (February 15, 1911): 565.

32. Peter Altenberg, "Ein Band Gedichte," in *Märchen des Lebens*, 5th and 6th rev. ed. (1907; repr., Berlin: Fischer, 1919), 209. The editor of the posthumously published *Altenbergbuch*, Egon Friedell, selected Ungar's poems—along with a reproduction of a postcard Altenberg had sent to Ungar—for inclusion alongside texts by Altenberg, Heinrich and Thomas Mann, Hugo von Hofmannsthal, Felix Salten, Alfred Polgar, and many others. Egon Friedell, ed., *Das Altenbergbuch* (Leipzig: Verlag der Wiener Graphischen Werkstätte, 1921), 293–99.

33. Werner Hofmann, "Das Fleisch erkennen," in *Ornament und Askese im Zeitgeist des Wien der Jahrhundertwende*, ed. Alfred Pfabigan (Vienna: Brandstätter, 1985), 120–29; Hilde Spiel, *Vienna's Golden Autumn 1866–1938* (London: Weidenfeld and Nicolson, 1987), 79–80, 82; Gemma Blackshaw and Leslie Topp, "Scrutinised Bodies and Lunatic Utopias: Mental Illness, Psychiatry and the Visual Arts in Vienna, 1898–1914," in *Madness and Modernity: Mental Illness and the Visual Arts in Vienna 1900*, ed. Gemma Blackshaw and Leslie Topp (Farnham: Lund Humphries, 2009), 21.

34. Hofmann, "Das Fleisch erkennen," 127, 125.

35. Scott Spector, "Beyond the Aesthetic Garden: Politics and Culture on the Margins of Fin-de Siècle Vienna," *Journal of the History of Ideas* 59, no. 4 (1998): 695.

36. Alessandra Comini has highlighted the "dramatized anatomical veracity" at the heart of much of Schiele's artistic production. Alessandra Comini, *Egon Schiele's Portraits* (Berkeley: University of California Press, 1974), 40. A recent exhibition of Schiele's works aptly highlighted his "radical nudes." Peter Vergo and Barnaby Wright,

eds., *Egon Schiele: The Radical Nude* (London: Courtauld Gallery in Association with Paul Holberton Publishing, 2014).

37. Jane Kallir, a leading Schiele scholar, has termed this series "gynecological watercolors." Jane Kallir, *Egon Schiele's Women* (Munich: Prestel, 2012), 87. In her catalogue raisonné, *Egon Schiele: The Complete Works* (New York: Abrams, 1990), Kallir identifies the drawings made at the Women's Clinic as Kallir D. 528–29, 531–35. My subsequent mentions of Schiele's works reference this cataloging system. Alessandra Comini speculates that several other watercolors of unidentified women from the same time period probably also belong to the same series of drawings from the Women's Clinic, including Kallir D. 536–40. Comini, *Egon Schiele's Portraits*, 212n64. At least six studies of newborn infants (Kallir D. 382–87) were likely executed simultaneously. Kallir, *Egon Schiele*, 391.

38. Gemma Blackshaw and Leslie Topp have highlighted how the aesthetic of Viennese modernism was influenced by contact with the medical establishment, though they focus foremost on the representation of mental illness in Viennese visual art. Blackshaw and Topp, "Scrutinised Bodies and Lunatic Utopias"; Gemma Blackshaw, "The Pathological Body: Modernist Strategising in Egon Schiele's Self-Portraiture," *Oxford Art Journal* 30, no. 3 (2007): 377–401.

39. Klaus Albrecht Schröder rightly points to the influence of photography on portraiture conventions around the turn of the century. He calls the veritable "flood" of pictures of the human body in the context of medicine, psychology, ethnology, and erotica "the decisive stylistic influence on Austrian Expressionism." Klaus Albrecht Schröder, *Egon Schiele: Eros and Passion*, trans. David Britt (Munich: Prestel, 1995), 48–49.

40. Though there are two examples from the German context: Käthe Kollwitz's etching *Pregnant Woman* (1910) was on display in November and December 1910 at the 37th Secession exhibition in Vienna, which was simultaneously the first exhibition of the Union of Austrian Women Artists (Vereinigung bildender Künstlerinnen Österreichs), titled *The Art of the Woman* (Die Kunst der Frau)—but this was months after Schiele had completed his series. *XXXVII. Ausstellung der Vereinigung bildender Künstler Österreichs Secession / Wien I. Ausstellung der Vereinigung bildender Künstlerinnen Oesterreichs / Die Kunst der Frau*, exhibition catalog (Vienna: Secession, November–December 1910) (Vienna: Kunstdruckerei Moriz Frisch, 1910), inventory number B40089, Wienbibliothek im Rathaus. Kollwitz's subject is, however, fully covered—in the vein of Klimt's *Hope II* (1907–8). The second example, perhaps the first nude self-portrait of an expectant mother, is Paula Modersohn-Becker's powerful *Self-Portrait on Her Sixth Wedding Anniversary* (1906)—executed, interestingly, not while the artist was actually pregnant.

41. Schiele's clinic series has, for the most part, been negatively assessed by leading scholars. Jane Kallir, for example, projects a misguided eroticizing, gynophobic, and psychobiographical interpretation onto the artist. She writes that Schiele feared these women and that "the patients threaten to devour the viewer with flesh-eating vaginas." Kallir, *Egon Schiele's Women*, 87. Elsewhere, she characterizes the sitters as "passive vehicles" and "empty vessels" for Schiele's erotic longings and sexualized voyeurism.

They attest, she claims, "to the inner-directed, rather primitive state of Schiele's sexual development." Kallir, *Egon Schiele*, 75, 226. Alessandra Comini alone registers Schiele's empathetic gaze. Comini, *Egon Schiele's Portraits*, 212n64.

42. An early hint of direct eroticism is, however, present in Schiele's *Nude Woman on Her Back* (1908), which presages the clinic drawings discussed here. Kallir D. 211, private collection, reproduced in Kallir, *Egon Schiele's Women*, 49.

43. I am referring to the drawings Kallir D. 526, 528, 529, 533a, and 539.

44. Bernhard Kathan, *Das Elend der ärztlichen Kunst: Eine andere Geschichte der Medizin* (Berlin: Kadmos, 2002), 225–38. See also Monika Ankele's research on the hospital bed, including "Wie das Krankenbett zum Medikament wurde," science.orf.at, accessed July 4, 2018, https://science.orf.at/stories/2847043/.

45. Elias Canetti, *Crowds and Power*, trans. Carol Stewart (New York: Continuum, 1978), 390.

46. Various hypotheses have been advanced to explain Schiele's recourse to extreme gestures and figural exaggeration, particularly in the groundbreaking series of self-portraits from 1910. Klaus Albrecht Schröder and Gemma Blackshaw have suggested that Schiele was familiar with photographs of psychiatric patients suffering from hysteria from Charcot's clinic. Schröder, *Egon Schiele*; Blackshaw, "Pathological Body." There is no indication, however, that Schiele ever came into direct contact with these images. Alexander Klee speculates that silent film was an influence. Alexander Klee, "Attitüde und Geste als Abbild des Geschlechterverständnisses," in *Egon Schiele: Selbstporträts und Porträts*, ed. Agnes Husslein-Arco and Jane Kallir (Munich: Prestel, 2011), 31–45. Schiele's affinity for modern dance has been noted by several scholars. See Patrick Werkner, *Austrian Expressionism: The Formative Years*, trans. Nicholas T. Parsons (Palo Alto: Society for the Promotion of Science and Scholarship, 1993); Arthur Roessler, "Erinnerungen an Egon Schiele: Marginalien zur Geschichte des Menschentums eines Künstlers," in *Das Egon Schiele Buch*, ed. Fritz Karpfen (Vienna: Verlag der Wiener Graphischen Werkstätte, 1921), 27–106; Comini, *Egon Schiele's Portraits*; Kirk Varnedoe, *Vienna 1900: Art, Architecture and Design* (New York: Museum of Modern Art, 1986); Kallir, *Egon Schiele.*

47. Specifically, Kallir D. 671. Not depicted. Kallir suggests this connection. Kallir, *Egon Schiele*, 75. Other drawings from the same time frame (1910 and 1911) include similar positions, among them Kallir D. 672, 720, 953.

48. Kallir D. 534. Not depicted.

49. See Michel Foucault, *The Birth of the Clinic: An Archaeology of Medical Perception*, trans. A. M. Sheridan Smith (New York: Vintage, 1994).

50. Tobias G. Natter and Thomas Trummer, *Die Tafelrunde: Egon Schiele und sein Kreis* (Cologne: DuMont, 2006), 26.

51. It was with these aesthetic developments and in this year, the critic Fritz Karpfen later argued, that Schiele's work began to be pegged as "unhealthy," the discourse of pathology applied to his portraiture. Fritz Karpfen, "Kunst und Zeit," in *Das Egon Schiele Buch*, ed. Fritz Karpfen (Vienna: Verlag der Wiener Graphischen Werkstätte, 1921), 22–23. The terminology must clearly be viewed in the context of discourses of criminal atavism and cultural decline. Max Nordau (1849–1923), a physician and prominent cultural critic for the *Neue Freie Presse*, expanded the Italian criminologist Cesare

Lombroso's (1835–1909) notion of a criminal atavism identifiable by the interpretation of physical signs into a critique of a supposedly declining modern society in his book *Degeneration* (Entartung, 1892). Nordau extended clinical analysis to a cultural critique of modern art and literature, applying a doctor's diagnostic gaze to art and society, which he claimed were afflicted by degeneration and hysteria. The artist and author Albert Paris Gütersloh—of the same generation as Schiele and the first to publish a monograph on his colleague—challenged the indiscriminate application of such labels, vehemently countering that artists and their art are not the "appropriate objects" upon which reviewers should attempt "to demonstrate their knowledge of pathological nomenclature." [Albert] Paris von Gütersloh, *Egon Schiele: Versuch einer Vorrede* (Vienna: Brüder Rosenbaum, 1911), n.p.

52. Jane Kallir has called this Schiele's "expressionist breakthrough" (1910–11). Agnes Husslein-Arco and Jane Kallir, eds., *Egon Schiele: Selbstporträts und Porträts* (Munich: Prestel, 2011), 84. See also Kallir, *Egon Schiele*, 391. A series of five large-scale oil paintings, all nudes—three self-portraits and two portraits of his sister Gerti—mark this break. Kallir, *Egon Schiele's Women*, 70.

53. As early as 1921, Fritz Karpfen attributed Schiele's shift to the formation of the New Art Group (Neukunstgruppe) in mid-1909. Karpfen, "Kunst und Zeit," 22–23. Recent art-historical research has pointed to possible influences of medical imagery from Charcot's clinic to Messerschmidt's character busts on Schiele's work. See Blackshaw, "Pathological Body," 377–401. Her ideas originate, however, in Schröder, *Egon Schiele*. The hypothesis that Schiele directly encountered photographs of hysterical patients from Charcot's clinic is largely speculative. Others suggest the influence of modern dance and silent film on the gestural repertoire and mimic expressiveness of Schiele's portraits. See Klee, "Attitüde und Geste," and Werkner, *Austrian Expressionism*.

54. Recent, revisionist scholarship on Klimt's ornamental iconography highlights a possible interface with scientific and medical advances of the day, particularly with regard to evolutionary biology in Darwin's wake. See Emily Braun, "Ornament as Evolution: Gustav Klimt and Berta Zuckerkandl," in *Gustav Klimt: The Ronald S. Lauder and Serge Sabarsky Collections*, ed. Renée Price (Munich: Prestel, 2007), 145–69. Eric R. Kandel picked up on Braun's ideas in *The Age of Insight: The Quest to Understand the Unconscious in Art, Mind, and Brain, from Vienna 1900 to the Present* (New York: Random House, 2012).

55. It was founded on June 17, 1909, and the students exmatriculated from the academy in the fall. Schiele was president and secretary of the group, whose fifteen founding members included Anton Faistauer, Erwin Osen, Anton Peschka (Schiele's future brother-in-law), and Franz Wiegele. Albert Paris Gütersloh, Anton Kolig, Oskar Kokoschka, and several others joined in 1911. For a summary of the petition Schiele and the others submitted to Griepenkerl, see A[rthur] R[oessle]r, "Neukunstgruppe: Ausstellung im Kunstsalon Pisko," *Arbeiter-Zeitung*, December 7, 1909, Morgenblatt edition, 7–8. The most detailed survey of the Neukunstgruppe's context and significance is Natter and Trummer, *Die Tafelrunde*.

56. Comini, *Egon Schiele's Portraits*, 48.

57. Kallir, *Egon Schiele*, 62.

58. Varnedoe, *Vienna 1900*, 167–68.

59. Alessandra Comini suggested as much in a footnote in 1974 but did not pursue the thought further. Comini, *Egon Schiele's Portraits*, 212n64.

60. Reininghaus was a major art collector and key supporter of Schiele and Klimt. For more on patronage networks, see Tobias G. Natter, *Die Welt von Klimt, Schiele und Kokoschka: Sammler und Mäzene* (Cologne: DuMont, 2003). For more on Berta Zuckerkandl's influential salon, see Markus Oppenauer, *Der Salon Zuckerkandl im Kontext von Wissenschaft, Politik und Öffentlichkeit: Populärwissenschaftliche Aspekte der Wiener Salonkultur um 1900* (Weitra: Bibliothek der Provinz, 2012).

61. See Tobias Natter, ed., *Die Galerie Miethke: Eine Kunsthandlung im Zentrum der Moderne* (Vienna: Jüdisches Museum der Stadt Wien, 2003), for the centrality of the gallery.

62. Kallir, *Egon Schiele*, 84.

63. Comini, *Egon Schiele's Portraits*, 72.

64. In addition to Schiele's supporter and facilitator, Graff, we might also note Schiele's lifelong acquaintance with Dr. Hermann Heller, an anatomist who taught an entire generation of young artists at the Akademie.

65. Biographical information on Graff, though scarce, is contained in Isidor Fischer, ed., *Biographisches Lexikon der hervorragenden Ärzte der letzten fünfzig Jahre*, 2 vols. (Berlin: Urban & Schwarzenberg, 1932), 526, and Kronfeld, "Doktor Erwin Graff." Graff's research focused on the early diagnosis of cancer, gynecological radiology, and, later, female infertility. He authored a number of works on these topics, including *Obstetrics for Practicing Physicians* (Geburtshilfe des praktischen Arztes, 1930). In 1931, Graff embarked on a lecture tour of the United States and, while there, accepted a professorship for obstetrics and gynecology at the University of Iowa in Iowa City. Letter from Erwin von Graff to Roland Graßberger, Dean of the University of Vienna's Medical School, dated June 20, 1931, from New York, box 117, MED PA 956, Archive of the University of Vienna. Graff never returned to Vienna, but the news of his suicide in 1935 traveled across the Atlantic and was registered in the *Wiener Zeitung*. "Selbstmord eines Wiener Professors in Amerika," *Wiener Zeitung*, March 8, 1935, Tagblattarchiv folder TP 016238, Wienbibliothek im Rathaus, Vienna. While Comini falsely gives 1952 as Graff's death date, the newspaper article incorrectly identifies his place of employ as Ohio.

66. Kronfeld, "Doktor Erwin Graff," 16; W. C. Kettel, *A History of the Department of Obstetrics and Gynaecology, The University of Iowa, 1848–1980* (Iowa City: University of Iowa, 1981), 53–54, quoted in Blackshaw, "Pathological Body," 391.

67. Comini, *Egon Schiele's Portraits*, 72, 212n64.

68. Erwin von Graff to Egon Schiele, May 18, 1910, inventory number 239, Egon Schiele Datenbank der Autographen; Christian M. Nebehay, *Egon Schiele 1890–1918: Leben, Briefe, Gedichte* (Salzburg: Residenz, 1979), 131 (document 102).

69. The impressive collection of the dentist Heinrich Rieger was among the best-documented instances of such exchange. See Natter, *Die Welt von Klimt, Schiele und Kokoschka*.

70. Alessandra Comini, "Egon Schiele: Redefining Portraiture in the Age of Angst," in *Egon Schiele: Portraits*, ed. Alessandra Comini (Munich: Prestel, 2014), 27; Rudolf Leopold, *Egon Schiele: Gemälde, Aquarelle, Zeichnungen* (Salzburg: Residenz Verlag,

1972), 550. Aside from the three preparatory sketches Schiele made for his painting of Graff, the portrait itself was completed at latest by mid-October 1910. Egon Schiele to Josef Hoffmann, c. October 15, 1910, inventory number 159463, Handschriftensammlung, Wienbibliothek im Rathaus, Vienna; Nebehay, *Egon Schiele 1890–1918*, 135–36 (document 123).

71. Anton Faistauer, *Neue Malerei in Österreich: Betrachtungen eines Malers* (Zurich: Amalthea, 1923), 18.

72. Faistauer, *Neue Malerei in Österreich*, 18.

73. Elana Shapira, *Style and Seduction: Jewish Patrons, Architecture, and Design in Fin-de-Siècle Vienna* (Waltham: Brandeis University Press, 2016), 7, 133.

74. Shapira, *Style and Seduction*, 133–37.

75. Faistauer, *Neue Malerei in Österreich*, 18.

76. In fact, until his later years and the portraits of his wife Edith, whom he married in 1915, Schiele had only two female takers for formal portraits: Ida Roessler in 1912 and Friederike Maria Beer in 1914. Kallir, *Egon Schiele*, 223, 276, 86. Beer would also, incidentally, pose for Klimt in 1916, to very different ends. See Stephanie Auer, "Egon Schieles Frauenbild: Zwischen Heiliger und Hure?," in *Egon Schiele: Selbstporträts und Porträts*, ed. Agnes Husslein-Arco and Jane Kallir (Munich: Prestel, 2011), 47–59.

77. Faistauer, *Neue Malerei in Österreich*, 18.

78. Kathryn Simpson, "Viennese Art, Ugliness, and the Vienna School of Art History: The Vicissitudes of Theory and Practice," *Journal of Art Historiography*, no. 3 (December 2010): 1. Already in 1974, Alessandra Comini noted the study of the "ugly" in both Klimt's work and in Austrian expressionism as a research desideratum. Comini, *Egon Schiele's Portraits*, 201n43.

79. Arpad Weixlgärtner, "Ausstellungen," *Mitteilungen der Gesellschaft für Vervielfältigende Kunst. Beilage der "Graphischen Künste"* 33, nos. 2/3 (1910): 55. The Salon Pisko was, aside from the Galerie Miethke, the most important private exhibition space in fin-de-siècle Vienna. Arthur Roessler similarly remarked that Schiele was uniquely concerned with the creaturely sufferings of his subjects. Roessler, "Erinnerungen an Egon Schiele," 31.

80. Karpfen, "Kunst und Zeit," 23.

81. Faistauer, *Neue Malerei in Österreich*, 18.

82. Herbert Waniek, "Egon Schiele und ich," ed. Karl F. Kocmata, *Ver! Auf daß der moderne Geist in Allem und Jedem zum Ausdruck komme*, no. 7 (November 15, 1917): 104. Emphasis in original.

83. Alys X. George, "Anatomy for All: Medical Knowledge on the Fairground in *Fin-de-Siècle* Vienna," *Central European History* 51, no.4 (2018): 535–62.

84. "Exterieur-Kunde," *Wiener Caricaturen*, November 9, 1913, 3.

85. See Richard T. Gray, *About Face: German Physiognomic Thought from Lavater to Auschwitz* (Detroit: Wayne State University Press, 2004).

86. "Vortrag über die Pathologie des Porträts," *Neue Freie Presse*, January 30, 1914, Morgenblatt edition. The announcement is for a later variant of the same lecture.

87. The 85th Assembly of German Scientists and Physicians was held in Vienna from September 21 through September 28, 1913. Kronfeld lectured at the University

of Vienna on September 24, on a panel about the history of medicine and science. Adolf Kronfeld, "Zur Pathologie des Porträts: Neurologisches und Psychiatrisches (mit Demonstrationen)," in *Tageblatt der 85: Versammlung Deutscher Naturforscher und Ärzte in Wien vom 21. bis 28. September 1913*, ed. Adolf Kronfeld (Vienna: 1913), 3:72. Kronfeld held versions of this lecture for the Viennese Society of Physicians (Gesellschaft der Ärzte) on June 14, 1912 (Isidor Fischer, *Geschichte der Gesellschaft der Ärzte in Wien 1837–1937* [Vienna: Springer, 1938], 157) and for the Union of Viennese Doctors (Vereinigung Wiener Mediziner) at the I. Anatomical Institute in Vienna on February 3, 1914 (Wiener Medizinische Wochenschrift). Kronfeld's repertoire also included other art-historical lectures, including one on classical bronzes and painted Greek vases (June 3, 1910) and the practice of facial tattooing among the ancients (December 3, 1909). His lecture on anatomy and the fine arts in the wake of Rembrandt's *The Anatomy Lesson of Dr. Nicolaes Tulp* (May 26, 1911) was later published separately in 1912 as *Die Entwicklung des Anatomiebildes seit 1632*. Another version of this lecture was held as late as 1931: "Geschichte des anatomischen Bildes," given on December 18, 1931 (Fischer, *Geschichte der Gesellschaft*, 223). Regarding the 1909 lecture on facial tattooing, it is tempting, given the year, to imagine that Kronfeld might have had in mind Adolf Loos's polemic "Ornament and Crime," which, though conventionally dated to 1908, was not held as a lecture in Vienna until 1910. Janet Stewart reconstructs the essay's genealogy in *Fashioning Vienna: Adolf Loos's Cultural Criticism* (London: Routledge, 2000), 173n5. See also Jimena Canales and Andrew Herscher, "Criminal Skins: Tattoos and Modern Architecture in the Work of Adolf Loos," *Architectural History* 48 (2005): 235–56.

88. Kronfeld completed his doctorate in medicine in 1887 and was active in numerous specializations at the Vienna General Hospital, as well as at the University of Vienna's Laboratory for Medical Chemistry. His initial editorial post at the *Wiener Medizinische Wochenschrift* commenced in 1899; in 1909 he became the journal's editor-in-chief until his death on June 14, 1938. Kronfeld was a frequent contributor to Viennese dailies, including the *Neue Freie Presse*. He was awarded Austria's highest award for service to the nation, the *Goldenes Ehrenzeichen für Verdienste um die Republik Österreich*, in 1934. The biographical information sketched here is drawn from the Literaturarchiv of the Österreichische Nationalbibliothek, http://data.onb.ac.at/nlv_lex/perslex/K/Kronfeld_Adolf.html, as well as from Fischer, *Biographisches Lexikon*, 827, and Franz Planer, ed., *Das Jahrbuch der Wiener Gesellschaft: Biographische Beiträge zur Wiener Zeitgeschichte* (Vienna: Verlag Franz Planer, 1929), 353.

89. The coauthored, two-volume *Comparative Folk Medicine* (Vergleichende Volksmedizin, 1908–9) sealed Kronfeld's notoriety, and his *Guide through Medical Vienna* (Führer durch das medizinische Wien, 1911) demonstrated his comprehensive knowledge of Vienna's medical history. Later in life, he penned a guidebook for the collection of the portrait gallery of the Liechtenstein Palace (1927). Kronfeld's other works included monographs on hysteria and the history of syphilis, as well as several volumes germane to our analysis: *Doctors and the Fine Arts in the Nineteenth Century* (Ärzte und die schönen Künste im 19. Jahrhundert, 1899), *The Doctor in Literature* (Der Arzt in der schönen Literatur), *The Development of the Anatomy Painting since 1632* (Die

Entwicklung des Anatomiebildes seit 1632, 1912), and *On the Pathology of the Artistic Portrait* (Zur Pathologie des künstlerischen Porträts).

90. Egon Schiele, notebook, 1913–15, n.p. [70 and 74], inventory number 159.474, Nachlass Hans Ankwicz-Kleehoven, Handschriftensammlung, Wienbibliothek im Rathaus, Vienna. The artist noted "Kronfeld—Saturday 10–12 o'clock—Monday 2–4 o'clock" alongside five male figure studies in motion on page 70 of the sketchbook, with the name "Dr. Kronfeld" several pages later. Cf. Christian Nebehay, ed., *Egon Schiele's Sketch Books* (London: Thames and Hudson, 1989), 356–57, and Blackshaw, "Pathological Body," 392. Blackshaw was the first to note the repeated presence of Kronfeld's name in Schiele's sketchbooks.

91. A letter from Osen to Schiele mentions the commission. Erwin Dominik Osen to Egon Schiele, August 15, 1913, inventory number 139, Egon Schiele Datenbank der Autographen. There is very little reliable information about Osen, but he and Schiele made numerous striking portraits of one another during the summer of 1910, an artistically pivotal time for Schiele, which he spent part of in Český Krumlov, his mother's birthplace, with Osen and the artist (and Schiele's future brother-in-law) Anton Peschka.

92. Osen to Schiele, August 15, 1913, inventory number 139, Egon Schiele Datenbank der Autographen. Three of Osen's portraits of patients from Steinhof used to illustrate Kronfeld's lecture are known to exist. These were first unearthed and published by Blackshaw, "Pathological Body," 377–401; they are also depicted in Gemma Blackshaw and Leslie Topp, eds., *Madness and Modernity: Mental Illness and the Visual Arts in Vienna 1900* (Farnham: Lund Humphries, 2009), 37–39.

93. "Vortrag über die Pathologie des Porträts," *Neue Freie Presse*, January 30, 1914, Morgenblatt edition.

94. Blackshaw, "Pathological Body," 393. Blackshaw points out that the information Osen included maps exactly onto the historical medical records at Steinhof.

95. Blackshaw and Topp, "Scrutinised Bodies and Lunatic Utopias," 37.

96. W. F. Bynum, *Science and the Practice of Medicine in the Nineteenth Century* (Cambridge: Cambridge University Press, 1994), 202–6.

97. Therese Schlesinger-Eckstein, "Auzug aus dem Bericht der Frau Therese Schlesinger-Eckstein für den Londoner Internationalen Frauencongress," ed. Auguste Fickert, Marie Lang, and Rosa Mayreder, *Dokumente der Frauen* 1, no. 9 (July 15, 1899): 248.

98. See Erna Lesky, *Die Wiener medizinische Schule im 19. Jahrhundert*, Studien zur Geschichte der Universität Wien 6 (Graz: Böhlau, 1965), 475.

99. Kathan, *Das Elend der ärztlichen Kunst*, 66.

100. Foucault, *Birth of the Clinic*; Kathan, *Das Elend der ärztlichen Kunst*, 30. See also Barbara Duden, *Der Frauenleib als öffentlicher Ort: Vom Mißbrauch des Begriffs Leben* (Frankfurt: Luchterhand, 1991).

101. "Die neuen Frauenkliniken," *Neue Freie Presse*, March 25, 1908, Morgenblatt edition, sec. Kleine Chronik, 12. A draft typescript of this article is held at the Medizinische Universität Wien, MUW-AS-003779. A handwritten note by Friedrich Schauta identifies its author as "Fr. Kronfeld," but the more likely author is "Dr. [Adolf] Kronfeld."

102. "Die neuen Frauenkliniken," *Neue Freie Presse*, March 25, 1908, Morgenblatt edition, sec. Kleine Chronik, 12.

103. Steinhof—officially, the Niederösterreichische Landes-Heil- und Pflege-anstalten für Geistes- und Nervenkranke 'am Steinhof'—was designed in part according to plans by Otto Wagner (1841–1918). Other prominent examples of such building projects are the private Sanatorium Purkersdorf, designed by Josef Hoffmann (1870–1956), and the Niederösterreichische Landes-Irrenanstalt Kierling-Gugging. A recent body of research has begun to document the links between institutional architecture and science in the Viennese context. See Nicole Imrie and Leslie Topp, "Modernity Follows Madness? Viennese Architecture for Mental Illness and Nervous Disorders," in *Madness and Modernity: Mental Illness and the Visual Arts in Vienna 1900*, ed. Gemma Blackshaw and Leslie Topp (Farnham: Lund Humphries, 2009), 76–99; Leslie Topp, *Architecture and Truth in Fin-de-Siècle Vienna* (Cambridge: Cambridge University Press, 2004), 63–95; Leslie Topp and Sabine Wieber, "Architecture, Psychiatry and the Rural Idyll: The Agricultural Colony at Kierling-Gugging," in *Psychiatrische Institutionen in Österreich um 1900*, ed. Eberhard Gabriel and Martina Gamper (Vienna: Verlagshaus der Ärzte, 2009), 109–20.

104. "Die neuen Frauenkliniken," 11–12.

105. Rudolf Chrobak and Friedrich Schauta, *Geschichte und Beschreibung des Baues der neuen Frauenkliniken in Wien* (Berlin: Urban & Schwarzenberg, 1911), 15.

106. Else Feldmann, "Aus dem Wasser gezogen," *Arbeiter-Sonntag*, July 8, 1934, 9.

107. Kathan, *Das Elend der ärztlichen Kunst*, 85–88. See Philipp Sarasin, *Reizbare Maschinen: Eine Geschichte des Körpers 1765–1914* (Frankfurt: Suhrkamp, 2001), for an analysis of the genealogy of the discourse about hygiene.

108. Chrobak and Schauta, *Geschichte und Beschreibung*, 76–80.

109. "Die neuen Frauenkliniken," 11; Chrobak and Schauta, *Geschichte und Beschreibung*, 58.

110. Kathan, *Das Elend der ärztlichen Kunst*, 230.

111. "Die neuen Frauenkliniken," 11. That the lecture hall's "picturesque" quality, heightened by space and light, would invite comparisons to the artist's studio was likely not lost on the contemporary commentators and architects. Both provide a negative space for the staging of subjects' (patients', models') bodies, a neutral backdrop for observation, study, and diagnosis.

112. Chrobak and Schauta, *Geschichte und Beschreibung*, 33, 78–79.

113. Wagner's designs often included modern building materials, such as iron, in their exteriors, rather than as concealed structural supports. His designs for the Vienna city railway project in the second half of the 1890s exemplify this. Schorske argues that Wagner's material modernism was not fundamentally functionalist in nature but was a kind of "ornamental supplement" to the Ringstraße's historicist façades, rather than in opposition to them. Schorske, *Fin-de-Siècle Vienna*, 78–81.

114. Chrobak and Schauta, *Geschichte und Beschreibung*, 65.

115. See Kathan, *Das Elend der ärztlichen Kunst*, 225–38.

116. Katrin Pilz, "Der schwangere Frauenkörper in der Wiener medizinischen Kinematografie," in *Die helle und die dunkle Seite der Moderne: Festschrift für Siegfried Mattl zum 60. Geburtstag*, ed. Werner Michael Schwarz and Ingo Zechner (Vienna:

Turia + Kant, 2014). See also Cartwright, *Screening the Body*, and Treichler, Cartwright, and Penley, *The Visible Woman*.

117. Chrobak and Schauta, *Geschichte und Beschreibung*, 74.

118. Wilhelm Weibel, "Der Film als Unterrichtsbehelf in der Geburtshilfe und Gynäkologie: Offizielles Protokol der Gesellschaft der Ärzte in Wien," *Wiener Klinische Wochenschrift* 33, no. 45 (November 4, 1920): 995.

119. Pilz, "Der schwangere Frauenkörper," 147, cites the *Verzeichnis der Filme der Staatlichen Film-Hauptstelle* (1924), 4.

120. Weibel, "Der Film als Unterrichtsbehelf," 995.

121. Weibel, "Der Film als Unterrichtsbehelf," 995.

122. Weibel, "Der Film als Unterrichtsbehelf," 995.

123. Pilz, "Der schwangere Frauenkörper," 145.

124. Weibel, "Der Film als Unterrichtsbehelf," 995–96.

125. "Cinematic Caesarean," *Time* 26, no. 6 (August 5, 1935): 26; see Pilz, "Der schwangere Frauenkörper," 148.

126. See Andreas Killen, *Homo Cinematicus: Science, Motion Pictures, and the Making of Modern Germany* (Philadelphia: University of Pennsylvania Press, 2017), 137–63; Ursula von Keitz, *Im Schatten des Gesetzes: Schwangerschaftskonflikt und Reproduktion im deutschsprachigen Film 1918–1933* (Marburg: Schüren Verlag, 2005); Ulf Schmidt, "'Der Blick auf dem Körper': Sozialhygienischer Film, Sexualaufklärung und Propaganda in der Weimarer Republik," in *Geschlecht in Fesseln: Sexualität zwischen Aufklärung und Ausbeutung im Weimarer Kino*, ed. Malte Hagener (Munich: Edition Text + Kritik, 2000), 23–46.

127. The film's opening credits list the cooperation partners. The Imperial Institute focused on the reduction of infant mortality—a most pressing problem of the age—and opened in 1915. It later became known as the Glanzing Children's Clinic of the City of Vienna (Kinderklinik der Stadt Wien Glanzing), named after its street address in Glanzinggasse.

128. For more on the clinic, see McEwen, *Sexual Knowledge*, 121–28, and Luft, "Thinking about Sexuality," 21–30.

129. McEwen, *Sexual Knowledge*, 121. See also Mark Mazower, *Dark Continent: Europe's Twentieth Century* (New York: Knopf, 1999), 76–103.

130. Cited here are the film's intertitles. The correspondence between the principles articulated in the film and later National Socialist family-planning manuals is striking. See Mazower, *Dark Continent*, 76.

131. "Theaterkino," *Arbeiterwille*, October 20, 1922, 2nd edition, sec. Grazer Lokalnachrichten, 5.

132. "Hygiene der Ehe," *Das Kino-Journal*, September 30, 1922, sec. Neuheiten auf dem Filmmarkte, 9; "Notizen," *Das Kino-Journal*, September 30, 1922, 4; "Hygiene der Ehe," 8.

133. R[oland] Graßberger, "Gutachten über den Film 'Hygiene der Ehe,'" *Wiener Medizinische Wochenschrift* 73, no. 40 (September 29, 1923): 1778. Emphasis in original.

134. Graßberger, "Gutachten," 1778; see Pilz, "Der schwangere Frauenkörper," 150.

135. Graßberger, "Gutachten," 1778. In point of fact, newspaper announcements for film screenings reveal that most screenings were for sex-segregated audiences.

136. Graßberger, "Gutachten," 1779.

137. Pilz, "Der schwangere Frauenkörper," 150.

138. Kathan, *Das Elend der ärztlichen Kunst*, 70.

139. Schlesinger-Eckstein, "Auzug aus dem Bericht," 248–49.

140. The dismal living conditions stood in marked contrast to the tenements' façades, which frequently replicated the grand architecture of the city center. For more on this "contradictory grammar" of suburban architecture, see Wolfgang Maderthaner and Lutz Musner, *Unruly Masses: The Other Side of Fin-de-Siècle Vienna*, trans. David Fernbach and Michael Huffmaster (New York: Berghahn, 2008), 52–57.

141. Else Feldmann, *Der Leib der Mutter* (1931; repr., Vienna: Wiener Frauenverlag, 1993), 55. This text will henceforth be cited parenthetically with page number.

142. For biographical information on Feldmann, see Adolf Opel and Marino Valdéz, "Nachwort: Else Feldmann—eine Auslöschung und eine Wiederfindung," in *Der Leib der Mutter* (Vienna: Wiener Frauenverlag, 1993), 209–25; Herbert Exenberger, "Auf den Spuren von Else Feldmann: Eine Wiener Schriftstellerin—Opfer des Holocaust," in *Dokumentationsarchiv des österreichischen Widerstandes, Jahrbuch 1990*, ed. Siegwald Ganglmair (Vienna: Österreichischer Bundesverlag, 1990), 56–75; Herbert Exenberger, ed., *Als stünd' die Welt in Flammen: Eine Anthologie ermordeter sozialistischer SchriftstellerInnen* (Vienna: Mandelbaum Verlag, 2000), 253–57; Lisa Silverman, "*Zwischenzeit* and *Zwischenort*: Veza Canetti, Else Feldmann, and Jewish Writing in Interwar Vienna," *Prooftexts* 26, nos. 1–2 (2006): 29–52; and the Tagblattarchiv folder TP "Else Feldmann, Diverses," Wienbibliothek im Rathaus, Vienna.

143. Quoted in Opel and Valdéz, "Nachwort," 220.

144. Else Feldmann, "'Zu den Müttern müßt ihr hinuntersteigen . . . ,'" *Der Abend*, March 29, 1917.

145. Foucault, *Birth of the Clinic*, 8.

146. See Cornelia Cabuk, *Carry Hauser: Monografie und Werkverzeichnis*, Belvedere Werkverzeichnisse 2 (Weitra: Bibliothek der Provinz, 2012), 111–17.

147. Contemporary reviewers, such as one for the Viennese daily *Der Tag* commenting on a 1924 exhibition of Hauser's works in the Viennese Galerie Würthle, already noted the striking subject matter. Cabuk, *Carry Hauser*, 138, 141.

148. Foucault, *Birth of the Clinic*, 121–22.

149. See Foucault, *Birth of the Clinic*, 109–10, for a description of how medical experience is collectively structured in the dual clinical pursuits of scientific knowledge and teaching.

150. E[ngelbert] Pernerstorfer, "Zu Arthur Schnitzlers neuestem Drama," *Arbeiter-Zeitung*, February 6, 1913, Morgenblatt edition, 2. Recent critics have focused largely on the political and religious conflicts central to the play, but Schnitzler himself conceived of the drama in broader terms as a "character comedy"—which by no means detracts from the play's political implications. Arthur Schnitzler, *Briefe 1913–1931*, ed. Peter Michael Braunwarth et al. (Frankfurt: Fischer, 1984), 1. For a perspective that traces Bernhardi's moral individualism to Kantian idealism—and offers the potential for Jewish self-assertion in light of fin-de-siècle anti-Semitism—see Helga Schreckenberger, "Reclaiming Moral Individualism: Jewish Identity in Arthur Schnitzler's *Professor Bernhardi*," *The German Quarterly* 90, no. 3 (2017): 283–98.

151. The reference is again to Elisabeth Bronfen, as in chapter 2. Judith Beniston, a co-investigator of the ongoing project "Digital Critical Edition of Middle-Period Works by Arthur Schnitzler (1862–1931)" with Andrew Webber and Robert Vilain, is an expert on the play and presented "Bodies and Power in Schnitzler's *Professor Bernhardi*" (Modern Language Association Convention, Chicago, January 5, 2019).

152. Foucault, *Birth of the Clinic*, 8.

153. Helmut Gruber, *Red Vienna: Experiment in Working-Class Culture, 1919–1934* (New York: Oxford University Press, 1991), 160.

154. Julius Tandler, *Wohltätigkeit oder Fürsorge?* (Vienna: Verlag der Organisation Wien der sozialdemokratischen Partei, 1925), 7.

155. Tandler, *Wohltätigkeit oder Fürsorge?*, 5.

156. Tandler, *Wohltätigkeit oder Fürsorge?*, 8.

157. See Felix Czeike, *Historisches Lexikon Wien*, 6 vols. (Vienna: Kremayr & Scheriau, 1992), 3:88–89. The program was terminated by the Austrofascists in 1934, a move that makes plain the political stakes of this social-democratic initiative from the First Republic. Despite its discontinuation, the popularity of the *Säuglingswäschepaket* was not forgotten during World War II. It was reinstated after the war with the help of the American occupying forces and the International Red Cross. In fact, the *Säuglingswäschepaket* remains a trademark of Viennese social programs to this day, and the program was even expanded in 2001 to include a modern diaper bag in backpack form (*Wickelrucksack*).

158. "Wie Wien für seine kleinsten Bürger sorgt," *Arbeiter-Zeitung*, March 17, 1927, Morgenblatt edition, 8.

159. Maderthaner and Musner, *Unruly Masses*, 56.

160. Among Carry Hauser's illustrations for Feldmann's *Arbeiter-Zeitung* serial is a grisly scene of Marie Miczek killing her child. Hauser clearly took cues in both style and technique from Oskar Kokoschka's well-known illustrations for his play *Murderer Hope of Women* (Mörder Hoffnung der Frauen), one of which appeared on the front page of Herwarth Walden's influential Berlin-based journal *Der Sturm* on July 14, 1910.

161. See Duden, *Der Frauenleib als öffentlicher Ort*, for the increasing role that medical technologies have played in such debates.

162. Karin Lehner, *Verpönte Eingriffe: Sozialdemokratische Reformbestrebungen zu den Abtreibungsbestimmungen in der Zwischenkriegszeit* (Wien: Picus Verlag, 1989). See also Sylvia Mattl-Wurm, "Schön, gesund und sittlich rein: Die Entsexualisierung des weiblichen Körpers durch Hygiene und Frauenbewegung," in *Aufbruch in das Jahrhundert der Frau? Rosa Mayreder und der Feminismus in Wien um 1900*, ed. Reingard Witzmann (Vienna: Eigenverlag der Museen der Stadt Wien, 1989), 118–27.

163. The law had been on the books since the institution of the Austro-Hungarian Imperial Code of Law (*Strafgesetzbuch*) of 1852, which itself was to a large extent a reiteration of the *Strafgesetzbuch* of 1803. Paragraph 144 established the criminality of abortion, while the subsequent paragraphs 145–48 regulated the sentencing of both the mother and anyone who had aided and abetted her. For the case of the interwar Austrian debate about elective abortion and the laws regulating it, see Maria Mesner, *Geburten/Kontrolle: Reproduktionspolitik im 20. Jahrhundert* (Vienna: Böhlau, 2010), 199–202.

164. "Unsere Forderungen im Nationalrat," *Arbeiterinnen-Zeitung*, March 15, 1921, 2.

165. See Alys X. George, "Hollywood on the Danube? Vienna and Austrian Silent Film of the 1920s," in *Interwar Vienna: Culture between Tradition and Modernity*, ed. Deborah Holmes and Lisa Silverman (Rochester: Camden House, 2009), 151–52.

166. Johann Ferch, "Paragraph 144: Die Hetzenjagd auf Frauen," *Bettauers Wochenschrift*, no. 15 (August 21, 1924): 12.

167. Poster "A Cry for Help" (Ein Notschrei. §144. Lesen Sie Nr. 11 von Bettauers Wochenschrift), (Vienna: Elbemühl—Graphische Industrie 1926), 63 × 95 cm, inventory number P-13319, Plakatsammlung, Wienbibliothek im Rathaus. See also Wiener Stadt- und Landesbibliothek, ed., *Tagebuch der Straße: Geschichte in Plakaten* (Vienna: Österreichischer Bundesverlag, 1981), 174.

168. This position mandated the right to terminate if either the mother's or child's health was at risk, or if the child's birth would pose undue economic burden on the family. Gruber, *Red Vienna*, 160; McEwen, *Sexual Knowledge*, 41–42. Austrian Social Democrats likewise pushed this agenda in cultural politics. A 1928 play *The Gynecologist* (Der Frauenarzt) by the German playwright and theater intendant Hans José Rehfisch (1891–1960) was excerpted in the party organ *Kunst und Volk*. The monthly journal appeared from 1926 to 1931 and was edited by David Joseph Bach (1874–1947), the influential writer and editor, who had assumed the directorship of the Social Democratic Arts Bureau (Sozialdemokratische Kunststelle) in 1919. Rehfisch's drama was quickly picked up for the repertoire of Vienna's Carltheater. Hans J. Rehfisch, "Der Frauenarzt," *Kunst und Volk: Mitteilungen des Vereines "Sozialdemokratische Kunststelle"* 3, no. 2 (October 1928): 14–16. See also Hans J. Rehfisch, *Der Frauenarzt. Schauspiel in drei Akten* (Berlin: Oesterheld, 1928).

169. Marie Frischauf and Annie Reich, *Ist Abtreibung schädlich?* (Vienna: Münster-Verlag, 1930). See Fallend, *Wilhelm Reich in Wien*, 134–36.

170. Maderthaner and Musner, *Unruly Masses*, 51.

171. The portfolio was published by the Verlag der k. k. Staatsdruckerei, known across the continent for its artistry and high-quality prints. Algraphy is an offset lithographic printing process that uses aluminum plates rather than stone surfaces. After her death, Heller-Ostersetzer faded into obscurity, and the portfolio went out of print until its rediscovery in the 1980s. Christoph Wagner, "Hermine Ostersetzer—Eine Annäherung," in *Hermine Ostersetzer: Malerin—Kämpferin—Frau, 1874–1909*, ed. Willibald Kranister (Vienna: Edition S, Verlag der Österreichischen Staatsdruckerei, 1988), 11.

172. Heller-Ostersetzer also furnished illustrations and covers for a variety of publications for the Social Democratic Party. In 1901, she had married the like-minded, noted bookseller Hugo Heller, who was deeply engaged in the Austrian social-democratic movement.

173. She was the recipient of, among other awards, the prestigious *Preis der Rothschild-Stiftung*. Art[h]ur Roessler, "Hermine Heller-Ostersetzer: Sätze und Ansätze zu einem Essai," *Erdgeist* 4, no. 9 (March 6, 1909): 325.

174. Roessler, "Hermine Heller-Ostersetzer," 325.

175. Although she does not mention Heller-Ostersetzer, Megan Brandow-Faller's rich dissertation stakes out the territory of so-called *Frauenkunst* in early twentieth-century Austria. Megan Brandow-Faller, "An Art of Their Own: Reinventing *Frauen-*

kunst in the Female Academies and Artist Leagues of Late-Imperial and First Republic Austria, 1900–1930" (PhD diss., Georgetown University, 2010). Julie M. Johnson's *The Memory Factory: The Forgotten Women Artists of Vienna 1900* (West Lafayette, IN: Purdue University Press, 2012) makes only passing mention of Heller-Ostersetzer, yet is a crucial revisionist art history of Viennese modernism.

176. Roessler, "Hermine Heller-Ostersetzer," 325.

177. Maderthaner and Musner, *Unruly Masses*, 68–70. This absence is also palpable in cultural historiography on the period, such as in Schorske.

178. Maderthaner and Musner, *Unruly Masses.*

179. See Rolf Schwendter, "Armut und Kultur der Wiener Jahrhundertwende," in *Die Wiener Jahrhundertwende: Einflüsse, Umwelt, Wirkungen*, ed. Jürgen Nautz and Richard Vahrenkamp (Wien: Böhlau, 1993), 677–93.

180. Maderthaner and Musner, *Anarchie der Vorstadt*, 70. These reporters were obviously working in the tradition of the photojournalist Jacob Riis's pioneering *How the Other Half Lives: Studies among the Tenements of New York* (1890). See Max Winter, *Expeditionen ins dunkelste Wien: Meisterwerke der Sozialreportage*, ed. Hannes Haas (Vienna: Picus Verlag, 2018). See also Werner Michael Schwarz, Margarethe Szeless, and Lisa Wögenstein, eds., *Ganz unten: Die Entdeckung des Elends: Wien, Berlin, London, Paris, New York* (Vienna: Brandstätter, 2007). Hugo Bettauer's novel *The Joyless Street* (1924), earlier serialized in *Der Tag*, would take up the theme in fictional form in the postwar inflationary years. G. W. Pabst soon made it into a film starring Asta Nielsen and Greta Garbo (1925). See Armin Loacker, ed., *Wien, die Inflation und das Elend: Essays und Materialien zum Stummfilm "Die freudlose Gasse"* (Vienna: Verlag Filmarchiv Austria, 2008).

181. Silverman, "*Zwischenzeit*," 35–36.

182. Emil Kläger and Hermann Drawe, *Durch die Wiener Quartiere des Elends und Verbrechens: Ein Wanderbuch aus dem Jenseits* (Vienna: Mitschke, 1908), 1. The book emulated Max Winter's reportages for the *Arbeiter-Zeitung*, which had appeared since 1898. Winter later published the book *Soziales Wandern* (1911). See Margarethe Szeless, "Die Sozialreporter Emil Kläger und Hermann Drawe," in *Wien: Die Stadt lesen: Diskurse, Erzählungen, Gedichte, Bilder*, ed. Hubert Christian Ehalt (Weitra: Bibliothek der Provinz, 2006), 61–68; Siegfried Mattl, "Das wirkliche Leben: Elend als Simulationskraft der Sicherheitsgesellschaft. Überlegungen zu den Werken Max Winters und Emil Klägers," in *Ganz unten*, eds. Schwarz, Szeless, and Wögenstein, 111–17; Christian Brandstätter, "Durch die Wiener Quartiere des Elends und Verbrechens: Anmerkungen zum Werk des Wiener Amateurfotografen Hermann Drawe," *Fotogeschichte* 2, no. 6 (1982): 23–40.

183. Wilhelm Petrasch, *Die Wiener Urania: Von den Wurzeln der Erwachsenenbildung zum lebenslangen Lernen* (Vienna: Böhlau, 2007), 42–43.

184. *Durch die Quartiere des Elends und Verbrechens* (1920), written and directed by Richard Land (a.k.a. Richard Liebmann, 1887–?). The film is considered lost. George, "Hollywood on the Danube?," 152.

185. Maderthaner and Musner, *Unruly Masses*, 49.

186. Feldmann had begun writing for *Der Abend* in 1916. Between 1917 and 1921 both she and Frei contributed regular reports from the Viennese juvenile justice system.

187. Bruno Frei, *Das Elend Wiens* (Vienna: Verlag der Wiener Graphischen Werkstätte, 1921), viii.

188. Frei, *Das Elend Wiens*, 99–100; photographs appended as numbers 27, 28, 35, and 36 (n.p.).

189. See Mattl, "Das wirkliche Leben."

190. Any number of Schiele's drawings of proletarian youths were hung in galleries or printed in art journals during his lifetime or shortly after his death. See Kallir, *Egon Schiele*; the catalogue raisonné details each artwork's exhibition history. For the feature article, which included *Two Crouching Boys* (Zwei hockende Knaben,1910 [Kallir D. 457]), see Arthur Roessler, "Egon Schiele," ed. Arthur Roessler, *Bildende Künstler: Monatsschrift für Künstler und Kunstfreunde*, no. 3 (1911): 118. Then there is the haunting *Sick Girl* (Krankes Mädchen, 1910 [Kallir D. 427]), her lustrous belly pulsating with the unnamed disease within. This drawing was shown in Vienna at Gustav Nebehay's gallery in 1919 as part of an exhibition of 162 works on paper by Schiele.

191. Nicole Fritz, "Lolitas in Glory: On the Development of the Child Portrait in the Work of Egon Schiele," in *Egon Schiele: The Beginning*, ed. Christian Bauer (Munich: Hirmer, 2013), 30–31. We might also consider Oskar Kokoschka, who likewise used vulnerable youth, including street children and juvenile circus performers, as preferred models in his early years. Oskar Kokoschka, *Mein Leben* (Munich: Bruckmann, 1971), 50–51. Kokoschka chose these models, he stated, because of their gaunt figures, which revealed the underlying joints, muscles, and tendons much more clearly. Interview with Oskar Kokoschka in Ludwig Goldscheider, *Kokoschka* (Cologne: Phaidon, 1963), 10–11. The results are apparent in the prints he executed for *The Dreaming Youths* (Die träumenden Knaben) in 1907–8—for example, "Das Mädchen Li und ich"—as well as in drawings such as *Der sogenannte Savoyardenknabe* (1912–13).

192. Roessler, "Egon Schiele," 114.

CHAPTER FOUR

1. Egon Friedell, "Prologue before the Film," in *The Promise of Cinema: German Film Theory, 1907–1933*, ed. Anton Kaes, Nicholas Baer, and Michael Cowan, trans. Don Reneau (Oakland: University of California Press, 2016), 180; Egon Friedell, "Prolog vor dem Film [1912]," in *Kino-Debatte: Texte zum Verhältnis von Literatur und Film, 1909–1929*, ed. Anton Kaes (Munich: Deutscher Taschenbuch Verlag, 1978), 45. Originally published in *Blätter des Deutschen Theaters* 2, no. 32 (1912–13): 508–12.

2. Friedrich Nietzsche, "On Truth and Lie in a Nonmoral Sense [1873]," in *On Truth and Untruth: Selected Writings*, ed. and trans. Taylor Carman (New York: Harper Perennial, 2010), 24; Friedrich Nietzsche, *Sämtliche Werke: Kritische Studienausgabe*, ed. Giorgio Colli and Mazzino Montinari, 15 vols. (Berlin: de Gruyter, 1967–88), 1:878.

3. Janik and Toulmin sum up its significance in Viennese modernism: "By the year 1900, the linked problems of communication, authenticity and symbolic expression had been faced in parallel in all the major fields of thought and art—by Kraus and Schönberg, Loos and Hofmannsthal, Rilke and Musil." Allan Janik and Stephen Toulmin, *Wittgenstein's Vienna* (New York: Simon and Schuster, 1973), 119.

4. The crisis of language is an emblematic strand of research on modernism, not

least because it decisively shaped the literary production of modernism and the avant-garde, from the Dadaist sound poems to *Finnegans Wake* and Beckett's stage silence. See Marjorie Perloff, *Wittgenstein's Ladder: Poetic Language and the Strangeness of the Ordinary* (Chicago: University of Chicago Press, 1996); Rolf Grimminger, "Der Sturz der alten Ideale: Sprachkrise, Sprachkritik um die Jahrhundertwende," in *Literarische Moderne: Europäische Literatur im 19. und 20. Jahrhundert*, ed. Rolf Grimminger, Jurij Murasov, and Jörn Stückrath (Reinbek bei Hamburg: Rowohlt, 1995), 169–200; Harold B. Segel, *Body Ascendant: Modernism and the Physical Imperative* (Baltimore: Johns Hopkins University Press, 1998); Susan Sontag, "The Aesthetics of Silence," in *Styles of Radical Will* (New York: Farrar, Straus and Giroux, 1969), 3–34; George Steiner, *Language and Silence: Essays on Language, Literature, and the Inhuman* (New York: Atheneum, 1967).

5. Isolde Schiffermüller, ed., *Geste und Gebärde: Beiträge zu Text und Kultur der klassischen Moderne* (Innsbruck: Studien-Verlag, 2001); Gabriele Brandstetter, *Poetics of Dance: Body, Image, and Space in the Historical Avant-Gardes*, trans. Elena Polzer and Mark Franko (New York: Oxford University Press, 2015), 23–24, 31–38; Hartmut Vollmer, *Die literarische Pantomime: Studien zu einer Literaturgattung der Moderne* (Bielefeld: Aisthesis, 2011), 21–28; Mary Fleischer, *Symbolist Playwright-Dancer Collaborations* (Amsterdam: Rodopi, 2007), 93–99; Segel, *Body Ascendant*, 14–15; Michael Hamburger, *Hofmannsthal: Three Essays* (Princeton, NJ: Princeton University Press, 1972), 15.

6. Gerhart Pickerodt, "Gebärdensprache, Sprachgebärde, musikalische Gebärde in der Oper *Elektra*," in *Geste und Gebärde*, ed. Schiffermüller, 143.

7. Friedell, "Prologue," 180; Friedell, "Prolog," 45. This assertion, in strikingly similar wording, was present already in the first half of the nineteenth century in an influential anatomy textbook for artists by the anatomist and artist Anton Franz Perger. He wrote, "We also know that at certain times one can say more with the simplest motion of a finger than one is capable of expressing through words." Anton Ritter von Perger, *Anatomische Studien des menschlichen Körpers für bildende Künstler* (Vienna: Gerold, 1848), 332.

8. Friedell, "Prologue," 180; Friedell, "Prolog," 45.

9. Hugo von Hofmannsthal, *Gesammelte Werke*, 10 vols., ed. Bernd Schoeller and Rudolf Hirsch (Frankfurt: Fischer, 1979–80), 7:568. This edition will henceforth be cited parenthetically with the abbreviation HGW, followed by the volume and page number.

10. Elements of this are apparent in Hermann Broch's formulation of Vienna's "gay apocalypse" and Ernst Mach's "unrettbare Ich." See also Peter Gay, *The Naked Heart*, vol. 4, *The Bourgeois Experience: Victoria to Freud* (New York: Oxford University Press, 1995). Significant for later developments in psychology, art, and literature, Gay describes the inward turn—a preoccupation with the self and expression of psychic processes—as a defining characteristic of the late nineteenth century.

11. Many analyses read Chandos as Hofmannsthal's doppelgänger. Janik and Toulmin are typical for this vein, calling "A Letter" Hofmannsthal's "literary apologia for giving up the medium of poetry." Janik and Toulmin, *Wittgenstein's Vienna*, 144. See also an otherwise excellent essay by Grimminger, "Der Sturz der alten Ideale," 169–200. For a biographico-historical interpretation, see Rainer Nägele, "Die Sprachkrise

und ihr dichterischer Ausdruck bei Hofmannsthal," *The German Quarterly* 43, no. 4 (1970): 720–32. Others place emphasis instead on the work's fictionality and its role in Hofmannsthal's wider oeuvre. See the chapter on Hofmannsthal in Hans Mayer, *Der Repräsentant und der Märtyrer: Konstellationen der Literatur* (Frankfurt: Suhrkamp, 1971); Jost Bomers, *Der Chandosbrief—die nova poetica Hofmannsthals* (Stuttgart: M & P Verlag, 1991); and Thomas A. Kovach, "Hofmannsthal's 'Ein Brief': Chandos and His Crisis," in *A Companion to the Works of Hugo von Hofmannsthal*, ed. Thomas A. Kovach (Rochester: Camden House, 2002), 85–95.

12. Michael Hamburger asserts, "It is characteristic of Hofmannsthal's works of every period, even the social comedies, that the most crucial thoughts and feelings of his personages cannot be rendered in words, only intimated by gesture, music, or silence." Hamburger, *Hofmannsthal*, 15. Just a year later, Hofmannsthal brought this thought to an even finer point, writing elsewhere, "when speaking we become estranged from ourselves" (HGW 10:413).

13. A *Gaukler* is more generally any kind of entertainer who uses his or her body to thrill audiences. In the figure of Clown Furlani, the *Gaukler* plays an important role in Hofmannsthal's later comedic drama *The Difficult Man* (Der Schwierige, 1921). A whole chapter, richly illustrated with photographs by Emil Mayer, is dedicated to various fairground *Gaukler* in Felix Salten, *Wurstelprater* (Vienna: Rosenbaum, 1911), 38–51.

14. Hofmannsthal hinted at a generalized multimedial principle in a letter to his parents from August 30, 1898: "[You] cannot dispense with any form of art, sooner or later [you] need each one, because one allows [you] to express things the others resist." Hugo von Hofmannsthal, *Briefe 1890–1901* (Berlin: Fischer, 1935), 265.

15. See Vollmer, *Die literarische Pantomime*, and Segel, *Body Ascendant*.

16. Margreth Egidi et al., eds., *Gestik: Figuren des Körpers in Text und Bild* (Tübingen: Gunter Narr, 2000), 35.

17. Georg Braungart, *Leibhafter Sinn: Der andere Diskurs der Moderne* (Tübingen: Niemeyer, 1995), 2.

18. For Hofmannsthal, the actor plays an ideal, archetypal role in cultural creation. See Michael Hamburger, "Art as Second Nature: The Figures of the Actor and the Dancer in the Works of Hugo von Hofmannsthal," in *Romantic Mythologies*, ed. Ian Fletcher (London: Routledge & Kegan Paul, 1967), 225–41. See the description of the actor as the "paradigm of expressive theory" in Petra Löffler, *Affektbilder: Eine Mediengeschichte der Mimik* (Bielefeld: transcript, 2004), 49–75.

19. Erika Fischer-Lichte details this shift in terms of a radical transformation in the notion of embodiment. Erika Fischer-Lichte, *Ästhetik des Performativen* (Frankfurt: Suhrkamp, 2004), 130–39.

20. Georg Fuchs, *Die Schaubühne der Zukunft* (Berlin: Schuster & Loeffler, 1905), 35–36. Fuchs elsewhere writes that acting and dance "are one and *the same art*." Georg Fuchs, *Der Tanz*, Flugblätter für künstlerische Kultur 6 (Stuttgart: Strecker & Schröder, 1906), 57, emphasis in original.

21. Fuchs, *Der Tanz*, 57. See also Fuchs, *Schaubühne*, 35–36.

22. Brandstetter, *Poetics of Dance*, 203. Fuchs believed that the emotional stirrings staged through gesture were also transferable to a healthier, more productively physical way of living in the world at large. His vision overlapped to some extent with the

physical culture craze detailed in chapter 1. In the training rooms for Fuchs's new stage, like-minded youth would meet with "aesthetically educated doctors," who would coach them in dietetics, drainage therapy, massage, calisthenics, skin and hair care, as well as providing instruction in dance, acrobatics, and acting technique. Fuchs, *Schaubühne*, 60. Like some strains of the life reform movement, to which Fuchs's thoughts are related, his writing is not free from the discourse of racial hygiene.

23. "Eleonora Duse: A Viennese Theater Week" (Eleonora Duse: Eine Wiener Theaterwoche [1892]), "Eleonora Duse: The Legend of a Viennese Week" (Eleonora Duse: Die Legende einer Wiener Woche [1892]), "Duse in the Year 1903" (Die Duse im Jahre 1903" [1903]), and "A Monograph" (Eine Monographie [1895]).

24. Her acting was a model for Anton Chekhov, brought Henrik Ibsen's dramas to a wide European audience, and inspired Konstantin Stanislavsky to create a wholly new method of acting. Helen Sheehy, *Eleonora Duse: A Biography* (New York: Knopf, 2003), 5.

25. Sheehy, *Eleonora Duse*, 5–6.

26. When Mitterwurzer died in 1897, Hofmannsthal even dedicated a poem to him, "To the Memory of the Actor Mitterwurzer" (Zum Gedächtnis des Schauspielers Mitterwurzer), praising the actor's physical expressivity: "His entire body was like the magic cape / In whose folds all things live" (HGW 1:71).

27. The earliest source to identify this as a trend is Donald G. Daviau, "Experiments in Pantomime by the Major Writers of Jung-Wien," in *Österreich in amerikanischer Sicht: Das Österreichbild im amerikanischen Schulunterricht*, ed. Herbert Lederer and Maria Luise Caputo-Mayr (New York: Austrian Institute, 1981), 19–26. Segel, *Body Ascendant*, 14–79, devotes a chapter to the broader European phenomenon of modernist pantomime, in which he also covers, in varying depth, Reinhardt, Hofmannsthal, and Schnitzler. The research gap has definitively been filled with the comprehensive study by Vollmer, *Die literarische Pantomime*, and with the anthology, Hartmut Vollmer, *Literarische Pantomimen: Eine Anthologie stummer Dichtungen* (Bielefeld: Aisthesis, 2012).

28. Hermann Bahr, *Die Überwindung des Naturalismus* (Dresden: Pierson, 1891), 46. Bahr devotes an entire chapter of the book to pantomime (44–49).

29. Stéphane Mallarmé, "The Mime," trans. Barbara Johnson, in *Selected Poetry and Prose*, ed. Mary Ann Caws (New York: New Directions, 1982). A convincing reading of Mallarmé with Jacques Derrida is found in Abigail Gillman, *Viennese Jewish Modernism: Freud, Hofmannsthal, Beer-Hofmann, and Schnitzler* (University Park: Pennsylvania State University Press, 2009), 64.

30. Richard Beer-Hofmann, *Große Richard Beer-Hofmann-Ausgabe in sechs Bänden*, ed. Günter Helmes, Michael M. Schardt, and Andreas Thomasberger, 6 vols. (Paderborn: Igel, 1993).

31. Arthur Schnitzler, *Gesammelte Werke in Einzelausgaben: Das dramatische Werk*, 8 vols. (Frankfurt: Fischer, 1977–78).

32. *Variété: Ein Buch der Autoren des Wiener Verlages* (Vienna: Wiener Verlag, 1902).

33. Ödön von Horváth, *Das Buch der Tänze* (Munich: Schahin-Verlag, 1922); Ödön von Horváth, *Gesammelte Werke: Kommentierte Werkausgabe in 14 Einzelbänden*, ed.

Traugott Krischke, vol. 11 (Frankfurt: Suhrkamp, 2001). Horváth's dance-pantomimes were performed and published, but the author—perhaps skeptical about the future of the genre—bought back the remainders of his book in 1926 and destroyed them.

34. See Vollmer, *Die literarische Pantomime*, 47–54; Martin Green and John Swan, *The Triumph of Pierrot: The Commedia dell'Arte and the Modern Imagination* (University Park: Pennsylvania State University Press, 1993); Karin Wolgast, *Die Commedia dell'arte im Wiener Drama um 1900* (Frankfurt: Peter Lang, 1993).

35. Green and Swan, *The Triumph of Pierrot*, 12.

36. Over the course of his career, Reinhardt directed more dramatic works by Hofmannsthal than by any other contemporary author. Fleischer, *Symbolist Playwright-Dancer Collaborations*, 103.

37. *Sumurûn* premiered in April 1910 at the Kammerspiele of the Deutsches Theater in Berlin and was the first pantomime Reinhardt staged. It was an international success, traveling to Vienna, London, Paris, and, ultimately, New York, marking Reinhardt's directorial debut in the United States. See Friedrich Freska, *Sumurûn: Eine Pantomime in neun Bildern nach orientalischen Märchenmotiven* (Berlin: Erich Reiss, 1910); Vollmer, *Die literarische Pantomime*, 282–311; Segel, *Body Ascendant*, 19–20. *The Miracle* was written by Karl Vollmoeller and modeled on a symbolist drama by Maurice Maeterlinck. Reinhardt's colossal staging recreated a Gothic cathedral interior and debuted at London's immense Olympia Hall (which held eight thousand viewers) in December 1911. In Vienna, it was performed in September and October 1912 in the Prater's vast exhibition hall, the Rotunde, which had been built for the World's Fair in 1873. After World War I, it was popular as a traveling production in North America, staged close to three hundred times in New York in 1924 alone. See J. L. Styan, *Max Reinhardt* (Cambridge: Cambridge University Press, 1982), 96; Segel, *Body Ascendant*, 19.

38. Freska, *Sumurûn*, 30.

39. Erika Fischer-Lichte, "Inszenierung des Fremden: Zur (De-)Konstruktion semiotischer Systeme," in *TheaterAvantgarde: Wahrnehmung—Körper—Sprache*, ed. Erika Fischer-Lichte (Tübingen: Francke, 1995), 187.

40. Grete Wiesenthal, "Tanz und Pantomime," *Hofmannsthal-Blätter* 34 (1986): 39.

41. The sketches are challenging to date. See Hugo von Hofmannsthal, *Sämtliche Werke: Kritische Ausgabe*, vol. 27, *Ballette, Pantomimen, Filmszenarien*, ed. Klaus-Dieter Krabiel and Gisela Bärbel Schmid (Frankfurt: Fischer, 2006), 670, 675, 677. (This edition will henceforth be cited parenthetically with the abbreviation HSW, followed by the volume and page number.) Hofmannsthal seems to have been inspired to work in pantomime after collaborating with Richard Beer-Hofmann for three days in spring 1893 on a German-to-French translation of Beer-Hofmann's own *Pierrot Hypnotiseur* (1892) in 1893. The pantomime was published only posthumously (HSW 27:665).

42. Hofmannsthal viewed the boundaries between dance and pantomime as relatively permeable. These pieces are perhaps best understood as "dance-intensive" pantomimes, characterized by strongly rhythmic components. Segel, *Body Ascendant*, 38.

43. HSW 27:670.

44. HSW 27:677–78. In the years that followed, dance seems to have captured Hofmannsthal's imagination, though only brief notes for the ballet projects *Apocalypse /*

Song of Songs (Apokalypse / Hohelied, 1893–94), *Children's Ballet* (Kinderballett, 1895-96), and *The Year of the Soul* (Das Jahr der Seele, 1898) resulted.

45. HSW 27:130.

46. Gillman, *Viennese Jewish Modernism*, 66. Her chapter "Hofmannsthal's Jewish Pantomime: *Der Schüler* (The Student, 1901)," 54–76, is the defining reading of this work.

47. HSW 27:263.

48. Hofmannsthal was able to win composer Alexander von Zemlinsky (after unsuccessfully petitioning Richard Strauss, Gustav Mahler, and Ernst von Dohnányi) to score *Triumph of Time*, which was intended for performance at the newly founded Darmstadt Center for Art (Darmstädter Zentrum für die Kunst) in 1901. He contracted Erich Julius Wolff to compose the musical accompaniment for *The Student*, which was written for performance at Felix Salten's cabaret Theater zum lieben Augustin in the Theater an der Wien. See Vollmer, *Die literarische Pantomime*, 111–36; Gillman, *Viennese Jewish Modernism*, 54–76; Donald G. Daviau, "Hugo von Hofmannsthal's Pantomime: *Der Schüler*. Experiment in Form—Exercise in Nihilism," *Modern Austrian Literature* 1, no. 1 (1968): 4–30; Karin Wolgast, "'Scaramuccia non parla, e dice gran cose': Zu Hofmannsthals Pantomime *Der Schüler*," *Deutsche Vierteljahresschrift für Literaturwissenschaft und Geistesgeschichte* 71, no. 2 (1997): 245–63; Wolfram Mauser, "Hofmannsthals 'Triumph der Zeit': Zur Bedeutung seiner Ballett- und Pantomimen-Libretti," in *Hofmannsthal und das Theater: Die Vorträge des Hofmannsthal Symposiums Wien 1979* (Vienna: Halosar, 1981), 141–48.

49. Gillman, *Viennese Jewish Modernism*, 59.

50. Gillman, *Viennese Jewish Modernism*, 57–58.

51. Gillman, *Viennese Jewish Modernism*, 66. In racist discourse around the turn of the century, Jewish males are equated with women, seen as feminized and thus negatively connoted. Otto Weininger's *Sex and Character* is perhaps the most notorious text asserting this correspondence. Otto Weininger, *Geschlecht und Charakter: Eine prinzipielle Untersuchung* (Vienna: Braumüller, 1903). See Sander L. Gilman, *The Jew's Body* (New York: Routledge, 1991), Sander L. Gilman, *Freud, Race, and Gender* (Princeton, NJ: Princeton University Press, 1993), and Klaus Hödl, *Die Pathologisierung des jüdischen Körpers: Antisemitismus, Geschlecht und Medizin im Fin de Siècle* (Vienna: Picus, 1997).

52. Gillman, *Viennese Jewish Modernism*, 68.

53. Gillman, *Viennese Jewish Modernism*, 68.

54. Gillman, *Viennese Jewish Modernism*, 65–66.

55. Gillman, *Viennese Jewish Modernism*, 67.

56. Gillman, *Viennese Jewish Modernism*, 59.

57. Gillman, *Viennese Jewish Modernism*, 58.

58. Gillman, *Viennese Jewish Modernism*, 62.

59. See Gerhard Austin, *Phänomenologie der Gebärde bei Hugo von Hofmannsthal* (Heidelberg: Winter, 1981).

60. The group that founded the Salzburg Festival in 1920 included Hugo von Hofmannsthal, Max Reinhardt, Richard Strauss, Alfred Roller, and Franz Schalk. See

Michael Steinberg, *Austria as Theater and Ideology: The Meaning of the Salzburg Festival* (Ithaca, NY: Cornell University Press, 2000).

61. See HSW, 27:585n18; "Reinhardt Forms 'Pantomime Society,'" *New York Times*, June 7, 1925; "International Pantomime," *New York Times*, June 15, 1925. The guiding principle behind the society was that pantomime was a "medium . . . for new ideas and expression which it would be impossible to portray in spoken drama." "Reinhardt Forms 'Pantomime Society,'" 27. Several others were involved in the founding, including the dancer and choreographer Ernst Matray, whom Reinhardt had cast in *Sumurûn*, *The Miracle*, and other productions.

62. See Hedwig Müller, "Von der äußeren zur inneren Bewegung: Klassische Ballerina—Moderne Tänzerin," in *Von der äußeren zur inneren Bewegung: Klassische Ballerina—Moderne Tänzerin*, ed. Renate Möhrmann (Frankfurt: Insel, 1989), 283–99. For a history of classical dance traditions in nineteenth-century Vienna, see Gunhild Oberzaucher-Schüller, "Institutionalisierter Tanz in Wien des 19. Jahrhunderts," in *Österreich tanzt: Geschichte und Gegenwart*, ed. Andrea Amort and Mimi Wunderer-Gosch (Vienna: Böhlau, 2001), 36–53.

63. How modernist innovations in theater—including a shift away from a naturalistic, mimetic conception of stage acting—shaped the reform notions that underlay free dance is articulated in Gabriele Brandstetter, *Tanz-Lektüren: Körperbilder und Raumfiguren der Avantgarde* (Frankfurt: Fischer, 1995), 90–92. Elsewhere, Brandstetter notes correspondences between the modernist *Sprachkrise* and the break with classical ballet, which resulted in two divergent tendencies in literature and in dance. On the one hand, it leads toward avant-gardism, i.e., increased abstraction and attempts to transcend the medium. In literature, the emphasis is on "pure" language, stripped of any signifying quality (the Dadaist sound poems come to mind here); in dance, it results in a focus on the body's physical materiality and on "pure" movement (the *Ausdruckstanz* strand of modern dance). The other tendency, Brandstetter argues, emphasizes naturalness and authenticity, for which the dances (and conceptions of the body) of foreign cultures and antiquity are the paradigms. This strand leads to free dance, as discussed here, and explains why proponents of free dance—both performers and theorists alike—often referred to Asian and classical Greek dances as models. Gabriele Brandstetter, "Tanz und Literatur I. Körperbilder der Jahrhundertwende," *Ballett-Journal: Das Tanzarchiv: Zeitung für Tanzpädagogik und Ballett-Theater* 40, no. 4 (1992): 10–15.

64. Hugo von Hofmannsthal and Carl J. Burckhardt, *Briefwechsel*, ed. Carl J. Burckhardt and Claudia Mertz-Rychner (Frankfurt: Fischer, 1991), 279. Emphasis in original.

65. Brandstetter, *Tanz-Lektüren*, 33.

66. The development of free dance in the Viennese context is detailed in Gunhild Oberzaucher-Schüller, "Der freie Tanz in Wien bis 1938," in *Österreich tanzt: Geschichte und Gegenwart*, ed. Andrea Amort and Mimi Wunderer-Gosch (Vienna: Böhlau, 2001), 54–69.

67. In her autobiography, St. Denis wrote that her encounters with Hofmannsthal had left a lasting impression, pushing her to articulate more in her performances than she thought possible. Ruth St. Denis, *An Unfinished Life: An Autobiography* (New York: Harper & Brothers, 1939), 94–96. See also Rolf-Peter Janz, "Zur Faszination des Tanzes in der Literatur um 1900: Hofmannsthals *Elektra* und sein Bild der Ruth

St. Denis," in *Fremde Körper: Zur Konstruktion des Anderen in europäischen Diskursen*, ed. Kerstin Gernig (Berlin: Dahlem University Press, 2001), 258–71.

68. St. Denis's program that evening included *Cobras*, *Incense*, and *Radha: The Dance of the Five Senses*. Hofmannsthal's essay discusses only *Radha*, a seven-part dance analyzed at length in Suzanne Shelton, *Divine Dancer: A Biography of Ruth St. Denis* (Garden City, NY: Doubleday, 1990), 62–65.

69. St. Denis acknowledged that dance was, for her, a spiritual discipline that made possible the physical expression of her deepest inner experiences. Freny Mistry, "On Hofmannsthal's 'Die unvergleichliche Tänzerin,'" *Modern Austrian Literature* 10, no. 1 (1977): 38.

70. Insightful analyses of the text can be found in Gabriele Brandstetter, "Der Traum vom anderen Tanz: Hofmannsthals Ästhetik des Schöpferischen im Dialog 'Furcht,'" *Freiburger Universitätsblätter* 112 (1991): 37–58, and Hamburger, "Art as Second Nature," 234–40.

71. Brandstetter, "Der Traum vom anderen Tanz," 45.

72. As Gabriele Brandstetter points out, the classical dance of the hetaera is a "culture-dance" (*Kultur-Tanz*)—a complex, culturally coded semiotic system that operates on the unity of dance, music, and verse and is staged as an artwork. The islanders' primal dance is, by contrast, an amimetic "nature dance" (*Naturtanz*) that exists outside of cultural conventions and semiosis, for it is pure, spontaneous rhythm in and of itself. Brandstetter, "Der Traum vom anderen Tanz," 48.

73. The close of Hofmannsthal's *Electra* likewise contains such a cathartic moment, expressible only through a dance, which ends in Electra's death. Stefan Andriopoulos has productively related the medical discourses of hysteria and hypnosis to Hofmannsthal's drama. See Stefan Andriopoulos, *Possessed: Hypnotic Crimes, Corporate Fiction, and the Invention of Cinema*, trans. Peter Jansen and Stefan Andriopoulos (Chicago: University of Chicago Press, 2007), 85–90.

74. Baum also wrote the screenplay for the blockbuster Hollywood movie (1932), which won the Academy Award for Best Picture. She recognized early on that the world of stage performance more generally was fascinating to her readership, as *Castle Theater* (Schloßtheater, 1921) and the novel *The Stage Door* (Der Eingang zur Bühne, 1920), her first Ullstein publication, demonstrate. One of her last novels, *Theme for Ballet* (1958), published in English in the United States, where Baum emigrated in 1932, again takes up dance, treating the career of a Viennese prima ballerina.

75. [Albert] Paris von Gütersloh, *Die tanzende Törin* (Munich: Georg Müller, 1913). Other contemporaries, including Hofmannsthal and Ödön von Horváth, actually wrote dances that were staged. In addition to the works by Hofmannsthal already mentioned, see Horváth, *The Book of Dances*.

76. Vicki Baum, *Schloßtheater* (Berlin: Egon Fleischel, 1921), 117–25. This text will henceforth be cited parenthetically with page number.

77. Three foundational sources are Gilman, *The Jew's Body*, Hödl, *Pathologisierung*, and Todd Samuel Presner, *Muscular Judaism: The Jewish Body and the Politics of Regeneration* (London: Routledge, 2007).

78. Gilman, *The Jew's Body*. See also Gilman, *Freud, Race, and Gender*, 49–69, for "the construction of the male Jew"—among other things, through circumcision.

79. For an analysis of the exoticizing gaze in St. Denis's *Radha* dance, see Jane Desmond, "Dancing out the Difference: Cultural Imperialism and Ruth St. Denis's 'Radha' of 1906," *Signs: Journal of Women in Culture and Society* 17, no. 1 (1991): 28–49.

80. Along with pathology, disease, and "ugliness"—all localized on the skin. Gilman, *The Jew's Body*, 171–76. As Gilman puts it, "nothing, not acculturation, not baptism, could wipe away the taint of race. No matter how they changed, they still remained diseased Jews. And this was marked on their physiognomy." Gilman, *The Jew's Body*, 179.

81. Lisa Silverman, *Becoming Austrians: Jews and Culture between the World Wars* (New York: Oxford University Press, 2012), 101. Silverman calls them "Vienna's 'invisible' Jewish women" (93–102). On the subject of invisible Jewish women, see also Ann Pelligrini, "Whiteface Performances: 'Race,' Gender, and Jewish Bodies," in *Jews and Other Differences: The New Jewish Cultural Studies*, ed. Jonathan Boyarin and Daniel Boyarin (Minneapolis: University of Minnesota Press, 1997), 108–49.

82. The story was serialized in two parts in the Berlin-based journal *Ost und West*. Not merely the first explicitly Jewish magazine, it was also the first illustrated and first "ethnic magazine" of Jewish "middlebrow" culture—which promoted cultural legitimacy for European Jews via an ostensibly more "nuanced" depiction of the diversity of Jewish cultures in Europe. David A. Brenner, "Neglected 'Women's' Texts and Contexts: Vicki Baum's Jewish Ghetto Stories," *Women in German Yearbook* 13 (1997): 101–21.

83. See Gilman, *The Jew's Body*.

84. For more on operative procedures intended to render Jewishness invisible, see Gilman, *The Jew's Body*, 181–91.

85. The historical iconography and discourses surrounding Jewish sexual difference in the form of purported hypersexuality and heightened incidence of sexually transmitted diseases have been definitively analyzed by Sander L. Gilman. See Gilman, *Freud, Race, and Gender*; Gilman, *The Jew's Body*.

86. Brenner describes the inclusive message of "Jewish particularism" advocated by *Ost und West*, the periodical in which "Rafael Gutmann" appeared. Brenner, "Neglected 'Women's' Texts and Contexts," 103.

87. Hugo Bettauer, *Die Stadt ohne Juden: Ein Roman von übermorgen* (Vienna: Gloriette-Verlag, 1922).

88. Gilman, *The Jew's Body*, 193.

89. Brenner, "Neglected 'Women's' Texts and Contexts," 102–3; Silverman, *Becoming Austrians*, 102.

90. Brenner, "Neglected 'Women's' Texts and Contexts," 112. Brenner spells out the notion of "Jewish self-hatred" in this context, but the deep rhetorical roots, specifically Viennese, from Otto Weininger and Theodor Herzl to Karl Kraus and Anton Kuh, are treated by Sander L. Gilman, *Jewish Self-Hatred: Anti-Semitism and the Hidden Language of the Jews* (Baltimore: Johns Hopkins University Press, 1986), and Paul Reitter, *On the Origins of Jewish Self-Hatred* (Princeton, NJ: Princeton University Press, 2012).

91. See Vollmer, *Die literarische Pantomime*, 268–81; Grete Wiesenthal, *Der Aufstieg: Aus dem Leben einer Tänzerin* (Berlin: Rowohlt, 1919), 207–9; Fleischer, *Symbolist Playwright-Dancer Collaborations*, 119–20.

92. Wiesenthal, *Der Aufstieg,* 169–70. See also Wiesenthal, "Tanz und Pantomime," 37.

93. Wiesenthal, "Tanz und Pantomime," 37. Emphasis mine.

94. Wiesenthal, "Tanz und Pantomime," 36–40.

95. The actual performances were a smash hit. After the rehearsal, the Wiesenthals performed on ten days in January. Claudia Feigl, "Die Chronologie der 'Fledermaus' 1907 bis 1913," in *Kabarett Fledermaus 1907 bis 1913: Ein Gesamtkunstwerk der Wiener Werkstätte: Literatur, Musik, Tanz,* ed. Michael Buhrs, Barbara Lesák, and Thomas Trabitsch (Vienna: Brandstätter, 2007), 181–83.

96. See Buhrs, Lesák, and Trabitsch, *Kabarett Fledermaus.*

97. Helga Malmberg, *Widerhall des Herzens. Ein Peter Altenberg-Buch* (Munich: Langen/Müller, 1961), 82.

98. Malmberg, *Widerhall des Herzens,* 85–87.

99. Malmberg, *Widerhall des Herzens,* 85.

100. Buhrs, Lesák, and Trabitsch, *Kabarett Fledermaus.*

101. Janet Stewart, "Egon Friedell and Alfred Polgar: Cabaret in Vienna at the Turn of the Last Century," in *From Perinet to Jelinek: Viennese Theater in Its Political and Intellectual Context,* ed. W. E. Yates, Allyson Fiddler, and John Warren (Bern: Peter Lang, 2001), 156.

102. Elana Shapira, *Style and Seduction: Jewish Patrons, Architecture, and Design in Fin-de-Siècle Vienna* (Waltham: Brandeis University Press, 2016), 147–51.

103. Shapira, *Style and Seduction,* 150.

104. Hugo von Hofmannsthal, "Erinnerung an Grete Wiesenthal," in *Grete Wiesenthal: Die Schönheit der Sprache des Körpers im Tanz,* ed. Leonhard M. Fiedler and Martin Lang (Salzburg: Residenz, 1985), 155.

105. Anton Kuh, "Der Strauß-Walzer als Gesinnung," in *Werke,* ed. Walter Schübler, vol. 4, *1926–1930* (Göttingen: Wallstein, 2016), 369–70.

106. See Oberzaucher-Schüller, "Institutionalisierter Tanz in Wien," 36–53; Walter Sorell, *Dance in Its Time* (New York: Columbia University Press, 1981).

107. Wiesenthal was surely inspired by Isadora Duncan's guest appearances in Vienna in 1902 at the Secession and in 1904 at the Carltheater, where Duncan danced, among other things, to the "Blue Danube" waltz, much to the audience's delight. Ludwig Hevesi, "Isadora Duncan" (January 8, 1904), in *Acht Jahre Sezession (März 1897—Juni 1905): Kritik—Polemik—Chronik* (Vienna: Konegen, 1906), 516.

108. Grete Wiesenthal, "Sphärischer Tanz (Ein Vortrag)," in *Grete Wiesenthal,* ed. Fiedler and Lang, 147–50.

109. Oscar Bie, "Grete Wiesenthal," in *Grete Wiesenthal: Holzschnitte von Erwin Lang mit einer Einleitung von Oskar Bie* (Berlin: Erich Reiss, 1910), n.p. [3, 1].

110. For more on *The Wind,* see Wiesenthal, "Tanz und Pantomime," 36–40. See also Fleischer, *Symbolist Playwright-Dancer Collaborations,* 117; Leonhard M. Fiedler, "Aus dem Leben einer Tänzerin," in *Grete Wiesenthal,* ed. Fiedler and Lang, 34–35. The writer Richard Billinger gave Wiesenthal the designation, which is typically applied to Alma Mahler-Werfel, as immortalized by Oskar Kokoschka in his painting *The Bride of the Wind* (1913). Richard Billinger and Erwin Lang, *Grete Wiesenthal und ihre Schule* (Vienna: Haybach, 1923), 4.

111. Bie, "Grete Wiesenthal," n.p. [2].

112. Bie, "Grete Wiesenthal," n.p. [1].

113. Max Lehrs, "Die Wiesenthals: Ein Epilog," *Der Tag*, April 25, 1908, Ausgabe B edition, n.p. [3].

114. Alfred Rosenzweig, "Grete Wiesenthal im heutigen Wien," in *Grete Wiesenthal*, ed. Fiedler and Lang, 143.

115. Bie, "Grete Wiesenthal," n.p. [4].

116. See Reingard Witzmann, "Grete Wiesenthal—eine Wiener Tänzerin," in *Die neue Körpersprache—Grete Wiesenthal und ihr Tanz*, ed. Reingard Witzmann (Vienna: Eigenverlag der Museen der Stadt Wien, 1985), 20. For more on spinning techniques in modern dance, see Brandstetter, *Poetics of Dance*, 206–23.

117. Hans Brandenburg, *Der moderne Tanz*, 2nd ed. (Munich: Müller, 1917), 69–70.

118. Wiesenthal, "Sphärischer Tanz (Ein Vortrag)," 147.

119. Brandstetter, *Poetics of Dance*, 221.

120. Wiesenthal's break with the Imperial Opera Ballet came full circle and was bridged almost eighty years after her departure, when the ballet school of the (now) Vienna State Opera began incorporating the Wiesenthal technique as part of its curriculum in 1986. As Andrea Amort notes, two specifically Viennese modern dance techniques—those of Wiesenthal and of Rosalia Chladek—are the only "living" forms of dance that originated from the turn-of-the-century European free dance movements and are still instructed to this day. Andrea Amort, "'Ich könnte mir eine moderne Tänzerin denken, die auf Krücken tanzt': Anmerkungen zum Paradigmenwechsel im künstlerischen Tanz am Beispiel des Tanzprogramms im Wiener Theater und Kabarett Fledermaus von 1907 bis 1913," in *Kabarett Fledermaus*, ed. Buhrs, Lesák, and Trabitsch, 151n6.

121. Leonhard M. Fiedler, "Die Schönheit der Sprache des Körpers im Tanz," in *Grete Wiesenthal*, ed. Fiedler and Lang, 8.

122. Hofmannsthal, "Erinnerung an Grete Wiesenthal," in *Grete Wiesenthal*, ed. Fiedler and Lang, 155.

123. Hugo von Hofmannsthal to Clemens von Franckenstein, May 27, 1914. Hugo von Hofmannsthal and Clemens von Franckenstein, "Briefwechsel 1894 bis 1928," ed. Ulrike Landfester, *Hofmannsthal-Jahrbuch zur europäischen Moderne* 5 (1997): 125.

124. In a letter to Wiesenthal from July 1910, Hofmannsthal wrote, "As I have been trying to clarify for myself the art form 'pantomime' originating from Reinhardt's 'mixed form,' it has also become clear to me the immense, rich possibilities it holds for you, the natural second stage of your development, boundless possibilities, really, to unfold your innermost being [*Ihr Inneres*], to develop the outer [*Äußeres*], endlessly multifarious, summoned from the inner" (quoted in HSW 27:361).

125. See Vollmer, *Die literarische Pantomime*, 311–40. For a detailed account of the relationship between the pantomime and film versions of *The Foreign Girl*, see Heinz Hiebler, *Hugo von Hofmannsthal und die Medienkultur der Moderne* (Würzburg: Königshausen & Neumann, 2003), 433–54.

126. The dance scene "Tanz der Küchenjunge" in the Molière adaptation *Der Bürger als Edelmann* as a prelude to *Ariadne auf Naxos* (1912); *The Bee* (Die Biene, 1914/16), a pantomime, debuted in November 1916 and based on a Chinese folktale; and two un-

finished works, a ballet, *Taugenichts* (1912), and *The Dark Brother* (Der dunkle Bruder) (1912/14/28), a pantomime. The idea for a further ballet, *Achilles auf Skyros* (1914/25), originated from time spent with Wiesenthal in 1914 but was first performed much later, in 1926, and without the Viennese dancer, who had by that time moved on and would soon open her own school of dance.

127. Harry Graf Kessler to Hugo von Hofmannsthal, June 25, 1911. Hugo von Hofmannsthal and Harry Graf Kessler, *Briefwechsel 1898–1929*, ed. Hilde Burger (Frankfurt: Insel, 1968), 331.

128. Harry Graf Kessler to Hugo von Hofmannsthal, May 28, 1909 and June 5, 1909. Hofmannsthal and Kessler, *Briefwechsel*, 435–36.

129. See Abigail Gillman's subtle reading of the ballet in her chapter "Mythic Memory Theater and the Problem of Jewish Orientalism in Hofmannsthal's Ballet *Josephslegende* (Legend of Joseph, 1912)." Gillman, *Viennese Jewish Modernism*, 128–49.

130. Like Wiesenthal and Nijinsky, the Norwegian dancer Lillebil Christensen (later Ibsen), a pupil of the Russian dancer and choreographer Michel Fokine, captured Hofmannsthal's and Reinhardt's attention. The two collaborated to complete two "ballet-pantomimes" with her as the lead: *The Green Flute* (Die grüne Flöte, 1916/23) and *Prima Ballerina: A Day in the Life of a Dancer* (Prima Ballerina: Ein Tag aus dem Leben einer Tänzerin, 1917). *The Green Flute* was a major success: it was included in multiple seasons of the Deutsches Theater's touring productions and again after World War I, when the aforementioned International Pantomime Society staged a 1925 revival at the Salzburg Festival under Reinhardt's direction and with the celebrated Viennese dancer Tilly Losch as the lead. See HSW, 27:584–85, and Leonhard M. Fiedler, "Hofmannsthals Ballettpantomime 'Die grüne Flöte': Zu verschiedenen Fassungen des Librettos," *Hofmannsthal-Blätter* 8/9 (1972): 113–45.

131. Fleischer, *Symbolist Playwright-Dancer Collaborations*, 147.

132. Alfred Polgar, "Grete Wiesenthal," in *Alfred Polgar: Kleine Schriften*, ed. Marcel Reich-Ranicki and Ulrich Weinzierl, vol. 6, *Theater II* (Reinbek: Rowohlt, 1986), 439–40.

133. The revolution brought about by the invention of film, particularly the reciprocal effects between modern urban life and cinema, has been amply documented. Two notable works in this area are Leo Charney and Vanessa R. Schwartz, eds., *Cinema and the Invention of Modern Life* (Berkeley: University of California Press, 1995), and Tom Gunning, "The Cinema of Attraction: Early Film, Its Spectator and the Avant-Garde," *Wide Angle* 8, nos. 3–4 (1986): 63–70. See Walter Benjamin's description of the effects of the medium on early twentieth-century city dwellers and politics: Walter Benjamin, "The Work of Art in the Age of Mechanical Reproduction," in *Illuminations*, ed. Hannah Arendt, trans. Harry Zohn (New York: Schocken, 1968).

134. Hugo von Hofmannsthal, "A Letter," in *The Lord Chandos Letter and Other Writings*, trans. Joel Rotenberg (New York: New York Review Books, 2005), 127/HGW 7:471.

135. Giorgio Agamben, *Infancy and History: The Destruction of Experience*, trans. Liz Heron (London: Verso, 1993), 138.

136. Georg Lukács, "Gedanken zu einer Ästhetik des Kinos," in *Kino-Debatte:*

Texte zum Verhältnis von Literatur und Film, 1909–1929, ed. Anton Kaes (Munich: Deutscher Taschenbuch Verlag, 1978), 115–16. Originally published in the *Frankfurter Zeitung*, September 10, 1913. Emphasis in original.

137. *Burgtheater* actors had to petition for consent to act in films. See Hiebler, *Hofmannsthal und die Medienkultur*, 433.

138. See Anton Kaes, "The Debate about Cinema: Charting a Controversy (1909–1929)," *New German Critique* 40 (1987): 7–33; Kaes, *Kino-Debatte*; Anton Kaes, Nicholas Baer, and Michael Cowan, eds., *The Promise of Cinema: German Film Theory, 1907–1933* (Oakland: University of California Press, 2016).

139. Béla Balázs, *Béla Balázs: Early Film Theory: Visible Man and The Spirit of Film*, ed. Erica Carter, trans. Rodney Livingstone (New York: Berghahn, 2010), 4, emphasis in original; Béla Balázs, *Der sichtbare Mensch oder die Kultur des Films* (Frankfurt: Suhrkamp, 2001), 10–11. The English translation will henceforth be cited parenthetically with page number.

140. See Mary Gluck, *Georg Lukács and His Generation, 1900–1918* (Cambridge, MA: Harvard University Press, 1985), 14–16.

141. Three of Balázs's films came to fruition: *Kaiser Karl* (1921), *The Unknown Man from Russia* (Der Unbekannte aus Rußland, 1922), and the episodic film *Modern Marriages* (Moderne Ehen, 1924), for which Balázs was one of three authors.

142. Balázs also penned theater reviews and feuilletons for the same publication. See Hanno Loewy's excellent biographical work on Balázs, including *Béla Balázs: Märchen, Ritual und Film* (Berlin: Vorwerk 8, 2003); "Space, Time, and 'Rites de Passage': Béla Balázs's Paths to Film," *October* 115 (2006): 61–76; and "Vom Schielen der Sinne: Feuilletons und Film: Béla Balázs—ein Dichter auf Abwegen," in *Wien und die jüdische Erfahrung 1900–1938: Akkulturation—Antisemitismus—Zionismus*, ed. Frank Stern and Barbara Eichinger (Vienna: Böhlau, 2009), 325–41.

143. The English-language film theories by Vachel Lindsay (*The Art of the Moving Picture*, 1915) and Hugo Münsterberg (*The Photoplay*, 1916) predate Balázs's work. Robert Musil was among the first to fully acknowledge the significance of Balázs's monograph. See Robert Musil, "Ansätze zu einer neuen Ästhetik: Bermerkungen über eine Dramaturgie des Films," in *Gesammelte Werke*, ed. Adolf Frisé (Reinbek: Rowohlt, 1978), 8:1137–54.

144. See Gertrud Koch, "Béla Balázs: The Physiognomy of Things," *New German Critique* 40 (1987): 167–77; William M. Johnston, *The Austrian Mind: An Intellectual and Social History, 1848–1938* (Berkeley: University of California Press, 1972), 384–85.

145. It is interesting to note the title of a novel in diary form Balázs coauthored with the Danish writer Karin Michaelis during a tumultuous affair in his Viennese exile years: *Beyond the Body: Diary of a Man and a Woman*. It was published in Hungarian in Vienna. Béla Balázs and Karin Michaelis, *Túl a testen: Egy férfi és egy nö naplója* (Vienna: Bécsi Magyar Kiadó, 1920). For the personal feud between Balázs and Michaelis over the book's publication, see Loewy, "Vom Schielen der Sinne," 328–29.

146. The wider cultural context of sports is detailed in Anne Fleig, *Körperkultur und Moderne: Robert Musils Ästhetik des Sports* (Berlin: de Gruyter, 2008).

147. Malcolm Turvey, "Balázs: Realist or Modernist?," *October* 115 (2006): 82.

148. See Koch, "Béla Balázs," 167–68. On *Lebensphilosophie*, see Nitzan Lebovic,

The Philosophy of Life and Death: Ludwig Klages and the Rise of a Nazi Biopolitics (New York: Palgrave Macmillan, 2013), esp. 155–81.

149. Balázs also makes some problematic racialist claims that need to be understood in the context of a Marxist strand of physiognomy advocated by Walter Benjamin, among others. See Laura Heins, "The 'Psyche of the White Man' and the Mass Face on Film: Béla Balázs between Racialist and Marxist Physiognomics," *New German Critique* 43, no. 1 (February 2016): 59–89.

150. Hugo von Hofmannsthal, "Three Small Observations," in *Hugo von Hofmannsthal and the Austrian Idea: Selected Essays and Addresses, 1906–1927*, trans. and ed. David S. Luft (West Lafayette, IN: Purdue University Press, 2011), 111–19; here 114. The English translation will henceforth be cited parenthetically with page number, along with the corresponding passages from the German original, HGW; here 9:142–43.

151. In his posthumously published notes from the year 1928, Hofmannsthal remarks that "the dangerous aspect of the [modern] condition is this: that *everything* . . . is conveyed to the audience through an excessively individualistic and impressionistic press language [*Pressesprache*]" (HGW 10:593). This assertion is reminiscent of Karl Kraus's comprehensive *Sprachkritik*.

152. This echoes a sentiment from one of Hofmannsthal's early poems, "Zukunftsmusik" (Music of the Future, 1891): "Words are formulas, they can't say it" (Worte sind Formeln, sie können's nicht sagen). It also calls to mind Musil's negative definition of the soul as "that which sneaks off at the mention of algebraic series." Robert Musil, *The Man without Qualities*, trans. Sophie Wilkins and Burton Pike, 2 vols. (New York: Vintage, 1996), 1:106.

153. The inventory of childhood dream spaces Hofmannsthal describes in this essay resonates strikingly with his description of the inanimate objects that stir Chandos's soul in "A Letter"—and bear more than a passing resemblance to aspects of Walter Benjamin's *Berlin Childhood around 1900*. Miriam Hansen relates Benjamin's thoughts on cinema to a utopian hopefulness he ascribes to children's access to the unconscious. Miriam Hansen, *Cinema and Experience: Siegfried Kracauer, Walter Benjamin, and Theodor W. Adorno* (Berkeley: University of California Press, 2012), 149–50. See also Assenka Oksiloff, "Archaic Modernism: Hofmannsthal's Cinematic Aesthetics," *The Germanic Review* 73, no. 1 (1998): 70–85.

154. As Hofmannsthal phrased it in his third "Vienna Letter," written in 1923 for the American modernist literary magazine *The Dial*, "We are without doubt on the arduous path toward creating a new reality for ourselves, and this creation only can occur through the complete doubtfulness about reality, that is, through the dream" (HGW 9:291). Interestingly, Antonin Artaud would later articulate aspects of his "Theater of Cruelty" along similar lines, striving—like a marriage of Balázs's celluloid gestures and Hofmannsthal's notion of film as a substitute for dreams—to create a language in which words achieve "something of the significance they have in dreams," a "language half-way between gesture and thought." Antonin Artaud, *The Theater and Its Double*, trans. Mary Caroline Richards (New York: Grove, 1958), 94, 89.

155. The journalist Alfred Polgar summed up the situation for the majority of Viennese, charging, "Access to the theater's world of illusion is barred by outrageous ticket prices, and even books are now affordable only for people who have so much money

that they no longer find it necessary to read at all." Alfred Polgar, "Geistiges Leben in Wien," in *Taschenspiegel*, ed. Ulrich Weinzierl (Vienna: Löcker, 1979), 96. Originally published in the *Prager Tagblatt*, November 14, 1920, 4. Hofmannsthal's—and Balázs's—ideas are found later in condensed form by the Social Democratic commentator Grete Ujhely, "Film als Volkskunst," *Kunst und Volk: Mitteilungen des Vereines "Sozialdemokratische Kunststelle"* 3, no. 6 (February 1929): 173–75.

156. Hiebler, *Hofmannsthal und die Medienkultur*, 457–66; here 466. Hiebler rightly argues that Hofmannthal's essay is best understood as a form somewhere between film theory and poetics. He relates the author's film projects to his attempts to revitalize Austrian-German literature in the wake of World War I. Hofmannsthal's postwar ventures into popular culture, his editorial and journalistic activities, and the Salzburg Festival likewise speak to his efforts to reach a wider audience. See also Alys X. George, "Editing Interwar Europe: *The Dial* and *Neue Deutsche Beiträge*," *Austrian Studies* 23 (2015): 16–34.

157. Two further film scenarios remained unrealized: *Daniel Defoe* (1922/26) and an untitled film collaboration between Hofmannsthal, Reinhardt, and the actress Lillian Gish (1928), star of D. W. Griffith's *Intolerance* (1916). Hiebler, *Hofmannsthal und die Medienkultur*, 427–513, analyzes the films in great detail. Aside from Hiebler's research, the best work on Hofmannsthal's relation to film has been done by Oksiloff, "Archaic Modernism," and Ernst Prodolliet, *Das Abenteuer Kino: Der Film im Schaffen von Hugo von Hofmannsthal, Thomas Mann und Alfred Döblin* (Freiburg [CH]: Universitätsverlag, 1991). See also Marion Faber, "Hofmannsthal and the Film," *German Life and Letters* 32, no. 3 (1979): 187–95, and Elke C. Furthman-Durden, "Hugo von Hofmannsthal and Alfred Döblin: The Confluence of Film and Literature," *Monatshefte* 78, no. 4 (1986): 443–55.

158. Hugo von Hofmannsthal to Richard Strauss; quoted in Prodolliet, *Das Abenteuer Kino*, 24.

159. See Hugo von Hofmannsthal to Alfred Walter Heymel, September 22, 1911. Hugo von Hofmannsthal and Alfred Walter Heymel, *Briefwechsel 1900–1914*, ed. Werner Volke (Freiburg: Rombach, 1998), 187.

160. Stiller is remembered today foremost as the director who gave Greta Garbo her big break.

161. It is worth recalling the close of both Hofmannsthal's *Electra* and the essay "Fear," which also end with the dancers' collapse.

162. Ludwig Klinenberger, "Ein Filmdrama von Hugo von Hofmannsthal," in *Kino-Debatte*, ed. Kaes, 107. Originally published in *Bühne und Welt* 15 (1913): 503–4.

163. The reviews are from the *Deutsche Montags-Zeitung* (Berlin), *Arbeiter-Zeitung* (Vienna), and *Berliner Tageblatt* (Morgenausgabe), respectively (quoted in HSW 27:818–19). See Hiebler, *Hofmannsthal und die Medienkultur*, 450–54.

164. Karl Kraus, "Ein Verlorener," *Die Fackel* 15, nos. 391/392 (1914): 18–19. Though Kraus also turned up his nose at Arthur Schnitzler and Felix Salten for their work in the industry, Leo A. Lensing has convincingly demonstrated the significance of cinema in Kraus's own work. See Leo A. Lensing, "'Kinodramatisch': Cinema in Karl Kraus' *Die Fackel* and *Die letzten Tage der Menschheit*," *The German Quarterly* 55, no. 4 (1982): 480–98.

165. Quoted in HSW 27:819. The most moderate voice was Klinenberger's: "Hof-

mannsthal has not fully worked out the technique of the cinema dramatist [*Kinodramatiker*]. Many scenes and images repeat themselves all too often, the plot does not progress quickly enough, but individual images are gripping and very beautiful." Klinenberger, "Ein Filmdrama," 109.

166. Hugo von Hofmannsthal, interview by Paul Frank, "Der Reinhardt-Hofmannsthal-Gish-Film: Hugo von Hofmannsthal schildert Entstehung und Inhalt des Werkes," *Münchner Telegrammzeitung*, December 31, 1928, 8; quoted in Hiebler, *Hofmannsthal und die Medienkultur*, 509.

167. *World's Pictorial News*, June 8, 1929, n.p. Press clipping in Orig. Album (Mirquette Hirmer album), 140, Bodenwieser-Dokumentation, Hilverding-Stiftung 4, Austrian Theater Museum, Vienna.

168. A note on terminology: scholars translate *Ausdruckstanz* variously. Brandstetter's translator, e.g., prefers "expressionist dance." Karl Toepfer chooses "expressive dance," while Susan Manning and Lucia Ruprecht opt for the more literal "dance of expression." Toepfer, Manning, and Ruprecht, however, retain the German original, as do I. Brandstetter, *Poetics of Dance*; Susan Manning and Lucia Ruprecht, eds., *New German Dance Studies* (Urbana: University of Illinois Press, 2012); Karl Toepfer, *Empire of Ecstasy: Nudity and Movement in German Culture, 1910–1935* (Berkeley: University of California Press, 1997).

169. Brandstetter, *Poetics of Dance*, 19–20. See also Gabriele Klein, *FrauenKörper-Tanz: Eine Zivilisationsgeschichte des Tanzes* (Berlin: Quadriga, 1992).

170. Oberzaucher-Schüller, "Der freie Tanz," 61.

171. Andrea Amort, "Ausdruckstanz in Österreich bis 1938," in *Ausdruckstanz: Eine mitteleuropäische Bewegung der ersten Hälfte des zwanzigsten Jahrhunderts*, ed. Gunhild Oberzaucher-Schüller (Wilhelmshaven: Noetzel, 1992), 384.

172. See Oberzaucher-Schüller, "Der freie Tanz," 61.

173. Bettina Vernon-Warren and Charles Warren, eds., *Gertrud Bodenwieser and Vienna's Contribution to Ausdruckstanz* (Amsterdam: Harwood, 1999).

174. Alfons Török, "Wiener Tanzabende," *Der Merker*, June 1, 1919, 421; quoted in Shona Dunlop MacTavish and Denny Hirschbach, eds., *Gertrud Bodenwieser: Tänzerin, Choreographin, Pädagogin, Wien—Sydney* (Bremen: Zeichen + Spuren, 1992), 20.

175. Hilde Holger, "The Early Days," in *Gertrud Bodenwieser*, ed. Vernon-Warren and Warren, 79.

176. Oberzaucher-Schüller, "Der freie Tanz," 61. See also Pia Janke, *Politische Massenfestspiele in Österreich zwischen 1918 und 1938* (Vienna: Böhlau, 2010).

177. Unidentified author and newspaper, presumably British, held in a facsimile copy of an album of press clippings about Bodenwieser, document 58, folder 49–66, 1–122, Bodenwieser-Dokumentation, Hilverding-Stiftung 1, Austrian Theater Museum, Vienna. Just ten years later, even before the "Anschluss," Bodenwieser would be forced to relinquish her professorship, as Austrian institutions were "Aryanized." She would escape via France, eventually settling in Australia, where she continued her career.

178. Holger, "Early Days," 77.

179. Duncan performed in 1902 at the Secession and in 1904 at the Carltheater. See, e.g., Hevesi, "Isadora Duncan," and Ludwig Hevesi, "Miß Duncan in der Sezession," in *Acht Jahre Sezession*, 368–70.

180. Advertisement in the Jewish weekly *Die Stimme* 1, no. 44 (November 1, 1928): 6. Additional advertisements can be found, e.g., in *Kunst und Volk* in 1928 and 1929.

181. [Karl Tschuppik] (tsch.), "Kindertanzabend," *Wiener Neueste Nachrichten*, February 12, 1928; reprinted in Denny Hirschbach and Rick Takvorian, eds., *Die Kraft des Tanzes: Hilde Holger: Wien, Bombay, London* (Bremen: Zeichen + Spuren, 1990), 65.

182. Program from the March 8, 1929, Urania performance, Liz Pisk Dokumentation, Hilverding-Stiftung, Austrian Theater Museum, Vienna. For more general information on the Urania as a site for public education, see Wilhelm Petrasch, *Die Wiener Urania: Von den Wurzeln der Erwachsenenbildung zum lebenslangen Lernen* (Vienna: Böhlau, 2007).

183. "Gymnastik für Werktätige," *Kunst und Volk: Mitteilungen des Vereines "Sozialdemokratische Kunststelle"* 3, no. 5 (January 1929): 148–49. Advertisement for the *Neue Schule für Bewegungskunst* in *Kunst und Volk: Mitteilungen des Vereines "Sozialdemokratische Kunststelle"* 3, no. 7 (March 1929): 215.

184. Edward Timms, *Dynamik der Kreise, Resonanz der Räume: Die schöpferischen Impulse der Wiener Moderne* (Weitra: Bibliothek der Provinz, 2013), 181.

185. Jarmila Weißenböck, "Expressionistischer Tanz in Wien," in *Expressionismus in Österreich: Die Literatur und die Künste*, ed. Klaus Amann and Armin A. Wallas (Vienna: Böhlau, 1994), 177.

186. Among them "The Artistic Dance in the Life of the Child" (Der künstlerische Tanz im Leben des Kindes) and "Dancing as a Factor in Education," folder 49–66, 1–122, Bodenwieser-Dokumentation, Hilverding-Stiftung 1, Austrian Theater Museum, Vienna.

187. See Deborah Holmes, *Langeweile ist Gift: Das Leben der Eugenie Schwarzwald*, trans. Esther Marian and Fanny Esterházy (Salzburg: Residenz Verlag, 2012).

188. Hilde Holger, quoted in *Kraft des Tanzes*, ed. Hirschbach and Takvorian, 61.

189. Zina Luca, *Die hygienisch-harmonische Gymnastik* (Vienna: Verlag der Vereinigung Bildender Künstlerinnen Österreichs, 1917), inventory number A201.281, Wienbibliothek im Rathaus.

190. Gertrud Bodenwieser, "Dancing as a Factor in Education," 169, folder 49–66, 1–122, Bodenwieser-Dokumentation, Hilverding-Stiftung 1, Austrian Theater Museum, Vienna.

191. Gertrud Bodenwieser, "Der künstlerische Tanz im Leben des Kindes," 9–10, folder 49–66, 1–122, Bodenwieser-Dokumentation, Hilverding-Stiftung 1, Austrian Theater Museum, Vienna.

192. Anonymous, *World's Pictorial News*, June 8, 1929, n.p., Orig. Album (Mirquette Hirmer album), 140, Bodenwieser-Dokumentation, Hilverding-Stiftung 4, Austrian Theater Museum, Vienna.

193. When critics drew comparisons between the choreographic styles of Mary Wigman and Gertrud Bodenwieser, the conclusion was often that Bodenwieser's dances were set apart by their lightness, gracefulness, or, simply, their distinctively "Viennese" character. But what qualifies as "typically Viennese"? As one reviewer wrote, it seemed to consist of "tasteful Expressionism." Anonymous, cited in Rudolph Lämmel, *Der moderne Tanz: Eine allgemeinverständliche Einführung in das Gebiet der rhythmischen Gymnastik und des neuen Tanzes* (Berlin: Oestergaard, 1928), 180. See

also Oberzaucher-Schüller, "Der freie Tanz," 60; Carol Brown, "Der stilistische Beitrag des Werks von Gertrud Bodenwieser zur Bewegung des Ausdruckstanzes," in *Gertrud Bodenwieser*, ed. MacTavish and Hirschbach, trans. Jürgen Dierking, 120; Alfred Sandt, "Gruppen- und Solotanz," *Der Tanz* 1, no. 3 (1926): 3. One critic saw Bodenwieser's choreography, for example, as a happy medium between the traditional danse d'école and the more radical Wigmanesque style of expressionism. Considering Bodenwieser's position "very wise," he argued that it allowed her to "secure the advantages of both schools." Arnold L. Haskell, "Further Studies in Ballet," *The Dancing Times*, October 1929, 12. The distinctions between Austrian and German *Ausdruckstanz* tend to parallel those made between the national styles of free dance. Holger's and Bodenwieser's dances (like many of Wiesenthal's) were often choreographed to familiar classical music (Mozart, Debussy, Schumann, Richard Strauss, both Johann Strausses, Schubert), popular Viennese folk songs (*Wienerlieder*), and operetta tunes (Lehár, Ziehrer, Kreisler). See Jarmila Weißenböck's "Choreochronicle" of Bodenwieser's work in *Gertrud Bodenwieser*, ed., Vernon-Warren and Warren, 177–85. and the "Werkverzeichnis" of Holger's choreographies and performances in *Kraft des Tanzes*, ed., Hirschbach and Takvorian, 82–85. Writing in 1935, Jeanette Rutherston reconstructs the "differing national temperaments" reflected in a genealogy of central European dance stemming from Laban. Mary Wigman is on the one extreme of the present *Ausdruckstanz*; Gertrud Bodenwieser on the other. Jeanette Rutherston, "The Central European Dance in England," *The Dancing Times*, October 1935, n.p., folder 99, 1–122, Bodenwieser-Dokumentation, Hilverding-Stiftung, Austrian Theater Museum, Vienna.

194. Hede Juer, "A Dancer Speaks," in *Gertrud Bodenwieser*, ed. Vernon-Warren and Warren, 81–82.

195. Haskell, "Further Studies in Ballet," 14.

196. Lämmel, *Der moderne Tanz*, 181–82.

197. See Hede Juer, "A Note on 'The Ford System,'" in *Gertrud Bodenwieser*, ed. Vernon-Warren and Warren, 83–84.

198. Although many of the dances are lost, Labanotation does exist for *Demon Machine* at the National Library of Australia, where Bodenwieser settled after being forced into exile following the "Anschluss" in 1938.

199. Oskar Schlemmer, "Mechanisches Ballett," in *Tanz und Reigen*, ed. Ignaz Genges (Berlin: Bühnenvolksbundesverlag, 1927).

200. Oskar Schlemmer, "Mensch und Kunstfigur," in *Die Bühne im Bauhaus*, Bauhausbücher 4 (Munich: Albert Langen Verlag, 1925), 7–24.

201. Schlemmer, "Mechanisches Ballett," 82. See also Dirk Scheper, "Oskar Schlemmers Tanzexperimente," in *Ausdruckstanz: Eine mitteleuropäische Bewegung der ersten Hälfte des zwanzigsten Jahrhunderts*, ed. Gunhild Oberzaucher-Schüller (Wilhelmshaven: Noetzel, 1992), 306–16.

202. For Schlemmer, as for Heinrich von Kleist and Edward Gordon Craig, the marionette was an exemplary figure because it embodies both the "unnatural" (*Unnatürliches*) and the "supernatural" (*Übernatürliches*). Schlemmer, "Mechanisches Ballett," 81. Kleist was such an important touchstone for Schlemmer that he had excerpts from "On the Marionette Theater" (Über das Marionettentheater) read aloud as a kind of preamble to the premiere of the *Triadic Ballet*. See Kate Elswit, "The Some of the Parts:

Prosthesis and Function in Bertolt Brecht, Oskar Schlemmer, and Kurt Jooss," *Modern Drama* 51, no. 3 (2008): 402.

203. Schlemmer, "Mensch und Kunstfigur," 18.

204. Egon Friedell, *A Cultural History of the Modern Age: The Crisis of the European Soul from the Black Death to the World War*, trans. Charles Frances Atkinson, 3 vols. (New York: Knopf, 1932), 3:475; Egon Friedell, *Kulturgeschichte der Neuzeit: Die Krisis der europäischen Seele von der schwarzen Pest bis zum Ersten Weltkrieg* (Munich: C. H. Beck, 2007), 1512.

205. Friedell, *Cultural History*, 3:475; Friedell, *Kulturgeschichte*, 1512. See also Johnston, *The Austrian Mind*, 383.

206. Friedell, *Cultural History*, 3:484, 3:483, 3:481; Friedell, *Kulturgeschichte*, 1523, 1522, 1519.

207. Friedell, *Cultural History*, 3:484; Friedell, *Kulturgeschichte*, 1523.

208. Friedell, "Prologue," 180; Friedell, "Prolog," 45.

EPILOGUE

1. Though largely forgotten, Brunngraber was a commercially successful author during his lifetime. His books were translated into eighteen languages and sold over a million copies. He was a committed Social Democrat, even promoted from deputy chairman to chairman of the Austrian Union of Socialist Authors in 1934, and worked at Otto Neurath's Social and Economic Museum (Gesellschafts- und Wirtschaftsmuseum) from 1928 to 1934, but his legacy is tainted by having later aligned himself with the National Socialists. While he returned to Social Democracy after World War II, Brunngraber was for a time a member of the Reich Chamber of Literature (Reichsschrifttumkammer) after the "Anschluss." Wendelin Schmidt-Dengler, "Statistik und Roman: Über Otto Neurath und Rudolf Brunngraber," in *Arbeiterbildung in der Zwischenkriegszeit: Otto Neurath—Gerd Arntz*, ed. Friedrich Stadler (Vienna: Löcker, 1982), 119–24; Christoph Fuchs, "Rudolf Brunngraber, 1901–1960," *Literatur und Kritik* 32, nos. 317–18 (1997): 103–9; Jon Hughes, "Facts and Fiction: Rudolf Brunngraber, Otto Neurath, and Viennese Neue Sachlichkeit," in *Interwar Vienna: Culture between Tradition and Modernity*, ed. Deborah Holmes and Lisa Silverman (Rochester, NY: Camden House, 2009), 206–23; and Evelyne Polt-Heinzl, "Das Kommando der Dinge oder Was ein Bimmerling lernen kann: Überlegungen zu Rudolf Brunngrabers Arbeitslosenroman 'Karl und des 20. Jahrhunderts' (1932)," *Studia austraica* 3 (1995): 45–63. For more on the Union of Socialist Authors, see Herbert Exenberger, "Vereinigung sozialistischer Schriftsteller," in *Als stünd' die Welt in Flammen: Eine Anthologie ermordeter sozialistischer SchriftstellerInnen*, ed. Herbert Exenberger (Vienna: Mandelbaum Verlag, 2000), 8–35.

2. See Freud's assertion in the *Introductory Lectures on Psychoanalysis* that "the motive of human society is in the last resort an economic one." Sigmund Freud, *The Standard Edition of the Complete Psychological Works of Sigmund Freud*, ed. and trans. James Strachey, 24 vols. (London: Hogarth Press, 1953), 16:311.

3. The phrase was central enough for Freud to use it twice: once in "On the Universal Tendency to Debasement in the Sphere of Love" (1912) and again in "The Dissolution of the Oedipus Complex" (1924).

4. Toril Moi, "Is Anatomy Destiny? Freud and Biological Determinism," in *Whose Freud? The Place of Psychoanalysis in Contemporary Culture*, ed. Peter Brooks and Alex Woloch (New Haven, CT: Yale University Press, 2000), 79. Few statements of Freud's have drawn such rancor from feminist scholars charging him with biological determinism. Moi decisively refutes this claim. Freud is, as Moi has pointed out, paraphrasing an encounter with Napoleon recounted by Goethe (75–76).

5. Moi, "Is Anatomy Destiny?," 88.

6. Brunngraber fancied himself a "poet-sociologist." Fuchs, "Rudolf Brunngraber," 103. Like Horváth, if we recall *Faith, Hope, and Charity* (chap. 2), Brunngraber integrated documentary materials into fictional works in the mode of the New Objectivity (Neue Sachlichkeit) of the late Weimar Republic. Consequently, he has been compared thematically to authors of the same time period: Alfred Döblin, Hans Fallada, Erich Kästner, Irmgard Keun, and Joseph Roth. From a formal standpoint, a key reference point might rather be John Dos Passos.

7. See Marx's *Das Kapital* and the description of labor power as commodity. Karl Marx, *Das Kapital*, in *Werke*, by Friedrich Engels and Karl Marx, 24th ed. 44 vols. (Berlin: Dietz, 2013), 23:182–83.

8. "A Newsreel Novel," *New York Times*, November 12, 1933, 24.

9. Rudolf Brunngraber, *Karl and the Twentieth Century*, trans. Eden and Cedar Paul (New York: William Morrow, 1933), 310; Rudolf Brunngraber, *Karl und das 20. Jahrhundert* (Frankfurt: Societäts-Verlag, 1933), 289–90.

10. Anson Rabinbach, *The Human Motor: Energy, Fatigue, and the Origins of Modernity* (New York: Basic Books, 1990).

11. See Mark Mazower, *Dark Continent: Europe's Twentieth Century* (New York: Knopf, 1999), 76–103, and Enzo Traverso, *The Origins of Nazi Violence*, trans. Janet Lloyd (New York: New Press, 2003).

12. As Sander L. Gilman, Klaus Hödl, and Todd Presner have detailed, the pathologizing of the Jewish body in medicine, science, and popular culture had strong roots long before the rise of National Socialism. See Sander L. Gilman, *Difference and Pathology: Stereotypes of Sexuality, Race, and Madness* (Ithaca, NY: Cornell University Press, 1985); Sander L. Gilman, *The Jew's Body* (New York: Routledge, 1991); Klaus Hödl, *Die Pathologisierung des jüdischen Körpers: Antisemitismus, Geschlecht und Medizin im Fin de Siècle* (Vienna: Picus, 1997); Todd Samuel Presner, *Muscular Judaism: The Jewish Body and the Politics of Regeneration* (London: Routledge, 2007).

13. Max Horkheimer and Theodor W. Adorno, *Dialectic of Enlightenment: Philosophical Fragments*, ed. Gunzelin Schmid Noerr, trans. Edmund Jephcott (Stanford: Stanford University Press, 2002), 195.

14. See Alys X. George, "Everyman and the New Man: Festival Culture in Interwar Austria," *Austrian Studies* 25 (2017): 198–214, and Pia Janke, *Politische Massenfestspiele in Österreich zwischen 1918 und 1938* (Vienna: Böhlau, 2010). Many of the dancers considered in chapter 4 were lead choreographers for similar political festivals in the late 1920s and early 1930s.

15. Claudia Spring, "Vermessen, deklassiert und deportiert: Dokumentation zur anthropologischen Untersuchung an 440 Juden im Wiener Stadion im September 1939

unter der Leitung von Josef Wastl vom Naturhistorischen Museum," *Zeitgeschichte* 32, no. 2 (2005): 92–93.

16. The memoir of survivor Gershon Evan, who was among the people measured, describes the scene in the stadium and his experience as the subject of these studies in depth. See Gershon Evan, *Winds of Life: The Destinies of a Young Viennese Jew 1938–1958* (Riverside, CA: Ariadne Press, 2000). The studies took place September 25–30, 1939, and involved 440 subjects. The materials and data collected from the prisoners at the stadium were rediscovered at the National History Museum in 1998 in the context of a provenience research project. They included over seven hundred black-and-white photographs, reams of documents, strands of hair, seventeen masks, and two busts. Spring, "Vermessen," 95.

17. See Spring, "Vermessen," and Margit Berner, "Die Bedeutung der biometrischen Erfassungsmethode in der österreichischen Anthropologie in der ersten Hälfte des 20. Jahrhunderts," in *Eugenik in Österreich: Biopolitische Strukturen von 1900–1945*, ed. Gerhard Baader, Veronika Hofer, and Thomas Mayer (Vienna: Czernin, 2007), 254.

18. The prehistory of this later development is detailed in Alys X. George, "Anatomy for All: Medical Knowledge on the Fairground in *Fin-de-Siècle* Vienna," *Central European History* 51, no. 4 (2018): 535–62.

19. For more on the relationship between anatomical science and National Socialism, see Sabine Hildebrandt, *The Anatomy of Murder: Ethical Transgressions and Anatomical Science during the Third Reich* (New York: Berghahn, 2016).

20. See Oliver Rathkolb, *The Paradoxical Republic: Austria, 1945–2005* (New York: Berghahn, 2010), 26.

21. Werner Hofmann, "Das Fleisch erkennen," in *Ornament und Askese im Zeitgeist des Wien der Jahrhundertwende*, ed. Alfred Pfabigan (Vienna: Brandstätter, 1985), 120–29.

22. Museum moderner Kunst Stiftung Ludwig Wien, ed., *Körper, Psyche und Tabu* (Vienna: Walther König, 2016).

23. Karl Kraus, "Sprüche und Widersprüche," *Die Fackel* 10, nos. 272/273 (1909): 43.

24. Friedrich Michael Fels, "Die Moderne [1891]," in *Die Wiener Moderne: Literatur, Kunst und Musik zwischen 1890 und 1910*, ed. Gotthart Wunberg (Stuttgart: Reclam, 1981), 194.

25. Norman O. Brown, *Love's Body* (New York: Random House, 1966), 155.

INDEX

Note: Page numbers in italics indicate illustrative material.

abortion, 135, 148, 152–53, 154, 158–61, 287n163, 288n168. *See also* Paragraph 144
Adorno, Theodor W., 63, 229, 232, 260n139
Agamben, Giorgio, 203, 269n93
Albert, Eduard, 264n34
Altenberg, Peter, *46*, *57*; *Ashantee*, 38–44, *39*, 57, 255nn68–70; *As I See It*, 57, 63; connection to dance, 196, 200; connection to Ungar, 123, 126–27, 276n32; criticism and praise of, 62–63, 260n139; fascination with pubescent girls, 42–43, 261n155; on health, 45–46, *46*, 54, *55*, 58–62; *Pròdrŏmŏs*, 56–63; visits to human displays, 28
Amor and Psyche (Hofmannsthal), 201, 202
Analysis of Sensations and the Relation of the Physical to the Psychical, The (Mach), 72
Anatomist, The (Max), 262n3
anatomy, 51–52, 64, 229; and anthropology, 10, 36; and dance, 218; pathological anatomy, 6–7, 14, 70, 75, 243n24 (*see also* dissection); and pathology, 4, 6, 7; representations of, 50, 118, 130, 138, 233; topographical anatomy, 80–81, 85–87. *See also* medicine
Anatomy (Matsch), 69, 70, 261–62n2, 262n4
Anatomy Lesson of Dr. Nicolaes Tulp, The (Rembrandt), 262n3, 266n53
"Anschluss," 12, 17, 234, 305n177, 307n198, 308n1
Anthropological Society in Vienna (Anthropologische Gesellschaft in Wien, AGW), 34, 36
anthropology and ethnography: in human display discourse, 31–32, 34–37, 41; physical anthropology, 35–37, 253nn46–47; study of Jewish prisoners, 233, 310n16
anthropometry, 32, 34, *35*, 36, 253n45
anti-Semitism, 136, 154–55, 160, 163, 191–94, 196, 231, 232–34, 286n150, 295n51, 309n12, 310n16
Arbeiterinnen-Zeitung (newspaper), 160
Arbeiter-Zeitung (newspaper), 26, 65, 151, 153, 155, 220
architecture, clinical, 140–44, *144*, 284n103, 284n111, 284n113
Arnheim, Rudolf, 205
Artaud, Antonin, 178, 303n154
Artmann, H. C., 235
Ashantee (Altenberg), 38–44, *39*, 57, 255nn68–70
Ashantis, *27*; anthropological objectification, 31–32, 41, 255n68; audience interactions, 30; literary depictions, 38–44, *39*; reception in media, 23, 25–26; village exhibit, 25, 250n8, 250n10
As I See It (Altenberg), 57, 63
Association of Viennese Artists. *See* Künstlerhaus (Association of Viennese Artists)
Auden, W. H., 12

Ausdruckstanz (expressive dance), 170, 190, 214–17, 218, 222–25, 305n168, 307n193
Austria, First Republic, 7, 17, 19, 49, 53, 54, 55, 56, 119, 159, 160, 229
Austria, Second Republic, 234
Austrian Women's Club, 275n16
Austrofascism, 151, 271n124, 275n20, 287n157
authenticity, discourse of, 29, 31, 33, 37–38, 41–44
autopsy. *See* dissection
"Autopsy Room" (Pappenheim), 79–80, 265n48

Bach, David Joseph, 220, 288n168
Bachofen-Echt, Elisabeth, 136
Bahr, Hermann, 1–4, 2, 13–14, 63, 170, 171, 174, 260n139; *Dear Augustin*, 178; "The Modern," 3–4; *Overcoming Naturalism*, 177; *The Pantomime of the Good Man*, 178
Baker, Josephine, 63–64, 66–67, 261n156
Balázs, Béla, 205, 302nn141–43, 303n149; *Beyond the Body* (with Michaelis), 302n145; *The Shadows*, 178; *The Visible Man*, 204–8, 227
ballet, classical, 185, 194–95, 200, 214–15. *See also* Imperial Opera Ballet
Ballets Russes (Diaghilev), 201–2
Balzac, Honoré de, 171
Bartók, Béla, *Bluebeard's Castle*, 205
Bauhaus, 224–25
Baum, Vicki, 189, 257n104; "The Boy and the Dancer," 185, 190–92, 193, 194; *Castle Theater*, 297n74; *The Dances of Ina Raffay*, 189–90; *Grand Hotel*, 189; "In the Old House," 192; "Rafael Gutmann," 192; *The Stage Door*, 297n74; *Theme for Ballet*, 297n74
Bayer, Konrad, 235
Beer, Friederike Maria, 281n76
Beer-Hofmann, Richard, 28, 170, 171, 174, 195, 294n41; *The Golden Horse*, 178; *Pierrot Hypnotiseur*, 178
Beller, Steven, 18, 20
Benjamin, Walter, 205; *Berlin Childhood around 1900*, 303n153; "Critique of Violence," 269n93; "The Storyteller," 89
Berg, Alban, 78
Berger, Hanna, 214
Bergson, Henri, 207
Berlin Childhood around 1900 (Benjamin), 303n153
Berman, Marshall, 12
Bermann, Richard A., 267n72, 267n74
Bettauer, Hugo, 102; *Bettauers Wochenschrift*, 160; *The City without Jews*, 193; *The Joyless Street*, 289n180
Beyond the Body (Balázs and Michaelis), 302n145
Bie, Oscar, 198
Billinger, Richard, 299n110
Billroth's Lecture Hall at the Vienna General Hospital (Seligmann), 262n3
Bilz, Friedrich Eduard, 52
blackness, 26–32, 64, 67, 192
Blei, Franz, 200
Bloch-Bauer, Adele, 136
Bluebeard's Castle (Bartók), 205
Blumenberg, Hans, 241n4
Boccioni, Umberto, 103
Bock, Anton and Hans, 164, *165*
Bodenwieser, Gertrud, 214, 217–18, 220–22, 305n177, 306–7n193; *Demon Machine*, 222–24, *224*, 225; *Mechanization (Ford System)*, 222, 224
body culture: defined, 4–5; historiography, 9–11
body language. *See* gesture, and crisis of language
Body of the Mother, The (Feldmann), 150–54, 155–56, 158–61. *See also* Hauser, Carry
Boeckl, Herbert, 127, 262n4
Book of Dances, The (Horváth), 178, 294n33, 297n75
Book of Hours, The (Rilke), 126
Book of the City, The (Hauser), 102–4, *105*, 110, 270n119
Bordo, Susan, 9–10
Bourdieu, Pierre, 37
bourgeois class: as audience at human displays, 28, 40; feminine ideals, 120; hypocrisy, 66; as Klimt's preferred subjects, 136
"Boy and the Dancer, The" (Baum), 185, 190–92, 193, 194
Boyer, John, 12
Brandenburg, Hans, *The Modern Dance*, 199–200
Brandstetter, Gabriele, 188, 200, 215, 296n63, 297n72, 300n116, 305n168
Breitner, Hugo, 156

Breuer, Josef, 7, 78–79, 173
Bride of the Wind, The (Kokoschka), 299n110
Broch, Hermann, 267n70, 291n10
Bronfen, Elisabeth, 71, 111, 151, 287n151
Brown, Norman O., 236
Brücke, Ernst von, 74, 139, 253n47
Brunngraber, Rudolf, 102, 109, 308n1, 309n6; *Karl and the Twentieth Century*, 229–31
Brus, Günter, 235
Burgtheater, 67, 115, 172, 175, 204, 235, 302n137
Butler, Judith, 9
Bynum, Caroline, 9, 10

Cabaret Fledermaus, 184, 195–96
cadavers. *See* corpses and fragmented bodies
Canetti, Elias, 131–32
Castle Theater (Baum), 297n74
Charcot, Jean-Martin, 243n15, 278n46, 279n53
Chekhov, Anton, 293n24
children: physical education, 53–54, 218–22; poverty-stricken, 163–67, *164*, *165*, 290nn190–91; in social welfare discourse, 156–61, 287n157
Chladek, Rosalia, 214, 300n120
Chosen One, The (Hofmannsthal), 180
Christensen, Lillebil, 301n130
Chrobak, Rudolf, 141
cinema. *See* film
City without Jews, The (Bettauer), 193
Civilization and Its Discontents (Freud), 108
civil war, Austrian, 151
class. *See* bourgeois class; working class
Clémenceau, Georges, 259n122
clinical gaze, 132, 140, 143–44, 150, 152–56
clinics. *See* medical clinics
Closing Time (Ungar), 123–27
"Coffee-House Spring: Nightlife" (Roth), 104–5, 107–8
colonialism, 38, 253n45
commedia dell'arte, 178, 179, 183
commercialization and commodification, 30, 48–49, 60–61, 109–11
Communist Party of Austria, 77, 106, 275n18
corporeal turn, 7, 9–11
corpses and fragmented bodies: discourses on human fragmentation, 89–95, 99–101; discourses on sociopolitical death, 104–8, 111–12; *Leichenbim*, 68–69, 103, 107, *107*, 271n122; visual presence of disfigured war veterans, 95–97, *96*, *98*, *99*; visual representations of social fragmentation, 102–3. *See also* dissection
Courbet, Gustave, *L'Origine du monde*, 130
Craig, Edward Gordon, 174, 178, 307n202
creatureliness, 89, 95, 101
criminal atavism, 278–79n51
crisis of language (*Sprachkrise*), 168–69, 171–77, 235, 290–91n4
"Critique of Violence" (Benjamin), 269n93
Cultural History of the Modern Age, A (Friedell), 168, 227–28
culture, defined, 19–20
Czermak, Emmerich, 52–53

Dalcroze, Émile Jaques-, 53, 215–16, 217
dance: *Ausdruckstanz*, 214–17, 218, 222–25, 305n168, 307n193; classical ballet, 185, 194–95, 200, 214–15; compared to pantomime, 183–84 (*see also* pantomime); connection to film, 203–4; exploration of identity, 189, 191–94; free dance, as genre, 185–89; free dance, Wiesenthal's style, 195–201, *197*, *199*, 300n120; nude performances, 63–64, 66; pedagogy, 53, 218–22, *221*; waltz, 197–98
Dancer and the Marionette, The (Mell), 194
Dances of Ina Raffay, The (Baum), 189–90
Dear Augustin (Bahr), 178
death. *See* corpses and fragmented bodies; dissection
Decline of the West, The (Spengler), 227
Delsarte, François, 215–16, 217
Demon Machine (Bodenwieser), 222–24, *224*, *225*
Derp, Clotilde von, 214
Diaghilev, Sergei, *Ballets Russes*, 201–2
dietetics, 58
Difficult Man, The (Hofmannsthal), 292n13
dissection: and commodification of bodies, 109–11, 272n134; and liminal space between life and death, 79–80, 81–83, 87–88, 104–8, 112; and self-vivisection, 71–75, 113; and visual observation, 84–87; visual representations, 69, 70, 104, *105*, 262n3
Dix, Otto, 102
Döblin, Alfred, 309n6
Doderer, Heimito von, 8
Dörmann, Felix, 102, 122, 178
Dos Passos, John, 309n6

Dostoevsky, Fyodor, 259n122
Drawe, Hermann, 163, 289n182
Dreaming Youths, The (Kokoschka), 290n191
Dream Story (Schnitzler), 83–88
Duncan, Isadora, 185, 189, 214–15, 218, 299n107, 305n179
Duse, Eleonora, 175–76, 184, 188, 293n24

Eberle, Josef, *98*
Ebner-Eschenbach, Marie von, 126
Ehalt, Hubert Christian, 5, 18
Electra (Hofmannsthal), 297n73, 304n161
Eley, Geoff, 18, 247n53
Elias, Norbert, 9, 37
Engels, Friedrich, 12
ethnography. *See* anthropology and ethnography; human displays
eugenics, 7, 18, 146, 231
eurythmics, 53
exhibitions. *See* human displays; hygiene exhibitions
Exner, Wilhelm, 95–96
Expectation (Schönberg), 78–79, 265n46
expressionism, 102, 127, 153, 215, 277n39, 281n78, 306–7n193

"Failed Putsch, The" (Roth), 106–8
Faistauer, Anton, 136–37, 279n55
Faith, Hope, and Charity (Horváth), 108–13, 271n124, 271n126
Fallada, Hans, 309n6
"Fear" (Hofmannsthal), 188–89, 304n161
Felbinger, Franz Ritter von, 261n1
Feldmann, Else, 16, 26, 119, 162, 163, 289n186; *The Body of the Mother*, 150–54, *154*, 155–56, 158–61 (*see also* Hauser, Carry); "Pulled from the Water," 141–42; *The Scream That Nobody Hears*, 151
Fels, Friedrich Michael, 236
femininity, 120
feminism, 77, 120
Ferch, Johann, 160
Ferdinand, Franz, 28
Fickert, Auguste, 77, 120
film: Balázs's theory of, 204–8; critical reception of Hofmannsthal's, 212–13, 304–5n165; Hofmannsthal's theory of, 208–12; *Kino-Debatte*, 204–5, 211, 213; as language of gesture, 203, 207–8, 211; and mechanization, 227; medical clinics as sets for, 144–49
"First Pregnancy" (Pappenheim), 121–22
Fischer-Lichte, Erika, 292n19
fitness, physical, 7, 49, 58, 232. *See also* physical education
Fleischmann, Trude, 257n104
Fokine, Michel, 301n130
Foreign Girl, The (Hofmannsthal), 201, 212–13, 304–5n165
Foucault, Michel, 2, 9, 10, 16, 70, 141, 153
fragmented bodies. *See* corpses and fragmented bodies
Franceschini, Robert, 26
Frank, Johann Peter, 257n96
Frankl, Oskar, 146
free dance: vs. *Ausdruckstanz*, 215; as genre, 185–89; Wiesenthal's style, 195–201, *197*, *199*, 300n120
Frei, Bruno, 162, 289n186; *Vienna's Misery*, 163–66, *164*, *165*
Freska, Friedrich, 179
Freud, Sigmund, 6, 229–30, 308n3, 309n4; *Civilization and Its Discontents*, 108; *The Interpretation of Dreams*, 3, 74–75; *New Introductory Lectures on Psycho-Analysis*, 263n21; *Studies on Hysteria* (with Breuer), 79
Friede, Der (journal), 53, 124, 257n101
Friedell, Egon, 168, 169, 213–14, 226–27, 276n32; *A Cultural History of the Modern Age*, 168, 227–28
Frischauf, Hermann, 77
Frischauf-Pappenheim, Marie. *See* Pappenheim, Marie
Fuchs, Georg, 174–75, 292n20, 292–93n22
Fuller, Loïe, 185, 214–15
Furies, The (Hofmannsthal), 202

Gait of Pregnant Women/Skeletal Anomalies (film), 145
Galerie Miethke, 134, 161, 162, 280n61, 281n79
Gaukler, 173, 292n13
Gay Science, The (Nietzsche), 73–74
gaze: clinical, 132, 140, 143–44, 150, 152–56; male, 42–43, 66, 85–87, 261n155
Geert, Gisa, 214
gender and sexuality: femininity, 120; male gaze, 42–43, 66, 85–87, 261n155; masculinity, 191, 295n51; sexual morality, 32, 64, 117, 233; women's medical training,

76–77, 274n10. *See also* pregnancy and childbirth
George, Stefan, 171
Gerstl, Richard, 78, 127
Gert, Valeska, 214
gesture, and crisis of language, 168–69, 171–77, 290–91n4. *See also* dance; film; pantomime
Gillman, Abigail, 20, 180–83
Gilman, Sander L., 10, 39–40, 191, 192, 193, 298n80, 298n85, 309n12
Girl Is Sold, A (Horváth), 272n135
Glöckel, Otto, 156
Gluck, Mary, 19–20
Godlewski, Carl, 217
Golden Horse, The (Beer-Hofmann), 178
Graff, Erwin von, 133–35, *134*, 274n13, 280n65
Grand Hotel (Baum), 189
Graßberger, Roland, 148–49
Green Flute, The (Hofmannsthal), 301n130
Griepenkerl, Christian, 133
Grillparzer, Franz, 83
Großmann, Stefan, 178
Grosz, George, 102
Guglia, Eugen, 172
Gütersloh, Albert Paris, 190, 279n51, 279n55
gymnastics, performances and exercise, 64–66, *65*, *216*, *221*; rhythmic, 215, 219, 220. *See also* physical education

Haberda, Albin, 106
Hagenbeck, Carl, 27–28, *29*, 31, 34
Hagenbund, 102, 166, 270n119
Hajnal, Eugen, 65–66
Hamburger, Michael, 292n12
Hammer-Purgstall, Joseph Freiherr von, 171
Handke, Peter, 235
Hartel, Wilhelm von, 115
Haßreiter, Josef, 194
Hau, Michael, 47
Hauser, Carry, 270n114, 286n147; *The Book of the City*, 102–4, *105*, 110, 270n119; illustrations for Feldmann's *The Body of the Mother*, 153–54, *154*, 287n160; *War Victim*, 95, 96
health. *See* hygiene and health
Hebra, Ferdinand, 75
Heller, Hermann, 280n64
Heller, Hugo, 179, 288n172
Hellerau School, 216, *216*
Heller-Ostersetzer, Hermine, 288nn172–73; *The Life of the Poor Is Bitterer Than the Death of the Rich*, 161–62, 288n171
Hertwig, Aura, 1–3, *2*
Herzl, Theodor, 28, 31, 32, 298n90
Hevesi, Ludwig, 115, 167, 299n107, 305n179
Hilferding, Margarethe, 274n10, 275n15
Hilpert, Heinz, 271n124
Hochstetter, Ferdinand, 34
Hödl, Klaus, 10, 20, 309n12
Hoffmann, E. T. A., 83
Hoffmann, Josef, 115–16, 194, 195, 284n103
Hofmann, Werner, 5, 7, 127, 234, 243n17
Hofmannsthal, Hugo von, 276n32; on Altenberg, 63; *Amor and Psyche*, 201, 202; *The Chosen One*, 180; connection to Wiesenthal, 186, 195, 196–98, 200–202, 212, 300n124; on dance, 183–84, 185–89, 294n42; *The Difficult Man*, 292n13; *Electra*, 297n73, 304n161; "Fear," 188–89, 304n161; *The Foreign Girl*, 201, 212–13, 304–5n165; *The Furies*, 202; *The Green Flute*, 301n130; "The Incomparable Dancer," 186–88; on language and gesture, 171–77, 183–84, 209, 235, 292n14, 303nn151–52, 303n154; *The Legend of Joseph*, 202; "A Letter," 168, 171, 172, 173, 174, 291n11, 303n153; *The Magical Telephone*, 179–80; on Mitterwurzer, 293n26; "A Monograph," 172–73, 174; *La mort du jeune homme voluptueux*, 202; *Narcissus and the School of Life*, 180; "On Characters in the Novel and in Drama," 171; "On Pantomime," 183, 201; *Der Rosenkavalier*, 212; *Sign of Love*, 179; *The Student*, 170, 180–83; "Three Small Observations," 208–12, 304n156; *Triumph of Time*, 180, 295n48; *Viennese Pantomime*, 179
Holger, Hilde, 214, 217, 218–20, *219*, 307n193; *Mechanical Ballet*, 222, 224–25, 226
Hope I (Klimt), 117, *118*, 127, 128, 136
Hope II (Klimt), 127, 128, 277n40
Horkheimer, Max, 229, 232
Horváth, Ödön von, 104; *The Book of Dances*, 178, 294n33, 297n75; *Faith, Hope, and Charity*, 108–13, 271n124, 271n126; *A Girl Is Sold*, 272n135; "Marianne, or The Decay," 273n141
Hudetz, Josef, 261n1
human displays, 27; Altenberg's fictional

human displays (*continued*)
depiction, 38–44, *39*; audience-display boundaries, 30–32, 37–38, 252n33; origins, 26–27, 251n25; scientific legitimacy, 29–30, 32–37; as spectacles, 27–30. *See also* hygiene exhibitions
"Human Fragments" (Roth), 94–95, 100–101
Hungarian Council (Soviet) Republic, 205
Huyssen, Andreas, 19, 266n63
hygiene and health, *8*; Altenberg on, 45–46, 54, 56–63; in clinical setting, 142; and life reform movement, 45–48, *48*, 203, 220; marital hygiene film, 146–49; and social democracy, 50–51, 231, 257n96
hygiene exhibitions, *45*, *50*; anatomical displays, 49–52; and life reform movement, 45–48; as phenomenon, 44–46; physical education displays, 52–53. *See also* human displays
Hynais, Vojtěch, 41
Hyrtl, Josef, 6, 75, 265n50

Ibsen, Henrik, 293n24
identity: explored through dance, 189, 191–94; explored through pantomime, 180–83; improvement of self, 47; understood through human displays, 29, 37–38; understood through self-vivisection, 71–74, 113; *Volkskörper* concept, 53
Illustrirtes Wiener Extrablatt (newspaper), 23, 25, 31–32
Imperial Opera Ballet, 194, 201, 215, 217. *See also* ballet, classical
"Incomparable Dancer, The" (Hofmannsthal), 186–88
industrialization and mechanization, 222–25, 226–27, 230–32
Internationale Klinische Rundschau (journal), 81
International Pantomime Society, 184, 296n61, 301n130
Interpretation of Dreams, The (Freud), 3, 74–75
"In the Old House" (Baum), 192
Irigaray, Luce, 117

Jahoda, Marie, 257n104
Janik, Allan, 18, 290n3, 291n11
Jewish identity and the body: in dance, 190–94; "difference" rhetoric, 190–94, 231, 298nn80–82; economic and social marginalization, 119, 151, 162–63, 192–93; masculinity, 190–92, 295n51; in pantomime, 180–83; "self-hatred," 298n90; treatment under National Socialists, 232–33, 310n16. *See also* anti-Semitism
Johnston, William, 6–7, 18
Jooss, Kurt, 214
Joseph, Jacques, 269n105
Josephus, Flavius, 90–91
Joyless Street, The (Bettauer), 289n180
Jubal, Elias, 271n124
Judson, Pieter, 18, 247n55
Juer, Hede, 223
Jugendstil, 5, 69, 197, 198
Junger, Erwin, 146

Kahn, Fritz, *The Life of Man*, 51
Karl and the Twentieth Century (Brunngraber), 229–30
Karpeles, Benno, 90, 257n101
Karpfen, Fritz, 137, 278n51, 279n53
Kästner, Erich, 309n6
Kessler, Harry Graf, 201–2
Keun, Irmgard, 309n6
Kisch, Egon Erwin, 257n101, 267n74
Kläger, Emil, 162; *Through the Viennese Quarters of Misery and Crime*, 163, 289n182
Kleist, Heinrich von, 307n202
Klimt, Gustav: compared to Schiele, 127, 128, 133, 136; *Hope I*, 117, *118*, 127, 128, 136; *Hope II*, 127, 128, 277n40; involvement in Viennese cultural elite, 194, 195; *Medicine*, 115–17, *116*, 262n2, 273n6; *Nuda Veritas*, 1–3, *2*, 22, 113, 137, 241n2; *Philosophy*, 116, 262n2; *Water Serpents II*, 69
Klinenberger, Ludwig, 212, 304–5n165
Kodály, Zoltán, 205
Kokoschka, Oskar, 127, 200, 220, 257n104, 279n55, 287n160, 290n191; *The Bride of the Wind*, 299n110; *The Dreaming Youths*, 290n191; *Murderer Hope of Women*, 287n160
Kolig, Anton, 279n55
Kollwitz, Käthe, 161; *Pregnant Woman*, 277n40
Körper, distinction from *Leib*, 2–3, 155, 167
Kracauer, Siegfried, 205
Krafft-Ebing, Richard von, 264n37
Kraus, Gertrud, 214

Kraus, Karl: criticism of human displays, 32, 37; criticism of Jugendstil, 5; and film, 213, 304n164; Jewish rhetoric, 298n90; and language criticism, 168, 235, 303n151; literary style, 102; support for Altenberg, 63, 260n139; support for Pappenheim, 76, 78, 121, 122; on Viennese culture, 236
Kristeva, Julia, 71, 113
Kristl, Lukas, 271n126
Kronfeld, Adolf, 138–39, 274n13, 281n87, 282nn88–89, 283n90
Krystufek, Elke, 235
Kubin, Alfred, 161
Kuh, Anton, 197–98, 257n101, 298n90
Kunst (journal), 123
Künstler-Compagnie, 261n2
Künstlerhaus (Association of Viennese Artists), 116
Kunstschau, 117, 161
Kunststelle (Social Democratic Arts Bureau), 220, 288n168

Laban, Rudolf von, 215, 216, 217
Lacan, Jacques, 241n3
Lang, Marie, 77, 120
Langer, Carl von, 80, 85, 253n47, 265n50, 266n53
language. *See* crisis of language (*Sprachkrise*); gesture, and crisis of language
Laqueur, Thomas, 69–70, 118
Lassnig, Maria, 235
League of Jewish Women, 265n45
Lebensphilosophie, 207, 302–3n148
Legend of Joseph, The (Hofmannsthal), 202
Lehrs, Max, 198
Leib, distinction from *Körper*, 2–3, 155, 167
Leichenbim (corpse tram), 68–69, 103, 107, *107*, 271n122
Leoster, Heinrich, 92
Le Rider, Jacques, 12
Lethen, Helmut, 89, 101, 111, 267n68, 269n95
"Letter, A" (Hofmannsthal), 168, 172, 173, 174, 291n11, 303n153
Life of Man, The (Kahn), 51
Life of the Poor Is Bitterer Than the Death of the Rich, The (Heller-Ostersetzer), 161–62, 288n171
life reform movement (*Lebensreformbewegung*): in Altenberg's literary discourse, 56–63; as concept, 45–48, 203, 220
Lindsay, Vachel, 302n143
Lombroso, Cesare, 252n40, 264n37, 278–79n51
Loos, Adolf, 5, 53–54, 61, 63–64, 220, 255n82, 261n155, 282n87
Losch, Tilly, 214, 301n130
Löwenstein, Hans Otto, 205
Lucian of Samosata, *On the Dance*, 183
Lueger, Karl, 163, 196
Luft, David, 6, 7–9
Lukács, Georg, 203, 205
Lumière brothers, 203
Luschan, Felix von, 34–37, 253nn46–47
Lyotard, Jean-François, 72

Mach, Ernst, 291n10; *The Analysis of Sensations and the Relation of the Physical to the Psychical*, 72
machine culture and industrialization, 222–25, 226–27, 230–32
Mackintosh, Charles Rennie, 198
Maderthaner, Wolfgang, 20, 21, 157–58, 161
Magical Telephone, The (Hofmannsthal), 179–80
Mahler, Gustav, 295n48
Mahler-Werfel, Alma, 299n110
male gaze, 42–43, 66, 85–87, 261n155
Mallarmé, Stéphane, 177
Malmberg, Helga, 195–96
Mann, Heinrich, 259n122, 276n32
Mann, Thomas, 61, 63, 276n32
Man without Qualities, The (Musil), 12
"Marianne, or The Decay" (Horváth), 273n141
Marital Hygiene (film), 146–49, *147*, 285n127, 285n135
Marx, Karl, 12, 208, 230, 309n7
masculinity, 191, 295n51
Matray, Ernst, 296n61
Matsch, Franz, *Anatomy*, 69, 70, 261–62n2, 262n4
Mattl, Siegfried, 20, 29
Mauss, Marcel, 37, 54
Mauthner, Fritz, 168, 173, 235
Max, Gabriel von, *The Anatomist*, 262n3
Mayreder, Rosa, 77, 120, 122, 264n37
Mbembe, Achille, 108–9, 272n128
McEwen, Britta, 146
Mechanization (Ford System) (Bodenwieser), 222, 224

mechanization and industrialization, 222–25, 226–27, 230–32

medical clinics: architecture, 140–44, *144*, 284n103, 284n111, 284n113; clinical gaze, 132, 140, 143–44, 150, 152–56; as film sets, 144–49; paintings of pregnant women in, 128–33, *129*, *130*, *131*; public access to patients in, 134–35, 139–40

medicine: and anthropology, 36, 253n47; forensic, 106; pathognomy, 138–39; pathological anatomy, 6–7, 70, 75, 243n24 (*see also* dissection); pathology, 38, 71, 106, 108, 137–40, 155, 166, 278n51, 298n80; physiology, 4, 6, 36, 51, 64, 71, 72, 74, 218; prostheses and orthopedics for wounded war veterans, 95–97, *98*, *99*, 269n102, 269n104; topographical anatomy, 80–81, 85–87. *See also* anatomy; hygiene and health; hygiene exhibitions; pathology; physiology

Medicine (Klimt), 115–17, *116*, 262n2, 273n6

Mell, Max, 170, 174, 195; *The Dancer and the Marionette*, 194

Mensendieck, Bess (Elizabeth Marguerite de Varel), 260n149

Messerschmidt, Franz Xaver, 279n53

Meyerhold, Vsevolod, 174, 178, 215

Meyers Konversations-Lexikon, 29, 39–40

Meynert, Theodor, 253n47

Michaelis, Karin, 302n145

militia (*Volkswehr*), 106

Minne, George, 198

Miracle, The (Reinhardt and Vollmoeller), 179, 218, 294n37

Mitterwurzer, Friedrich, 172, 175, 176–77, 293n26

"Modern, The" (Bahr), 3–4

Modern Dance, The (Brandenburg), 199–200

"Modern Vehicles" (Roth), 271n122

Modersohn-Becker, Paula, *Self-Portrait on Her Sixth Wedding Anniversary*, 277n40

Moll, Leopold, 146

"Monograph, A" (Hofmannsthal), 172–73, 174, 176–77

Monte Verità, 215, 258n112

morality, sexual, 32, 64, 117, 233

Morena, Erna, 54, *55*

mort du jeune homme voluptueux, La (Hofmannsthal), 202

Moscow Declarations, 234

Moser, Koloman, 69, 115, 194, 195, 198

Mosse, George, 5

motherhood, 119–20, 124–25. *See also* pregnancy and childbirth

Mühl, Otto, 235

Müller-Cohen, Anitta, 162

Municipal Marriage Advice Center, 146–47, 148

Münsterberg, Hugo, 302n143

Murderer Hope of Women (Kokoschka), 287n160

Musil, Robert, 8, 21, 71–74, 93, 257n101, 302n143; *The Man without Qualities*, 12

Muskete, Die (journal), 124

Musner, Lutz, 20, 21, 157–58, 161

My Youth in Vienna (Schnitzler), 162

Napoleon Bonaparte, 229

Narcissus and the School of Life (Hofmannsthal), 180

National Socialism, 18, 64, 138, 151, 228, 231–34, 285n130

Neue Freie Presse (newspaper), 25, 28, 141

Neues Wiener Tagblatt (newspaper), 23, 25–26, 30, 32

Neue Tag, Der (newspaper), 90, 267n74

Neukunstgruppe (New Art Group), 133, 136, 137, 279n53, 279n55

Neumann, Robert, 102

New Art Group. *See* Neukunstgruppe (New Art Group)

New Healing Practice, The (Bilz), 52

New Introductory Lectures on Psycho-Analysis (Freud), 263n21

New School for Movement Art, 218–20

Nietzsche, Friedrich, 9, 13, 58, 61–62, 168, 172, 173; *The Gay Science*, 73–74; *On the Genealogy of Morality*, 73

Nijinsky, Vaslav, 201–2

Nitsch, Hermann, 235, 244n27

Nordau, Max, 252n40, 278–79n51

Normal Birth, The (film), 145

Nuda Veritas (Klimt), 1–3, *2*, 22, 113, 137, 241n2

nude performances, 63–66

Nude Woman on Her Back (Schiele), 278n42

Olbrich, Joseph Maria, 1, 116

Olden, Rudolf, 267n72

Olympia (Riefenstahl), 231

"On Characters in the Novel and in Drama" (Hofmannsthal), 171

"On Pantomime" (Hofmannsthal), 183, 201
On the Dance (Lucian of Samosata), 183
On the Genealogy of Morality (Nietzsche), 73
operating theaters, 142–44, *144*
Oppenheimer, Max, 127
orientalism, 193, 197
Origine du monde, L' (Courbet), 130
Osen, Erwin Dominik, 139, 279n55, 283nn91–92, 283n94
Österreichische Rundschau (journal), 123
Other and Othering, 29, 38–39, 190–94
Our War Invalids (Spitzy), 97, *99*
Overcoming Naturalism (Bahr), 177

Pabst, G. W., 289n180
Palucca, Gret, 214
pantomime: compared to dance, 183–84; connection to film industry, 203–4; explorations of identity, 180–83; forms, 178–80; revival, 170, 177–78
Pantomime of the Good Man, The (Bahr), 178
Paoli, Betty, 126
Pappenheim, Bertha, 78–79, 265n45
Pappenheim, Else, 257n104
Pappenheim, Marie: "Autopsy Room," 79–80, 265n48; "First Pregnancy," 121–22; literary career, 77–79, 275n20; marginalized, 126; medical training, 75–76; social justice work, 121, 161, 275n18
Paragraph 144, 159–61, 287n163. *See also* abortion
pathognomy, 138–39
pathology, 38, 71, 106, 108, 137–40, 155, 166, 278n51, 298n80. *See also* anatomy: pathological anatomy
Pavlova, Anna, 201
performing arts. *See* dance; film; pantomime
Perger, Anton Franz, 52, 291n7
Pernerstorfer, Engelbert, 155
Perutz, Leo, 267n74
Peschka, Anton, 279n55
Pfundmayr, Hedy, 214
Philosophy (Klimt), 116, 262n2
physical anthropology, 35–37, 253nn46–47
physical education: dance pedagogy, 218–22, *221*; gymnastics performances, 64–66, *65*; at hygiene exhibitions, 52–53; in sociopolitical discourse, 53–55, 219–20, 225–26
physiognomy, 5, *11*, 32, *33*, 41, 138, 208, 252nn40–41, 303n149
physiology, 4, 6, 36, 51, 64, 71, 72, 74; and dance, 218
Pierrette's Veil (Schnitzler), 178
Pierrot Hypnotiseur (Beer-Hofmann), 178
Pinthus, Kurt, 56
Plachy, Franz, 163, *164*
Plessner, Helmut, 241n4
Polgar, Alfred, 49–50, 90, 109, 113, 200, 202, 257n101, 276n32, 303–4n155
politics and nation: physical education discourse, 53–55, 219–20, 225–26; social welfare discourse, 16, 50, 51, 119, 138, 144, 146, 156–61, 231, 287n157
Polt-Heinzl, Evelyne, 18, 254n59
Popp, Adelheid, 77
Popular Austrian Health Newspaper, 47
Portrait of Dr. Erwin von Graff (Schiele), 133, *134*, 135, 281n70
Prager, Wilhelm, *Ways to Strength and Beauty*, 231
Prater park, 25, 28, 44, 232–33
Präuscher, Hermann, 29, 233–34
pregnancy and childbirth: abortions, 135, 148, 152–53, 154, 158–61, 287n163, 288n168; and clinical gaze, 132, 140, 143–44, 150, 152–56; discourses on struggle of, 121–22, 124–25, 149–50; in obstetrical and gynecological films, 144–49; in social welfare discourse, 156–61, *159*, 287n157; in visual art, *116*, 117, *118*, 128–33, *129*, *130*, *131*
Pregnant Woman (Kollwitz), 277n40
Pregnant Woman (Schiele), *129*, *130*, *131*
Primavesi, Eugenie, 136
Pròdrŏmŏs (Altenberg), 56–63
Professor Bernhardi (Schnitzler), 154–55, 160, 286nn150–51
"Prosector" (Schnitzler), 80, 81
prostheses, 95–97, *98*, *99*, 269n102, 269n104
prostitution, 111
pseudosciences, 32–33
psychological turn vs. corporeal turn, 7

Rabinbach, Anson, 58, 230–31
race, 10, 37, 169, 193, 233; and entertainment vs. education, 66; Jewish "difference," 191–94, 231, 298nn80–82. *See also* anthropology and ethnography; blackness
"Rafael Gutmann" (Baum), 192

Rathenau, Walther, 229
Rebellion (Roth), 105–6
"Reconstruction of Man, The" (Roth), 269n105
Rehfisch, Hans J., 288n168
Reich, Annie, 161
Reich, Wilhelm, 77, 121, 161, 275n18
Reichel, Oskar, 134, 135
Reinhardt, Max, 170, 174, 178–79, 184, 186, 198, 271n124, 294n36, 295–96n60, 300n124; *The Miracle* (with Vollmoeller), 179, 218, 294n37; *Sumurûn*, 179, 201, 294n37
Reininghaus, Carl, 134, 280n60
Rembrandt, *The Anatomy Lesson of Dr. Nicolaes Tulp*, 262n3, 266n53
"Resurrection of the Spirit, The" (Roth), 93–94
Riefenstahl, Leni: *Olympia*, 231; *Triumph of the Will*, 232
Rieger, Heinrich, 135, 280n69
Riethof, Willy, 11, *11*
Rilke, Rainer Maria, 101, 200, 258n112; *The Book of Hours*, 126
Roessler, Arthur, 134, 161–62, 166–67, 281n79
Roessler, Ida, 281n76
Rokitansky, Carl von, 6, 36, 75, 243n24
Roller, Alfred, 295–96n60
Rosenkavalier, Der (Hofmannsthal), 212
Rosenzweig, Alfred, 198
Roth, Joseph, 267n75, 268n90, 309n6; "The Failed Putsch," 106–8; "Human Fragments," 94–95, 100–101; *Rebellion*, 105–6; "The Reconstruction of Man," 269n105; "Sick Humanity," 90, 92–93; Viennese Symptoms essays, 90–91, 92–94, 97–99, 104–5, 107–8, 271n122; *The White Cities*, 89; *Zipper and His Father*, 91
Rühm, Gerhard, 235

Salten, Felix, 28, 151, 178, 276n32, 292n13, 295n48, 304n164
Salzburg Festival, 295–96n60, 301n130, 304n156
Santner, Eric, 89, 101
Sarasin, Philipp, 7, 48
Scarry, Elaine, 12–13
Schatz, Otto Rudolf, 270n115
Schauta, Friedrich, 141
Schiele, Edith, 281n76
Schiele, Egon: access to pregnant patients, 134–35; artistic style and influences, 127–28, 133, 276n36, 278n46, 279n53; clinic series, 127–32, *129*, *130*, *131*, 277–78n41; connection to Heller, 280n64; connection to Kronfeld, 139, 283n90; connection to Osen, 139, 283n91; *Nude Woman on Her Back*, 278n42; physiognomic illustrations, 32, *33*, 252n41; *Portrait of Dr. Erwin von Graff*, 133, *134*, 135, 281n70; *Pregnant Woman*, *129*, *130*, *131*; *Seated Male Nude with Lowered Head*, 132; sexual misconduct and imprisonment, 261n155; subjects and models, 136–37, 166–67, 281n76, 281n79, 290n190
Schlemmer, Oskar, *Triadic Ballet*, 225, 307n202
Schlesinger-Eckstein, Therese, 149–50
Schmidt, Kurt, 224
Schmidt-Dengler, Wendelin, 18
Schnitzler, Arthur: "Andreas Thameyer's Last Letter," 251n18; connection to Feldmann, 151; connection to Freud, 15, 83, 89, 104; *Dream Story*, 83–88; and film, 304n164; and human displays, 28, 251n18; medical training, 75–76, 80–81, 266n53; *My Youth in Vienna*, 81, 83, 86, 162; pantomimes, 174, 178; *Pierrette's Veil*, 178; *Professor Bernhardi*, 154–55, 160, 286nn150–51; "Prosector," 80, 81; *Reigen*, 111; "Spring Night in the Autopsy Room," 82–83; *The Transformation of Pierrot*, 178; and Young Vienna, 171
Schnitzler, Johann, 81
Schönberg, Arnold, 220, 257n101, 257n104; *Expectation*, 78–79, 265n46
School for Rhythm, Music, and Physical Training, 216
Schorske, Carl, 3–4, 12, 18, 19, 20, 235, 273n3, 284n113, 289n177
Schubert, Franz, 197
Schwartz, Vanessa R., 28–29
Schwarz, Werner Michael, 29, 37, 250n6, 252nn33–35
Schwarzkogler, Rudolf, 235
Schwarzwald, Eugenie "Genia," 53–54, 220, *221*, 257n104, 267n74
scientific knowledge: vs. entertainment, 29–30, 37; in human displays, 29–30, 32–37

scientific materialism, 6
Scream That Nobody Hears, The (Feldmann), 151
Seated Male Nude with Lowered Head (Schiele), 132
Sebald, W. G., 44, 86, 91
Secession, 115–16, 117, 127, 136, 161, 198, 218, 277n40, 299n107, 305n179
second Vienna medical school, 4, 6, 7, 15, 36, 74, 243n18
Seitz, Karl, 156
Self-Portrait on Her Sixth Wedding Anniversary (Modersohn-Becker), 277n40
self-vivisection, 71–75, 113
Seligmann, Adalbert Franz, *Billroth's Lecture Hall at the Vienna General Hospital*, 262n3
semipermeable exhibition spaces, 30–32
Semmelweis, Ignaz, 142
Sex and Character (Weininger), 295n51
sexuality. *See* gender and sexuality
Shadows, The (Balázs), 178
Shapira, Elana, 20, 136, 196
"Shoelaces, please!" (Roth), 97–99
"Sick Humanity" (Roth), 90, 92–93
Sign of Love (Hofmannsthal), 179
silent film. *See* film
Silverman, Lisa, 20, 162–63, 192, 193–94, 298n81
Simmel, Georg, 207
Simplicissimus (journal), 123
Skeletal Anomalies/Gait of Pregnant Women (film), 145
Škoda, Josef, 6, 75
Social Democratic Arts Bureau. *See* Kunststelle (Social Democratic Arts Bureau)
Socialist Society for Sexual Advice and Sexual Research, 77, 121, 161, 275n18
social welfare, 16, 50, 51, 119, 138, 144, 146, 156–61, 231, 287n157
spectacular realities, 28–29
Spector, Scott, 17, 18, 21
Spengler, Oswald, *The Decline of the West*, 227
spherical dance, 199–200
Spiel, Hilde, 5, 257n104
Spitzy, Hans, 96–97, 146, 269n101; *Our War Invalids*, 97, 99
Sprachkrise (crisis of language), 168–69, 171–77, 235, 290–91n4
Spring Awakening (Wedekind), 160
"Spring Night in the Autopsy Room" (Schnitzler), 82–83
Stage Door, The (Baum), 297n74
Stanislavsky, Konstantin, 293n24
St. Denis, Ruth, 184, 185, 186–87, *187*, 189, 190, 195, 214–15, 296n67, 297nn68–69
Steinhof, 139, 141, 255n82, 283n92, 284n103
Stiller, Mauritz, 212, 304n160
"Storyteller, The" (Benjamin), 89
Strauss, Richard, 184, 197, 201, 202, 212, 295n48, 295–96n60
Student, The (Hofmannsthal), 170, 180–83
Studies on Hysteria (Freud and Breuer), 79
Sturm, Der (journal), 123, 287n160
Suján, Paul, 269n104
Sumurûn (Reinhardt), 179, 201, 294n37
Swieten, Gerard van, 243n18
Szeps-Zuckerkandl, Berta. *See* Zuckerkandl, Berta

Tandler, Julius, 51, 55, 59, 77, 119, 121, 138, 146, 156–57, 231
Taylorism, 230
Teisinger, Heinrich, 99, 270n107
Teltscher, Georg, 224
Theater für 49, 271n124, 272n131
Theme for Ballet (Baum), 297n74
therapeutic nihilism, 6–7, 155–56
"Three Small Observations" (Hofmannsthal), 208–12, 304n156
Through the Viennese Quarters of Misery and Crime (Kläger and Drawe), 163, 289n182
Thun-Hohenstein, Maximilian Graf von, 64–66, *65*
Timms, Edward, 21, 244n25
Toepfer, Karl, 5, 305n168
Toulmin, Stephen, 290n3, 291n11
Trakl, Georg, 126
Transformation of Pierrot, The (Schnitzler), 178
Trčka, Anton Josef (Antios), 226
Triadic Ballet (Schlemmer), 225, 307n202
Triumph of the Will (Riefenstahl), 232
Triumph of Time (Hofmannsthal), 180, 295n48

Ujhely, Grete, 304n155
Ungar, Ilka Maria, 122–23, 275–76n22, 276n32; *Closing Time*, 123–27
Union of Austrian Artists. *See* Secession

Union of Austrian Women Artists, 221, 277n40
Union of Socialist Authors, 151, 308n1
Union of Viennese Doctors, 138, 282n87
Urania, 163, 182

Valéry, Paul, 22
Ver Sacrum (journal), 117
veterans of war: and discourses on human fragmentation, 89–95, 99–101; prostheses for wounded, 95–97, *98*, *99*, 269n102, 269n104; visual presence of wounded, 95–97, *96*, *98*, *99*
Vienna's Misery (Frei), 163–66, *164*, *165*
Viennese modernism: centrality of human body, overview, 5–9; and crisis, 12–14; historiography, 18–21
Viennese Pantomime (Hofmannsthal), 179
Virchow, Rudolf, 6, 75
Visible Man, The (Balázs), 204–8, 227
vivisection, 71–75, 113
Völkerschau, as term, 23, 26. *See also* human displays
Volksgemeinschaft, 15
Volkskörper, 53, 228
Volksstück, 109
Volkstheater, 235
Vollmoeller, Karl, *The Miracle*, 294n37

Waerndorfer, Fritz, 136, 196
Wagner, Otto, 143, 195, 284n103, 284n113
waltz, 197–98
Wang, Cilli, 214
War Victim (Hauser), 95, *96*
Wastl, Josef, 233
Water Serpents II (Klimt), 69
Ways to Strength and Beauty (Prager), 231
Webern, Anton, 78
Wedekind, Frank, *Spring Awakening*, 160
Weibel, Wilhelm, 145–46
Weigel, Helene, 257n104
Weininger, Otto, 8, 77, 298n90; *Sex and Character*, 264n37, 295n51
Weixlgärtner, Arpad, 137
welfare. *See* social welfare
Wertheimer, Paul, 126
White Cities, The (Roth), 89
Wiegele, Franz, 279n55
Wiene, Robert, 212
Wiener Aktionismus (Viennese Actionism), 235
Wiener Gruppe (Vienna Group), 235
Wiener Medizinische Presse (journal), 81
Wiener Werkstätte, 194
Wiener Zeitung (newspaper), 26
Wiesenthal, Berta, 195–96, 198, 216–17
Wiesenthal, Elsa, 195–96, 198, 216–17
Wiesenthal, Grete: collaborations with Hofmannsthal, 186, 200–202, 212–13, 300n124; dissatisfaction with classical ballet, 194–95; free dance style, 195–200, *197*, *199*, 216–17, 300n120; on pantomime, 179
Wigman, Mary, 214, 306–7n193
Winter, Max, 162, 289n182
Wittels, Fritz, 77
Wittgenstein, Ludwig, 168, 173, 235
Wolff, Erich Julius, 295n48
Woman and Child (exhibition), 157, *158*
women's bodies. *See* pregnancy and childbirth; working class
Women's Documents (journal), 120
women's rights, 158–60
working class: experience of poverty and injustice, 124, 125–26, 151–52; medical care for, 120–21, 140, 142, 149–50, 152–55; physical education initiatives, 220; as Schiele's subjects, 136–37; in social welfare discourse, 156–61, 287n157; visual and journalistic depictions of, 161–65, *164*, *165*
World of Yesterday, The (Zweig), 162
Worpswede, 258n112

Young Vienna (literary circle), 1, 170, 178

Zelezny, Franz, 56, 57
Zemlinsky, Alexander von, 78, 295n48
Zipper and His Father (Roth), 91
zoological and animal gardens, 31, 252n31
Zuckerkandl, Berta, 77, 117, 134, 249n71, 280n60
Zuckerkandl, Emil, 77, 266n53
Zweig, Stefan, 20, 108; *The World of Yesterday*, 89, 162